T0231094

Applied Semantic Web Technologies

Applied Semantic Web Technologies

Edited by
Vijayan Sugumaran
Jon Atle Gulla

CRC Press
Taylor & Francis Group
Boca Raton London New York

CRC Press is an imprint of the
Taylor & Francis Group, an **informa** business
AN AUERBACH BOOK

CRC Press
Taylor & Francis Group
6000 Broken Sound Parkway NW, Suite 300
Boca Raton, FL 33487-2742

© 2012 by Taylor & Francis Group, LLC
CRC Press is an imprint of Taylor & Francis Group, an Informa business

Printed in the United States of America on acid-free paper
Version Date: 20110808

International Standard Book Number: 978-1-4398-0156-7 (Hardback)

Library of Congress Cataloging-in-Publication Data

Applied semantic web technologies / editors, Vijayan Sugumaran, Jon Atle Gulla.
   p. cm.
  Includes bibliographical references and index.
  ISBN 978-1-4398-0156-7 (hardback)
  1. Semantic Web. I. Sugumaran, Vijayan, 1960- II. Gulla, Jon Atle. III. Title.

TK5105.88815.A67 2011
025.04'27--dc23
                                     2011031717

Visit the Taylor & Francis Web site at
http://www.taylorandfrancis.com

and the CRC Press Web site at
http://www.crcpress.com

Contents

v

SECTION IV SEMANTIC APPLICATIONS

Acknowledgment

The work of Vijayan Sugumaran has been partially supported by the Sogang Business School's World Class University Program (R31-20002) funded by the Korea Research Foundation.

Editors

Vijayan Sugumaran is a professor of management information systems in the Department of Decision and Information Sciences at Oakland University, Rochester, Michigan. He is also a visiting professor in the Department of Service Systems Management and Engineering at Sogang University, Seoul, South Korea. He earned a PhD in information technology from George Mason University, Fairfax, Virginia. His research interests are in the areas of service science, ontologies and semantic web issues, intelligent agent and multiagent systems, and component-based software development. He has published over 140 peer-reviewed articles in journals, conference proceedings, and books and edited eight books and two special journal issues. He is the editor-in-chief of the *International Journal of Intelligent Information Technologies* and serves on the editorial boards of seven other journals. He was the program co-chair for the 13th International Conference on Applications of Natural Language to Information Systems (NLDB 2008) and also acted as the chair of the Intelligent Agent and Multi-Agent Systems track for the Americas Conference on Information Systems (AMCIS 1999–2010). He regularly serves as a program committee member for international and national conferences.

Dr. Sugumaran has obtained research funding from several international agencies. He is a co-principal investigator on a multimillion dollar grant funded by the Korea Research Foundation. As part of this World Class University program, Dr. Sugumaran works with colleagues at Sogang University on a project titled Service Systems Engineering for the Creation of a New Growth Engine based on Knowledge Service.

Jon Atle Gulla has been a professor of information systems since 2002 and heads the Department of Computer and Information Science at the Norwegian University of Science and Technology. He earned his MSc in 1988 and a PhD in 1993, both in information systems, at the Norwegian Institute of Technology, along with an MSc in linguistics from the University of Trondheim and another MSc in management

(Sloan Fellow) from the London Business School. He previously worked as a manager in Fast Search and Transfer in Munich and as a project leader for Norsk Hydro in Brussels. Gulla's research interests include text mining, semantic search, ontologies, and enterprise modeling. He has taken part in national and international research projects on semantic technologies and co-founded several companies that make use of semantics and linguistics in industrial applications.

Contributors

Rajendra Akerkar
Vestlandsforsking
Sogndal, Norway

Donato Barbagallo
Dipartimento di Elettronica e
    Informazione
Politecnico di Milano
Milan, Italy

Sebastian Blohm
(Formerly) Institute AIFB
Universität Karlsruhe
Karlsruhe, Germany

Tobias Bürger
STI Innsbruck
University of Innsbruck
Innsbruck, Austria

Felix Burkhardt
Deutsche Telekom Laboratories
Bonn, Germany

Krisztian Buza
ISMLL
Universität Hildesheim
Hildesheim, Germany

Maria Laura Caliusco
CIDISI
Universidad Tecnologica Nacional
Santa Fe, Argentina

Cinzia Cappiello
Dipartimento di Elettronica e
    Informazione
Politecnico di Milano
Milan, Italy

Olga Cerrato
Det Norske Veritas
Oslo, Norway

Omar Chiotti
Consejo Nacional de Investigaciones
Cientificas y Tecnicas
Universidad Tecnologica Nacional
Santa Fe, Argentina

Philipp Cimiano
Semantic Computing Group
Universität Bielefeld
Bielefeld, Germany

Michael Elhadad
Department of Computer Science
Ben-Gurion University of the Negev
Beer Sheva, Israel

Anna Fensel
Forschungszentrum
    Telekommunikation Wien GmbH
Vienna, Austria

Chiara Francalanci
Dipartimento di Elettronica e
    Informazione
Politecnico di Milano
Milan, Italy

David Gabay
Department of Computer Science
Ben-Gurion University of the Negev
Beer Sheva, Israel

Maria Rosa Galli
Consejo Nacional de Investigaciones
Cientificas y Tecnicas
Universidad Tecnologica Nacional
Santa Fe, Argentina

Jon Atle Gulla
Department of Computer and
    Information Science
Norwegian University of Science and
    Technology
Trondheim, Norway

Veronika Haderlein
Det Norske Veritas
Oslo, Norway

Sung-Kook Han
Wan Kwang University Korea
Seoul, Korea

Jon Espen Ingvaldsen
Norwegian University of Science and
    Technology
Trondheim, Norway

Dae-Ki Kang
Division of Computer and
    Information Engineering
Dongseo University
Busan, Korea

Larry Kerschberg
Department of Computer Science
George Mason University
Fairfax, Virginia, USA

Stefan Kirn
Information Systems II
Universität Hohenheim
Stuttgart, Germany

Konstantinos Kotis
Department of Information and
    Communication Systems
    Engineering
University of the Aegean
Karlovasi, Samos, Greece

Monika Lanzenberger
Vienna University of Technology
Vienna, Austria

Joerg Leukel
Universität Hohenheim
Stuttgart, Germany

Jin Liu
T-Systems
Bonn, Germany

Michael Luger
STI Innsbruck
University of Innsbruck
Innsbruck, Austria

Maristela Matera
Dipartimento di Elettronica e
  Informazione
Politecnico di Milano
Milan, Italy

Robert Meersman
VUB STARLab
Department of Computer Science
Brussels, Belgium

Saravanan Muthaiyah
Faculty of Management
Multimedia University
Cyberjaya, Malaysia

Per Myrseth
Det Norske Veritas
Oslo, Norway

Yael Netzer
Department of Computer Science
Ben-Gurion University of the Negev
Beer Sheva, Israel

Andreas Papasalouros
Department of Mathematics
University of the Aegean
Karlovasi, Samos, Greece

Mariela Rico
CIDISI
Universidad Tecnologica Nacional
Santa Fe, Argentina

Jennifer Sampson
Statoil
Bergen, Norway

Lars Schmidt-Thieme
ISMLL
Universität Hildesheim
Hildesheim, Germany

Michael Schwanzer
University of Applied Sciences
Technikum Wien
Vienna, Austria

Elena Simperl
Karlsruhe Institute of Technology
Karlsruhe, Germany

Katharina Siorpaes
STI Innsbruck
University of Innsbruck
Innsbruck, Austria

Milan Stefanovic
E-Smart Systems DOO
Beograd, Serbia

Vijanan Sugumaran
Department of Decision and
  Information Sciences
Oakland University
Rochester, Michigan, USA
and
Department of Service Systems
  Management and Engineering
Sogang University
Seoul, South Korea

Yan Tang
VUB STARLab
Department of Computer Science
Brussels, Belgium

Slobodanka Tomic
Forschungszentrum
  Telekommunikation Wien GmbH
Vienna, Austria

Jan Vanthienen
Department of Decision Sciences and
  Information Management
Katholieke Universiteit Leuven
Leuven, Belgium

Mirna Kojic Veljovic
E-Smart Systems DOO
Beograd, Serbia

Christian Weiss
Deutsche Telekom Laboratories
Bonn, Germany

Stephan Wölger
STI Innsbruck
University of Innsbruck
Innsbruck, Austria

Jianshen Zhou
Deutsche Telekom Laboratories
Bonn, Germany

INTRODUCTION

I

Chapter 1

Applied Semantic Web Technologies: Overview and Future Directions

Vijayan Sugumaran
Oakland University, Rochester, MI; Sogang University, Seoul, Korea and

Jon Atle Gulla
Norwegian University of Science and Technology, Trondheim, Norway

Contents

1.1   Introduction

Since Tim Berners-Lee's original idea for a global system of interlinked hypertext documents from 1989, the World Wide Web has grown into the world's biggest pool of human knowledge. Over the past few years, the Web has changed the way people communicate and exchange information. It has created new business opportunities and obliterated old business practices. As a borderless source of information, it has been instrumental in globalization and cooperation among people and nations. Importantly, it has also helped individuals join virtual communities and take part in social networks that cross physical, cultural, and organizational barriers. The rapid growth of information on the World Wide Web has, however, created a new set of challenges and problems.

Information overload—In 1998, the size of the Web was estimated to exceed 300 million pages with a growth rate of about 20 million per month (Baeza-Yates and Ribeiro-Neto, 1999). The real size of the Web today is difficult to measure, although Web search indices cite a lower band number of unique and meaningful Web pages. The Google search index was measured around 500 million pages in 2000, 8 billion in 2004, and more than 27 billion today. This constitutes an enormous amount of information about almost any conceivable topic. While the early Web often suffered from a lack of high-quality relevant pages, the present Web now contains far too many relevant pages for any user to review. As an example, at the time of this writing, Google is returning about 18.6 million pages for the "World Wide Web" search phrase. If you fail to mark it as a phrase, an astonishing 113 million pages are found to be relevant and presented on the result page. In addition, the deeper Web generates information dynamically based on users' queries.

Poor retrieval and aggregation—The explosion of Web documents and services would not be so critical if users could easily retrieve and combine the information needed. Since Web documents are at best semi-structured in simple natural language text, they are vulnerable to obstacles that prevent efficient content retrieval and aggregation. An increasing problem is the number of languages used on the Web. Studies of Langer (2001) suggested that almost 65% of Web pages were in English in 1999; data from Internet World Stats* indicate a more balanced use of languages. The English using population at the end of 2009 constituted only 27.7% of total online users. The plethora of languages now used on the Web prevents search applications from applying language-specific strategies, and they still depend on content-independent statistical models. In a similar vein, the many

---

* www.internetworldstats.com

misspellings and general syntactic variations in documents hamper the reliability of statistical scores of document relevance.

Stovepipe system—All components of a stovepipe system application are hard-wired to work only together (Daconta et al., 2003). Information flows only inside an application and cannot be exchanged with other applications or organizations without access to the stovepipe system. Many enterprises and business sectors suffer from stovepipe systems that use their own particular database schemas, terminologies, standards, etc. and prevent people and organizations from collaborating efficiently because one system cannot understand the data from another system.

1.2 History

The *Semantic Web* term was popularized by Tim Berners-Lee and later elaborated in 2001. The first part of his vision for the Semantic Web was to turn the Web into a truly collaborative medium—to help people share information and services and make it easier to aggregate data from different sources and different formats. The second part of his vision was to create a Web that would be understandable and processable by machines. While humans can read and comprehend current Web pages, Berners-Lee envisioned new forms of Web pages that could be understood, combined, and analyzed by computers, with the ultimate goal of enabling humans and computers to cooperate in the same manner as humans do among each other. Berners-Lee did not think of the Semantic Web as a replacement of the current Web. It was intended as an extension for adding semantic descriptions of information and services. Central to the Semantic Web vision is the shift from applications to data. The key to machine-processable data is to make the data smarter. As seen from Figure 1.1, data progress along a continuum of increased intelligence as described below.

Text and databases—In this initial stage, most data is proprietary to an application. The application is responsible for interpreting the data and contains the intelligence of the system.

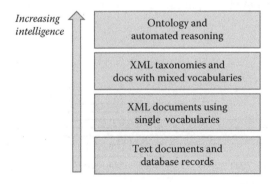

Figure 1.1   Smart data continuum.

XML documents for single domains—The second stage involves domain-specific XML schemas that achieve application independence within the domain. Data can flow between applications in a single domain but cannot be shared outside the system.

Taxonomies—In this stage, data can be combined from different domains using hierarchical taxonomies of the relevant terminologies. Data is now smart enough to be easily discovered and combined with other data.

Ontologies and automated reasoning—In the final stage, new data can be inferred from existing data and shared across applications with no human involvement or interpretation. Data is now smart enough to understand its definitions and relationships to other data.

In the Semantic Web these smart data are assumed to be application-independent, composable, classified, and comprise parts of a larger terminological structure. Ontologies play a very important role in the Semantic Web community. According to Gruber (1995), an ontology is an explicit specification of a conceptualization. It represents a common understanding of a domain and its relevant terminology. Technically, ontologies describe concepts and their taxonomic and nontaxonomic relationships. For the Semantic Web, ontologies enable us to define the terminology used to represent and share data within a domain. As long as the applications define their data with reference to the same ontology, they can interpret and reason others' data and collaborate without manually defining any mapping between the applications. Figure 1.2 illustrates language.

The W3C consortium devised a number of standards for defining and using ontologies. The *Resource Description Framework (RDF)* was available already in 1999 as a part of W3C's Semantic Web effort. It uses triplets (subjects, property, objects) to describe resources and their simple relationships to other resources. It is used as a simple ontology language for many existing applications for content management, digital libraries, and e-commerce.

DAML (DARPA Agent Markup Language) was proposed by DARPA, a U.S. government research organization, as part of a research program started in 2000. The definition of DAML is published at daml.org, which is run as part of the

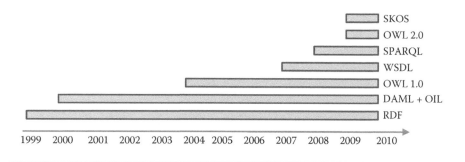

Figure 1.2   Important language standards of Semantic Web.

DAML program. DAML is a semantic language targeting the Semantic Web, although it can also be used as a general knowledge representation language. The OIL (Ontology Inference Layer) semantic markup language is a European initiative involving some of the continent's best artificial intelligence researchers. OIL is not very different from DAML, and both languages provide powerful mechanisms for defining complex ontologies. The DAML+OIL standard from 2001 is a markup language for Web resources that tries to capture some of the best features of both DAML and OIL.

In 2004, the Web Ontology Language (OWL), Version 1.0, was recommended by the W3C consortium. It replaces DAML+OIL as a semantic language designed for applications that need to process the content of information instead of simply presenting information to humans. OWL facilitates greater machine interpretability of Web content than that supported by XML and RDF by providing additional primitives along with improved formal semantics from Description Logic. The three increasingly expressive sublanguages of OWL are OWL Lite, OWL DL, and OWL Full. OWL DL is the most commonly used language today. Version 2.0 was introduced in 2009. OWL is now the dominant language for describing formal ontologies in enterprises and on the Web.

Several supporting standards have emerged recently. The Web Service Definition Language (WSDL), Version 2.0, from 2007, is one of many languages for specifying Web services. SPARQL (2008) is an RDF-based query language for accessing information in ontologies. SKOS (Simple Knowledge Organization System; 2009) is a light weight data model for sharing and linking knowledge organization systems via the Web. These and similar standards intend to simplify the use of Semantic Web technologies in practical applications.

1.3 Semantic Web Layers

As noted above, several standard specifications and technologies are contributing to the realization of the Semantic Web. It is evolving based on a layered approach, and each layer provides a set of functionalities (Breitman et al., 2007). The assortment of tools, technologies, and specifications that lay the foundation for the Semantic Web can be broadly organized into four major layers: (1) data and metadata, (2) semantics, (3) enabling technology, and (4) environment. Figure 1.3 illustrates some of the essential specifications and technologies that contribute to each layer. The four layers and key components are briefly described below.

1.3.1 Data and Metadata Layer

The data and metadata layer is the lowest; it provides standard representations for data and information and facilitates the exchanges among various applications and systems. The Unicode provides a standard representation for character sets in

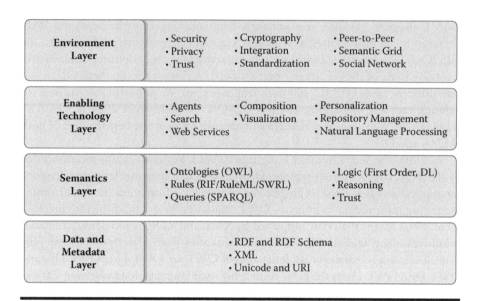

Environment Layer	• Security • Privacy • Trust	• Cryptography • Integration • Standardization	• Peer-to-Peer • Semantic Grid • Social Network
Enabling Technology Layer	• Agents • Search • Web Services	• Composition • Visualization	• Personalization • Repository Management • Natural Language Processing
Semantics Layer	• Ontologies (OWL) • Rules (RIF/RuleML/SWRL) • Queries (SPARQL)		• Logic (First Order, DL) • Reasoning • Trust
Data and Metadata Layer	• RDF and RDF Schema • XML • Unicode and URI		

Figure 1.3   Semantic Web layers.

different languages used by different computers and the URI provides a standard way to uniformly indentify resources such as Web pages and other forms of content. The Unicode and URI together enable us to create content and make these resources available for others to find and use in a simple way. XML enables us to structure data using user-defined tags that have well defined meanings that are shared by applications. This helps improve data interoperability across systems.

Namespaces and schemas provide the mechanisms to express semantics in one location for access and utilization by many applications. The next component in this layer is the Resource Description Framework (RDF) that conceptually describes the information contained in a Web resource. It can employ different formats for representing triplets (subjects, predicates, objects), can be used to model disparate abstract concepts, and is effective for knowledge management. RDF Schema is a language for declaring basic classes and types for describing the terms used. It supports reasoning to infer different types of resources.

1.3.2 Semantics Layer

The semantics layer incorporates specifications, tools, and techniques that help add meaning or semantics to characterize the contents of resources. It facilitates the representation of Web content that enables applications to access information autonomously using common search terms. The important ingredients of this layer are ontology language, rule language, query language, logic, reasoning mechanism, and trust. As noted earlier, ontologies express basic concepts and the relationship between concepts that exist in a domain. They form the backbone for the Semantic Web and are used to reason about entities in a particular domain and manage knowledge sharing and reuse. Ontologies can be used to specify complex constraints on the types of resources and their properties. OWL is the most popular ontology language used by applications for processing content from a resource without human intervention. Thus, it facilitates machine interoperability by providing the necessary vocabulary along with formal semantics. OWL Lite, OWL DL, and OWL Full are the three OWL sublanguages.

Rule languages help write inferencing rules in a standard way that can be used for reasoning in a particular domain. A rule language provides kernel specification for rule structures that can be used for rule interchange and facilitates rule reuse and extension. Among several standards, such as RIF (Rule Interchange Format), and Datalog RuleML, SWRL (Semantic Web Rule Language) is gaining popularity. It combines OWL DL, OWL Lite, and Datalog RuleML and includes a high-level abstract syntax for Horn-like rules in both OWL DL and OWL Lite.

Querying Web content and automatically retrieving relevant segments from a resource by an application is the driving force behind the SPARQL Web query language. It provides both a protocol and a language for querying RDF graphs via pattern matching. It supports basic conjunctive patterns, value filters, optional patterns, and pattern disjunction. Logic and reasoning are also integral parts of the semantics layer. A reasoning system can use one or more ontologies and make new inferences based on the content of a particular resource. It also helps identify appropriate resources that meet a particular requirement. Thus, the reasoning system enables applications to extract appropriate information from various resources. Logic provides the theoretical underpinning required for reasoning and deduction. First order logic, description logic, and others are commonly used to support reasoning. Trust is also an important ingredient in this layer; it is basic to the whole reasoning process. All the applications expect and demand that resource content be trustworthy and of high quality.

1.3.3 Enabling Technology Layer

This layer consists of a variety of technologies that can develop applications on the Semantic Web and accomplish different types of tasks or operationalize specific aspects of the Semantic Web. For example, intelligent agents or multiagent systems can be used to access and process information automatically on the Semantic Web. Some well-established technologies can be used synergistically to create valuable Semantic Web applications. Some of the technologies relevant to this layer are agents, search, Web services, composition (information and service composition), visualization, personalization, repository management, and natural language processing. Software agents and Web services are closely associated with the Semantic Web and are used in a variety of applications. For example, Klapiscak and Bordini

(2009) describe the implementation of an environment that combines agent-oriented programming and ontological reasoning. Similarly, Gibbins et al. (2004) discuss agent-based Semantic Web services for situational awareness and information triage in a simulated humanitarian aid scenario. Search (information and service) and composition (information and service) are other important technologies utilized in numerous applications on the Semantic Web.

Personalization on the Semantic Web is similar to creating individual views on Web data according to special interests, needs, requirements, goals, access context, etc. of the user (Baldoni et al., 2005). The availability of a variety of reasoning techniques, all fully integrated with the Web, opens the way for the design and development of different modes of interaction and personalization. Information visualization strives to make the information more accessible and less structured to improve usability. In the context of the Semantic Web, visualization supports the user in managing large amounts of data and performing interactive processes such as searching (Albertoni et al., 2004). Visualization of semantic metadata helps users gain insight into the structure and relationships in the data that are hard to see in text (Mutton and Golbeck, 2003). Natural Language Processing (NLP) technologies play an important role in materializing the Semantic Web with specific applications such as ontology-based information extraction, ontology learning and population, and semantic metadata generation. NLP techniques are increasingly used in ontology engineering to minimize human involvement. Much work remains to be done in the use of controlled natural language, representation of linguistic information in ontologies, and effective techniques for ontology learning from unstructured text.

1.3.4 Environment Layer

The environment layer deals with the surroundings and the infrastructure in which the Semantic Web applications execute and meet the basic expectations of these applications in terms of data quality and information assurance. It is also concerned with the operating environment and the degrees of interoperability of various domains. Some of the key aspects of this layer are security, privacy, trust, cryptography, application integration, standards, and environments such as peer-to-peer, semantic grid, and social networks.

Security and privacy are two important requirements that must be satisfied in the Semantic Web environment. Any two applications can interact automatically, and since the identities of the parties are not known in advance, a semantically enriched process is needed to regulate access to sensitive information (Olmedilla, 2007). Thus, security and privacy protections must be implemented carefully for a variety of Semantic Web scenarios. Cryptography, encoding, and secure transfer protocols are some of the ways to ensure certain levels of security and privacy on the Semantic Web. The critical issue of trust within the Semantic Web has been gaining attention recently. Just like the Web for which no attempts were made to centrally control the quality of information, it is infeasible to do so on the Semantic Web. By having each user explicitly specify a set of trusted users, the resulting web of trust may be used recursively to determine a user's trust in any other user or resource (Richardson et al., 2003).

Application and information integration along with standardization are also important for the success of the Semantic Web. Information integration is still an outstanding issue and the host of technologies of the Semantic Web bring several relevant and useful tools and techniques that can exploit the interoperability context. The environment layer also includes mechanisms to develop Semantic Web applications that take advantage of some of the contemporary network computing paradigms such as peer-to-peer, semantic grid, and social networks. Such advances can facilitate larger scale permeation of Semantic Web technologies and applications.

1.4 Future Research Directions

Semantic applications attempt to understand the meaning of data and connect data in meaningful ways. After almost a decade of intense research, we now have a number of practical semantic applications in use. A few commercial semantic search systems like Powerset have been launched commercially, and specialized semantic applications are now used for travel planning and user profiling, among other functions. Ontologies are to some extent used for integrating large-scale applications and reporting data from heterogeneous systems. While domains like medicine and petroleum production already have advanced users of Semantic Web technologies, most industries have only limited experience with semantic applications. There are probably many reasons for slow adoption of new technologies, and fundamental challenges of the Semantic Web relate to the scale, vagueness, inconsistency, and instability of data.

The massive amounts of data on the Web and in enterprises represent fundamental challenges for logic-based approaches like the Semantic Web. Specifying the semantic content of data is a tedious and error-prone process that requires deep expertise in logic and modeling. When the specifications are at hand, serious performance issues with ontology querying and reasoning arise. For some ontologies, like those specified in OWL Full, reasoning is not possible. Most textual data are formulated in natural languages that suffer from vagueness and uncertainty. Human beings can relate to terms like *tall* and *heavy* if they know the context of their use. Computers, on the other hand, need precise and complete definitions that allow them to apply the terms and interpret descriptions in which they are used.

Textual data also tend to show inconsistencies that we can reconcile or accept in our everyday life. Humans can deal with different and inconsistent definitions of terms like *tall* and still use such terms in conversations and text. A computer application can in principle deduce anything—right or wrong—from an inconsistent ontology.

In recent years, the challenges of unstable and evolving terminologies have become more apparent. Since semantic applications must understand the meanings of text and other data, they must update their underlying terminologies as domains change to interpret the data correctly. This is a continuous process that is costly to implement and difficult to organize.

Current research on the Semantic Web is diverse and spans many scientific disciplines. A number of unresolved theoretical questions are being addressed by the research community. For the practical use of Semantic Web technologies, a few areas carry particular significance.

Ontology learning or creation—These techniques allow semi-automatic or fully automatic creation of (parts of) ontologies from representative domain texts. Early work on ontology learning used text mining and computational linguistics to extract prominent terms in text and suggest these as candidate classes and individuals. Later research concentrated on extracting relationships and properties using statistical methods like association rules and simple phrasal searches like the Hearst patterns (Cimiano, 2006; Gulla et al., 2009). The quality of these techniques is, however, not impressive and we are still far from learning complete ontologies with classes, individuals, properties, and rules.

Performance—With current technologies, retrieval, storing, and manipulation of ontologies are computationally too demanding for many large-scale applications. Initial work on more efficient methods for storing and reasoning over complex ontologies has started, but more progress is needed for semantic applications to scale up.

Ontology quality and selection—As the number of available ontologies increases, their evaluation becomes more difficult. Existing approaches focus on the syntactic aspects of ontologies and do not take into account the semantic aspects and user contexts and familiarities. While many research efforts address the issues of ontology searching and quality separately, none has considered ontology evaluation and selection together. Research also has not considered task characteristics, application semantics, and user contexts. Hence, we still have a great need for developing a semi-automatic framework for selecting the best ontology appropriate for a specific task within the Semantic Web.

Linked data—In 2006, Tim Berners-Lee introduced the notion of linked data as a simplified approach to semantic applications. The approach is based on concepts and technologies for combining and integrating data using RDF triplets only. Linked data allows more scalable applications to be built and has already been used in a number of small Web applications and enterprise data architectures (Bizer et al., 2009). Whether the approach can handle functionally demanding tasks due to the limited expressiveness and lack of formality remains unclear.

Trust, Security, and Privacy—Semantic Web applications assume and expect that the information content of resources is of high quality and can be trusted.

Similarly, security and privacy of sensitive information on the Semantic Web must be ensured. While initial research has yielded interesting results, much work remains in developing comprehensive solutions and techniques to assess and ensure the trustworthiness, security, and privacy of Semantic Web content.

These and other areas of research will be central to the industrial adoption of semantic technologies in the years to come.

1.5 Organization of Book

This book is divided into four parts. The first contains this introductory chapter by the book editors. The second part, titled "Ontologies," covers the fundamentals of ontologies, ontology languages, and research related to ontology alignment, mediation, and mapping. "Ontology Engineering and Evaluation" is the third part dedicated to the issues and tools related to ontology engineering and some methodologies and processes used to create ontologies. It also covers several aspects of ontology evaluation and social ontologies. The fourth and final "Semantic Applications" part highlights the use of semantics in several applications and the employment of ontologies and other semantic technologies in various domains. Examples of real-life applications of semantic technologies in areas such as logistics, smart home environments, business process intelligence, and decision making are included. The following section is a brief summary of the salient aspects and contributions of each chapter.

1.5.1 Part I: Introduction

Part I contains this single introductory chapter. We briefly outline the history and the state of the art in the Semantic Web technologies arena and point out future research directions.

1.5.2 Part II: Ontologies

Part II contains four chapters. In Chapter 2, Akerkar provides an introduction to ontology fundamentals and languages. Specifically, he discusses Web Ontology Language (OWL) in detail and reveals that ontology creation consists of defining all ontology components through an ontology definition language. Ontology creation is initially informal through the use of either natural language or diagram technique, and is then encoded in a formal knowledge representation language such as RDF Schema or OWL. Chapter 2 also discusses different types of existing ontologies, parameters for constructing an ontology, interoperability, reasoning issues, and ontology representation languages such as XML Schema and RDF Schema.

Chapter 3 explores ways to provide semantic interoperability among information systems. Specifically, Rico et al. present a method for enriching the representations of entity semantics in an ontology by making contextual features explicit with the aim of improving the matching of heterogeneous ontologies. This ontology matching is used to establish meaningful information exchange among peers on a network. This chapter also presents a case study based on a peer-to-peer information sharing scenario in which each peer belongs to a different context.

In Chapter 4, Lanzenberger et al. present AlViz, a tool for ontology alignment that uses information visualization techniques. They argue that the use of these techniques to graphically display data from ontology mappings can facilitate user understanding of the meaning of the ontology alignment. Based on similarity measures of an ontology matching algorithm, AlViz helps assess and optimize alignment results at different levels of detail. Clustered graphs enable the user to examine and manipulate the mappings of large ontologies.

Chapter 5 by Muthaiyah and Kerschberg introduces a hybrid ontology mediation and mapping approach called the Semantic Relatedness Score (SRS) that combines both semantic and syntactic matching algorithms. They show that SRS provides better results in terms of reliability and precision when compared to purely syntactic matching algorithms. SRS has been developed through a process of rigorously testing 13 well-established matching algorithms and producing a composite measure from 5 of the best combinations of the 13. The authors contend that the workloads of ontologists may be significantly reduced by SRS measures since they select from fewer concepts; hence their productivity improves drastically.

1.5.3 Part III: Ontology Engineering and Evaluation

Part III consists of five chapters. Chapter 6 presents a collaborative ontology engineering tool that extends Semantic MediaWiki (SMW). Simperl et al. argue that unlike other wiki-based ontology editors, their tool focuses on light-weight ontology modeling that can be carried out through appropriate interfaces by technically savvy users who have no knowledge engineering background. Their method leverages existing knowledge structures into ontologies, and improves the results of the modeling process through knowledge repair techniques that identify potential problems and make suggestions to users.

In Chapter 7, Kotis, and Papasalouros discuss key issues, experiences, lessons learned, and future directions in creating social ontologies from the World Wide Web. This chapter reports on experiences and challenges related to automated learning of useful social ontologies based on a holistic approach in terms of the different types of content that may be involved in the learning process, i.e., Web, Web 2.0, and even Semantic Web content. The authors also address some of the challenges in resolving the Semantic Web content creation bottleneck.

Chapter 8 by Blohm et al. discusses relation extraction for the Semantic Web. It introduces Taxonomic Sequential Patterns (TSPs) as generalizations of many pattern classes adopted in the literature. The authors explore whether TSPs are superior to other types of patterns by looking at the precision–recall trade-off. They also present a principled mining algorithm as an extension of the well known ECLAT algorithm that allows mining of taxonomic sequential patterns.

Kang's Chapter 9 discusses data-driven evaluation of ontologies using machine learning algorithms. He introduces a few cutting-edge taxonomy-aware algorithms for automated construction of taxonomies inductively from both structured and unstructured data. These algorithms recursively group values based on a suitable measure of divergence among the class distributions associated with the values to construct taxonomies. They generate hierarchical taxonomies of nominal, ordinal, and continuous valued attributes.

In Chapter 10, Elhadad et al. present a method for functional evaluation of search ontologies in the entertainment domain using natural language processing. Their methodology evaluates the functional adequacy of an ontology by investigating a corpus of textual documents anchored to the ontology.

1.5.4 Part IV: Semantic Applications

Part IV contains six chapters. Tang et al. examine the addition of semantics to decision tables in Chapter 11. They propose a new approach to data and knowledge engineering using a Semantic Decision Table (SDT) defined as a semantically rich decision table supported by ontology engineering. They also discuss applications of SDT to demonstrate its usefulness and show how it can assist in ontology-based data matching processes.

In Chapter 12, Barbagallo et al. explore semantic sentiment analysis based on the reputation of Web information sources. They propose a platform for analyzing the Web reputation of a company's products and services. Their approach offers a self-service environment for the construction of personalized dashboards. The key ingredients are the selection and composition of trustworthy services for information access and processing.

Gulla et al. examine semantics and search in Chapter 13. They provide a summary of prominent approaches to semantic search and explain the principles behind them. They also discuss semantic indexing techniques, the use of semantics on search result pages, and techniques for semantic navigation of the result set. The temporal or evolutionary dimension of search is also delineated.

In Chapter 14, Leukel and Kirn discuss semantics-based service composition in transport logistics. Specifically, they propose a semantic model for transport services and demonstrate its usefulness in the domain of distribution logistics. They define the problem of finding the best solution for a given set of customer requirements as a subclass of service composition, thus combining and linking (logistics) services. They contend that a key prerequisite for determining compositions is a rich conceptualization that allows specification of relevant constraints that must be fulfilled.

Ingvaldsen examines various aspects of ontology-driven business process intelligence in Chapter 15. He highlights the importance of ontologies in the process analysis approach and demonstrates how ontologies and search are fundamental for structuring process mining models and analysis perspectives and providing an explorative analysis environment.

Finally, in Chapter 16, Tomic et al. discuss the use of semantics for energy efficiency in smart home environments. They use ontology-based modeling and service-oriented design for the integration of the building automation and advanced metering in a truly flexible system controlled by user-generated policies. Their system is designed to operate on a common semantically described framework of multimodal factors including preferences and policies of users; operational factors of peripheral devices, sensors, and actuators; and external information characterizing the availability and cost of energy.

Acknowledgment

The work of Vijayan Sugumaran has been partially supported by Sogang Business School's World Class University Program (R31-20002) funded by the Korea Research Foundation.

References

Albertoni, R., Bertone, A., and De Martino, M. 2004. Semantic Web and Information Visualization. In *First Italian Workshop on Semantic Web Application and Perspective*, Dipartimento di Elettronica, Intelligenza Artificiale e Telecomunicazioni, Ancona, December 10, pp. 108–114.

Baeza-Yates, R. A. and Ribeiro-Neto, B. 1999. *Modern Information Retrieval*. Addison-Wesley Longman, Boston.

Baldoni, M., Baroglio, C., and Henze, N. 2005. Personalization for the Semantic Web. In *REWERSE 2005: Lecture Notes on Computer Science* 3564, pp. 173–212.

Berners-Lee, T., Hendler, J., and Lassila O. 2001. The Semantic Web. *Scientific American*, May 2001, pp. 34–43.

Bizer, C., Heath, T., and Berners-Lee, T. 2009. Linked Data: The Story So Far. *International Journal of Semantic Web and Information Systems*, Special Issue on Linked Data, 5, 1–22.

Breitman, K. K, Casanova, M. A., and Truszkowski, W. 2007. *Semantic Web: Concepts, Technologies and Applications*. Springer Verlag, London.

Cimiano, P. 2006. *Ontology Learning and Population from Text: Algorithms, Evaluations, and Applications*. Springer Verlag, Berlin. Originally published as PhD thesis, Universitat Karlsruhe, Germany.

Daconta, M. C., Obrst, L. J., and Smith K. T. 2003. *The Semantic Web: A Guide to the Future of XML, Web Services, and Knowledge Management*. Wiley, Indianapolis.

Davies, J., Studer, R., and Warren, P. 2006. *Semantic Web Technologies: Trends and Research in Ontology-Based Systems*. Wiley. DOI: 10.3395/reciis.v3i1.245pt

Gibbins, N., Harris, S., and Shadbolt, N. 2004. Agent-Based Semantic Web Services. *Web Semantics: Science, Services and Agents on the World Wide Web, 1,* 141–154.

Gruber, T.S. 1995. Toward Principles for the Design of Ontologies Used for Knowledge Sharing. *International Journal of Human–Computer Studies, 43,* 907–928.

Gulla, J. A., Brasethvik, T., and Sveia-Kvarv, G. 2009. Association Rules and Cosine Similarities in Ontology Relationship Learning. In *Enterprise Information Systems: Lecture Notes in Business Information Processing,* Vol. 19, Springer Verlag, Berlin.

Hitzler, P., Krtzsch, M., and Rudolph, S. 2009. *Foundations of Semantic Web Technologies.* Chapman & Hall/CRC, Boca Raton, FL.

Klapiscak, T. and Bordini, R. H. 2009. JASDL: A Practical Programming Approach Combining Agent and Semantic Web Technologies. In *DALT 2008: Lecture Notes in Artificial Intelligence* 5397, pp. 91–110.

Langer, S. 2001. Natural Languages and the World Wide Web. *Bulletin de linguistique appliquée et générale, 26,* 89–100. <http://www.cis.unimuenchen.de/people/langer/veroeffentlichungen/bulag.pdf>

Mutton, P. and Golbeck, J. 2003. Visualization of Semantic Metadata and Ontologies. In *Proceedings of Information Visualization,* July 16–18, London.

Olmedilla, D. 2007. Security and Privacy on the Semantic Web. In *Security, Privacy, and Trust in Modern Data Management,* Part V, Springer Verlag, Berlin, pp. 399415. DOI: 10.1007/978-3-540-69861-6_26.

Richardson, M., Agrawal, R., and Domingos, P. 2003. Trust Management for the Semantic Web. In *ISWC 2003, Lecture Notes in Computer Science* 2870, pp. 351–368.

ONTOLOGIES

Chapter 2

Ontology: Fundamentals and Languages

Rajendra Akerkar

Vestlandsforsking, Sogndal, Norway

Contents

2.1 Introduction

The vision of the Semantic Web is to enable machines to interpret and process information on the World Wide Web to provide quality support to mankind in carrying out various tasks involving information and communication technology. The challenge of the Semantic Web is to provide necessary information with well-defined meanings, understandable by different parties and machines in such a way that applications can provide customized access to information by meeting the individual needs and requirements of the users.

Several technologies have been developed for shaping, constructing, and developing the Semantic Web. Ontology plays an important role as a source of formally defined terms for communication. The prime objective of ontology is to facilitate *knowledge sharing and reuse on a distributed platform.* While some dispute surrounds what encompasses ontologies, they generally include a taxonomy of terms, and several ontology languages allow supplementary definitions using some kind of logic. Moreover, although the words *ontology* and *vocabulary* are often used interchangeably, a *vocabulary* is a collection of terms used in a specific domain; it can be hierarchically arranged as a *taxonomy*, and combined with rules, constraints, and relationships to form an *ontology*. Ontology creation consists of defining all ontology components through an ontology definition language. Creation is initially an informal process using either natural language or diagram technique. The ontology is encoded in a formal knowledge representation language such as RDF schema or Web ontology language (OWL). This chapter introduces ontology fundamentals and languages and discusses ontology and OWL at a certain level of detail to enable the reader to see the potential of the language.

The next subsection presents terminology for taxonomy, thesauri, and ontology and will cover various issues related to ontology and its applications. Section 1.2

presents types of ontologies. Section 1.3 discusses construction parameters. Sections 1.4 and 1.5 deal with interoperability and Semantic Web issues. Section 1.6 explains traditional application areas for ontology. Reasoning issues are presented in Section 1.7. Section 1.8 discusses ontology languages, including representation types such as XML schema and RDF schema, to provide contexts for understanding OWL. We also discuss the basics of OWL—properties and examples. Section 1.9 describes integration of ontology and rule languages. Section 1.10 describes ontology-driven information integration. Finally, Section 1.11 presents useful Semantic Web tools.

2.1.1 Definitions

In the broad context of the Semantic Web, applications must be understood by machine, with the help of a meaning associated with each component stored on the Web. Such capability of understanding is not covered by the traditional tools like markup languages and protocols utilized on the World Wide Web platform. A component representation scheme called ontology is a requirement. Ontology interweaves human and computer understandings and interpretations of symbols (also known as terms). Ontology provides means for conceptualizing and structuring knowledge and allows semantic annotation of resources to support information retrieval, automated inference, and interoperability among services and applications across the Web.

Ontologies provide in-depth characteristics and classes such as inverses, unambiguous properties, unique properties, lists, restrictions, cardinalities, pair-wise disjoint lists, data types, and so on. Ontologies often allow objective specification of domain information by representing a consensual agreement on the concepts and relations that characterize the manner in which knowledge in a domain is expressed. This specification can be the first step in building semantically aware information systems to support diverse enterprise, government, and personal activities. The original definition of *ontology* comes from the field of philosophy (Definition 1) and is included in *Webster's Revised Unabridged Dictionary* (http://www.dict.org/). The more modern Definition 2 relates to systems.

Definition 1—That department of the science of metaphysics which investigates and explains ontology as the nature and essential properties and relations of all beings, as such, or the principles and causes of being.

Definition 2—Ontology is an abstract model which represents a common and shared understanding of a domain.

The word *ontology* has a very long history in philosophy starting with the works of Aristotle. Defined as the science of being, it comes from the Greek *ontos* (being) and *logos* (language or reason). Ontology is then the branch of metaphysics that deals with the nature of being. From the view of phenomenology, a more modern philosophy that started with the 19th century German philosophers, ontology is a systematic account of existence. However, based on a phenomenological approach, being and existence are different notions and cannot be combined or considered simultaneously. While philosophers build ontology from the top down, practitioners of computer science usually build an ontology from the bottom up.

As a matter of fact, one can retain three dimensions in an ontology: *knowledge, language,* and *logic,* i.e., *language* to speak about the world, *conceptualization* to understand the world, and *representation* to manipulate our understanding.

Ontology has been a well-known concept for many years in the artificial intelligence and knowledge representation communities. It addresses ways of representing knowledge so that machines can reason and thus make valid deductions and inferences. Ontology generally consists of a list of interrelated terms and inference rules and can be exchanged between users and applications. An ontology may be defined in a more or less formal way, from natural language to description logics. OWL belongs to the latter category. It is built upon RDF and RDFS and extends them to express class properties. The pioneer definition of ontology in the sense of the Semantic Web was proposed by Tom Gruber (Gruber, 1993):

Definition 3—Ontology is a formal explicit specification of a shared conceptualization.

In the 1990s, knowledge engineers borrowed the ontology term as a systematic account of existence rather than a metaphysical approach of the nature of being. As a matter of fact, for artificial intelligence systems, what exists is that which can be represented in a declarative language. Ontology is then an explicit formal specification of how to represent objects, concepts, and relationships assumed to exist in some area of interest—what Gruber called "a specification of a conceptualisation" (like a formal specification of a program) of the concepts and relationships of an agent or a community of agents. A conceptualization is an abstract simplified view of the world that one wishes to represent for some purpose. The ontology is a specification because it represents conceptualization in a concrete form. It is explicit because all concepts and constraints used are explicitly defined. *Formal* means the ontology should be machine understandable. *Shared* indicates that the ontology captures consensual knowledge.

Ontology-based semantic structures replace the jumbles of ad hoc rule-based techniques common to earlier knowledge representation systems. This makes knowledge representation languages easy to manage by combining logic and ontology. In the context of the Semantic Web, we can further modify the ontology definition as follows:

Definition 4—Computer ontologies are formally specified models of known knowledge in a given domain.

Metadata and ontology are complementary and constitute the Semantic Web's building blocks. They avoid meaning ambiguities and provide more precise answers. In addition to better query result accuracy, another goal of the Semantic Web is to describe the semantic relationships of the answers. Any general ontology model represents only a consensual agreement on the concepts and relations that characterize the way knowledge in a domain is expressed. Higher level ontology may simply model common knowledge instead of specific data. Important notions in connection with Web-related ontology are a vocabulary of basic terms and a precise specification of their meanings. The consensus standard vocabularies can be handled by defining reusable vocabularies, and customizing and extending them. A number of well-known ontologies arose from linguistics and knowledge engineering areas:

- *WordNet is a top-down ontology (in upper layer) in the linguistic domain containing a structured English language vocabulary with lexical categories and semantic relations.*
- *Cyc is a common ontology consisting of knowledge captured from different domains.*
- *SENSUS is a linguistic domain ontology built by extracting and merging information from existing electronic resources for the purpose of machine translation.*

2.1.2 Taxonomy, Thesauri, and Ontology

Taxonomy is a science of classification that provides guidelines about how to categorize, organize, label, and arrange information in hierarchical fashion. It can be considered classification based on similarities. Taxonomy includes presentations of vocabularies, application profiles, and development of metadata schemes, if any. Taxonomies and thesauri do not appear on the Semantic Web stack as they were not specifically designed for the Web; they, however, belong to the Semantic Web picture. The taxonomy can be defined as follows:

Definition 5—Taxonomy is a hierarchically organized controlled vocabulary. The world has a number of taxonomies, because humans naturally classify objects. Taxonomies are semantically weak and are commonly used when navigating without a precise research goal in mind.

As an example, a sample taxonomy from a typical tourism area is presented in this section. A tourism destination is primarily described by enumerating its features. However, since a taxonomy is only a collection of names, each item of a tourism area taxonomy must be characterized so that each description carries interesting information about the destination. This requires a vocabulary of terms that represent relevant concepts. Figure 2.1 illustrates a common (but incomplete) vocabulary that may serve this purpose. The relative meanings of the terms are reflected in the taxonomic ordering. The leaf terms are primary; the other terms are secondary and may be introduced by terminological definitions.

A thesaurus is intended to facilitate document retrieval. WordNet organizes English nouns, verbs, adverbs, and adjectives into a set of synonyms and defines relationships among synonyms.

Definition 6—A thesaurus is a controlled vocabulary arranged in a known order and structured so that equivalence, homographic, hierarchical, and associative relationships among terms are displayed clearly and identified by standardized relationship indicators.

```
Attraction
    Human artifacts
        Museum
    Visitor center
    Art gallery
    Architecture
            Stave church
            Stone church
            Memorial
            Monument
Viewpoint
Picnic area
Natural sites
    Fjord
    Waterfall
    Mountain pass
    National park
Activity
    Skiing
            Ski lift
            Ski tracks
    Rafting
    Fishing
    Walking
    Climbing
    Cycling
    Kayaking
Excursion
    Guided tour
    Fjord tour
    Canyon tour
    Glacier tour
    ..........
```

Figure 2.1   Hierarchical representations of tourist attractions.

Accommodation	Bed and breakfast
	Cabin
	Farm house
	Hotel
	Pension
Activities	Climbing
	Cycling
	Fishing
	Hiking
	Kayaking
	Rafting
	Ski tracking
	Skiing
	Walking
....	....
Events	Cultural
	Sport
Excursions	Canyon tour
	Fjord tour
	Glacier tour
	Guided tour
	Railway

Figure 2.2   Example of thesaurus.

A thesaurus can be modeled by concept- and term-oriented models. The International Organization for Standardization (ISO) provides two standards that deal with thesauri: ISO 2788 for monolingual thesauri and ISO 5964 for multilingual thesauri. Figure 2.2 is a partial thesaurus example (sorted alphabetically) for a typical tourism industry system. Both taxonomies and thesauri provide vocabularies of terms and simple relationships. Therefore, taxonomies and thesauri are above XML, namespaces, and controlled vocabulary in the Semantic Web stack.

However, the relationships they express are not as rich as those provided by RDF or Topic Maps, and consequently by ontology. In general, ontology consists of a taxonomy combined with relationships, constraints, and rules; the rules may be used with RDF or Topic Maps.

Ontology enables us to agree upon the meanings of terms used in a precise domain, knowing that several terms may represent the same concept (synonyms) and several concepts may be described by the same term (ambiguity). Ontology consists of a hierarchical description of important concepts of a domain and a description of each concept's properties. Ontology is at the heart of information retrieval from nomadic objects from the Internet and from heterogeneous data sources. An address can be modeled as shown in Figure 2.3.

In semantic-based information retrieval, ontology directly specifies the meanings of concepts to be searched. XML-based systems have very limited utility in this context unless the independent site content authors agree on the semantics of the terms they embed in source metadata. Ontology reduces such semantic ambiguities by offering a single interpretation resource. Furthermore, ontology can also enable software to map and transform information stored using variant terminologies.

Some researchers adopt modeling terminology and consider ontology as a metamodel, defined as an explicit description of the constructs and rules needed to

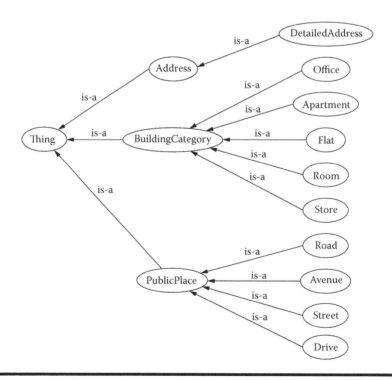

Figure 2.3   Example of address ontology.

build specific models within a domain of interest. A specific model can be created by instantiating the types and relating instances to each other according to the relationships in the meta-model; a model of the domain; and an example of a more general model, i.e., a meta-meta model. In order for a meta-model to act as an ontology, three properties must hold: (1) it must be expressed in a formal language to enable consistency checks and automated reasoning (formalization), (2) it must be agreed upon by a community (consensuality), and (3) it must be unambiguously identified and ubiquitously accessible over the Internet (identifiability).

2.1.3 Properties and Characteristics

The key characteristics of ontology are ease of use, comprehensibility, good formation, utility, limited proliferation, and reliance on technology (Kavi and Sergei, 1995). More particularly, it should include ease of representation and use and also support conversion of content from one ontology to another. It must also be easy to browse and present. Ontology should completely describe the intended content and be internally consistent in structure, naming, and content based on well-developed guidelines. It must ultimately aid language processing in resolving a variety of ambiguities and making necessary inferences. Situated development limits the size of an ontology, although presumably any piece of knowledge could be useful. An ontology is not limited to its domain but is more developed in the chosen domain. Acquisition and utilization are made more tractable by the deployment of recent technologies such as faster machines, color graphical user interfaces, graphical browsers and editors, on-line lexicons, corpora, other ontologies, semi-automated tools for consistency maintenance, and interfaces for lexicographer interactions.

2.2 Types of Ontologies

An ontology can be classified by the type of knowledge it conveys (Akerkar, 2009). A generic ontology, also known as a top ontology, specifies general concepts defined independently of a domain of application and can be used in different application domains. Time, space, mathematics, and other components are examples of general concepts. A domain ontology is dedicated to a particular domain that remains generic for this domain and can be used and reused for particular tasks in the same domain. Chemical, medical, enterprise modeling, and other uses represent domain ontologies. An application ontology gathers knowledge dedicated to a particular task, including more specialized knowledge of experts for the application. In general, application ontologies are not reusable. A meta-ontology or representation ontology specifies the knowledge representation principles used to define concepts of domain and generic ontologies; it defines, a class, a relation, and/or a function. Ontologies can also be classified as heavyweight and lightweight based on the expressiveness of their

Table 2.1   Parameters of Expressiveness of Ontology

Controlled vocabulary	List of terms
Thesaurus	Relations between terms such as synonyms provided
Informal taxonomy	Explicit hierarchy (generalization and specialization are supported) but no strict inheritance; instance of a subclass is not necessarily also an instance of a super class
Formal taxonomy	Strict inheritance
Frames	Frame (or class) has a number of properties inherited by subclasses and instances
Value restrictions	Property values restricted (e.g., by data type)
General logic constraints	Values may be constrained by logical or mathematical formulas using values from other properties
First-order logic constraints	Very expressive ontology languages allow first order logic constraints between terms and more detailed relationships such as disjoint classes, disjoint coverings, inverse relationships, part–whole relationships, etc.

contents. The parameters for such expressiveness were introduced by McGuinness (2003) and are summarized in Table 2.1.

According to Corcho et al. (2003), a lightweight ontology includes concepts, properties that describe concepts, relationships among concepts, and concept taxonomies. Heavyweight ontologies are complex and include axioms and constraints. A systematic evaluation of ontologies and related technologies may lead to a consistent level of quality and thus acceptance by industry. Future efforts may also achieve standardized benchmarks and certifications.

2.3 Parameters for Building Ontologies

Because of the complexity of the task and the many demands on ontology in terms of usability and reusability, many engineering methodologies have been developed. As stated earlier, ontology quality is measured in terms of criteria like clarity, coherence, extendibility, minimal encoding bias, and minimal ontological commitment (Gruber, 1995; Kalfoglou, 2000). Table 2.2 briefly lists the criteria. To gain the maximum benefit, ontology must be shared and reused. Existing ontologies may be combined to create new ones. This ability makes an ontology independent, reusable, and sharable for many applications. The parameters must be considered during ontology engineering. Many models have been utilized in designing and

Table 2.2 Design Criteria for Ontology Engineering

Clarity	Intended meaning of term should be clear and not permit multiple interpretations
Coherence	Ontology must be logically and formally consistent
Extendibility	Adding new terms and extending definitions should be easy and not require revision of existing definitions
Minimal encoding bias	Ontology should be as independent as possible from applications and implementation tools that will use the ontology and independent of formatting schemes
Minimal ontological commitment	Even if ontology is independent of platform of implementation and formatting schemes, it can be reusable if the content represented through the ontology is less committed

evaluating ontologies. The classical "skeletal" model (Uschold and King, 1995) presents a framework for designing and evaluating an ontology:

- *Identifying purpose and scope*
- *Building the ontology*
- *Capturing the ontology*
- *Coding the ontology*
- *Integrating existing ontology*
- *Evaluation*
- *Documentation*

Uschold et al. (1996; 1998) further modified the approach by adding six more steps:

Scoping (brainstorming to produce all potentially relevant terms and phrases; grouping terms into work areas)

- *Producing definitions (deciding next steps)*
- *Determining meta-ontology*
- *Addressing each work area individually*
- *Defining terms (reaching agreement in natural language)*
- *Reviewing and revising definitions*
- *Developing meta-ontology*

2.4 Standards and Interoperability

Contents and systems on the Semantic Web must share, exchange, and reuse data and utilities based on their intended meanings. This process is called *semantic interoperability*. Achieving semantic interoperability among different information systems is very laborious, tedious, and error-prone in a distributed and heterogeneous environment like the World Wide Web (WWW). The three levels of information heterogeneity are syntax, structure, and semantics (Stuckenschmidt and Harmelen, 2005). Syntactic heterogeneity is the simplest problem and arises from the use of different data formats. To solve syntactic heterogeneity, standardized formats such as XML [http://www.w3.org/TR/2004/REC-xml-20040204], RDF/RDFS [http://www.w3.org/TR/2004/REC-rdf-primer-20040210] and OWL [http://www.w3.org/TR/2003/CR-owl-features-20030818] have been widely used to describe data in a uniform way that makes automatic processing of shared information easier.

Although standardization plays an important role for syntactic heterogeneity, it does not overcome structural heterogeneity resulting from the way information is structured even in homogeneous syntactic environments (Ming, 2008). Manually encoded transformation rules and some middleware components have been used to solve structural heterogeneity problems (Wiederhold, 1992). Information heterogeneity can be defined as follows:

Definition 7—Semantics is an individual's interpretation of data according to his or her understanding of the world.

Definition 8—Interoperability is the ability of two or more systems to exchange information and use the information exchanged.

Definition 9—Semantic interoperability is the capability of different information systems to communicate information consistent with the intended meaning of the encoded information (Patel et al., 2005).

Definition 10—Information heterogeneity is information difference. It occurs at syntax, structure, and semantics levels (Stuckenschmidt and Harmelen, 2005).

2.5 Semantic Web and Ontology

As stated earlier, the Semantic Web enables machines to interpret and process information on the platform of the WWW. To meet the challenge of providing customized information with well-defined meanings, several technologies have been developed for shaping, constructing and developing the Semantic Web. Figure 2.4 represents a typical Semantic Web structure. The first layer works as an interface containing utilities and agents facilitating interface to one or more ontologies utilized in the language and standard layer that contains representations and management methodologies corresponding to the ontologies it accommodates.

The ontology of the Semantic Web helps share common understandings of the structure of information among people or software utilities and enables reuse of domain knowledge. It makes domain assumptions and relationships of contents explicit and understandable, and hence allows effective analysis of domain content; it separates domain knowledge from operational knowledge (Noy et al., 2001).

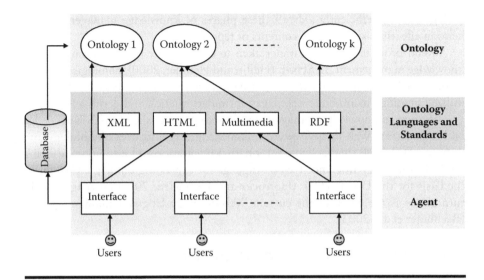

Figure 2.4   Structure of Semantic Web.

The Semantic Web presents much promise and many challenges, from scalability to effective assessment of the components of the Web. Semantic Web data are likely to increase significantly and associated techniques will have to evolve. The new tagging and ontology formats require new representations and navigation paradigms. The multiplicity of ontologies raises the issue of their integration; this area has been widely explored and solutions have been proposed, even though some problems remain. The highly dynamic nature of the Semantic Web makes the evolution and maintenance of semantic tagging and ontology difficult. The ultimate challenge is the automation of semantics extraction.

2.6 Applications

The traditional application areas for ontology are knowledge representation (Brachman and Schmolze, 1985) and knowledge-based systems (Akerkar and Sajja, 2009; Studer et al., 1998). Fensel (2003) mentions three important application areas in which the applications of ontology may exert huge impacts: knowledge management, enterprise application integration (EAI), and e-commerce; e-learning and e-governance are additional areas of potential impact.

2.6.1 Knowledge Management

Knowledge management deals with discovery, utilization, searching, and sharing the required knowledge from organization-wide repositories. A prime requirement is that ontology efficiently aids all these phases of knowledge management and helps in effective assessment of contents of repositories.

Several projects have been undertaken to demonstrate the use of ontology in knowledge management. In SHOE (Heflin and Hendler, 2000), ontologies are used to annotate Web pages to facilitate information retrieval. Fensel et al. (1998; 2000) utilized ontology to annotate web pages, formulate queries, and derive answers.

A European knowledge management research project called On-To-Knowledge on the Semantic Web [http://www.ontoknowledge.org/] focuses on ontology and Semantic Web tools that facilitate information integration and mediation, utilizing the OIL (Ontology Inference Layer) language for expressing ontology. OIL forms the basis for the DAML+OIL (Horrocks and Harmelen, 2001) language that in turn serves as the basis for the current Web ontology language known as OWL (Bechhofer et al., 2003).

2.6.2 Enterprise Application Integration

Enterprise-wide applications encompass several loosely coupled subsystems containing many heterogeneous types of knowledge, and hence must work with different ontologies. One example is customer relationship management (CRM; Bruijn, 2003). According to Bruijn, a company's customer data may be maintained in several different applications requiring different ontologies that must be integrated. Such ad hoc integration is not scalable and the creation of many ad hoc transformations introduces maintenance problems. A business requires a purpose-driven, extendable, and reusable approach to application integration. Ontologies are inherently extendable and reusable. They explicate the data in applications and thereby enable purpose-driven integration (Fensel, 2003).

2.6.3 e-Commerce

e-Commerce applications are broadly classified as B2C (business-to-consumer) and B2B (business-to-business). Ontology can be applied in both areas to increase efficiency and make cooperation easier. In the B2C area, ontology can be used to facilitate so-called shopbots, webbots, and marketing agents for activities like price comparison and meeting agents and buyers. In B2B, a lot of work has already been done to standardize the representation formats of electronic messages between businesses with EDIFACT [http://www.unece.org/trade/untdid/], XML [http://www.w3.org/xml], RosettaNet [http://www.rosettanet.org/], and VerticalNet [http://www.verticalnet.com/]. Applications for B2B can effectively mediate different product and service ontologies, as well as different e-business ontologies (Ding et al. 2002).

2.6.4 e-Learning

e-Learning is a cognitive activity that differs from person to person. It is necessary for e-learning systems to consider individual aspects of learners and ignore the different needs specific to existing cognitive profiles. Gomes et al. (2006) presented an approach to e-learning personalization based on an ontology. A student model is integrated with an ontology, enabling a personalized system to guide a student's learning process. Additional academic projects using OWL have been developed, for example:

Friend of a Friend or FOAF [http://www.foaf-project.org/]—This development is for communities and includes home pages of people, links among them, and objects they create and activities they pursue. Coverage treats a person as 1 concept with 10 properties.

Semantic Web Portal or SWP [http://sw-portal.deri.org/ontologies/swportal.html]—This ontology is for scientific portals. Coverage (main concept) is by person (agent or organization), publication, and conference and includes 68 classes, 21 data properties, and 57 object properties.

MarcOnt [http://www.marcont.org/]—This development applies to digital libraries, is ongoing and still under construction; mapping covers Marc21, DC, and BibTeX formats.

Other ontology applications include corporate intranets, knowledge management, ontology-based searching, information retrieval, group common access, and virtual enterprises. Summaries and useful links related to knowledge-based systems and ongoing ontology projects can be accessed at http://www.cs.utexas.edu/users/mfkb/related.html and http://ksl-web.stanford.edu/kst/ontology-sources.html.

2.7 Reasoning

Reasoning is the process of inferring new information from an ontology and its instance base. It may be performed on demand or by materialization (Kiryakov et al. 2004). Retrieval by query answering is an example of the former, often implemented by a backward chaining strategy in which the system is charged to establish only the information satisfying the request. Materialization means that inference is performed and the results stored for further usage (also known as forward chaining). Facts within the instance base, along with their relationships and constraints, are exploited to infer new facts that can be added to the base. A well known mechanism uses IF–THEN rules representing associations of concepts. If the ontology has been obtained by integration, rules can be classified as *internals* or *bridges*. Internal rules specify associations among elements of one source, as in:

$$\text{Internal Rule}: \frac{<O:Fi>}{<O:Fj>}$$

The schema can be read: If *Fi* (antecedent) is a true formula within ontology O, then *Fj* (consequent) is true in the same *O*. Internal rules support reasoning within an ontology to answer its competence questions. Bridge rules specify associations among elements of two or more ontologies, for example:

$$\text{Bridge Rule}: \frac{< Oi : Fi >}{< Ok : Fj >}$$

The schema reads: If *Fi* is a true formula within ontology *Oi*, then *Fj* is true in the ontology *Ok*. Bridge rules support reasoning across ontologies. Embedding production rules have been addressed at the symbolic level too. In a hybrid approach, a separation is maintained between the predicates used in the ontologies and those in the rules. In a homogeneous approach, both ontologies and rules are represented with the same language.

2.8 Ontology Languages

To use ontologies within an application, they must be specified. Obviously, an ontology must be delivered via some concrete representation. A variety of languages may be used to represent conceptual models with varying characteristics in terms of expressiveness, ease of use, and computational complexity. The field of knowledge representation (KR) has, of course, long been a focal point of research in the artificial intelligence community. Languages used for specifying ontologies are usually categorized as (1) vocabularies defined using natural language, (2) object-based knowledge representation languages such as frames and UML, and (3) languages based on predicates expressed in logic, e.g., description logics. The next subsections present brief overviews of frame-based and logic-based languages.

2.8.1 Frame-Based Languages

Frame-based systems are based on frames or classes that represent collections of instances. Each frame has an associated collection of slots or attributes that can be filled by values or other frames. In particular, a frame may include a "kind-of" slot allowing the assertion of a frame taxonomy. This hierarchy can then be used for inheritance of slots, allowing a sparse representation. Along with frames representing concepts, a frame-based representation may also contain instance frames that represent specific instances. Frame-based systems (Akerkar et al., 2009) have been used extensively in the KR world, particularly for applications in natural language processing. The best known frame system is Ontolingua. Frames are popular because frame-based modeling is similar to object-based modeling and is intuitive for many users.

Frame-based ontology (Gruber, 1993) defining concepts such as frames, slots, and slot constraints is a representational methodology. A frame is a single place in which facts about a class are gathered (Bechhofer et al., 2001) in a simple fashion. During modeling, the frames and their properties can be visualized by a tool in such a way that all relevant properties are available simultaneously. A frame ontology does not contain any static knowledge about the real world. Instead it is a representational mechanism for creating an ontology that describes knowledge about the real world.

Ontolingua (Gruber, 1993) is a system specially developed for representing ontologies so that they may be translated easily into other ontology languages. The syntax and semantics of definitions in Ontolingua are based on knowledge information formats (KIFs). A very influential frame-based knowledge representation standard is Open Knowledge Base Connectivity (OKBC; Chaudhri et al., 1998). In OKBC, a frame consists of either a class along with its properties and axioms (expressing logic constraints) or an instance along with its property values.

According to Bruijn (2003), the general problem with using a frame-based language as an ontology language is the lack of the well-defined semantics that enable computers to "understand" an ontology, or at least process it according to well-defined rules. For example, it is often not clear in frame-based systems whether a slot constraint is universally or existentially quantified (Bechhofer et al., 2001). SHOE (Heflin et al., 1999], based on a frame language (F-logic), was an early attempt to develop an ontology definition language to embed semantics inside HTML. Naturally, the ontology definitions in SHOE consist of class name, inheritance, and slots. The simplified syntax for the class inheritance diagram can be seen as follows:

```
[gen .base . SHOEEntity]
[...]
Address
Person
    Employee
```

In the above syntax, one can see two classes: *Employee* and *Person*. The employee class inherits from the person class and also from the address class. The following syntax gives a property of the STRING literal type that defines the city property of an address class:

```
addressCity(Address, .STRING)
[..]
homeAddress(Person, Address)
[..]
father(Person:"child", Person:"father")
friend(Person, Person)
[..]
```

SHOE supports the import of other ontologies and also allows us to define inference rules.

2.8.2 Logic-Based Languages

To represent, access, and reuse knowledge effectively and efficiently, frame-based ontologies are not sufficient. An alternative to frame-based methodology is logic, notably description logic (DL; Baader et al., 2003), also called terminological logic. A DL describes knowledge in terms of concepts and relations that are used to automatically derive classification taxonomies. Concepts are defined in terms of descriptions using other roles and concepts. A model is built from small pieces in a descriptive way rather than through assertion of hierarchies. (Baader et al., 1991).

DL forms a decidable subset of first order logic. This decidability is very convenient for reasoning about ontology. However, serious limitations surround the expressiveness of DL, e.g., the absence of variables (Bruijn, 2003). This limited expressiveness, however, ensures decidability and improves tractability. DL provides many reasoning services that allow the construction of classification hierarchies and the checking of consistency of the descriptions. These reasoning services can then be used by applications that prefer to use the knowledge represented in the ontology.

DLs vary in expressivity, which determines the computational complexity of the reasoning algorithms for each language. In DLs, class can include disjunction and negation along with constraints on the relations to other classes. A relation between a class (its domain) and another class (its range) can be constrained in cardinality and type. Relations can also be given definitions and thus have subclasses too. Class partitions can be defined by specifying a set of subclasses that represent the partitions. These partitions may be exhaustive if all instances of the class belong to some partition or disjoint if the subclasses do not overlap. A class can be denoted as primitive and not given a definition; in that case, the subclasses and instances must be explicitly shown.

DL systems use these definitions to automatically organize class descriptions in a taxonomic hierarchy and automatically classify instances into classes whose definitions are satisfied by their features. Specifically, description logic reasoners provide two key capabilities:

- *Class subsumption in which a C1 class subsumes another class (C2) if its definition includes a superset of the instances included in C2*
- *Instance recognition in which an instance belongs to a class if its features (roles and role values) satisfy the definition of the class*

Early DL systems include KL-ONE (Brachman and Schmolze, 1985) and CLASSIC (Borgida et al., 1989). Knowledge in DL is represented in a hierarchical structure of classes (or concepts) that are defined intentionally via descriptions that specify the properties that objects must satisfy to belong to a concept (Fensel, 2003). Obviously, DL presents advantages in comparison to other knowledge representation languages (Baader et al., 1991). Declarative semantics clearly indicate that the meaning of a construct is not given operationally, but provided by the description and its models. Well investigated algorithms have verified a number of properties of an ontology (correctness, completeness, decidability, complexity). Ontology languages for the Semantic Web based on description logics are now de facto W3C standards.

One major difference between frame-based and DL-based languages is that the former relies completely on explicit statements of class subsumption and the latter can efficiently compute the subsumption relationship between classes on the basis of the intentional definition of the classes. Moreover, frames usually offer a rich set of language constructs but impose very restrictive constraints on how they can be used to define a class. DL involves a more limited set of language constructs, but allows primitives to be combined to create defined concepts. The taxonomy for these defined concepts is automatically established by the logic reasoning system of the DL.

2.8.3 Ontology Representation Languages

In the 1990s, Knowledge Interchange Format (KIF) was seen as the standard for ontology modeling and ontology was applied slowly to the World Wide Web. In 1999, the RDF language (http://www.w3.org/RDF/) was developed to annotate Web pages with machine-processable meta-data. RDF can be used to express knowledge.

Figure 2.5 shows the layers of languages used for the Semantic Web (Berners-Lee, 2005). The components on the bottom layers mention Unicode URI and XML schema along with defined standards and provide a syntactical basis for Semantic Web languages. Unicode provides an elementary character encoding scheme used by XML. The URI (Uniform Resource Identifier; Beckett, 2003) standard provides

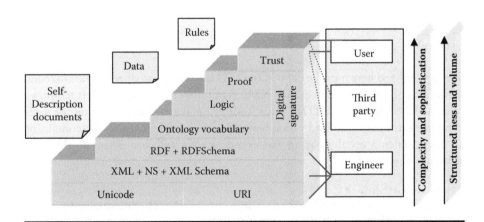

Figure 2.5   Layers of Semantic Web languages.

a means to uniquely identify content and other resources on the Web. All concepts used in higher languages are specified using Unicode and are uniquely identified by URIs. Layers atop the Unicode and URI bottom layer facilitate XML and RDF for content representation and utilization. The next layer defines and describes vocabulary used in ontology. Logic, proof, and trust layers provide functionalities of background logic, facility of deductive reasoning, and trust mechanisms by applying digital signatures and certifications from third parties. According to Eiter et al. (2006a), for the realization of the Semantic Web, the integration of different layers of its conceived architecture is a fundamental issue. In particular, the integration of rules and ontology is currently under investigation and many proposals have been made.

2.8.3.1 XML Schema

An XML schema formally describes the structure of an XML document. The schema may be considered a definition language that enables us to constrain conforming XML documents to a specific vocabulary and specific hierarchical structure. XML schemas are analogous to database schemas that define column names and data types in database tables. XML schema became a W3C recommendation (synonymous with standard) on May 5, 2001. Each schema should accompany document type definitions (DTDs) and presentation cascade style sheets (CSSs). A DTD contains a grammar describing a language. Using a schema to specify an XML vocabulary gets us much closer to a true type declaration. We may define our tour for a system in a tourism domain as follows:

```
<tour>
     <tour_name> …. </tour_name>

     <tour_description> …… </tour_description>
     …..
     …..
</tour>
```

The tags utilized here must be defined in DTD documents to provide grammar and definitions of user-defined tags. The XML is not presentation oriented; it requires a separate CSS along with a DTD. This leads to the benefits of presenting the same content in different fashion by simply providing multiple CSSs. A file containing an XML schema usually has an xsd extension. We will now illustrate the basic structure of such a file:

```
<?xml version = "1.0"?>
<xsd:schema xmlns:xsd="http://www.w3.org/2001/XMLSchema">
     <!-- global declarations go here -->
</xsd:schema>
```

Global declarations state the elements in documents that instantiate the schema:

```
<xsd:element name = "tag1" type = "Tag1Type"/>
<xsd:element name = "tag2" type = "Tag2Type"/>
<xsd:element name = "tag3" type = "Tag3Type"/>
```

An element declaration usually specifies the name and type of element, for example a built-in:

```
xsd:string ::= <char>+
xsd:boolean ::= false | true
xsd:decimal ::= (+ | -)?<digit>+(.<digit>*)?
xsd:double ::= IEEE double precision float
xsd:float ::= IEEE single precision float
xsd:integer ::= (+|-)?<digit>+
xsd:duration ::= P<int>Y<int>M<int>DT<int>H<int>M<int>S
xsd:time ::= <hours>:<mins>:<secs>
<hours>, <mins> ::= <int>, <secs> ::= <decimal>
xsd:date ::= <CCYY>-<MM>-<DD>
xsd:anyURI ::= <URI>
xsd:ID ::= <NCName>
xsd:IDREF ::= <NCName>
xsd:QName ::= <URI>:<NCName>
xsd:Name ::= <XMLName>
```

A declaration may be a complex type declared by the user. In this case the type schema will also contain global type declarations:

```
<xsd:complexType name = "Tag1Type">
     <!-- tag1 elements and attributes declared here -->
</xsd:complexType>
<xsd:complexType name = "Tag2Type">
     <!-- tag2 elements and attributes declared here -->
</xsd:complexType>
<xsd:complexType name = "Tag3Type">
     <!-- tag3 elements and attributes declared here -->
</xsd:complexType>
```

2.8.3.1.1 Constraints for Elements and Attributes

An element declaration may specify the minimum and maximum number of occurrences. The default value for both is 1. The maximum number of occurrences may be set to "unbounded" to indicate one or more. A default value (content) may also be specified:

```
<xsd:element name = "tag" type = "TYPE"
     minOccurs = "MIN"
```

```
     maxOccurs = "Max"
     default = "0" />
where: "0" <= Min <= Max <= "unbounded"
```

For example, assume the following declaration is made:

```
<xsd:element name = "members_tour">
     <xsd:complexType>
          <xsd:sequence>
               <xsd:element name = " members_tour " type =
"xsd:integer"
                         minOccurs = "0" maxOccurs = "3" default =
"2" />
          </xsd:sequence>
     <xsd:complexType>
</xsd:element>
```

Notice that the type of element declaration can be declared globally or locally. In the example above we declare the type on *nums* by an anonymous local declaration. Alternatively, we could have used a global declaration:

```
<xsd:element name = " members_tour " type = " members_
tourType"/>
<xsd:complexType name = " members_tourType">
     <xsd:sequence>
          <xsd:element name = " members_tour " type =
"xsd:integer"
               minOccurs = "0" maxOccurs = "3" default = "2"/>
     </xsd:sequence>
<xsd:complexType>
```

Here are a few sample *members_tour* elements:

```
     //------an empty ' members_tour' ----
     < members_tour />
//------an empty ' members_tour' ----
< members_tour >
</ members_tour >
//------an example ' members_tour' ----
     < members_tour > 3 </ members_tour >
```

The following declaration is inconsistent:

```
<xsd:element name = " members_tour " type = "xsd:integer"
     minOccurs = "0" default = "2"/>
```

Instead of a default value, we can specify that a fixed value should be used:

```
<xsd:element name = " members_tour " type = "xsd:integer"
     minOccurs = "0" maxOccurs = "3" fixed = "2"/>
```

We can utilize the *use* attribute to specify whether an attribute is optional, required, or prohibited. We can also use the default attribute to set a default value. For example:

```
<xsd:element name = "tourname" type = "xsd:string">
    <xsd:attribute name = "duration" use = "optional" default
= "11"/>
</xsd:element>
```

Here are a few sample elements:

```
<tourname duration = "5"> "Rameshwaram" </ tourname >
< tourname > "Kerala" </ tourname >
```

The duration of the Kerala trip is 11 days, that is, it is equivalent to:

```
< tourname duration = "11"> "Kerala" </ tourname >
```

Let's change the declaration to:

```
<xsd:element name = " tourname " type = "xsd:string">
    <xsd:attribute name = "duration" use = "optional" fixed =
"11"/>
</xsd:element>
```

Now the element:

```
< tourname duration = "5"> "Rameshwaram" </ tourname >
```

is illegal because it specifies a duration attribute different from 11 days. If we change the optional status to required:

```
<xsd:element name = " tourname" type = "xsd:string">
    <xsd:attribute name = "duration" use = "required" fixed =
"11"/>
</xsd:element>
```

Now both of the following elements are illegal:

```
< tourname duration = "5"> "Rameshwaram" </ tourname >
< tourname > "Kerala" </ tourname >
```

2.8.3.1.2 Creating Complex Types

It is simple to declare an element with text content such as:

```
< tourname >"Rameshwaram"</ tourname >
```

This is just:

```
<xsd:element name = " tourname " type = "xsd:string"/>
```

But what happens if the element also has an additional attribute?

```
<person duration = "11"> "Kerala" </ tourname >
```

Unfortunately, we must declare a complex type:

```
<xsd:element name = " tourname" type = "TourType"/>
```

TourType uses a *simpleContent* element that extends the simple type string by adding an attribute:

```
<xsd:complexType name = "TourType">
    <xsd:simpleContent>
        <xsd:extension base = "xsd:string">
          <xsd:attribute name = "duration" type
="xsd:positiveInteger"/>
        </xsd:extension>
    </xsd:simpleContent>
</xsd:complexType>
```

Example 2.1: Consider an online train booking site that enables issuance, reservation, and cancellation of tickets for different tourist sites. Part of the data is as follows:

```
<!-- trains.xml -->
<?xml version="1.0"?>
<!DOCTYPE trains SYSTEM "trains.dtd">
< trains >
  < trains id="1">
    <name>"National Express" </name>
  </ trains >
< trains id="2">
    <name>"Super Fast Express" </name>
  </ trains >
</trains>
```

The DTD and schema definition can be given as follows:

```
<!DOCTYPE trains [
  <!ELEMENT trains (trains*)>
  <!ELEMENT trains(name)>
  <!ELEMENT name (#PCDATA)>
  <!ATTLIST train id ID #REQUIRED>
]>
```

The XML schema definition of *train* is:

```
<xsd:schema xmlns:xsd="http://www.w3.org/2001/XMLSchema">
  <xsd:element name="trains">
    <xsd:complexType>
      <xsd:sequence>
        <xsd:element name="trains" type="TrainType"
                     minOccurs="1" maxOccurs="unbounded"/>
      </xsd:sequence>
    </xsd:complexType>
  </xsd:element>
  <xsd:complexType name="trainsType">
    <xsd:sequence>
      <xsd:element name="name" type="xsd:string">
    </xsd:sequence>
    <xsd:attribute name="id" type="xsd:id" use="required"/>
  </xsd:complexType>
</xsd:schema>
```

The XML schema is written in XML and offers more than a DTD. Thus it is more complex DTDs for the same class of XML documents. The XML schema allows the specification of many types of constraints and thus is a more suitable candidate for an ontology language than DTD.

2.8.3.2 RDF Schema

The Resource Description Framework (RDF) is considered the most relevant standard for data representation and exchange on the Semantic Web. RDF provides better support for interoperability and describes more than the document contents. The basic RDF model includes resources, properties, and statements. More advanced concepts in RDF include a container model and descriptions of statements. The container model has three types of objects (bags, sequences, alternatives). RDF is a universal language that provides the facility to describe resources using their own vocabularies. While it efficiently describes resources with classes, properties, and values, application-specific classes and properties must be defined. To meet this requirement, a schema is proposed as an RDF extension. A schema is a type of dictionary that includes interpretations of terms used in sentences.

An RDF schema is defined as a vocabulary (URI reference is http://www. w3.org/2000/01/rdf-schema#). It does not provide actual application-specific classes and properties. Instead, an RDF schema provides a framework to describe application-specific classes and properties. Classes in RDF schema are much like classes in object-oriented programming languages. A class is any resource having an rdf:type property whose value is rdfs:Class.

Example 2.2: In the following schema, the *train* resource is a subclass of the *vehicle* class.

```
<?xml version="1.0"?>
<rdf:RDF
xmlns:rdf= "http://www.w3.org/1999/02/22-rdf-syntax-ns#"
xmlns:rdfs="http://www.w3.org/2000/01/rdf-schema#"
xml:base= "http://www.vehicle.org/vehicles#">
<rdf:Description rdf:ID="vehicle">
  <rdf:type
   rdf:resource="http://www.w3.org/2000/01/rdf-schema#Class"/>
</rdf:Description>
<rdf:Description rdf:ID="train">
  <rdf:type
   rdf:resource="http://www.w3.org/2000/01/rdf-schema#Class"/>
  <rdfs:subClassOf rdf:resource="#vehicle"/>
</rdf:Description>
</rdf:RDF>
```

As an RDF schema, class is an RDF resource. We can modify the above example with the help of rdfs:Class instead of rdf:Description, and drop the rdf:type information; thus we have:

```
<?xml version="1.0"?>
<rdf:RDF
xmlns:rdf= "http://www.w3.org/1999/02/22-rdf-syntax-ns#"
xmlns:rdfs="http://www.w3.org/2000/01/rdf-schema#"
xml:base= "http://www.vehicle.org/vehicles#">
<rdfs:Class rdf:ID="vehicle" />
<rdfs:Class rdf:ID="train">
  <rdfs:subClassOf rdf:resource="#vehicle"/>
</rdfs:Class>
</rdf:RDF>
```

Furthermore, the RDF schema allows us to define the domain and range for every property. However, it has limitations; for example, it cannot be used to define whether a property is symmetric or transitive. To model such axioms within ontologies, W3C established a Web Ontology Language (OWL) Working Group in 2001.

2.8.3.3 Web Ontology Language

This subsection covers OWL—an ontology language for the Web. OWL is one of the main constituents of the Semantic Web. It involves common formats for integration and combination of data drawn from diverse sources, whereas the original Web mainly concentrated on the interchange of documents. It is also about language for recording how data relates to real-world objects. A simpler definition for OWL is that it represents knowledge about a particular domain; it is also recognized as a specification of conceptualization. OWL is semantically based on description logics (Baader et al., 2003).

The W3C has designed OWL as a revision of DAML+OIL. It is based on W3C standards (XML, RDF, and RDFS) and extends them with richer modeling primitives. Moreover, OWL is based on DL; thus it is an ontology language that can formally describe the meanings of terminologies used in Web documents. Both RDF and Topic Maps lack expressive power. OWL, layered on top of RDFS, extends the capabilities of RDFS and adds various constructors for building complex class expressions, cardinality restrictions on properties, characteristics of properties, and mapping between classes and individuals. Ontology in OWL is a set of axioms describing classes, properties, and facts about individuals.

OWL allows class information and data-type information, defines class constructs, and permits the Boolean combination of class expressions. OWL has quantifier forms. Standardized formal semantics and additional vocabulary allow OWL to explicitly represent term descriptions and the relationships among entities. Figure 2.6 illustrates the class hierarchy.

OWL allows the formalization of a domain by defining classes and their properties, defines individuals and asserts properties about them, and permits reasoning about classes and individuals. OWL is used in a three-step approach to improve term descriptions in a schema vocabulary:

■ *Formalize a domain by defining classes and their properties*
■ *Define individuals and assert properties about them*
■ *Reason out these classes and individuals to the degree permitted by the formal semantics of OWL languages*

OWL extends the notion of classes and properties defined in RDF schema and also provides additional axioms to define advanced characteristics and constraints of classes and properties. OWL offers three sublanguages with increasing expressiveness. OWL Full is the entire language that allows an ontology to enhance the meaning of a predefined (RDF or OWL) vocabulary. However, it offers no computational guarantees. OWL DL has theoretical properties of description logic and permits efficient reasoning. Every legal OWL DL document is a legal RDF document. OWL DL is useful where completeness and decidability are important. The third sublanguage, OWL Lite, uses simple constraints and reasoning and has the least formal complexity among the sublanguages. It is basically for class hierarchies and limited constraints.

OWL Full contains all the OWL language constructs and provides the free, unconstrained use of RDF constructs. In OWL Full, owl:Class is equivalent to rdfs:Class. OWL Full permits classes to be individuals. A class can even be a property of itself. In OWL Full, owl:Things and rdfs:Resource are equivalents. This

Figure 2.6   Class hierarchy.

means that object properties and data type properties are not disjoint. The advantage is that this jointness provides high expressive power. Unfortunately, the drawback is that it is computationally undecidable. As the result, it is very difficult to build a reasoning tool for OWL Full. Although theoretically it can be processed via an FOL engine, it cannot guarantee complete answers.

An OWL Lite ontology should be an OWL DL ontology and must additionally satisfy the constraints. For example, some constructors such as, owl:oneOf, owl:disjointWith, owl:unionOf, owl:complementOf, owl:hasValue and owl:DataRange are not allowed; owl:equivalentClass statements can no longer be made between anonymous classes and are permitted only between class identifiers. Cardinality statements (minimal, maximal, exact cardinality) can be made only on values 0 or 1 and not on arbitrary non-negative integers.

Ontology developers adopting OWL must consider which sublanguage best matches their requirements. The choice between OWL Lite and OWL DL depends on the extent to which users require the more expressive constructs provided by OWL DL and OWL Full. The choice of OWL DL or OWL Full depends on the extent to which users require the meta-modeling facilities of RDF schema.

Recently, Web Ontology Language has undergone a revision originally designated OWL 1.1 and now named OWL 2; it is an extension of the original version. OWL 2 introduces a new functional style syntax that will replace the OWL 1 abstract syntax. OWL 2 does not yet provide RDF-style semantics. Therefore, the transformation of ontologies in functional style syntax into RDF graphs is a purely syntactic process in OWL 2.

2.8.3.3.1 Ontology Header

A header contains information about an ontology such as the version number and collaborations with other ontologies. An ontology is basically a component of a software system and naturally changes over time. While changing the Semantic Web ontologies, documents should be copied and given new URLs. In order to connect a document to the original version, OWL offers versioning properties such as owl:priorVersion and owl:backwardCompatibleWith. These two properties have no formal semantics. The owl:priorVersion provides a link to its previous version and can be used to track the version history of an ontology. owl:backwardCompatibleWith and owl:incompatibleWith indicate compatibility or the lack thereof with previous ontology versions. For ontologies to exert maximum impacts, they must be widely shared. To minimize the intellectual effort required, ontologies must be reused. owl:DeprecatedClass and owl:DeprecatedProperty indicate that a class or property is preserved for backward compatibility purposes only and may be phased out in the future.

2.8.3.3.2 OWL Classes

OWL classes provide an abstraction mechanism for grouping resources with similar characteristics. A class has an intentional meaning that is related but not equal to its class extension. OWL has six types of class descriptions, namely:

- *A class identifier (URI reference)*
- *An exhaustive enumeration of individuals that together form instances of a class*
- *A property restriction*
- *An intersection of two or more class descriptions*
- *A union of two or more class descriptions*
- *A complement of a class description*

Two OWL class names are predefined: owl:Thing and owl:Nothing. The class extension of owl:Thing is the set of all individuals in the domain of discourse. The class extension of owl:Nothing is the empty set. The *Class* identifier describes a class through a name. It is represented as an instance of owl:Class, a subclass of rdfs:ClassL:

```
<owl:Class rdf:ID="Destination">
```

In OWL, you can specify taxonomies for both classes and properties. To provide extra information describing a class, one can include properties from the RDFS and/or OWL vocabularies. The rdfs:subClassOf property can be used to relate a class to more general classes. The following short OWL ontology provides an idea of the general structure of an OWL document; *Hotel* is a subclass of *Accommodation*.

```
<!DOCTYPE rdf:RDF [
<!ENTITY owl "http://www.w3.org/2002/07/owl#">]>
<rdf:RDF xmlns:owl ="http://www.w3.org/2002/07/owl#"
xmlns:rdf ="http://www.w3.org/1999/02/22-rdf-syntax-ns#"
xmlns:rdfs="http://www.w3.org/2000/01/rdf-schema#">
<owl:Ontology rdf:about="">
<rdfs:label>My Ontology</rdfs:label>
<rdfs:comment>An example tourism ontology</rdfs:comment>
</owl:Ontology>
<owl:Class rdf:ID="Accommodation" />
<owl:Class rdf:ID="Hotel" />
<rdfs:subClassOf rdf:resource="#Accommodation" />
</owl:Class>
<owl:ObjectProperty rdf:ID="hasService" />
<owl:ObjectProperty rdf:ID="hasFacility">
<rdfs:subPropertyOf rdf:resource="#hasService" />
</owl:ObjectProperty>
<owl:DatatypeProperty rdf:ID="hasFacilityName" />
<owl:ObjectProperty rdf:ID="hasGuestRoom">
<owl:inverseOf rdf:resource="#hasConferenceRoom" />
</owl:ObjectProperty>
<owl:ObjectProperty rdf:ID="isExpensiveThan">
<rdf:type rdf:resource="&owl;TransitiveProperty" />
</owl:ObjectProperty>
<owl:ObjectProperty rdf:ID="hasRoomNumber">
<rdf:type rdf:resource="&owl;FunctionalProperty" />
<rdf:type rdf:resource="&owl;InverseFunctionalProperty" />
</owl:ObjectProperty>
</rdf:RDF>
```

The root of the above OWL document is an rdf:RDF element because all OWL documents are RDF documents only if some degree of compatibility exists between the two standards. The purpose of the owl:Ontology element is to identify the current document as an ontology; it also serves as a container for metadata about the ontology. By using the empty string as the value for the rdf:about attribute, we indicate that the base URL of the document should be used as its URI.

2.8.3.3.3 Enumeration

A class description of *enumeration* defines an anonymous class that contains exactly the enumerated individuals. It is defined with the owl:oneOf property that points to a list of individuals that serve as instances of the class. It is essential to describe the complete set of members and subelements for each member. In the example below, the class owl:Thing is used but more particular classes could be used too.

```
<owl:IndianSubcontinent>
    <owl:oneOf rdf:parseType="Collection">
            <owl:Thing rdf:about="#India"/>
            <owl:Thing rdf:about="#Bangala Desh"/>
            <owl:Thing rdf:about="#Pakistan"/>
    </owl:oneOf>
</owl:IndianSubcontinent>
```

2.8.3.3.4 Property Restrictions

A local property restriction defines an anonymous class of all individuals that satisfy the restriction:

```
<owl:Restriction>
        <owl:onProperty>
          <owl:ObjectProperty rdf:ID="hasRoom"/>
        </owl:onProperty>
        <owl:someValuesFrom>
          <owl:Class rdf:ID="Guestroom"/>
        </owl:someValuesFrom>
</owl:Restriction>
```

OWL distinguishes two kinds of restrictions.

2.8.3.3.4.1 Value Restrictions—A value restriction puts constraints on the value range of a property when applied to this particular class description. The three types of value restrictions are:

owl:allValuesFrom
owl:someValuesFrom
owl:hasValue

An owl:allValuesFrom restriction property links a restriction class to either a class description or a data range:

```
<owl:Restriction>
    <owl:onProperty>
      <owl:ObjectProperty rdf:about="#hasRoom"/>
```

```
      </owl:onProperty>
      <owl:allValuesFrom>
        <owl:Class>
          <owl:unionOf rdf:parseType="Collection">
            <owl:Class rdf:about="#Guestroom"/>
            <owl:Class rdf:ID="ConferenceRoom"/>
          </owl:unionOf>
        </owl:Class>
      </owl:allValuesFrom>
</owl:Restriction>
```

An owl:allValuesFrom restriction is analogous to the universal (for-all) quantifier of predicate logic. Similarly, the value restriction owl:someValuesFrom is a property that links a restriction class to a class description or a data range. The owl:someValuesFrom restriction is analogous to the existential quantifier of predicate logic. Also, the owl:hasValue restriction is a property that links a restriction class to a value V that may be an individual or data value.

2.8.3.3.4.2 Cardinality Restrictions—OWL provides three constructs for restricting the cardinality of properties locally within a class context:

> owl:maxCardinality
> owl:minCardinality
> owl:cardinality

A restriction containing an owl:maxCardinality statement describes a class of all individuals that have *at most* specified distinct range values (individuals or data values) for the property concerned. The following example describes a class of individuals that have at most two activities:

```
<owl:Restriction>
      <owl:onProperty rdf:resource="#has_Activities" />
      <owl:maxCardinality rdf:datatype="&xsd;nonNegativeInteger
"> 2
      </owl:maxCardinality>
</owl:Restriction>
```

A restriction containing an owl:minCardinality statement describes a class of all individuals that have *at least* specified distinct range values (individuals or data values) for the property concerned. The following example describes a class of individuals that have at least two activities:

```
<owl:Restriction>
        <owl:onProperty rdf:resource="#has_Activities" />
        <owl:minCardinality rdf:datatype="&xsd;nonNegative
Integer"> 2
        </owl:minCardinality>
</owl:Restriction>
```

A restriction containing an owl:cardinality statement describes a class of all individuals that have *exactly* specified distinct range values (individuals or data values) for the property concerned. The example given below describes a class of individuals that have exactly two activities:

```
<owl:Restriction>
        <owl:onProperty rdf:resource="#has_Activities" />
        <owl:cardinality rdf:datatype="&xsd;nonNegative
        Integer">2
        </owl:cardinality>
</owl:Restriction>
```

2.8.3.3.5 Operators

The three operators in OWL are given standard set operator names: intersection, union, and complement. These operators can be used to define Boolean combinations of classes and may be defined in OWL. owl:intersectionOf describes the class extension containing precisely those individuals that are members of the class extension of all class descriptions in the range list:

```
<owl:Class>
     <owl:intersectionOf rdf:parseType="Collection">
     <owl:Class rdf:about="#GuestRoom"/>
     <owl:Class rdf:about="#ConferenceRoom"/>
      </owl:intersectionOf>
</owl:Class>
```

owl:intersectionOf can be viewed as analogous to a logical conjunction. owl:unionOf is analogous to logical disjunction:

```
<owl:Class>
     <owl:unionOf rdf:parseType="Collection">
       <owl:Class rdf:about="#Event"/>
       <owl:Class rdf:about="#Infrastructure"/>
     </owl:unionOf>
</owl:Class>
```

owl:complementOf means items *do NOT belong to*. Here owl:complementOf is analogous to logical negation, but restricted to individuals only. The statement *Neither GuestRoom Nor ConferenceRoom* could be written as:

```
<owl:Class>
     <owl:complementOf>
          <owl:Class>
                           <owl:unionOf
rdf:parseType="Collection">
                           <owl:Class
```

```
rdf:about="#GuestRoom"/>
                                    <owl:Class
rdf:about="#ConferenceRoom"/>
                              </owl:unionOf>
                    </owl:Class>
              </owl:complementOf>
</owl:Class>
```

Note that every Boolean operator takes one or more classes as operands. Such classes may be named *classes* or *complex classes* formed from descriptions.

2.8.3.3.6 Properties

A property is a binary relationship between individuals or between individuals and data values. Properties let us assert general facts about the members of classes and specific facts about individuals. Every property has a domain and a range. A domain is a set of individuals to which the property can be applied; a range is a set of individuals that the property may have as values. rdfs:domain links a property to a class description that asserts that the domain values of the property must belong to the class extension of the class description. Both the domain and range of a property are global restrictions. A restriction is stated on a property and not only on a property when it is associated with a specific class. Both the domain and range of a property may be used to infer the type of individual. For a property, one can define multiple rdfs:domain statements that will be interpreted as a conjunction. Further, a domain can be a disjunction of multiple classes (owl:unionOf).

```
<owl:ObjectProperty rdf:ID="hasTimePeriod">
    <rdfs:comment
     rdf:datatype="http://www.w3.org/2001/XMLSchema#string"
    >This property links an individual representing a date
period.</rdfs:comment>
    <rdfs:range rdf:resource="#TimePeriod"/>
    <rdfs:domain>
      <owl:Class>
        <owl:unionOf rdf:parseType="Collection">
          <owl:Class rdf:about="#OpeningHours"/>
          <owl:Class rdf:about="#Event"/>
        </owl:unionOf>
      </owl:Class>
    </rdfs:domain>
</owl:ObjectProperty>
```

An rdfs:range links a property to either a class description or a data range. It asserts that the range values of the property must belong to the class extension of the class description or to data values in the specified data range. As with rdfs:domain, conjunctions of multiple rdfs:range statements are allowed, and different combinations of class descriptions such as owl:unionOf can be used.

2.8.3.3.7 Datatypes

OWL allows two types of data range specifications:

- *User defined XML schema datatypes such as xsd:string, xsd:integer, xsd:positiveInteger*
- *Enumerated datatypes that make use of the owl:oneOf construct; the range value of owl:oneOf is a list of literals*

Most XML schema datatypes are supported by OWL 2 DL. Additionally, OWL 2 introduced some new datatypes and now supports owl:boolean, owl:string, xsd:integer, xsd:dateTime, xsd:hexBinary, and a number of datatypes derived from them by placing various restrictions on them. In addition, xsd:decimal, xsd:double, and xsd:oat will most likely be complemented with owl:real (it is interpreted as the set of all real numbers). OWL 2 also provides a datatype restriction construct allowing new datatypes to be defined by restricting the built-in datatypes in various ways.

2.8.3.3.7.1 Individual and Axiom—An *individual* is a member of some defined classes. Two different names of individuals do not mean that the names refer to different individuals. Remember that OWL does not support multidefined datatypes. Individual ordering is not important for defining individuals. The definition of a specific individual can be divided into various parts in an ontology. Every individual in the OWL world is a member of the class owl:Thing:

```
< owl:Thing rdf:ID="Accommodation"/>
Accommodation ∈ Thing
```

An individual can be a member of a specific class:

```
<Camping rdf:ID="Accommodation"/>
 Accommodation ∈ Camping
```

An individual may be a member of more than one class:

```
<owl:Individual rdf:about="#Accommodation">
  <rdf:type>
<owl:Class rdf:about="#Camping"/>
  </rdf:type>
  <rdf:type>
```

```
<owl:Class rdf:about="#Hotel"/>
  </rdf:type>
</owl:Individual>
```

An *axiom* is defined as a class, property, or individual. Axioms are used to associate class and property identifiers with partial or complete specifications of their characteristics and reveal other logical information about classes and properties. Figure 2.7 illustrates the language construct using OWLviz. The three OWL language constructs for class axioms are rdfs:subClassOf, owl:equivalentClass, and owl:disjointWith. In the following example (see figure), we present disjoint classes using the owl:disjointWith property; it shows that DatePeriod and TimePeriod have no instances in common.

```
<owl:Class rdf:ID="DatePeriod">
    <owl:disjointWith rdf:resource="#TimePeriod">
</owl:Class>
```

There is a difference in the owl:disjointWith and owl:complementOf properties. Using owl:complementOf, we can infer that *period* is not a *date*; it is a *time*. We cannot make the same inference using the owl:disjointWith property. In another example, we specify the rdfs:subClassOf property. This class is a concrete representation of the concept of seasons

```
<owl:Class rdf:ID="Season">
  <rdfs:subClassOf>
    <owl:Class rdf:ID="DateTime"/>
  </rdfs:subClassOf>
</owl:Class>
```

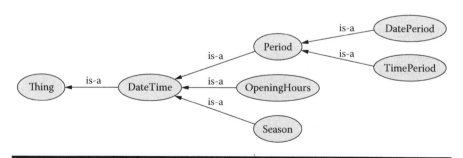

Figure 2.7 Language construct using OWLviz.

2.8.4 OWL 2 Profiles

OWL 2 provides three profiles: OWL 2 EL, OWL 2 QL, and OWL 2 RL. Each profile targets diffierent application scenarios. OWL 2 profiles are defined by placing restrictions on the functional style syntax of OWL 2. An ontology written in any of these profiles is a valid OWL 2 ontology. Each profile is designed to trade some expressive power for efficiency of reasoning. For example, the OWL 2 EL profile trades expressivity for the benefit of polynomial time subsumption testing. Similarly, reasoning for the OWL 2 RL profile can be implemented using a rule engine. The important modeling features of OWL 2 EL are class conjunction and SomeValuesFrom restrictions. The use of negation, disjunction, AllValuesFrom restrictions, and cardinality restrictions are not allowed to achieve tractability. To preserve its good computational properties, the datatypes supported by OWL 2 EL were selected to ensure that their intersection is either empty or infinite. Many large-scale ontologies may be captured using this profile.

OWL 2 QL is basically designed for data-driven applications and provides a suitable means for RDF vendors to include some kind of OWL support without excluding the advantages of a database type implementation. OWL 2 QL is based on the DL Lite family of description logics. Its special quality is the inclusion of many features required for capturing conceptual models. This profile is suitable when a limited extension of RDF schema is desired.

OWL 2 RL was designed to allow the smooth adoption of OWL by vendors of rule-based inference tools. Naturally, it offers better interoperability with knowledge representation languages based on rules. It allows for most constructs of OWL 2, but to permit rule-based implementations of reasoning, the use of these constructs in axioms is restricted.

2.9 Integration of Ontology and Rule Languages

Integrating Semantic Web ontology with logic programming and business rules has proven a challenge. According to Brachman et al. (1990), attempts to combine rules with description logics were made in the days of the classic system. Semantic Web Rule Language (SWRL) [http://www.w3.org/Submission/SWRL/] is a step in this direction. SWRL was first named OWL Rules Language before gaining built-in atoms and a more RuleML [http://www.ruleml.org/] flavored syntax. In that form, it was published as a W3C member submission. The decidability of SWRL rules with the DL safety condition was established by Motik et al. in 2004 and 2005 and further elaborated by Motik (2006).

Another tool named Description Logic Program (DLP) inherits its semantics from OWL and may be transformed syntactically into Logic Programming syntax, thus providing a kind of basic interoperability between OWL and Logic Programming. According to an analysis by Volz (2004), most existing OWL ontologies are almost completely contained in DLP. Another example is the Semantic Web Research Community (SWRC) ontology (Sure et al., 2005). DLP was originally presented in the works of Grosof et al. (2003) and Volz (2004).

Hybrid systems comprising both classical OWL reasoning and traditional rule-based approaches like logic programming in different variants present concerns. One hybrid solution is the MKNF knowledge base discussed by Motik et al. (2006; 2007). Another approach is based on integration of OWL DL reasoning with Answer Set programming through the dlvhex system (Eiter et al., 2006b and c; Schindlauer, 2006). According to Hitzler and Parsia (2009), such integration is not as strong as hybrid MKNF knowledge bases and basically consists of two reasoning engines that interact bidirectionally when reasoning over knowledge bases.

2.10 Ontology-Driven Information Integration

Data sets of interest to computational biologists are often heterogeneous in structure, content, and semantics. Such data sources are large, diverse in structure and content, typically autonomously maintained, and need integration before utilization. The next generation of computer-based information requires capabilities to deal with such heterogeneous data sources available in distributed fashion, i.e., on the Web. Ontology plays a key role. Ontology-driven information systems (ODIS) are based on explicit use of technologies for computer-based information systems (Guarino, 1998). As stated earlier, a software specification role for ontology was suggested by Gruber (1991).

It is obvious that ontology can be generated using different representation languages based on various knowledge representation paradigms (description logics, frame logics, etc.). According to Yildiz and Miksch (2007), to reduce the integration and run-time costs of ontology, ontology engineering should be automated to a large extent and ontology management services must be provided in form of an ontology management module (OMM). Information integration incorporates three phases: (1) ontology generation, (2) ontology management, and (3) ontology integration. Ontology and information system integration remain challenges because of the nature of ontology. Ontologies were conceived as backbones of semantic networks to represent content efficiently on the Web. Because information systems do not share the characteristics of the Semantic Web, it is difficult to add Semantic Web ontology to information systems.

Yildiz and Miksch (2007) cited requirements for fostering the wide acceptance of ontology-driven information system development. These requirements constitute an abstract ontology model for representing additional semantic knowledge and for ontology integration: (1) evolutional properties to indicate the expected behaviors of particular components over time; (2) quality properties to indicate confidence levels of ontology components; and (3) temporal properties to mark transaction times and valid times of components.

2.11 Ontology Tools

This section presents some useful Semantic Web software tools. They may be classified into three major categories: ontology and metadata editors, plug-ins, and inference tools. We will also take a short look at useful reasoning tools.

2.11.1 Protégé

Protégé is a free, open source ontology editor and knowledge acquisition system. It was developed at Stanford University in collaboration with the University of Manchester in 1987. It resembles Eclipse and acts as a basis for which a range of other projects suggests plug-ins. The application is written in Java and heavily uses Swing to create a complex user interface.

The objective of Protégé I was to assist the knowledge acquisition process by helping engineers build tools that would help experts in knowledge acquisition. Protégé II is an extension of the project supporting ontology, problem-solving mechanisms, and mapping among ontologies. It is the most popular Semantic Web ontology editor. Its extensible open-source platform supports several ontology formats including CLIPS (Protégé's native format), various XML dialects, databases, DAML+OIL, and RDFS. Storage plug-ins for Unified Modeling Language (UML) and OWL were added recently. Protégé supports two ways of modeling ontology—via Protégé–Frames and Protégé–OWL editors. The Protégé–OWL plug-in extends Protégé to a graphical software development environment that supports writing of OWL ontology. The Protégé Website provides more than 50 plug-ins. Protégé–OWL Viz is a major tool developed by the CO-ODE group to allow visualizing and navigating through the class hierarchy of an OWL ontology.

2.11.2 OntoEdit

OntoEdit is an ontology editor developed by the On-To-Knowledge project. It implements an ontology construction process of three steps: requirement specification, refinement, and evaluation. The editor stores the ontology conceptual model in the Sesame repository and produces RDF concrete representations.

2.11.3 KAON2

KAON2 is a reasoner and ontology management API for OWL DL and (parts of) SWRL. Motik wrote it in Java in cooperation with the University of Manchester, FZI, and the University of Karlsruhe. Its features include an API for programmatic management of OWL-DL, SWRL, and F-Logic ontology; a stand-alone server providing access to ontology in a distributed manner using RMI; an inference engine for answering conjunctive queries; an interface that allows access from tools such as Protégé; and a module for extracting ontology instances from relational databases. KAON2 is based on OWL-DL and F-Logic. It does not implement the tableaux calculus. Its reasoning is implemented by different algorithms that reduce a SHIQ(D) knowledge base to a disjunctive datalog program.

2.11.4 Pellet

Pellet is an open-source Java based OWL DL reasoner that may be used in conjunction with Jena and OWL API libraries. It provides a DIG interface and is an OWL DL reasoner based on tableaux algorithms developed for expressive DLs. It supports the full expressivity of OWL DL. As a result, the owl:oneOf and owl:hasValue constructs can be used freely.

The basis of Pellet is the tableaux reasoner that checks the consistency of a KB, i.e., an ABox and TBox pair. The reasoner is coupled with a datatype oracle that can check the consistency of conjunctions of simple XML schema datatypes. The OWL ontologies are loaded to the reasoner after species validation and ontology repair to guarantee that all the resources have appropriate type triples, and missing type declarations are added via heuristics. During the loading phase, axioms about classes (subclass, equivalent class, disjointness axioms) are put into the TBox component and assertions about individuals (type and property assertions) are stored in the ABox. TBox axioms undergo the standard preprocessing of DL reasoners before they are supplied to the tableaux reasoner.

2.11.5 FaCT++

FaCT++ is a well known FaCT OWL-DL reasoner. It uses conventional FaCT algorithms with special internal architectures. Moreover, FaCT++ is implemented using C++ to create an efficient software tool and maximize portability.

2.11.6 TopBraid Composer

TopBraid is a commercial visual modeling environment for developing and managing domain models and ontologies in RDF schema and OWL standards of the Semantic Web. It has a commercially available triple store to build a multiuser Web-accessible system that supports collaborative authoring. TopBraid is based on the Eclipse platform and uses Jena as its underlying API to support the rapid development of semantic applications on a single platform. It may be used to edit RDFS and OWL files in various formats and provides scalable database backends (Jena, AllegroGraph, Oracle 10g, and Sesame) along with multiuser support. It is a very flexible platform that enables Java programmers to add customized extensions and develop stand-alone Semantic Web applications.

2.11.7 SemanticWorks

Altova's SemanticWorks software is a commercially available application that provides good performance and flexibility for ontology creation and editing. Its built-in semantic reasoner allows a user to find flaws in coding or logic and correct any ontology issues. SemanticWorks supports all three OWL dialects in addition to fully supporting RDF and RDFS. It allows users to create complex ontologies visually using intelligent entry helpers, a fairly intuitive icon system, and shortcuts; it also auto-generates RDF-XML or N-Triple codes corresponding to user design.

2.11.8 CMapTools Ontology Editor (COE)

The COE application provides an outlet to create ontologies in the form of concept maps. CMap Server allows a group to collaborate online and provide feedback to each other. With CmapTools, a user may import various types of XML and text documents and export ontologies in OWL, N-Triple (and its various formats), and Turtle. It offers validation and concept suggestion tools. The major benefit is that a user needs only a very fundamental understanding of ontologies.

2.11.9 Other Tools

Sesame is a platform-independent data repository and search mechanism for data in RDF format offering export and search mechanisms and supporting the RQL, RDQL, and SeRQL query languages. For details, visit http://www.ontoknowledge.org.

OWL Validator is an online tool for validating OWL code. Validator reads an OWL file and examines it for probable errors. It then generates a list of errors and warnings, notes locations in files, and provides some insight into the nature of a problem. It requires a valid RDF input file.

JENA is an open-source Java API developed by Hewlett-Packard and intended to support the development of Semantic Web applications. It supports RDF, RDF schema, and OWL. It also includes an inference mechanism. JENA transforms ontology into an object-oriented abstract data model and permits its classes and relationships to be treated as objects.

Virtuoso is a novel universal server platform that delivers enterprise-level data integration and management solutions for SQL, RDF, XML, Web services, and business processes. Its hybrid server architecture facilitates delivery of distinct server functionality within a single product offering. It enables a single multithreaded server process that implements multiple protocols. The open source edition of Virtuoso is also known as OpenLink Virtuoso.

BOWiki is a semantic Wiki component for collaborative editing of biomedical ontology and gene data in a system based on OWL ontology. It includes a description logic reasoner to perform consistency checks and queries; it uses the general formal ontology (GFO) and concepts and relations defined in the OWL version of GFO to verify the consistency of semantic information. The biological core ontology provides biological type and background knowledge.

References

Akerkar, R. 2009. *Foundations of the Semantic Web: XML, RDF and Ontology*. New Delhi: Narosa.

Akerkar, R. and Sajja, P.S. 2009. *Knowledge-Based Systems*. Sudbury, MA, Jones & Bartlett.

Baader, F., Bürckert, H.J., Heinsohn, J. et al. 1991. Terminological knowledge representation: a proposal for a terminological logic. In *Proceedings of International Workshop on Terminological Logics*, DFKI Document D-91-13.

Baader, F., Calvanese, D.L., McGuinness, D. et al. 2003. *The Description Logic Handbook*. Cambridge: Cambridge University Press.

Bechhofer, S., Goble, C., and Horrocks, I. 2001. DAML+OIL is not enough. *In Proceedings of First Semantic Web Working Symposium*, California, pp. 151–159.

Bechhofer, S., Harmelen, F., Hendler, J. et al. August 18, 2003. OWL Web Ontology Language Reference. W3C Candidate Recommendation.

Beckett, D. October 10, 2003. RDF/XML Syntax Specification (Revised). W3C Working Draft.

Berners-Lee, T. 2005. Web for real people. Keynote Speech at 14th International Conference on World Wide Web, Chiba, Japan.

Borgida, A., Brachman, R.J., McGuinness, D.L. et al. 1989. CLASSIC: A structural data model for objects. In *Proceedings of ACM SIGMOD International Conference on Management of Data*, San Diego, CA, pp. 59–67.

Brachman, R. and Schmolze, J. 1985. An overview of the KL-ONE knowledge representation system. *Cognitive Science, 9*: 171–216.

Brachman, R., McGuiness, D.L., Peter, F. et al. 1990. Living with CLASSIC: When and how to use a KL-ONE-like language. In *Principles of Semantic Networks*, San Mateo, CA: Morgan Kauffman.

Bruijn, J. 2003. Using ontologies: Enabling knowledge sharing and reuse on the Semantic Web. Technical Report, Digital Enterprise Research Institute, University of Innsbruck.

Chaudhri, V.K., Farquhar, A., Fikes, R. et al. 1998. OKBC: A programmatic foundation for knowledge base interoperability. In *Proceedings of 15th National Conference on Artificial Intelligence*, Madison, WI, pp. 600–607.

Corcho, O., Fernández-López, M., and Gómez-Pérez, A. 2003. Methodologies, tools, and languages for building ontologies: Where is their meeting point? *Data and Knowledge Engineering, 46*: 41–64.

Ding, Y., Fensel, D., Klein, M. et al. 2002. The Semantic Web: Yet another hype? *Data and Knowledge Engineering, 41*: 205–227.

Eiter, T., Ianni, G., Polleres, A. et al. 2006a. Reasoning with rules and ontologies. In *Reasoning Web, Second International Summer School, Lisbon, Tutorial Lecture* 4126, Lecture Notes in Computer Science, pp. 93–127.

Eiter, T., Ianni, G., Polleres, A. et al. 2006b. Effective integration of declarative rules with external evaluations for Semantic Web reasoning. In *Proceedings of Third European Semantic Web Conference*, Budva, Montenegro, pp. 273–287.

Eiter, T., Ianni, G., Polleres, A. et al. 2006c. DLVHEX: A prover for Semantic Web reasoning under the answer-set semantics. In *Proceedings of IEEE/WIC/ACM International Conference on Web Intelligence,* Hong Kong, pp. 1073–1074.

Fensel, D. 2003. *Ontologies: A Silver Bullet for Knowledge Management and Electronic Commerce,* Springer Verlag, Berlin.

Fensel, D., Decker, S., Erdmann, M. et al. 1998. Ontobroker: A very high idea. In *Proceedings of 11th International FLAIRS Conference,* Sanibel Island, FL pp. 131–138.

Fensel, D., Decker, S., Erdmann, M. et al. 2000. Lessons learned from applying AI to the Web. *International Journal of Cooperative Information Systems, 9:* 361–382.

Gomes, P., Antunes, B., Barbeira, J. et al. 2006. Using ontologies for e-learning personalization. In *Proceedings of E-learning Conference,* Coimbra, Portugal.

Grosof, B., Horrocks, I., Volz, R. et al. 2003. Description logic programs: Combining logic programs with description logics. In *Proceedings of WWW.* Budapest, pp. 48–57.

Gruber T.R. 1991. Role of common ontology in achieving sharable, reusable knowledge bases. In *Principles of Knowledge Representation and Reasoning,* Cambridge: MIT Press, pp. 601–602.

Gruber, T.R. 1993. A translation approach to portable ontology specifications. *Knowledge Acquisition, 5:* 199–220.

Gruber, T.R. 1995. Toward principles for the design of ontologies used for knowledge sharing. *International Journal of Human Computer Studies, 43:* 907–928.

Grüninger, M. and Fox, M.S. 1995. Methodology for the design and evaluation of ontologies. In *Proceedings of IJCAI Workshop on Basic Ontological Issues in Knowledge Sharing,* Montreal.

Guarino, N. 1998. *Formal Ontology and Information Systems.* Amsterdam: IOS Press.

Heflin, J., Hendler, J., and Luke, S. 1999. SHOE: A knowledge representation language for Internet applications. Technical Report CS-TR-4078 (UMIACS TR-99-71), Department of Computer Science, University of Maryland, College Park.

Heflin, J. and Hendler, J. 2000. Dynamic ontologies on the Web, In *Proceedings of 17th National Conference on Artificial Intelligence,* Menlo Park, CA, pp. 443–449.

Hitzler, P. and Parsia, B. 2009. Ontologies and rules. In *Handbook on Ontologies,* 2nd Ed., Berlin: Springer Verlag, pp. 111–132.

Horrocks, I. and Harmelen, F. March 2001. Reference description of DAML+OIL. Ontology Markup Language Technical Report.

Kalfoglou, Y. 2000. Deploying ontologies in software design, PhD Thesis, University of Edinburgh.

Kavi, M. and Sergei, N. 1995. A situated ontology for practical NLP. *In Proceedings of Workshop on Basic Ontological Issues in Knowledge Sharing,* International Joint Conference on Artificial Intelligence), Montreal.

Kiryakov, A., Ognyanov, D., and Kirov, V. 2004 An ontology representation and data integration (ORDI) framework. DIP project deliverable D2.2. http://dip.semanticweb.org

McGuinness, D.L. 2003. Ontologies come of age. *In Spinning the Semantic Web: Bringing the World Wide Web to Its Full Potential,* Cambridge: MIT Press.

Ming, M. 2008. Ontology mapping: Towards semantic interoperability in distributed and heterogeneous environments, PhD Thesis, University of Pittsburgh, Pittsburgh, PA.

Motik, B. 2006. Reasoning in description logics using resolution and deductive databases. PhD Thesis, Universität Karlsruhe, Germany.

Motik, B. and Rosati, R. 2007. A faithful integration of description logics with logic programming. In *Proceedings of 20th International Joint Conference on Artificial Intelligence*, Hyderabad, India, pp. 477–482.

Motik, B., Horrocks, I., Rosati, R. et al. Can OWL and logic programming live together happily ever after? In *Proceedings of Fifth International Semantic Web Conference*, Athens, GA, pp. 501–514.

Motik, B., Sattler, U., and Studer, R. 2004. Query answering for OWL-DL with rules. In *International Semantic Web Conference*, Hiroshima, pp. 549–563.

Motik, B., Sattler, U., and Studer, R. 2005. Query answering for OWL-DL with rules. *Journal of Web Semantics, 3*: 41–60.

Noy, N. and McGuinness, D. 2001 Ontology Development 101: A guide to creating your first ontology. Knowledge Systems Laboratory Technical Report KSL-01-05/Medical Informatics Technical Report SMI-2001-0880, Stanford University, Palo Alto, CA.

Patel, M., Koch, T., Doerr, M. et al. 2005. *Semantic Interoperability in Digital Library Systems*. DELOS Network of Excellence on Digital Libraries, European Union, Sixth Framework Programme Deliverable D5.3. http://www.ukoln.ac.uk/ukoln/staff/t.koch/publ/SI-in-DLs.doc

Schindlauer, R. 2006. Answer set programming for the Semantic Web. PhD Thesis, Vienna University of Technology.

Stuckenschmidt, H. and Harmelen, F. 2005. *Information Sharing on the Semantic Web*. Advanced Information and Knowledge Processing Series, Vol. 19, Berlin: Springer Verlag.

Studer, R., Benjamins, V.R., and Fensel, D. 1998. Knowledge engineering: Principles and methods. *Data and Knowledge Engineering, 25*: 161–197.

Sure, Y., Bloehdorn, S., Haase, P. et al. 2005. SWRC ontology: A Semantic Web for research communities. In *Proceedings of 12th Portuguese Conference on Artificial Intelligence*, Covilha, pp. 218–231.

Uschold, M. and Grüninger, M. 1996. Ontologies: Principles methods and applications. *Knowledge Engineering Review, 11*: 93–155.

Uschold, M. and King, M. 1995. Toward a methodology for building ontologies. In *Proceedings of IJCAI Workshop on Basic Ontological Issues in Knowledge Sharing*, Montreal.

Uschold, M., King, M., Morale, S. et al. 1998. The enterprise ontology. *Knowledge Engineering Review, 13*: 31–89.

Volz, R. 2004. Web ontology reasoning with logic databases. PhD Thesis, Universität Fridericiana zu Karlsruhe, Germany.

Wiederhold, G. 1992. Mediators in the architecture of future information systems. *IEEE Computer, 25*: 38–49.

Yildiz, B. and Miksch, S. 2007. Ontology-driven information systems: Challenges and requirements. In *Proceedings of International Conference on Semantic Web and Digital Libraries*, Bangalore, India.

Chapter 3

Toward Semantic Interoperability between Information Systems

Mariela Rico, Maria Laura Caliusco,
Maria Rosa Galli, and Omar Chiotti

Universidad Tecnologica Nacional, Santa Fe, Argentina

Contents

3.1 Introduction

During recent decades, the evolution of information systems and communication technologies, particularly those related to the Internet, has led to the implementation of peer-to-peer (P2P) communication models among heterogeneous information systems. In this scenario, the main challenge is how to guarantee interoperability at four levels: system, structure, syntactic, and semantic. A large body of work built during the 1980s and 1990s dealt with heterogeneity at the first three levels and proved to be very effective [23]. However, the issue of interoperability at the semantic level is only partially solved [17].

Semantic interoperability requires that an information system understands both the semantics of the information sent or requested by another system, as well as the semantics of its information sources [8]. In recent years, ontologies have been used as artifacts to represent information semantics [13]. Even when two ontologies belong to the same domain of interest, they may present minor differences such as naming conventions or structures or the ways in which they represent information semantics [8]. This situation presents a new challenge: how to allow the interoperability between heterogeneous ontologies (each representing an information source) to guarantee semantic interoperability between P2P information systems that share information between these sources.

Ontology matching is a plausible solution to allow interoperability between heterogeneous ontologies [8,10,11]. It aims to find correspondences between semantically related entities of different ontologies by applying matching strategies that deal with issues like those described above. To this aim, matching techniques and tools such as HMatch [6], CATO [4], and Prompt [18] have been proposed.

Recent proposals focused on improving ontology matching by providing a better basis for matching. Stuckenschmidt and van Harmelen [27] presented a methodology for enriching class hierarchies with ontological information by supporting approximate matchings of class hierarchies plainly based on subsumption reasoning. Sviáb-Zamazal et al. [28] show that improving and systematizing the naming of concepts can improve matching. However, a thorough representation of information semantics in ontologies generally involves more than organization of class hierarchies or naming conventions.

Real entities may have features whose representations in an ontology are implicit; although they may be inferred by a human agent, they cannot be inferred by a machine agent. Moreover, interpretations of some of these features (contextual features) depend on the context in which the entities are considered. These features are not required to be made explicit when the entities are considered within the same context, but that becomes necessary when the entities must be interpreted in another context. The main contribution of this chapter is a method for enriching the representation of entity semantics in an ontology by making contextual features explicit with the aim of improving the matching between heterogeneous ontologies.

Recently, P2P information sharing has gained the attention of many researchers because it is the base for enabling inter-enterprise integration by maintaining enterprise autonomy and privacy [3,5]. Ontology matching is used to establish an exchange of meaningful information between peers [10]. Enterprises participating in information sharing usually belong to different contexts; and since the effectiveness of these applications depends on the accuracy of the matching process, they require more explicit conceptual models. This chapter focuses on a case study based on a P2P information sharing scenario in which each peer belongs to a different context. Section 3.2 defines the terminology around the main concepts. Section 3.3 introduces the role of ontology matching in P2P information sharing. Section 3.4 shows how the matching results may be improved by making contextual features explicit. Section 3.5 presents a method for making contextual features explicit. Section 3.6 shows an application of the method. Finally, Section 3.7 is devoted to conclusions.

3.2 Background

This section covers ontology and context definitions and, in accordance with these definitions, the ontology heterogeneity conflicts are characterized. A discussion about how to face the problem of integrating heterogeneous ontologies is presented.

3.2.1 Defining Ontology and Context

According to Smith et al. [26], an entity is anything that exists including objects, processes, qualities, and states at all three levels:

- Level 1: objects, processes, qualities, states, etc. in reality.
- Level 2: cognitive representations of this reality on the part of a cognitive subject. The representational units of a cognitive representation are ideas, thoughts, or beliefs in the mind of a cognitive subject.
- Level 3: concretizations of these cognitive representations in representational artifacts. A representational artifact can serve to make cognitive representations publicly accessible to both human and machine agents. These artifacts

are not composed of representations that refer to the cognitive ones. The constituent units of representational artifacts should be seen as referring to the same entities in reality (Level 1). The smallest constituent subrepresentations are called representational units.

For the sake of simplicity, in this chapter we will use *entity* to refer to entities in reality (Level 1). A *domain* is a portion of reality that forms the subject matter of a single science, technology, or mode of study [26], e.g., the domains of computer science, communications, e-learning, e-commerce, and others. A *domain ontology* (or simply *ontology*) is a representational artifact indicating the semantics of a given domain of discourse. It provides vocabularies about entities within a domain and their relationships, about the activities taking place in the domain, and about the theories and elementary principles governing the domain [13]. The representational units of an ontology or *ontology elements* are the following:

- *Terms* are words or groups of words that represent entities in a given domain and are normally cited inside the ontology by unique identifiers [2].
- *Properties* represent the features of entities in a given domain, e.g., the name of an organization or person.
- *Relations* are elements that join other ontology elements. They can be divided into hierarchical (is-a), mereological (part-of), semantic equivalence (synonym), opposite (antonym), and particular (defined by the ontology designer) relations among others [3].
- *Axioms* represent sentences that are always true in a domain [14]. They are usually formalized into a logic language and represent characteristics or restrictions about entities that cannot be formally defined by the other ontology elements. Thus, axioms restrict the interpretations of entities.
- *Instances* refer to individuals of an entity in a given domain [2]. A term representing an entity and its instances is related by the instance of relation. For example, a particular product is an instance of the Product entity.
- A *context* is defined as a circumstance in which something exists or occurs [22]. In a context, it can be distinguished as a set of characteristics that describe the environment and differentiate it from other contexts and a set of entities that constitute its content. An entity can be part of the content of more than one context and its interpretation will depend on the characteristics of the context in which it is considered. Thus, the context acts as a container of a set of characteristics that affects the meaning of the entities it contains [21]. A context may consist of other contexts. For example, in the context of an enterprise, each department constitutes a different context. Sales information is managed in certain departments such as human resources and the marketing department, but its interpretation depends on the characteristics of the department in which it is considered.
- The interpretation of a *contextual feature* of an entity belonging to the content of a context depends on the characteristics of the context.

3.2.2 Characterizing Ontology Heterogeneity Conflicts

Since the information sources of two information systems may be described semantically by heterogeneous ontologies, the need for communication between them turns ontology heterogeneity into a problem. The literature cites different classifications of ontology heterogeneity conflicts [1,7,10,12]. In this chapter, they are classified in four categories based on the previous ontology definition:

- *Terminological conflicts* are differences in names—alternatives that depict the same reality, for example, using distinct terms for the same entity. They can arise from the use of different natural languages (Chapter versus Capítulo), different technical sublanguages (Paper versus Memo), or synonyms (Paper versus Article).
- *Data versus metadata conflicts* are disagreements about what constitute data and metadata. An instance of an ontology can be represented as a term in another ontology.
- *Instance conflicts* are discrepancies in the representation or interpretation of instantiated data values arising from differences in measurement units, precision levels, and spellings. For example, the value of an instance of Size is 1000; in a given context, 1000 could be interpreted via an equation and in another context could be interpreted in liters.
- *Structural conflicts* result from using different structures to represent a single entity. For example, a Car entity could be represented in one ontology by a single term such as Automobile and in another ontology by several terms (Automobile, Color, and Year) plus their relations.

3.2.3 Approaches for Overcoming Ontology Heterogeneity Problem

To overcome such conflicts, ontology matching (finding semantic correspondences between elements of different ontologies) has been recognized as a plausible solution [8,10,11]. To this aim, different matching strategies have been implemented in the matching process. These strategies were developed by combining some basic techniques. Each technique tries to solve one or more of the conflicts described. Thus, according to the classification of techniques of Euzenat and Shvaiko [10], language- and string-based techniques along with linguistic resources are often used to address terminological conflicts while graph- and taxonomy-based techniques, among others, are used to face structural conflicts.

However, these techniques are unable to solve certain conflicts. An example concerns how entities represented in ontologies are interpreted. For example, if the Product term appears in an ontology of a packaging industry, one should not conclude that it is equivalent to the Product term in an ontology of a dairy industry. Associated with each of these terms is an intended use of the entity they represent, generally missing in the representation of that entity. When ontologies are developed without this consideration, it is impossible for a matching process to detect whether those terms are equivalent or not. In such cases, improving matching strategies or techniques is not useful because the conflicts relate to incomplete representations in the ontologies to be matched.

The treatment of incomplete information has been widely addressed in database research [11]. The most common technique is to model missing data with a pseudo-description called a *null* to denote missing information. Another approach [30] based on possibility theory provides an explicit distinction between incompleteness due to data unavailability and incompleteness due to data inapplicability. Since sharing information in P2P information systems is crucial to represent real meanings of shared entities, it is not appropriate to apply the aforementioned treatments. Thus, we propose improving the representations of entities in ontologies as a way of addressing conflicts resulting from poor representations.

3.3 Ontology-Based Peer-to-Peer (P2P) Information Sharing

P2P is a distributed communication model in which parties (peers) have equivalent functional capabilities in providing each other with data and services [31]. This communication model is a suitable solution to implement communications among heterogeneous information systems by maintaining some forms of peer privacy and autonomy. If peers are meant to be totally autonomous, they may use different terminologies and metadata models to represent their data even if they refer to the same domain of interest [10]. Thus, to exchange meaningful information between systems, it is necessary to define the semantics of the information to be shared by using ontologies and then establishing a relation between the ontologies belonging to all peers. To this aim, the following steps must be followed:

1. Identify, characterize, and establish correspondences between entities as represented in ontologies.
2. Define conversion rules for translating instances of one ontology into the instances of another.
3. Validate conversion rules defined earlier.
4. Execute conversion rules.

These steps correspond to an ontology-based P2P information sharing process (Figure 3.1). The first step is ontology matching [10]. The input is a pair of ontologies. The output is a set (alignment) of correspondences between the elements of the ontologies *A*. From this alignment, the Conversion Rule Definition Process carries out the second and third steps to yield a set of validated conversion rules *VCR*. The Information Integration Process will execute the conversion rules at run time

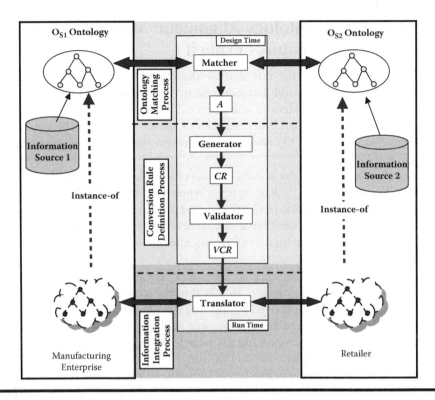

Figure 3.1   Ontology-based P2P information sharing process.

to allow meaningful information sharing. The quality of the *VCR* largely depends on the accuracy of the *A*. Improvement of the alignment is crucial to facilitate the generation of conversion rules.

Two alternatives can be followed to improve the *A* alignment: (1) improve the Ontology Matching Process and (2) improve the inputs to the process. A substantial body of work focuses on implementation of increasingly better strategies and matching systems [10,19,20,24]. In another approach, recent proposals may provide better inputs to the matching process; see the works of Stuckenschmidt and van Harmelen [27] and Sviáb-Zamazal et al. [28].

To provide better inputs for a matching process, it is convenient to represent entities whose instances must be translated with the necessary degree of detail. The features that should be made explicit are those whose interpretation depends on the characteristics (contextual features) of the context in which they are considered. The ontologies that represent the semantics of the sources are called *original ontologies*, and ontologies that result from making the contextual features explicit are called *extended ontologies*. The following section shows via example that the matching of extended ontologies is better than the matching of original ones.

3.4 Improving Ontology Alignment: Making Contextual Features Explicit

Suppose there is a need for information sharing between two enterprises: a manufacturing enterprise and a retailer. Source 1 contains information about the products of the manufacturer and Source 2 contains information about the products sold by the retailer. The semantics of the data stored in the sources is represented by ontologies, O_{s1} and O_{s2}, respectively. Figure 3.2 shows fragments of these ontologies.

It can be observed that the entities in these ontologies are represented in different ways. For example, the Package entity is represented by the Product, Type, and Size terms plus their relations in O_{s1} (Figure 3.2.a), and by the PackageType term in O_{s2} (Figure 3.2.b). This heterogeneity is difficult to solve by ontology matching techniques due to the structural conflict and also the intended use of the entity Package is not represented.

The objective of this section is to show how this problem can be solved by making contextual features explicit. To this aim, the section is organized in three parts. First, the alignment obtained by applying a matching process to the original ontologies is presented. Then an improvement in the representations of the entities in the ontologies is developed and the same matching process is applied to the resulting extended ontologies.

Even though a number of available ontology matching tools and techniques may provide matching between two different input ontologies (S-Match [25], CATO [4], Prompt [18], and COMA [9], to name few), HMatch Protégé Plugin 1.5 [6] was used. HMatch was chosen because it (1) can deal with different ontology specification languages, particularly OWL Full, in which the ontologies to be matched

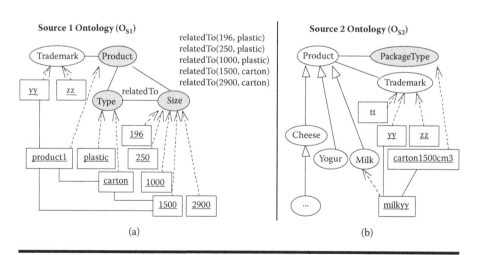

(a)   (b)

Figure 3.2 Fragments of two original ontologies to be matched.

are implemented; (2) considers both the names given to ontology elements and the relations they have with other elements; and (3) can deal with different levels of richness in ontology descriptions. The HMatch algorithm provides a ranking of similarity between the terms of two ontologies. A semantic affinity of two terms is calculated by considering their linguistic and contextual affinities. The first terms refer to the names of ontology elements and their meanings. The second terms refer to the properties and terms directly related to them.

To compare the alignments, the Ontology Alignment Evaluation Initiative (OAEI) criteria are followed and the next measurements calculated: *precision*, P, measures the ratio of correctly found correspondences (true positives – $E \hat{E} A$) over the total number of returned correspondences A; *recall*, R, measures the ratio of correctly found correspondences over the total number of expected correspondences E; F_2 weights recall twice as much as precision; and $F_{0.5}$ weights precision twice as much as recall.

3.4.1 Matching Original Ontologies

Figure 3.3 shows the alignment A_1 between the O_{S1} and O_{S2} ontologies (Source Concepts and Comparison Concepts columns, respectively), and the measure of semantic affinity of two terms in the range [0, 1] (Matching Value). The deep matching model was used to perform the matching. The model considers term names, term properties, and the set of terms that participate in semantic relations with all other terms. The minimum level of semantic affinity required to consider two terms as matching was set at 0.6, and the one-to-many (1:n) strategy was used to define a set of mappings for each term of O_{S1}. In addition, the impact of the linguistic affinity was set to equal the impact of the contextual affinity. The expected correspondences were:

$$\text{Product = PackageType,} \quad \text{Type = PackageType} \quad \text{(E1)}$$

$$\text{Size = PackageType,} \quad \text{Trademark = Trademark}$$

Alignment A_1 shows a correspondence between the Product terms of both ontologies; this is not the case in the set of expected correspondences E_1. In O_{s1}, Product refers to the different types of packages manufactured by the enterprise. In O_{s2},

Source concepts	Comparison concepts	Matching value
Product	Product	0.815
Trademark	Trademark	1.0
Type	PackageType	0.8

Figure 3.3   Matching results between the original O_{s1} and original O_{s2} ontologies with HMatch.

Product refers to dairy products sold by the retailer. Associated with these terms is an intended use of the entities that such terms represent that is not explicit in the ontologies. The values obtained for the precision P, recall R, F_2, and $F_{0.5}$ measurements are:

$$P(A_1, E_1) = \frac{E_1 \cap A_1}{A_1} = \frac{2}{3} = 0,66 \quad R(A_1, E_1) = \frac{E_1 \cap A_1}{E_1} = \frac{2}{4} = 0,5$$

$$F_2(A_1, E_1) = (1 + 2^2) \times \frac{P(A_1, E_1) \times R(A_1, E_1)}{(1 + 2^2) \times P(A_1, E_1) + R(A_1, E_1)} = 5 \times \frac{0,66 \times 0,50}{4 \times 0,66 + 0,50} = 0,53$$

$$F_{0.5}(A_1, E_1) = (1 + 0,5^2) \times \frac{P(A_1, E_1) \times R(A_1, E_1)}{(1 + 0,5^2) \times P(A_1, E_1) + R(A_1, E_1)}$$

$$= 1,25 \times \frac{0,66 \times 0,50}{0,25 \times 0,66 + 0,50} = 0,62$$

3.4.2 *Improving Representation of Entities*

The Package entity represented by PackageType in O_{s2} (Figure 3.2.b) has implicit association with a representation dimension that is not metric; it is an enumeration of possible values. To make this dimension explicit, a term representing it must be added to the original ontology. Figure 3.4 shows what the portion of interest of the extended ontology would be (the shaded term was added in the extended ontology). Additionally, this figure shows how the 1500 cm³ carton instance is represented. Note that the instance has been divided in two parts in the extended ontology packagetype1instanceOf PackageType and carton1500-cm3instanceOfPackageDimension; these two new instances are related by the associatedWith relation.

Similarly, the Package entity represented by the Product, Type, and Size terms plus their relations in O_{S1} (Figure 3.2.a) has an implicit association with a set of representation dimensions called multidimension. These dimensions are qualities that cannot be assigned a value on one dimension without giving them a value on the other; they are also called integral dimensions [15]. In Figure 3.5, the TypeDimension and SizeDimension terms represent integral dimensions that define the product multidimension represented as ProductMultiDimension. In its definition, this term includes a set of rules constraining the relations between its constituting dimensions shown by a note related to the ProductMultiDimension term.

Type Dimension is an enumeration of possible values (such as carton and plastic), and the Size Dimension is metric, i.e., its possible values are in nonnegative

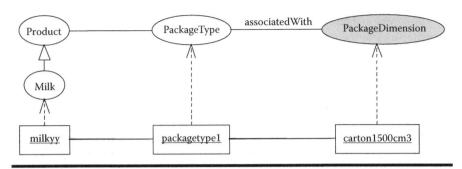

Figure 3.4   Portion of extended O_{s2}, and 1500 cm³ carton instance representation.

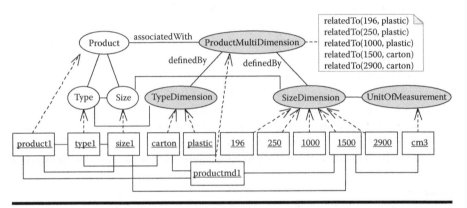

Figure 3.5   Portion of extended O_{s1}, and equivalent of 1500 cm³ carton instance representation.

numbers (196, 250, etc.). Additionally, Size Dimension has an associated metric unit represented by the UnitOfMeasurement term, indicating that all the possible values of Size Dimension are expressed in the cubic centimeter (cm³) metric unit. The Type term in O_{s1} is implicitly associated with the Type Dimension and the Size term in O_{s1} is implicitly associated with the Size Dimension.

The lower part of Figure 3.5 shows how the equivalent of the 1500 cm³ carton instance would be represented in the extended O_{s1} by defining the productmd1 instance defined by two instances of integral dimensions: carton and 1500. The carton dimension is an instance of the TypeDimension term and is the value of the type1 instance in the manufacturing enterprise context, i.e., the value of the type of product. 1500 is an instance of the SizeDimension term and represents the value of the size1 instance in the manufacturing enterprise context, i.e., the value of the size of product. Finally, cm³ indicates 1500 units, i.e., the size of product is expressed in cubic centimeter units.

The contextual features, whose representation and interpretation depend on the characteristics of the context in which the entities are considered, can be observed in Figures 3.4 and 3.5. In the retailer context, the Package entity requires a representation so simple that it can be represented by a dimension, whereas in the manufacturing enterprise context, it requires of a set of dimensions.

To facilitate meaningful information integration and provide better inputs to the matching process, it is proposed to represent the entities whose instances must be integrated with the necessary degree of detail. However, the inclusion of detail does not guarantee that the translation of instances of an entity from one context to another can be done in isolation. The translation process must identify correctly the set of ontology elements that represent an entity and its semantics in a given context. For example, in the extended O_{s2} (Figure 3.4), the absence of an ontology element that designates the semantics of the entity represented by the PackageType term can be noticed. The same happens in the extended O_{s1} (Figure 3.5) with the Product, Type, and Size terms plus their relations. The missing ontology element in both figures is the Package term. Figure 3.6 shows the two resulting extended ontologies in which the ProductMultiDimension term from the extended O_{s1} was renamed PackageMultiDimension with the aim of properly referring to the semantics of the entity.

The Package term refers to the semantics of an entity whose representation and interpretation depend on the characteristics of the context in which it is considered. In the context of the retailer, the Package term is associated with a dimension, whereas in the context of the manufacturing enterprise it is associated with multiple

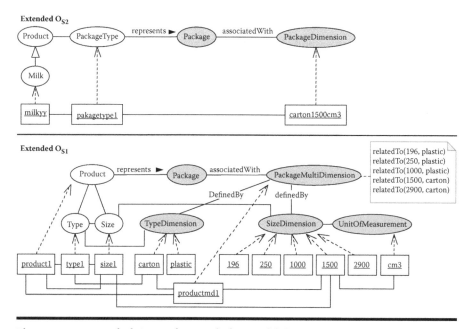

Figure 3.6   Extended O_{s2} and extended O_{s1} with instances.

dimensions. Thus, Package represents a common feature to both contexts whose instances must be translated between the two ontologies. This kind of term will be used to facilitate the generation of the conversion rules that will be executed automatically by the translation process to allow semantic interoperability between both enterprises. Additionally, considering that the conversion rules are generated from an alignment, entities represented in this way are steps toward the complete identification of the elements to translate and their features by the matching process.

In order to evaluate the richness of the extended ontologies, the OntoQA metric is used [29]. Table 3.1 shows the relationship richness (RR) and inheritance richness (IR) metrics of the O_{s2} ontology and the extended O_{s2} ontology. The RR is defined as the ratio of the number of relationships divided by the sum of the number of subclasses plus the number of relationships. An ontology that has an RR close to 1 would indicate that most of the relationships are other than class–subclass. An ontology that contains many relations other than class–subclass relations is richer than a taxonomy with only class–subclass relationships. Based on Table 3.1, the extended O_{s2} ontology is richer than the O_{s2} ontology.

The IR measurement describes the distribution of information across different levels of the ontology inheritance 3 or the fan-out of parent classes. An ontology with a low IR has a vertical nature that may reflect a very detailed type of knowledge that the ontology represents, while an ontology with a high IR would be of a horizontal nature—it represents a wide range of general knowledge. Table 3.1 indicates that the extended O_{s2} ontology represents a more detailed knowledge and is therefore richer than the knowledge of the original O_{s2} ontology.

3.4.3 Matching Resulting Extended Ontologies

The alignment A_2 between the extended ontologies (Figure 3.6) is shown in Figure 3.7. These results correspond to the same option set for obtaining A_1. The expected alignment was:

Package = Package,   Product = PackageType

PackageMultiDimension = PackageDimension,   Type = PackageType (E_2)

TypeDimension = PackageDimension,   Size = PackageType

SizeDimension = PackageDimension,   Trademark = Trademark

Table 3.1 Evaluation of Ontology Representation Improvement

Metric	O_{s2} Ontology	Extended O_{s2} Ontology
Relationship Richness (RR)	0.4	0.57
Inheritance Richness (IR)	0.5	0.375

Source concepts	Comparison concepts	Matching value
Package	Package	0.71033
PackageMultiDimension	PackageDimension	0.64
Product	Product	0.61571
SizeDimension	PackageDimension	0.64
Trademark	Trademark	1.0
Type	PackageType	0.8
TypeDimension	PackageDimension	0.64

Figure 3.7 Matching results between extended O_{s1} and extended O_{s2} ontologies with HMatch.

Although alignment A_2 still shows correspondence between the Product terms of both ontologies, its semantic affinity decreased from 0.815 (Figure 3.3) to 0.61571 (Figure 3.7). At the same time, it can be observed that in the alignment ([EQUATION]) there is a correspondence between the terms Package that designate the semantics of the entity Package in both ontologies, with a semantic affinity of 0.71033. The values obtained for the precision P, recall R, and F measurements are:

$$P(A_2, E_2) = \frac{E_2 \cap A_1}{A_1} = \frac{6}{7} = 0,85 \quad R(A_1, E_2) = \frac{E_2 \cap A_1}{E_2} = \frac{6}{8} = 0,75$$

$$F_2(A_2, E_2) = (1 + 2^2) \times \frac{P(A_2, E_2) \times R(A_2, E_2)}{(1 + 2^2) \times P(A_2, E_2) + R(A_2, E_2)} = 5 \times \frac{0,85 \times 0,75}{4 \times 0,85 + 0,75} = 0,77$$

$$F_2(A_2, E_2) = (1 + 0, \ 50^2) \times \frac{P(A_2, E_2) \times R(A_2, E_2)}{(1 + 0,50^2) \times P(A_2, E_2) + R(A_2, E_2)}$$

$$= 1,25 \times \frac{0,85 \times 0,75}{0,25 * 0,85 + 0,75} = 0,83$$

Judging by these preliminary results, it can be inferred that R, P, F_2, and $F_{0.50}$ measures are better when the matching process is applied to the extended ontologies.

3.5 Making Contextual Features Explicit

The previous section shows that making contextual features explicit improved the alignment of ontologies. The objective of this section is to present a method to guide the task of making these contextual features explicit in a given ontology. The proposed method is composed of five processes as shown in Figure 3.8 and described in the following subsections.

1. Identify the entities represented in the ontology and their features.
2. Identify the ontology elements that represent the entities.
3. Identify the features that must be made explicit.
4. Make the features of each entity explicit.
5. Designate a bridge term that refers to each entity.

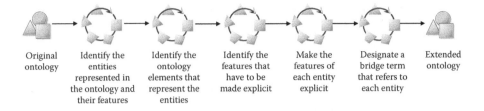

| Original ontology | Identify the entities represented in the ontology and their features | Identify the ontology elements that represent the entities | Identify the features that have to be made explicit | Make the features of each entity explicit | Designate a bridge term that refers to each entity | Extended ontology |

Figure 3.8   Method for making contextual features explicit.

3.5.1 Process 1: Identify Entities Represented in Ontology and Their Features

Any improvement on the representation of entities involves prior knowledge about the entities to which the representations relate. The objective of this process is to clarify what the entities, their features, and their relationships with other entities are, according to the way they are represented in the ontology. The process allows the ontologist to identify the features that are generally implicit in the representation of an entity; although they may be inferred by a human agent, they cannot be inferred by a machine agent. These features are not required to be made explicit when the entities are considered within the same context, but the entities must be explicit when they must be interpreted in another context.

The outputs of this process are lists of the entities and their relationships and a list of the features of each entity whose semantics are affected by the context in which the entity is considered. The list of the entities can be obtained by exploring the documentation associated with the ontology. The list of the features can be made by encoding the knowledge required to understand the corresponding entities, namely searching and representing the underlying knowledge that, according to domain experts, should be present to achieve accurate interpretations of the meanings of the entities in different contexts.

3.5.2 Process 2: Identify Ontology Elements Representing Entities

Terms, relations between terms, axioms, and other components used to represent each entity, its relationships, and features must be identified. Depending on the perspective, an entity may be represented by a simple term or a set of ontology elements.

3.5.3 Process 3: Identify Features That Must Be Explicit

When representing an entity, it is possible that some of its features are implicit or their representations are incomplete. Therefore, their explicitness becomes necessary for improving the representation of the real entity semantics. Based on the outputs of Processes 1 and 2, these features can be detected. Since not all of these features must be made explicit, answering the following questions could help to identify those that must be explicit.

■ Are there any implicit features in the representation of an entity that may be inferred by a human agent but cannot be inferred by a machine agent? If the answer is yes, can these features be inferred incorrectly in contexts different from the one considered? If the answer is yes, these features should be made explicit.

■ Are there any entities whose representations and/or meanings may change based on the context in which the entities are considered? If the answer is yes, are the representations and meanings completely explicit in the ontology? If the answer is no, the representations and meanings should be made explicit.

■ What are the quality dimensions used to represent a feature? Are they the same regardless of the context in which the feature is considered? If the answer is no, are they explicit in the ontology? If the answer is no, these quality dimensions should be made explicit.

3.5.4 Process 4: Make Features of Each Entity Explicit

After the features and their representation dimensions have been identified, they must be made explicit. For this purpose, integrating existing and widely accepted ontologies should be considered. Examples of such ontologies are:

■ OWL–Time ontology [16] for modeling most of the basic temporal concepts and relations, i.e., a vocabulary for expressing facts about topological relations among instants, intervals, and events, along with information about durations, dates, and times

■ ISO 3166 Country Codes Ontology (http://www.daml.org/2001/09/countries/iso-3166-ont) for modeling official country names

■ A portion of an ontology implementing ISO currency codes published in Standard ISO 4217:2008, such as the PCS ontology for the representation of currencies and funds (http://www.ifpi.com/pcs/)

■ A portion of an ontology implementing ISO 80000, the successor of ISO 31, for modeling physical quantities and units of measurement, e.g., the United Nations Centre for Trade Facilitation and Electronic Business (UN/CEFACT) (http://www.unece.org/cefact/codesfortrade/codes_index.htm)

When it is not possible to reuse an ontology to improve the representation of a feature, it is necessary to identify whether the feature is simple or complex. A simple feature does not exhibit multiple qualities and is associated with a one-dimensional representation in human cognition [15], e.g., the weight of an object. Thus, two elements should be added to an ontology: (1) a term denoting the representation dimension and (2) a relation between this term and the term that represents the simple feature.

A complex feature bears multiple qualities and is associated with a set of integral dimensions that are separable from all other dimensions [15]. In an integral dimension, it is not possible to assign a value to an object in one dimension without giving it a value in another. For instance, color can be represented in terms of the integral dimensions of hue, saturation, and brightness. By contrast, weight and hue dimensions are said to be separable. Each integral dimension is associated with a simple feature. To improve the representation of a complex feature, the following elements should be added to the ontology:

■ A term representing the set of integral dimensions and a relation between this term and the term that represents the complex feature
■ For each integral dimension, a term representing it and a relation between this term and the term that represents the set of integral dimension
■ For each term representing an integral dimension, a relation between this term and the term that represents the corresponding simple feature

In addition, for each term representing a one-dimensional representation or integral dimension, a term representing the unit of measurement of the dimension and a relation between these two terms should be added to the ontology. This term affects the granularity of the dimension but not its structure. For example, a weight dimension has positive real numbers as values regardless of whether the metric units are kilograms or tons.

3.5.5 Process 5: Designate Bridge Term for Each Entity

The intended uses of an entity in the context considered should be represented by terms called bridges because they allow linking different meanings and representations of the same entity in different contexts. These terms should also be interpreted as representing contextual features because the intended use depends on the context in which the entity is considered. Thus, it is necessary to determine whether an existing term designates the intended use of each entity; if such a term is absent, it must be added. Bridge terms should also relate to the elements that represent the entity whose intended use they represent. An entity may be represented by a single element or a set of elements. In the former case, a relation between the single element and the bridge term should be added. In the latter, the most representative term should be chosen and then a relation between this term and the bridge term should be added. As the bridge term represents a contextual feature, it should also relate to the term that represents its representation dimension.

3.6 Application Example

Suppose there is a collaborative relationship between a packaging industry (supplier) and a dairy industry (customer). Both trading partners must exchange the information shown in Table 3.2 to reach an agreement on a replenishment plan. The structure and semantics of this information are initially reflected in an *EBD ontology* as shown in Figure 3.9. To improve the representation of entities in this ontology, the proposed method is applied.

3.6.1 Process 1: Identify Entities and Their Features

The entities whose information must be translated are: (1) trading partners that assume two roles: supplier and customer; a relevant feature of a trading partner is its address; (2) a replenishment plan that refers to the agreed plan between the trading partners; some plan features are the time period during which the plan is valid, the products to be exchanged, the quantities of products, and periods within the horizon during which these products are exchanged, among others; (3) the products involved in the replenishment plan (manufactured by the packaging industry and the packages containing the dairy industry products). Product features include trademark, type, and size.

Table 3.2 Examples of Necessary Information for Devising Replenishment Plan

Horizon: 6/04–31/05 (Day/Month)					
Period	Product Identification	Trademark	Type	Size	Quantity
7/04–13/04	20320101	yy	Carton	1000	4400
	20320102			2900	2880
	20070231		Plastic	196	1600
	20070232			250	1800
	20320101	zz	Carton	1000	2200
	20320102			2900	8064
	20070232		Plastic	250	1800
	20070235			1000	6500
14/04–20/04	...	...	...	...	...

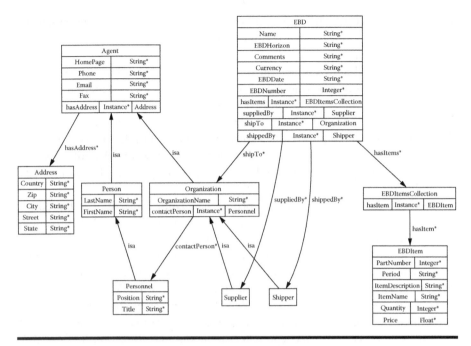

Figure 3.9 Original EBD ontology.

3.6.2 Process 2: Identify Ontology Elements

A trading partner assuming a supplier role is represented by the Agent, Organization, and Supplier terms, their properties, and the relations between these terms. A customer is represented by means of the Agent and Organization terms, their properties, and the relations between them. Their addresses are represented by the Address term and the hasAddress relation. The replenishment plan and its features are represented by EBD, EBDItem, and EBDItemsCollection terms, their properties, and the hasItems, and hasItem relations. EBD refers to documents exchanged by the trading partners. EBDItemsCollection and EBDItem represent the structures of the documents. The products and their features are represented by the following properties of the EBDItem term: PartNumber, ItemName, and ItemDescription.

3.6.3 Process 3: Identify Features That Must Be Explicit

As noted, a relevant feature for a trading partner is its address (represented by the Address term). According to Smith et al. [26], this term represents a quality existing in reality and cites a mailing address—not an e-mail address, for example. The features of a mailing address are street, number assigned to building or entity on street, floor, apartment, city, postal code, province or state, and country. In the ontology, some items (floor or apartment, for example) need not be explicit if they do not prevent a correct interpretation of the entity in any context in which the entity is considered. A reason for making these features explicit could be to achieve a more complete representation of the entity.

The time period during which the replenishment plan is valid is represented by the EBDHorizon property, whose data type is string. This representation does not reveal whether the horizon is expressed as an amount of time or an interval, and thus does not satisfy the minimal encoding bias criterion [14]. Based on Table 3.2, the representation should make the feature explicit as a calendar interval since the horizon is a quantity of time and also a location on the time line. A similar analysis can be made for periods within the horizon (represented by the Period property of EBDItem).

Another feature of a replenishment plan is the quantity ordered of each product. This feature is represented by the Quantity property (integer data type). At this point, some questions arise. What unit of measurement expresses this quantity? The answer could cite units of products or units of product packs, for example. Will any information system that deals with such information make a correct interpretation of it? If any misunderstanding is possible, the unit of measurement should be made explicit.

Products are represented by the following properties of the EBDItem term: PartNumber (integer data type), ItemName, and ItemDescription (both of string data type). PartNumber represents the product identification in Table 3.2. ItemName and ItemDescription do not represent, at least at first glance, any of the other product features. ItemDescription can appear in the natural language of the product. However, the ItemName property should be replaced by three terms that represent trademark, type, and size features.

3.6.4 Process 4: Make Features of Each Entity Explicit

To make a feature explicit, it is important to distinguish when that feature is an entity and when it is not. For example, the Country feature of an address may be considered an entity and be represented by a Country term instead of a property. In this case, a formal relation [15] that joins the Address and Country terms is needed. By contrast, the feature Floor is existentially dependent on the address in the context under consideration, in which case a property is more appropriate to represent it.

Taking the OWL–Time ontology [16] into account, the feature horizon of the Replenishment Plan entity should be represented by means of a different term derived from the CalendarClockInterval term and linked to the EBD term by a formal relation. The same treatment applies to the periods within the horizon.

Since the quantity ordered of each product is a simple feature, four elements should be added to the ontology: (1) a QuantityDimension term denoting the representation dimension, (2) a UnitOfMeasure term representing the measurement unit of the dimension, (3) a relation between these two terms, and (4) a relation between QuantityDimension and the term that represents the simple feature. However, quantity is represented by a property, not by a term. Although it

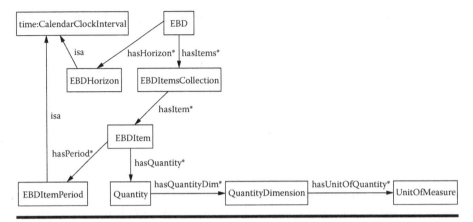

Figure 3.10 Portion of extended EBD ontology representing temporal and quantity features.

is possible to think about quantity as a property instead of an entity, it is necessary to represent it by a term to follow the minimal encoding bias criterion [14]. Additionally, this Quantity term must be related to the EBDItem term by a formal relation. Figure 3.10 shows a portion of the ontology after making the quantity and temporal features explicit.

To represent the features of products, three terms are added: Type, Size, and Trademark. The Trademark term is related to another term, Trademark Dimension, covering the representation dimension of the feature trademark. This representation dimension is an enumeration of possible values, not a metric. In the same way, the Type term that represents the type of material with which the packages are made is related to the TypeDimension term which is an enumeration of possible values (such as carton or plastic). Finally, the Size term representing package capacity is related to the SizeDimension term indicating the representation dimension of feature size. This dimension is metric, i.e. its possible values are nonnegative numbers (196, 250, etc.). Since the capacity of a packages is an amount associated with a unit of measure, the SizeDimension term has a relation with the UnitOfMeasure term mentioned earlier.

Up to this point, only the features of the Product entity have been represented, but Product lacks its own representation. Thus, a Product term must be added to the ontology and related to the EBDItem, Trademark, Type, and Size terms. Additionally, the PartNumber and ItemDescription must be properties of the Product term and not of the EBDItem term.

A product is both an entity and a feature of the Replenishment Plan entity. Thus it is a complex feature related to a set of representation dimensions (multidimension) and represented by the ProductMultiDimension term. The dimensions that compose this set are integral and represented by TrademarkDimension, TypeDimension, and SizeDimension.

3.6.5 Process 5: Designate Bridge Term for Each Entity

An important feature that should be made explicit is the intended use of an entity in the context considered. However, Trading Partners are the roles they assume, not physical entities. The treatment of entities that represent roles is postponed to future work. The intended use of the Replenishment Plan entity is to represent the agreed plan of the trading partners. Since the EBD term refers to the documents exchanged by the trading partners, particularly the replenishment plan, this term can be used to designate the intended use of the entity.

The products covered by the replenishment plan can be misunderstood, depending on their intended use. They are manufactured by the packaging industry and used for the dairy industry products. Thus, in an ontology from the collaborative relationship context such as the EBD ontology, two bridge terms should be added: Product and Package to represent the intended use of the entity in the packaging industry and dairy industry contexts, respectively. Since Product is already in the ontology, only Package must be added and related to the Product term. As bridge terms represent contextual features, they must also relate to the terms encompassing their representation dimension in human cognition. In the dairy industry context, packages are associated with a representation dimension that is an enumeration of possible values. Figure 3.11 shows a portion of the EBD ontology with the changes made to adequately represent the feature product.

3.7 Conclusions

This chapter discussed the problem of semantic interoperability between P2P information systems that share information from their sources. To solve this problem, we

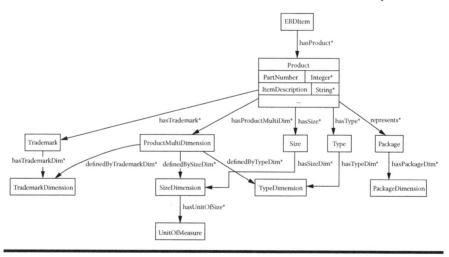

Figure 3.11   Portion of extended EBD ontology representing products.

proposed improving the results of the matching process between the ontologies that represent the semantics of the information sources by providing thorough representations of entities. To this aim, we suggested a method for making the contextual features of entities explicit. This approach significantly improves the output of the ontology matching process and facilitates the generation of conversion rules that constitute the core of information system interoperability. Regardless of the domain in which ontologies are used, in practice they suffer from different kinds of modeling errors. The proposed method can also be applied to existing ontologies to overcome some of these errors.

Acknowledgments

The authors are grateful to Universidad Tecnológica Nacional, Consejo Nacional de Investigaciones Científicas y Técnicas, and Agencia Nacional de Promoción Científica y Tecnológica for their financial support.

References

1. Bouquet, P., Ehrig, M., Euzenat, J. et al. February 2, 2005. D2.2.1 specification of a common framework for characterizing alignment. KWEB 200-4/D2.2.1, Version 2.0. Knowledge Web Consortium.
2. Brusa, G., Caliusco, M.L., and Chiotti. 2008. Towards ontological engineering: A process for building a domain ontology from scratch in public administration. *Expert Systems, 25*: 483–502.
3. Caliusco, M.L. 2005. A semantic definition support of electronic business documents in e-collaboration. PhD Thesis, Universidad Tecnologica Nacional, Santa Fe, Argentina.
4. Breiman, K., Felicissimo, C., and Casanova, M. 2005. CATO: A lightweight ontology alignment tool. In *Proceedings of 17th Conference on Advanced Information Systems Engineering*, Porto, Portugal.
5. Castano, S., Ferrara, A., and Montanelli, S. 2006. Dynamic knowledge discovery in open distributed and multi-ontology systems. In *Web Semantics and Ontology*, Group Publishing, Hershey, PA, pp. 226–258.
6. Castano, S., Ferrara, A., Montanelli, S. et al. 2004. Semantic information interoperability in open networked systems. In *Semantics for Grid Databases*, Springer Verlag, Berlin, pp. 215–230.
7. Corcho, O. 2004. A declarative approach to ontology translation with knowledge preservation. PhD Thesis, Universidad Politecnica de Madrid.
8. Davies, J., Studer, R., and Warren, P. 2007. *Semantic Web Technologies: Trends and Research in Ontology-Based Systems*. John Wiley & Sons, London
9. Do, H.H. and Rahm, E. 2002. COMA: A system for flexible combination of schema matching approaches. In *Proceedings of 28th International Conference on Very Large Databases*, pp. 610–621.
10. Euzenat, J. and Shvaiko, P. 2007. *Ontology Matching*. Springer Verlag, Berlin.
11. Gal, A. and Shvaiko, P. 2009. Advances in ontology matching. In *Advances in Web Semantics I: Ontologies, Web Services and Applied Semantic Web*, Springer Verlag, Berlin, pp. 176–198.

12. Ghidini, C. and Giunchiglia, F. 2004. A semantics for abstraction. In *Proceedings of 16th European Conference on Artificial Intelligence*, pp. 343–347.
13. Gomez-Perez, A., Fernandez-Lopez, M., and Corcho, O. 2004. *Ontological Engineering*, 2nd ed., Springer Verlag, Berlin.
14. Gruber, T. 1995. Toward principles for the design of ontologies used for knowledge sharing. *International Journal of Human– Computer Studies, 43*: 907–928.
15. Guizzardi, G. 2005. Ontological foundations for structural conceptual models. PhD Thesis, University of Twente, Enschede, Netherlands.
16. Hobbs, J.R. and Pan, F. 2003. An ontology of time for the semantic web. *ACM Transactions on Asian Language Information Processing, 3*: 66–85.
17. Mao, M., Peng, Y., and Spring, M. 2010. An adaptive ontology mapping approach with neural network-based constraint satisfaction. *Web Semantics, 8*: 14–25.
18. Noy, N. and Musen, M. 2003. The PROMPT suite: Interactive tools for ontology merging and mapping. *International Journal of Human–Computer Studies, 59*: 983–1024.
19. Noy, N.F. 2004. Semantic integration: A survey of ontology-based approaches. *SIGMOD Record, 33*: 65–70.
20. Rahm, E. and Bernstein, P.A. 2001. A survey of approaches to automatic schema matching. *VDLB Journal, 10*: 334–350.
21. Rico, M., Caliusco, M.L., Chiotti, O., and Galli, M.R. 2006. Combining contexts and ontologies: A case study and conceptual proposal. In *Proceedings of Second Internal Workshop on Contexts and Ontologies*, Riva del Garda, Italy.
22. Rico, M., Caliusco, M.L., Galli, M.R. et al. 2007. A comprehensive framework for representing semantics via context and ontology in the collaborative commerce area. In *Proceedings of Fifth Latin American Web Congress*, Santiago, Chile, pp. 110–119.
23. Sheth, A. 1998. Changing focus on interoperability in information systems: From system, syntax, and structure to semantics. *Interoperating Geographic Information Systems, 47*: 5–29.
24. Shvaiko, P. and Euzenat, J. 2005. A survey of schema-based matching approaches. *Journal of Data Semantics, 4*: 146–171.
25. Shvaiko, P., Giunchiblia, F., and Yatskevich, M. 2010. Semantic matching with S-Match. In *Semantic Web Information Management: A Model-Based Perspective*, Springer Verlag, Berlin, pp. 283–302.
26. Smith, B., Kusnierczyk, W., Schober, D. et al. 2006. Toward a reference terminology for ontology research and development in the biomedical domain. In *Proceedings of Second International Workshop on Formal Biomedical Knowledge Representation*, pp. 57–66.
27. Stuckenschmidt, H. and van Harmelen, F. 2004. Towards semantic interoperability between information systems. In *Information Sharing on the Semantic Web: Advanced Information Processing*, Springer Verlag, Berlin, Ch. 1.
28. Sviab-Zamazal, O., Sviatek, V., Meilicke, C. et al. 2008. Testing the impact of pattern-based ontology refactoring on ontology matching results. In *Proceedings of Third International Workshop on Ontology Matching*.
29. Tartir, S., Arpinar, B., Moore, M. et al. 2005. ONTOQA: Metric-based ontology quality analysis. In *IEEE Workshop on Knowledge Acquisition from Distributed, Autonomous, Semantically Heterogeneous Data and Knowledge Sources*.
30. Tsichritzis, D. and Klug, A.C. 1978. The ansi/x23/sparc DBMS framework report of the Study Group on Database Management Systems. *Information Systems, 3*: 173–191.
31. Zaihrayeu, I. 2006. Towards peer-to-peer information management systems. PhD Thesis, University of Trento, Trento, Italy.

Chapter 4

AlViz: A Tool for Ontology Alignment Utilizing Information Visualization Techniques

---

Monika Lanzenberger
Vienna University of Technology, Vienna, Austria

Jennifer Sampson
Statoil, Bergen, Norway

Contents

4.1 Introduction to Ontology Alignment

The main purpose of ontology alignment is to determine which entities or expressions in one ontology, correspond to other entities in a second ontology. Like Ehrig et al. [2005], we define an ontology as a tuple: $O = (C, H_C, R_C, H_R, I, R_I, A)$. Concepts C are organized in a subsumption hierarchy H_C. Relations R_C are between pairs of concepts and may also be arranged in a hierarchy H_R. The instances of specific concepts I are interconnected through relational instances R_I. A represents the axioms used for inferring knowledge. We define ontology alignment as given two ontologies O_1 and O_2, each describing a set of discrete entities (concepts C, relations R, and instances I), and find the relationships (equal, syntactically equal, broader than, narrower than, similar to, and different) that hold between these entities [Sampson, 2007]. Ontology alignment also includes evaluating the correspondences, sometimes bringing about the need to transform one or more input ontologies.

The use of terms cannot be expected to be consistent between related but separate ontologies. Different parts of the ontologies may contain conflicting or ambiguous elements for concepts, instances, and relations. However, we can find correspondences between ontologies in three main ways. First, intentional methods compare ontology schemas from terminological and structural perspectives. Terminological correspondences between entities are based on names, labels, or descriptions of entities. When comparing labels or names, techniques such as string equality, string dissimilarity, or edit distance may be used, resulting in what we define as a syntactical match.

String equality returns 0 if the strings compared are not the same and 1 if they are the same. The edit distance between two strings is the minimal number of changes required to transform one string into another. The structures of entities in two ontologies can also be compared from internal and external perspectives. Comparing the internal structures of ontologies involves checking their property ranges, cardinalities, and the transitivities and/or symmetries to determine similarities of the structures. These types of comparisons are most often used in conjunction with other techniques for alignment as they are not good indicators for similarity when used alone.

External structure comparison involves comparing the hierarchical positions of the entities in two ontologies. The intuition is that if two entities are similar, then often their neighbors are similar. Second, extensional methods compare the set of instances of the classes in the ontologies. This type of comparison can be used when the classes share the same instances or when they do not share the same instances. Testing for intersection between two classes is one extension comparison approach. The technique can be refined through the calculation of the symmetric difference between the two extensions. Third, a semantic comparison involves comparing the interpretations of the entities in the ontologies. Semantic methods have model-theoretic semantics, that is, they use deductive methods to verify the results. For example, description logics techniques such as the subsumption test can be used to establish relations between classes during ontology alignment. In the FOAM [Ehrig, 2005] algorithm, all three types of comparisons are made between entities. The resulting similarities provide evidence that two entities are the same (or similar) and can potentially be aligned. Calculating the similarity between two entities requires a range of similarity functions that combine different features of the ontologies with appropriate similarity measures. Section 4.4 provides a detailed example of ontology alignment.

4.2 Introduction to Information Visualization

Visualization has appealing potential when it comes to creating, exploring, or verifying complex and large collections of data such as ontologies. In particular, Information Visualization (InfoVis), which deals with abstract and non-spatial data, offers a bundle of techniques to represent hierarchical or semi-structured data. Thus it is no surprise that many ontology tools integrated visualization in some fashion during the past decade. Many tools rely on simple types of visualizations like two-dimensional trees or graphs. Usually the nodes stand for concepts and the edges represent relationships of concepts, but other approaches exist as well.

A literature study indicated a broad interpretation of ontology visualization differing among the various tools. InfoVis uses visual metaphors to ease the interpretation and understanding of multidimensional data to provide users with relevant information. A visual metaphor consists of graphical primitives such as point, line, area, or volume and utilizes them to encode information by position in space, size, shape, orientation, color, texture, and other visual cues, connections and enclosures, temporal changes, and viewpoint transformations [Card et al., 1999]. The goal of InfoVis is to promote a more intuitive and deeper level of understanding of the investigational data and foster new insights into the underlying processes [Tufte, 2001].

An enormous amount of work was done in the field of InfoVis in recent years. The methods range from geometric techniques such as scatter plots and parallel coordinates [Inselberg and Dimsdale. 1990]), glyphs like InfoBug [Chuah and Eick, 1997], icon-based techniques like Chernoff faces [Chernoff, 1973], stick figures [Pickett and Grinstein, 1988], pixel-oriented recursive patterns [Keim et al., 1995], and spiral and axis techniques [Keim, 1996] to interactive visualizations for hierarchical information such as cones or cam trees [Robertson et al., 1991], hyperbolic trees [Lamping et al., 1995], graph-based techniques such as small world graphs [van Ham and van Wijk, 2004], maps such as themescape [Wise et al., 1995], distortion-oriented methods like the fisheye lens [Furnas, 1986], other focus + context techniques [Pirolli et al., 2001], and hybrids like Stardinates [Lanzenberger et al., 2003].

Combining several views is well known as multiple view visualization, which offers several advantages such as improved user performance, discovery of unforeseen relationships, and desktop unification [North and Shneiderman, 1997]. Generally, in InfoVis the exploration process is characterized by cognitive abstraction. In addition, visualization often reduces information or emphasizes certain aspects of the data in order to ease goal-oriented interpretation. Combining distinct visualizations yields different kinds of abstractions from the data that allow for diverse approaches of exploration. An important challenge of multiple view visualization is its complexity for the users. They need to switch between different views and contexts.

4.3 Visualization for Mapping and Alignment

A few visualization tools support users with ontology mapping and alignment. We identified six such tools: OLA, Coma++, PromptViz, CogZ, Optima, and AlViz.

OLA [OWL Lite Alignment; Euzénat et al., 2004], a stand-alone program, uses graph-based visualizations to represent ontologies. In particular, an extended JGraph API is applied. The graph structure of OLA makes relationships between language elements explicit, e.g., if a class c refers to another class c' via an owl:allValuesFrom restriction, a labeled path between the corresponding nodes in the OL graph is shown such that the connection between both classes is perceived intuitively. Besides common subclass relationships, users can activate a display of edges between objects that are reverse, symmetric, or transitive.

Coma++ [Aumueller et al., 2005], a stand-alone tool for schema and ontology matching, uses simple lines to connect mapping pairs in list views. However, its main focus is the mapping algorithm, not the visualization of mapping results.

PromptViz [Perrin, 2004] is a visualization tool for Protégé's Prompt tool [Noy, 2004]. It provides visual representations of the differences between two versions of an ontology using histograms within a tree map. The bars in the histograms represent the percentages of descendants classified as unchanged, added, deleted, moved from, moved to, and directly changed, respectively. A histogram is divided into four linked frames: (1) an expandable horizontal tree layout of the ontology showing the differences; (2) a tree map layout of the ontology embedded in a zoomable user interface; (3) a path window that shows the location of the currently selected concepts within the is-a hierarchy of the ontology; and (4) a detailed list of the changes (if any) to the currently selected concept.

Implemented as a user interface plug-in extension to Prompt, the CogZ tool [Falconer and Storey, 2007] offers visual mapping functionality. It enables users to examine, add, or remove temporary or permanent mappings. A bundle of filtering options help handle the complexity of ontology mapping. Moreover, neighborhood graphs, fisheye lenses, and other tree map or pie chart views offer efficient means for exploration of the mappings. (see Figures 4.1 and 4.2).

Optima [Kolli and Doshi, 2008] is a Jena-based alignment tool using a graph-theoretic algorithm to find the most likely match between two ontologies (optimization) and computes the likelihood using the expectation maximization (EM)

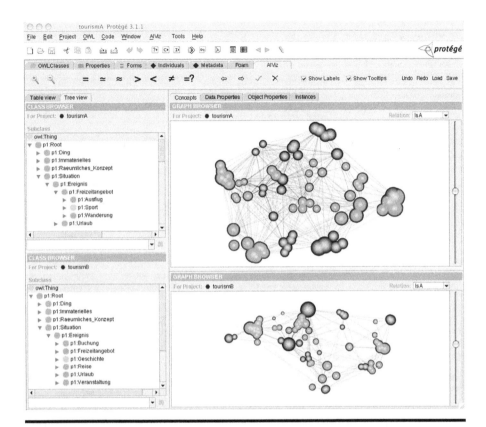

Figure 4.1 AlViz: the four views of the tool visualize two ontologies named tourismA and tourismB. The nodes of the graphs and dots next to the list entries represent the similarities of the ontologies by color. The sizes of the nodes result from the number of clustered concepts. The graphs show the IsA relationship among the concepts. Light gray/green indicates similar concepts available in both ontologies. Dark gray/red nodes represent equal concepts. The sliders to the right adjust the level of clustering. (The figure is available in color at: http://www.ifs.tuwien. ac.at/~mlanzenberger/alviz/graphics/ASWT/Figure41_AlVizScreenShot1.pdf)

technique. It involves structural and lexical similarities between schemas. Both ontologies are visualized as graphs available with several different layouts such as tree, circle, etc. However, this tool does not integrate other alignment algorithms and is not linked to an ontology editor.

AlViz [Lanzenberger and Sampson, 2006] is a research prototype for visual ontology alignment implemented as a multiple-view plug-in for Protégé (see Figures 4.1 and 4.2). Based on similarity measures of an ontology matching algorithm like FOAM [Ehrig, 2005], AlViz helps assess and optimize the alignment results at different levels of detail. Clustered graphs enable users to examine and manipulate mappings of large ontologies. In AlViz in conjunction with FOAM,

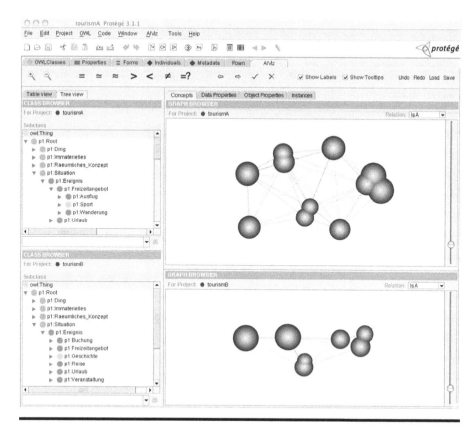

Figure 4.2 **AlViz showing a highly clustered view of alignment results for tourismA and tourismB ontologies. Different concepts are colored light gray/yellow to represent entities that occur in only one of the two source ontologies. Gray/orange represents syntactically equal concepts. (The figure is available in color at: http://www.ifs.tuwien.ac.at/~mlanzenberger/alviz/graphics/ASWT/Figure42_AlVizScreenShot2.pdf)**

additional alignment algorithms can be exploited for similarity calculations [Gradwohl, 2009]; we use the API ontology alignment [Euzénat, 2004] as a common interface. More details about AlViz are described in the next section.

4.4 AlViz: Multiple View Visualization for Semi-Automatic Alignment of Ontologies

AlViz supports the visual alignment of two ontologies by making the type of similarity between entities explicit. The tool [Banovic, 2009] consists of two types of views coupled by a linking and brushing technique. AlViz applies J-Trees as one of two types of views. Such trees consist of a root node, expanded or collapsed branch nodes, and leaf nodes displaying the hierarchical structure by indentation. They support the access and manipulation of instances and single items within classes effectively and are well established within the Protégé community. But such J-Trees bear shortcomings regarding the representation of large or complex ontologies because they become cluttered and do not provide adequate overview functionality.

To overcome this problem, another visualization type was integrated: small world graphs [van Ham and van Wijk, 2004]. Therefore, as a second view, such graphs help a user examine the structure of an ontology intuitively. This method uses clusters to group the nodes of a graph according to the selected level of detail. The nodes represent the entities (concepts or instances) connected to each other according to the selected relations, also called mutual properties, such as IsA, IsPart, IsMember, locatedIn, and IsDistinct. Each source ontology is visualized as a clustered graph whose edges represent the selected mutual property (a cumulation of properties is possible as well).

When aligning ontologies visually, users are interested in the global questions about the data. Are there any distinct groups of items that are strongly interconnected (i.e., graph clusters)? How do these split into separate clusters and how do the clusters relate? Small world graphs [Milgram, 1967] in social networks exhibit small average path length (average shortest path between nodes) compared to the number of nodes, but show a high degree of clustering compared to a random graph of the same size. Informal evaluation of structures of different ontologies showed the same property, which makes clustering a suitable approach.

An adequate visualization for clusters should communicate the underlying structure efficiently. The number of visible elements in a graph must be reduced, but at the same time we must maintain the global structure of the graph. That means finding a representative visual abstraction of the original graph. Although the small world graphs, like all spring-embedded algorithms, bear the problem of high computational complexity—usually $O(N^3)$—clustering the graph improves program interactivity. The tool is fast enough to perform at interactive speeds because, on average, only $O(Log(N))$ clusters are visible. The current implementation manages about a thousand entities per ontology and will be able to deal with some tens of thousands of entities per ontology.

Each ontology is visualized by both views, the J-Tree and the small world graph, resulting in four linked views making the ontologies available at different levels of detail and overview. Figure 4.1 shows AlViz visualizing the alignment of two ontologies about tourism with a high degree of detail. Clustering the nodes (Figure 4.2) allows a visualization to emphasize the hierarchical structure in the graph. Both figures visualize the same source ontologies on different levels of detail. The colors of the nodes and the dots next to the entity names represent the degree of similarity or type of association, respectively.

Six categories of association between entities are distinguished: equal, syntactically equal, broader-than, narrower-than, similar, and different. Tables 4.1

and 4.2 list these association categories and the assigned rules applied by the similarity algorithm for concepts, instances, data, and object properties. The input file representing these associations is discussed in detail later in this section. By default, an entity of one ontology equal to an entity in the other ontology is colored red; a syntactically equal entity is orange; an entity broader than an entity in the other ontology appears blue; a narrower entity is violet, a similar entity is green; and finally, an entity different from all entities in the other ontology is yellow.

Table 4.1   Comparison Relations of Concepts and Instances in Ontologies

OWL Ontology Construct	Comparison Relationship	Description
Concept	Equal	URIs equal
		Class member instance equal
	Syntactically equal	Labels are the same
	Similar	Superclasses are the same
		Subclasses are the same
		Data properties are the same
		Object properties are the same
		Similar low and high fraction of instances
	Broader than	Subclass–superclass comparison
	Narrower than	Superclass–subclass comparison
	Different	Class different from all classes of second ontology
Instance	Equal	URIs equal
	Syntactically equal	Labels are the same
	Similar	Instances of same concept
		Property members are the same
		Two instances linked via same property to another instance
	Different	Instance different from all instances of second ontology

Table 4.2 Comparison Relations among Properties in Ontologies

OWL Ontology Construct	Comparison Relationship	Description
Data Properties	Equal	URIs equal
	Syntactically equal	Labels are the same
	Similar	Data property domains are the same
		Data super properties are the same
		Data subproperties are the same
		Data properties members are the same
	Different	Data property is different from all data properties of second ontology
Object Properties	Equal	URIs equal
	Syntactically equal	Labels are the same
	Similar	Object property domains are the same
		Object super properties are the same
		Object subproperties are the same
		Object properties members are the same
	Different	Object property is different from all object properties of second ontology

In the graphs, the clusters of nodes inherit the colors of the underlying nodes in accordance to the selected comparison strategy. Three comparison strategies are available. The first emphasizes similarities of entities, the second highlights differences among entities, and the third represents the entities according to the dominant types of associations. If a user focuses on similarity, the colors of nodes indicating more similarity have priority over the colors of nodes with less similarity. Particularly, clustering an equal and a syntactically equal node into a single node results in a red cluster. Of course, higher levels of detail are also possible, maintaining two differently colored nodes as individuals but combined within one cluster. However, this case is simple. If a cluster is represented by a single node, a priority approach is necessary.

Interacting with a graph involves a number of tasks. Beside the zooming functionality, a selection and/or highlighting function, several alignment functions, and tracking buttons for questionable associations are implemented. Selecting a node with a mouse click results in highlighting three other items. In particular, the entity (or group of entities) of the same ontology is highlighted in a tree view. While navigating the nodes (entities) in ontology O_1, the associated nodes in O_2 are highlighted. This interaction technique is known as linking and brushing.

If the association is equality, then the equal entity (or group of entities) in the other ontology is highlighted as well. This results in linking together entities between both ontologies, O_1 and O_2, in both views—a graphical (over) view and a text-based (detailed) view. The same holds for the other types of association, i.e., syntactical equality, broader-than and narrower-than relations, and similarity.

The alignment functions allow for adapting the automatically derived associations by assigning the type of association manually and thus approving or rejecting the alignment result. A user can select an entity in the graph or in the text list, then activate the required type of association, e.g., equality, followed by a selection of the associated entity (or group of entities) within the other ontology.

Such changes of the alignment are rather complex. However, the interactive manner of the graph visualization makes this task easier and more manageable. Undo and redo functions combined with a history of applied interactions, labeling, and tool tips are included. AlViz supports users in understanding the alignment process and manipulating its results to improve and maintain quality [Sampson, 2007].

In terms of perception, small world graphs utilize features of the Gestalt tradition, in particular, the Gestalt law of organization: "When we are presented with a number of stimuli, we do not as a rule experience a number of individual things…. Instead larger wholes…are given in experience, their arrangement and division are concrete and definite" [Wertheimer, 1967]. Gestalt psychologists thought that the way in which parts of a figure are influenced by such factors as proximity, good continuation, and closure reflects a natural tendency toward good forms in our experience [Coren and Girgus, 1980].

In addition to features such as lie position, size, and shape, color is an outstanding property that supports the perception that items belong together. Another aspect is explained by Asch's concept of unit Formation: It is easier to remember two or more objects if you see them as one unitary pattern. Gestalt psychologists believed the reason is that unitary patterns are much more coherent perceptually and can be remembered as units. When switching among different levels of clustering, a user perceives the various groups of nodes as units and this helps him or her to remember the positions of the individual entities. A detailed discussion of the perceptional features of AlViz exceeds the scope of this chapter.

4.5 Ontology Alignment in AlViz

The basic elements of ontologies are concepts, properties, and instances. They describe (by necessary conditions) or define (by necessary and sufficient conditions) a knowledge domain for a certain purpose. Ontology alignment requires analysis of these elements or entities to identify overlapping parts in two ontologies.

According to Ehrig [2007] entities are the same if their features are the same or similar enough. In ontologies, features represent a certain meaning of an entity. We will list some examples of such features below. If an alignment algorithm determines low similarity among entities of two ontologies, evidence for an alignment may be absent. If good similarity is found, we may have strong evidence. To estimate similarities, we must consider the features of the neighborhood because entities may be the same if their neighborhoods are the same or similar enough. That means entities are also defined by their positions in the ontological structure. Structure similarity is expressed through the similarity of the other entities in the structure.

In a first round of the alignment algorithm, only basic comparison methods such as string similarity are applied; even manually predefined alignments are used. In further rounds, already computed pairs serve as bases to measure structural similarities, but not all types of similarities are of equal importance. Therefore, we must judge and emphasize the relevant similarities. The alignment process is executed iteratively and it stops after a fixed number of iterations, at a specific time, or when the number of newly identified alignments is below a certain defined threshold. As in Ehrig's work [2007], ten iterations were used because that number proved efficient and appropriate in practice.

Human interaction was involved in the second part in which the results are visualized and presented to the user. She or he investigates and may correct the alignments in an iterative manner as well. This may be followed by an automatic recalculation of the similarities going back to the first part. In this case, the manually changed alignments, such as predefined entity pairs, serve as additional inputs for the algorithm. The user decides whether or how often this recalculation is done.

4.5.1 Alignment Algorithm

This section describes such a general alignment process based on the work of Ehrig [2007]. The generic process was extended to include the human-mediated alignment steps [Lanzenberger and Sampson. 2007].

Feature engineering and compatibility—This step determines the input ontologies for alignment. When a choice of ontologies can be made, a user may assess the ontologies for compatibility with respect to their scenarios and complexities and also validate them prior to alignment. Additionally, this step extracts characteristics of both ontologies, i.e., features of their ontological entities such as (1) ontology language primitives (range and domain definitions for properties), (2) identifiers (unified resource identifiers or URIs), (3) derived features exploiting the inheritance structure, and (4) external features (additional text files describing instance data). When measuring similarity, these features will allow comparison of entities.

Search step selection—Two initial entities from the two ontologies are chosen for comparison. Every entity pair may be compared or only an efficient subset may be chosen using heuristics to lower the number of mappings [Ehrig, 2007]. We can reduce the number of candidates by comparing entities of the same type only.

Similarity assessment—Based on the features of the selected candidate pairs, similarity computation is performed. As stated in Ehrig [2007], comparing two ontology entities goes far beyond syntax level. It considers their relations (meanings) to the real world entities they represent and their purposes (usages) in the real world. Therefore, a semiotic view is used and the similarity measures are classified into three layers: data, ontology, and context. On the first layer, data types such as integers, strings, etc. are compared by operations like relative distance and edit distance. Second, on the ontology layer, we measure the similarities of ontological objects such as comparing the domains and ranges of two properties. Finally, we consider the context. For example, two books may be similar if their authors co-authored many publications. We must consider domain knowledge for all three layers, for example domain-specific vocabularies like Dublin Core in the bibliographic domain.

Similarity aggregation—The individual measures from the previous step are input to the similarity aggregation. They are weighted and combined via a sigmoid function that emphasizes high individual similarities and de-emphasizes low individual similarities.

Determination—The aggregated numbers, a threshold, and an interpretation strategy are used to generate actual alignments. Borderline alignments are marked as questionable. The threshold determines whether similarities are high enough to align a candidate pair. Everything above the threshold is aligned; lower values indicate different entities.

Visualization—This tool uses input from the algorithm and renders preliminary alignments. Each ontology is shown as a detail and overview visualization capable of displaying a high number of items. In Figure 4.3, AlViz visualizes two ontologies using a J-Tree (detail) on the left side and a graph (overview) on the right side. Each concept of both ontologies is represented by a node in the graph and an entry in the J-Tree. The similarity of concepts is encoded by color; green shows all similar concepts.

Clustering and navigation—The user changes the level of detail according to need. For validation, the user selects individual items connected in the different views by linking and brushing. In Figure 4.3, the concepts marked as similar would be highlighted in green/light gray. The user selected the House node in the first ontology. As a result of this interaction, similar concepts in the second ontology were highlighted in both the J-Tree and graph visualizations—an approach called linking and brushing. In this example, both visualizations show detail views. In the

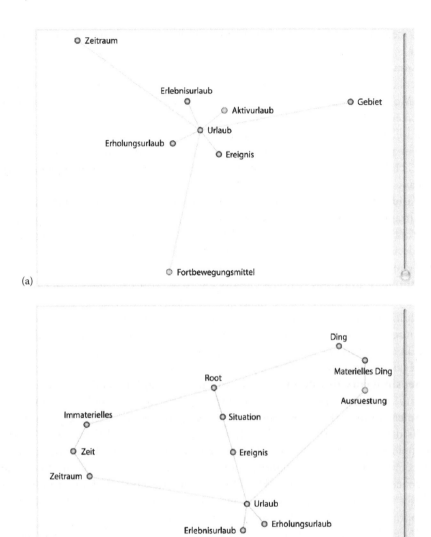

Figure 4.3 Small world graph visualizations of two ontologies in the tourism domain. The focus of the graph is on the Urlaub (vacation) entity, showing all related concepts for both ontologies. Labeling is activated. The colors represent the type of alignment based on the results of the alignment algorithm. Orange indicates at least one syntactically equal entity in the other ontology; green indicates similarity with at least one entity of the other ontology based on the neighborhood. In this view, the nodes are not clustered; each node of the graph represents one entity. (Figure 4.3_top_km1.pdf and Figure 4.3_bottom_km4. pdf are available in color at: http://www.ifs.tuwien.ac.at/~mlanzenberger/alviz/graphics/ASWT/).

graph view, it is possible to zoom out and thus cluster several concepts to be shown as one node.

Competency questions—To check whether specific alignments make sense, the user collects competency questions that should be answered by the aligned ontologies. Moreover, results of earlier competency questions are reviewed again. Such competency questions play an important role in developing an ontology. When an ontology engineer develops a formal representation of a domain, the questions serve as a starting point for defining concepts, hierarchies, and relations. A similar approach is helpful for alignment since the two or more aligned ontologies may be seen as a new domain(s) model.

Validation—Appropriate changes may be made to the alignments based on visualization analysis. The user may verify questionable alignments by accepting or rejecting the suggestions. Moreover, all alignments may be subject to change if the user decides to assign other types of alignments. Based on Figure 4.3, a user could decide to select a narrower alignment instead of the one defined automatically.

Ontology update—Ontology alignment may involve changes to one or both source ontologies. To obtain better targets for similarity assessment, a user can create additional entities. Before updating is done, the user must consider the usage of the source ontologies carefully. For example, Building could serve as an additional concept defined in one of the two ontologies in Figure 4.3, thus providing an additional target entity available for alignment with House or Private Dwelling.

Set similarity threshold—An algorithm threshold for identifying alignments is a crucial value. Sometimes it is necessary to adapt the threshold to obtain better alignment results. If a user finds many missing alignments and the preliminary results derived from the algorithm show a high number of different entities, the threshold may be too high. On the other hand, the threshold may be too low. For example, an alignment algorithm may detect a similarity between House and Pet concepts because both have Has Owner properties. If enough other properties describe the concepts, this similarity may be detected with a low value. With an appropriate threshold this alignment could be excluded.

These phases are not applied in a linear process, but rather the alignment results are refined when users iteratively work through the various thematic or hierarchical subareas of the ontologies at different levels of detail. The next subsection gives an example of the human-mediated alignment process.

4.5.2 *Interpretation of Alignments*

To ease the understanding of the process, parts of only two source ontologies are visualized. AlViz (compare Figure 4.1) looks a bit different because it arranges the two ontologies horizontally and provides interaction functionality. However, to describe an example of a verification task practically, it is appropriate to reduce the complexity of the user interface. In addition to data, only the clustering sliders are depicted. Figure 4.4(a) shows a subgraph of the first ontology called tourismA.

Sometimes it is not necessary to see the whole ontology—clustered or not. Moreover, too many visual objects not relevant for a specific tasks may impede exploration. Therefore, a user can focus on a certain entity so that the graph only represents the related entities, thus emphasizing the context of the specific entity. This view includes all subentities (transitive relations) and directly related entities (nontransitive relations), supplemented with all relations and entities among them within a previously defined number of hops (relations). The second source ontology (tourismB) is visualized in Figure 4.4(b).

In this example, the labeled nodes represent concepts, the edges represent three types of relations, and the Urlaub entity (vacation) is focused. In tourismA, the depicted relations are: IsA, HasPeriod (hatReisedauer), GoesToRegion (hatZiel), UsesVehicle (hatReisemittel). The IsA paths are shorter than the others because we gave these edges a higher weight. In order to distinguish different types of relations such as functional, transitive, or nontransitive, we apply different weights that a user can modify according to the exploration needs. In a simpler version of graph visualization, a user may select one type of relation only. However, showing all relations of the central entity at once gives an impression of its context. On the right side, the tourismB subgraph consists of: IsA, HasAPeriod (hatEineDauer), EquipmentNeeded (manBenoetigtAusruestung) and HasAGoal (hatEinZiel). Thus tourismA has three subclasses of the central concept and tourismB has only two.

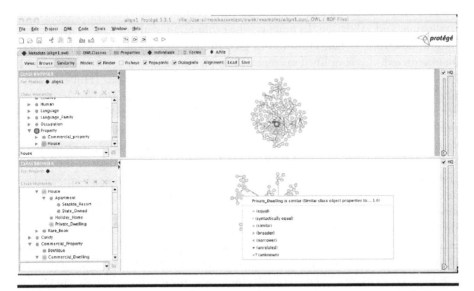

Figure 4.4 Context menu of the Private Dwelling concept shows automatically generated type of similarity relation (similar class object property) to the House concept. It also offers other types of similarities to users. (The figure is available in color at: http://www.ifs.tuwien.ac.at/~mlanzenberger/alviz/graphics/ASWT/Figure44_AlViz_Alternate1.pdf)

Although the entities Erholungsurlaub (recreation) and Erlebnisurlaub (adventure) are identified as syntactically equal in both ontologies, a third called Aktivurlaub (active vacation) in tourismA, with no directly corresponding entity in tourismB, was found similar to another entity by the alignment algorithm. By highlighting this concept, we perceive the associated concept in the other ontology: Erlebnisurlaub. Based on similar object properties inherited from the superclass (Urlaub), on the one hand, and a smaller distance (in terms of characters to be changed) between Aktivurlaub and Erlebnisurlaub than between Aktivurlaub and Erholungsurlaub on the other, the alignment algorithm calculates the association stating that Aktivurlaub and Erlebnisurlaub are similar. Similar concepts are colored green/light gray; syntactically equal concepts are orange/gray.

Obviously, in this subgraph the algorithm found many syntactically equal concepts and only a few similar concepts. For the moment, we ignore the other green nodes and investigate the concept of Aktivurlaub only. The graphs show that the neighborhoods of Aktivurlaub in tourismA and of Erlebnisurlaub in tourismB are similar, strengthening the claim that both concepts are closely associated. But Erlebnisurlaub in tourismA is also related to Erlebnisurlaub in tourismB; they are syntactically equal. Now the user must decide whether changes of one or both ontologies are required and confirm or reject the alignment of similar types between Aktivurlaub in tourismA and Erlebnisurlaub in tourismB.

Although our application example is static, the process of exploration is highly interactive. For our alignment framework, this example involves steps of clustering, navigation, and validation. In practice, the exploration of alignments is more complex, as described earlier. However, to give an idea how ontology alignments may be interpreted, this simplified example is complex enough.

As an alternative approach, we also developed a version [Huber, 2009; Koglgruber, 2009] of AlViz that enables users to explore the similarities of one entity in the first ontology with all entities in the second ontology (1 to *n*). The exploration of ontology alignment details is supported more efficiently with this version. Figure 4.5 visualizes the two ontologies (align1 and align2) together with the similarity values generated by FOAM. In the upper part (align1), the House entity was selected and the properties of the concept are shown in a pop-up window next to the selected node. It lists one datatype property and three relations (object properties). The automatic alignment algorithm identified four similar entities in the second ontology (they would be marked in light gray/green). Private Dwelling privies listed as a similar concept. The second pop-up window shows the properties of this concept. Obviously, both concepts have Has Owner properties and some similarity exists between Has Location and Has Country. Thus, the user can see the reasons for the automatically detected similarity. Sometimes automatic alignments are not optimal and need correction. The pop-up window in Figure 4.3 shows the current similarity rule (similar class object properties to… with value 1.0) for Private Dwelling and House. If a user wants to manually update the similarity type, he or she selects another entry on the list, e.g., narrowing to indicate a subclass relation.

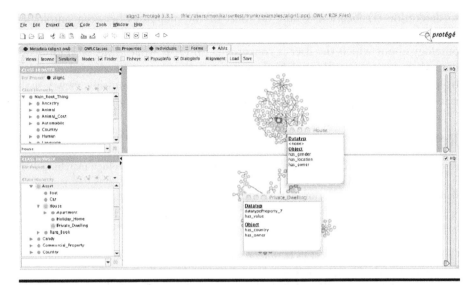

Figure 4.5 For the House concept in the first ontology, AlViz visualizes all similar concepts in the second ontology (light gray/green nodes). One is the Private Dwelling concept. Properties of both concepts are shown in a pop-up window. (The figure is available in color at: http://www.ifs.tuwien.ac.at/~mlanzenberger/ alviz/graphics/ASWT/Figure45_AlViz_Alternate2.pdf)

4.6 Need for Visualization in Ontology Alignment

Understanding semantic relations between entities of different ontologies is a cognitively difficult task [Noy, 2004]. To align domain ontologies, a developer or end user is required to define the mapping between the ontologies manually or by using a semi-automated tool. Ontology mapping is largely a human-mediated process, although numerous tools can help identify differences between ontologies.

The reason is that most conflicts or mismatches discovered by such tools require a human to recognize that different symbols represent the same concept or that a single symbol may represent different concepts. The OpenGALEN reference model comments that in an ideal situation the easiest way to answer questions about two different ontologies is to have the designers of the two original ontologies get together and merge them, but in practice this approach is not always feasible.

Instead, during the establishment of aligned concepts, the user performing the alignment must make the decisions. While many alignment tools generate mappings between entities, it is difficult to analyze and validate the alignments without examining every pair-wise correspondence in the output files, and even then the task is overwhelming. The use of visualization techniques to graphically display data from ontology mappings can facilitate user understanding of the meaning of the ontology alignment. The AlViz alignment visualization tool provides support to determine (1) location: where do most of the mappings between ontologies occur? (2) impact: do the mapping choices directly or indirectly affect parts of the ontology about which the user is concerned? (3) type: what kinds of alignments occur between the ontologies? (4) extent: how different is the aligned ontology from the source ontologies? By exploring such questions in a multiple view visualization, a user may be able to understand and enhance the alignment results.

References

Aumueller, D., Do, H.H., Massmann, S. et al. 2005. Schema and ontology matching with Coma++. *SIGMOD.*

Banovic, S. 2009. Visualisation and verification of ontology alignment results. Master's Thesis, Vienna University of Technology.

Card, S., Mackinlay, J., and Shneiderman, B., Eds. 1999. *Readings in Information Visualization.* Morgan Kaufman.

Chernoff, H. 1973. The use of faces to represent points in k-dimensional space graphically. *Journal of the American Statistical Association, 68:* 361–368.

Chuah, M. and Eick, S. 1997. Glyphs for software visualization. In *Proceedings of Fifth International Workshop on Program Comprehension,* pp. 183–191.

Coren, S. and Girgus, J. 1980. Principles of perceptual organization and spatial distortion: the Gestalt illusion. *Journal of Experimental Psychology, 6.*

Ehrig, M. 2005. FOAM: framework for ontology alignment and mapping. http://www.aifb.uni-karlsruhe.de/WBS/meh/foam/.

Ehrig, M., Haase, P., Stojanovic, N. et al. 2005. Similarity for ontologies: comprehensive framework. In *Proceedings of Tenth European Conference on Information Systems.*

Ehrig, M. and Sure, Y. 2004. Ontology mapping: An integrated approach. In *Proceedings of First European Semantic Web Symposium,* pp. 76–91.

Ehrig, M. 2007. *Ontology Alignment: Bridging the Semantic Gap.* Springer Verlag, New York.

Euzénat, J. 2004. An API for ontology alignment. In *Proceedings of Third International Semantic Web Conference,* Hiroshima, Japan, pp. 698–712.

Euzénat, J., Loup, D., Touzani, M. et al. 2004. Ontology alignment with ola. In *Proceedings of Third International Semantic Web Conference.*

Falconer, S. and Storey, M.A. 2007. A cognitive support framework for ontology mapping. In *Proceedings of Sixth International Semantic Web Conference,* pp 114–127.

Furnas, G. W. 1986. Generalized fisheye views. *SIGCHI Bulletin, 17:* 16–23.

Gradwohl, M. 2009. Integration of ontology alignment algorithms in AlViz. Master's thesis, Vienna University of Technology.

Huber, M. 2009. Visual support of ontology alignments. Master's thesis, Vienna University of Technology.

Inselberg, A. and Dimsdale, B. 1990. Parallel coordinates: A tool for visualizing multi-dimensional geometry. In *Proceedings of First IEEE Conference on Visualization,* IEEE Computer Society Press, Los Alamitos, CA, pp. 361–378.

Keim, D., Kriegel, H.P., and Ankerst, M. 1995. Recursive pattern: A technique for visualizing very large amounts of data. In *Proceedings of Sixth IEEE Conference on Visualization,* IEEE Computer Society Press, Los Alamitos, CA, pp. 279–286.

Keim, D. A. 1996. Pixel-oriented visualization techniques for exploring very large databases. *Journal of Computational and Graphical Statistics, 5:* 58–77.

Koglgruber, C. 2009. Visualization of small world graphics. Bachelor's thesis, Vienna University of Technology.

Kolli, R. and Doshi, P. 2008. OPTIMA: Tool for ontology alignment with application to semantic reconciliation of sensor metadata for publication in sensor map. In *ICSC*, IEEE Computer Society, Press, Los Alamitos, CA, pp. 484–485.

Lamping, J., Rao, R., and Pirolli, P. 1995. A focus + context technique based on hyperbolic geometry for visualizing large hierarchies. In *Proceedings of SIGCHI Conference on Human Factors in Computing Systems,* Addison-Wesley/ACM, New York, pp. 401–408.

Lanzenberger, M., Miksch, S., and Pohl, M. 2003. The stardinates: Visualizing highly structured data. In *Proceedings of Third International Conference on Information Visualization,* IEEE Computer Society Press, Los Alamitos, CA, pp. 47–52.

Lanzenberger, M. and Sampson, J. 2006. AlViz: A tool for visual ontology alignment. In *Proceedings of International Symposium of Visualization of the Semantic Web,* IEEE Computer Society, Los Alamitos, CA.

Lanzenberger, M. and Sampson, J. 2007. Human-mediated visual ontology alignment. In *Proceedings of 12th International Conference on Human–Computer Interaction, Lecture Notes in Computer Science,* Springer Verlag, Berlin, pp. 394–403.

Milgram, S. 1967. The small world problem. *Psychology Today, 2:* 60–67.

North, C. and Shneiderman, B. 1997. A taxonomy of multiple window coordinations. Technical Report CS-TR-3854. citeseer.nj.nec.com/north97taxonomy.html

Noy, N.F. 2004. Ontology management with the Prompt plug-in. In *Proceedings of Seventh International Protégé Conference,* Bethesda, MD.

OpenGALEN Common Reference Model. http://www.opengalen.org/themodel/summary.html

Pickett, R. and Grinstein, G. 1988. Iconographic displays for visualizing multidimensional data. In *Proceedings of IEEE International Conference on Systems, Man, and Cybernetics,* Vol. 1, pp. 514–519.

Pirolli, P., Card, S. K., and Wege, M.M. 2001. Visual information foraging in a focus + context visualization. In *Proceedings of SIGCHI Conference on Human factors in Computing Systems*, Addison-Wesley/ACM, New York, pp. 506–513.

Perrin, D. 2004. Prompt-Viz: Ontology version comparison visualizations with tree maps. Master's Thesis, University of Victoria, British Columbia, Canada. http://www.thechiselgroup.org/promptviz

Robertson, G.G., Mackinlay, J.D., and Card, S. K. 1991. Cone trees: Animated three-dimensional visualizations of hierarchical information. In *Proceedings of SIGCHI Conference on Human Factors in Computing Systems,* Addison-Wesley/ACM, New York, pp. 189–194.

Sampson, J. 2007. A comprehensive framework for ontology alignment quality. PhD thesis, Norwegian University of Science and Technology, Bergen.

Tufte, E. 2001. *The Visual Display of Quantitative Information. 2nd. Ed.* Graphics Press, Cheshire, CT.

van Ham, F. and van Wijk, J. 2004. Interactive visualization of small world graphs. In *Proceedings of IEEE Symposium on Information Visualization*, IEEE Computer Society Press, Los Alamitos, CA, pp. 199–206.

Wertheimer, M. 1967. Laws of organization in perceptual forms. In *A Source Book of Gestalt Psychology.* Humanities Press, New York.

Wise, J., Thomas, J., Pennock, K. et al. 1995. Visualizing the non-visual: Spatial analysis and interaction with information from text documents. In *Proceedings IEEE Symposium on Information Visualization*, IEEE Computer Society Press, Los Alamitos, CA, p. 51.

Chapter 5

SRS: A Hybrid Ontology Mediation and Mapping Approach

Saravanan Muthaiyah
Multimedia University, Cyberjaya, Malaysia

Larry Kerschberg
George Mason University, Fairfax, Virginia, USA

Contents

5.1 Introduction

Ontology mediation is a process for establishing schema or data interoperability between two or more domain ontologies, whereas ontology mapping is the process of identifying concept and attribute correspondences between domain ontologies, usually via a matching process. Both ontology mediation and mapping enable ontologists to borrow and reuse rich schema definitions from existing domain ontologies already developed by other experts in their respective domains.

The practice of matching ontology schemas today is very labor-intensive. Although semi-automated systems have been introduced, they are largely based on syntactic matching algorithms and do not produce reliable results. This chapter introduces a hybrid approach known as Semantic Relatedness Score (SRS) that combines both semantic and syntactic matching algorithms and provides better results in terms of reliability and precision when compared to purely syntactic matching algorithms. SRS was developed by rigorously testing 13 well established matching algorithms and a composite measure was produced from 5 of the best combinations.

5.2 Background

It is impossible to find an ontology that is perfect and ontologists must be able to reuse knowledge and share data definitions from multiple ontologies. However, a fully automated system for ontology mediation and mapping without human intervention is not impossible. For that reason, we introduce a semi-automated approach in this chapter. The objective is to reduce the workloads of ontologists while providing more reliable results.

A review of current ontology mediation initiatives such as InfoSleuth, XMapper, ONION, FOAM, FCA-Merge, KRAFT, CHIMERA, PROMPT, and OBSERVER, among others, revealed that the state-of-art of ontology mediation is to a large extent based on mainly syntactic schema matching that supports binary schema matches (1:1) only. Our approach however, is capable of many-to-many (M:N) matching and the SRS algorithm selects the best candidates for matching from the source and target ontologies and eliminates candidates that are not suitable for matching; in other words, noise is eliminated efficiently.

5.3 Literature Review

Ontologies are meant to allow machine processable metadata to be executed efficiently. Different ontologies may include different sets of definitions and may have not been developed in a unified fashion. Since no standards govern the creation of ontologies at present, two or more ontologies may contain similar data definitions or labels that are named differently such as <cost>$5</cost> in one ontology and <quote>$5</quote> in another. Unless semantics or contextual analysis is used, machines will not be able to comprehend equivalent data labels and hence may not be able to match them.

Without semantics, the creation of rich data specifications for a shared conceptualization will not be possible (Fowler et al. 1999; Muthaiyah and Kerschberg 2006). Although rules can be specified to enable machines to reason data in more useful ways and understand their semantic nuances (Missikoff, Schiappelli and Taglino 2003), this approach is not flexible and scalable, as thousands of rules would be needed. A more reasonable approach is mediating ontologies (Maedche et al. 2002; Muthaiyah and Kerschberg 2007) via their data labels to achieve data heterogeneity. Present ontology mediation systems are mostly semi-automated. They eliminate extraneous data by filtering out data labels that are not syntactically similar and present the results for manual input. The ontologist manually selects semantically related data labels and matches them individually to the target ontology (TO). Many current techniques such as MAFRA (Maedche et al. 2002), IF-Map (Kalfoglou and Schorlemmer 2003), SMART (Noy and Musen 1999), and PROMPT (Noy and Musen 2000) use match algorithms based on string, prefix, and suffix matches. Other techniques are applicable only to relational schemas in databases or XML type data. Researchers have also attempted to use machine learning systems (Doan et al. 2002) for the same purpose, but as noted earlier, they lack flexibility.

5.3.1 Similarity Measures

Many current methods allow computing of semantic relatedness of concepts and include dictionary-based (Lesk 1986), ontology-based (Lesk 1986; Weeds and Weir 2005), information-based (Budanitsky and Hirst 2006; Leacock and Chodorow 1998), and distributional (Weeds and Weir 2005) methods. The knowledge sources used for computing relatedness can be as different as dictionaries, ontologies, or large corpora. Budanitsky and Hirst (2006) explain three prevalent approaches for evaluating SR measures: (1) mathematical analysis, (2) application-specific evaluation, and (3) comparison with human judgments. Mathematical analysis can assess a measure with respect to some formal properties but cannot tell us whether a measure closely resembles human judgments. The next sections describe the existing approaches and measures.

5.3.1.1 Leacock–Chodorow Measure (LC)

The LC method (Leacock and Chodorow 1998) uses the length of the shortest path [len (c1, c2)] of two synonym sets (synsets) to measure similarity. The method counts the number of links between the two synsets. The shorter the length of the path, the more related they are. The measure performed well for a medical taxonomy called MeSH (http://www.nlm.nih.gov/mesh/). However, it is limited to is-a links and scales the path length by the maximum depth D of the taxonomy of noun hierarchies in WordNet. The following formula is used to compute semantic relatedness:

$$Sim_{LC}(c1, c2) = \frac{-\log len\ (c1,\ c2)}{2D} \tag{5-1}$$

where c1, c2 are synsets, sim is similarity, LC denotes Leacock–Chodorow, D indicates maximum depth of noun hierarchies in WordNet, and len is length of path.

5.3.1.2 Resnik Measure (RS)

Resnik (1995) devised the first similarity approach to include ontology and corpus. Similarity between two concepts is defined as the information content of their lowest super-ordinate (most specific common subsumer) designated lso (c1, c2). The p variable denotes the probability of encountering an instance of a synset c in the corpus (Resnik 1992 and 1998). The formula below is used to compute similarity:

$$sim_R(c1, c2) = -\log p\ (lso(c1, c2)) \tag{5-2}$$

where c1, c2 are synsets, R denotes Resnik, lso is the lowest super-ordinate, and p represents the probability of encountering an instance.

5.3.1.3 Jiang–Conrath Measure (JC)

This method (Jiang and Conrath 1997) uses information content in the form of the probability of encountering an instance of a child synset given the instance of a parent synset. Information content of two nodes and their most specific subsumer are important. Semantic distance is measured instead of semantic similarity. The formula below is used to compute distance:

$$dist_{JC}(c1, c2) = 2\log (p\ (lso(c1, c2))) - (\log (p\ (c1)) + \log (p(c2))) \tag{5-3}$$

where c1, c2 are synsets, dist denotes distance, JC stands for Jiang–Conrath, lso is the lowest super-ordinate, and p denotes the probability of encountering an instance.

5.3.1.4 Lin Measure (LN)

Lin (1998) uses the theory of similarities of arbitrary objects. This measure uses the same elements such as dist $_{JC}$ with slight changes. The formula is as follows:

$$\text{sim}_L(c1, c2) = \frac{2 \times \log p(lso \text{ len } (c1, c2))}{\log p(c1) + \log p(c2)} \tag{5-4}$$

where c1, c2 are synsets, sim is similarity, L denotes Lin, lso is the lowest super-ordinate, len indicates length of path, and p is the probability of encountering an instance.

5.3.1.5 Hirst–St-Onge Measure (HS)

Hirst and St-Onge (1998) assumed that two lexicalized concepts are semantically close if a path that is not too long and does not change often connects their WordNet synsets. They measure semantic similarity with the following formula:

$$\text{rel}_{HS}(c1, c2) = C - \text{path length} - k \times d \tag{5-5}$$

where rel denotes relation, HS indicates Hirst–St-Onge, d is the number of changes of direction in the path of synsets, and C and k are constants. If a path does not exist then rel $_{HS}$(c1, c2) = 0 and synsets are deemed unrelated.

5.3.1.6 PMI Measure (PM)

Turney (2001) computes the similarities of word pairs based on this algorithm, also referred to as PMI-IR (Pointwise Mutual Information) and IR (Information Retrieval) algorithms. It is successful for approximating human semantics. A test match for 80 synonyms on TOEFL (Test of English as a Foreign Language) and 50 synonyms on ESL (English as a Second Language) tests produced higher scores compared to LSA (Latent Semantic Analysis) and LSI (Latent Semantic Indexing). The following formula is used to measure similarity:

$$\text{PMI}(c1, c2) = \log_2 \frac{P(c1, c2)}{P(c1) \times P(c2)} \tag{5-6}$$

It is based on the probability (P) of finding two concepts of interest (c1 and c2) within the same text window versus the probability (P) of finding the concepts separately. P (c1, c2) is the probability of finding both c1 and c2 in the same window. P (c1) and P (c2) are the probabilities of finding c1 and c2 separately.

5.3.1.7 NSS Measure (NS)

Cilibrasi and Vitanyi (2007) introduced the Normalized Search Similarity (NSS) adapted from Normalized Google Distance (NGD). They measured similarities between two concepts using probability of co-occurrences as demonstrated by the following equation:

$$\text{NGD}\,(c1,\,c2) = \frac{\max\,\{\log f(c1),\,\log f(c2)\} - \log f(c1,\,c2)}{\log M - \min\,\{\log f(c1),\,\log f(c2)\}} \tag{5-7}$$

M is the number of searchable Google pages, and *f(x)* is the number of pages that Google search returns for searching *x*. NGD is based on the Google search engine. The equation may also be used with other text corpora such as Wikipedia, New York Times, Project Gutenberg, Google groups, and Enron E-mail corpus.

5.3.1.8 GLSA, LSA, and SA Measure (SA)

Landauer and Dumais (1997) introduced LSA (Latent Semantic Analysis). It uses Singular Value Decomposition (SVD) to analyze relationships of concepts in a collection of text. It is a fully automatic computational technique for representing the meaning of text. A passage is viewed as a linear equation and its meaning is a sum of words such as m (passage) = m (word$_1$) + m (word$_2$) + m(word$_n$). Eigenvalue is used for ordering the vector and cosine values are used to represent similarities:

$$\cos\theta_{xy} = x.y \,/\, |x|\,|y| \tag{5-8}$$

LSA provides better results than keyword matching; for example, *doctor–doctor* match gives a 1.0 score for both LSA and keyword match. However, *doctor–physician* scores 0.8 for LSA and 0 for keyword match. This is why LSA is better. GLSA (Generalized LSA) computes term vectors for vocabulary V of document collection C using corpus W (Matveeva et al. 2007). Anderson and Pirolli (1984) introduced Spreading Activation (SA) that uses a semantic network to model human memory using a Bayesian analysis. The following is their formula to measure similarity:

$$\text{SA}(w1,\,w2) = \log \frac{P(X = 1|Y = 1)}{P(X = 1|Y = 0)} \tag{5-9}$$

5.3.1.9 WordNet Similarity Measure (WN)

The similarity measure program is an open-source Perl module developed at the University of Minnesota. It allows a user to measure the semantic similarities between a pair of concepts. It provides six measures of similarity and three measures of relatedness based on the WordNet lexical database. The measures of similarity are based on WordNet's *is-a* hierarchy and the program uses Resnik (RS), Lin (LN), Jiang–Conrath (JC), Leacock–Chodorow (LC), Hirst–St-Onge (HS), Wu–Palmer (WP), Banerjee–Pedersen (BP), and Patwardhan–Pedersen (PP).

5.3.1.10 Gloss Vector (GV)

This measure forms second order co-occurrence vectors from the glosses of concept definitions. It primarily uses WordNet definitions to measure similarity or relatedness of two or more concepts and determines the similarities of two concepts by determining the cosine of the angle between their gloss vectors. It augments glosses of concepts with glosses of adjacent concepts as defined by WordNet relations to resolve data sparsity problems due to extremely short glosses.

5.4 Semantic Relatedness Score (SRS)

As discussed previously, measures of similarity have been researched widely in the areas of cognitive sciences, databases, natural language processing (NLP), and artificial intelligence (AI). A popular usage of these measures is in word sense disambiguation, information retrieval, and malapropism detection. SRS is a similarity score representing a function of the above measures. Semantic similarity can thus be represented by:

$$SRS = f_x \{LC, RS, JC, LN, HS, PM, NS, LSA, WN, GV, SYN\} \quad (5\text{-}10)$$

Although 13 measures were explored to build the SRS function, empirical tests show that only 5 provided the highest degrees of relevance, precision, and reliability. Empirical data based on studies at Princeton by Miller and Charles (1991) were used to test the revised SRS function. Results also showed a higher degree of correlation (92%) when compared with human cognitive evaluation of 60 concept words. This makes the revised SRS function more reliable. The measures used in combination with SYN were Lin (LN), Gloss Vector (GV), WordNet (WN), and LSA. Lin (LN) and Gloss Vector (GV) measures were obtained via an API service supported by Ted Pedersen and Jason Michelizzi from the University of Minnesota.* WordNet and LSA measures were obtained through an API service provided by Rensselaer's MSR server.† Scores were aggregated to derive SRS. Thus the revised SRS function is represented as:

$$SRS = f_x \{LN, LSA, WN, GV, SYN\} \quad (5\text{-}11)$$

---

* Ted Pedersen and Jason Michelizzi - http://marimba.d.umn.edu/cgi-bin/similarity.cgi
† Rensselaer MSR Server - http://cwl-projects.cogsci.rpi.edu/msr/

SRS is unique because it adopts both cognitive and syntactic measures to calculate similarities between concepts, making it more reliable. Current research on ontology mediation focuses mainly on binary mappings (1:1) and does not use cognitive measures to determine semantic similarity for concept matching. Most research utilizes only syntactic matching. One of the contributions of this chapter is to include multiple mappings (1:*n*, *n*:1, and *m*:*n*) and provide SRS scores as a composite measure for similarity. The scores are used to populate a similarity matrix that serves as a major part of the proposed mediation framework and architecture.

5.4.1 Experiment Design and Results

Table 5.1 illustrates the 30-word pair rank. Fifty questionnaires were distributed to domain experts for this experiment. The respondents were carefully selected and only high school English teachers who taught English as a second language were picked. The idea was to choose only people who were highly skillful in the language to be able to rank the 30 word pairs. Obviously, if we were to evaluate the domain of neurons, we would use neurologists because they understand that domain better. Of the 50, we received 38 responses; we rejected 12 because they were incomplete. Thus, the study had a 76% response rate. The questionnaire focused on testing human judgment for similarities of 30 word pairs (see table).

Scores by respondents are labeled as *HCR Rank,* and *Syn Rank* denotes syntactic scores. *Sem Rank* denotes semantic scores, and *SRS Rank* is the hybrid score combining semantic and syntactic scores. Respondents were asked to rank all 30 word pairs on a scale of 0 to 10. Rank 0 was for unrelated word pairs and 10 was for highly related pairs according to the respondents' cognitive similarity judgments. They were instructed not to assign the same rank twice for the same word category, e.g., if "lad" appeared twice for a word pair, they were not to assign the same rank for a second instance that included "lad." This was to ensure that previous answers did not have an effect on new answers and also prevent bias. Higher scores by respondents meant that the similarity of a word pair was higher based on their cognitive reasoning.

Figure 5.1 shows the results obtained for all four ranks (*Sem Rank, HCR Rank, Syn Rank*, and *SRS Rank*) and the symbols used to represent the 30 word pairs (*a* to *ad*). All ranks were scored on a scale of 1 to 10 and higher scores indicated greater similarities of the word pairs. The *a* symbol or car–automobile scored 10 by semantic match (*Sem Rank*) and 0 by syntactic match (*Syn Rank*) and so on. Semantic scores (*Sem Rank*) revealed the closest match to human response (*HCR Rank*)—a 92% match. When combined with syntactic scores (*Syn Rank*), correlation of the hybrid score was 80%.

However, the pure syntactic scores were clearly inaccurate: they showed a week and negative correlation with the *HCR Rank*. This supported our hypothesis that pure syntactic scores are not accurate for matching data labels as part of ontology mediation. We still use syntactic scores to eliminate erroneous data labels, then apply semantic match results to obtain the closest match to human domain experts'

Table 5.1 Word Pair Ranks

Word Pair	SEM Rank	HCR Rank	SYN Rank	SRS Rank
Car–automobile	10	8	0	5
Gem–jewel	0	2	6	3.21
Journey–voyage	8	8	5	6.53
Boy–lad	8	8	7	7.43
Coast–shore	6	7	5	5.715
Asylum–madhouse	8	8	4	5.845
Magician–wizard	10	8	3	6.5
Midday–noon	10	10	4	7
Furnace–stove	6	6	4	4.88
Food–fruit	3	3	6	4.485
Bird–cock	7	6	6	6.275
Bird–crane	4	4	5	4.29
Tool–implement	4	4	2	2.77
Brother–monk	4	2	4	4.145
Lad–brother	4	2	4	4.12
Crane–implement	2	1	2	1.795
Journey–car	4	2	4	4.085
Monk–oracle	1	4	4	2.645
Cemetery–woodland	1	2	4	2.31
Food–rooster	1	4	6	3.655
Coast–hill	2	2	6	4.185
Forest–graveyard	1	1.2	2	1.45
Shore–woodland	1	1	4	2.535
Monk–slave	3	2	6	4.255
Coast–forest	2	0	8	4.825
Lad–wizard	1	0	6	3.26
Chord–simile	1	0.6	6	3.38
Glass–magician	1	0	4	2.33
Rooster–voyage	0	0	6	3.205
Noon–string	1	1	6	3.47

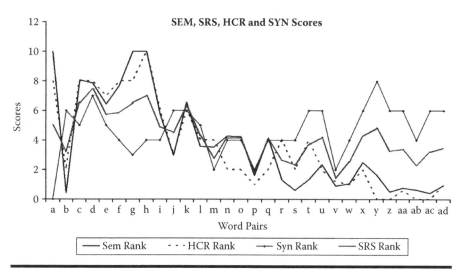

Figure 5.1   SEM, SRS, HCR, and SYN scores.

rankings. Semantic agreement and semantic affinity measurement use cognitive measures derived from WordNet including synonymy, meronymy, antonymy, functions, and polysemy associations (Resnik 1995; Budanitsky and Hirst 2006). In the next section we discuss hypothesis tests to validate our approach.

5.4.2 Hypothesis Tests and Results

Thirty word pairs were used in our experiment. Ten were highly related (scores between 7 and 10), 10 were intermediately related (scores between 3 and 6), and 10 were unrelated (scores between 0 and 2). SRS scores were calculated based on *Sem Rank* scores and *Syn Rank* scores that were summed and averaged (see Table 5.1). *HCR Rank* scores were obtained from domain experts who ranked the 30 word pairs. The results were compared with the combined syntactic and semantic scores. To prove the hypothesis that combined scores (*SRS Rank*) provided a better match with *HCR Rank*, the following hypothesis test was carried out:

(H_0): SRS scores do not match expert responses (*HCR Rank*)
(H_1): SRS scores match expert responses (*HCR Rank*)

Table 5.2 illustrates the significant relationship between SRS and HCR ranks. It shows a significant positive correlation between the two scores ($r = 0.806$ or 80.6%). The asterisks indicate significant correlation at 0.01, level (two-tailed). The significance value (p) for this two-tailed test is <0.05. Thus $r = 0.806$; $p < 0.05$ rejects the null hypothesis (H_0) and accepts the alternate hypothesis (H_1). Thus, to achieve the Semantic Web dream, both syntactic and semantic matching must be given importance.

Table 5.2   Correlation of SRS and HCR

		SRS Rank	HCR Rank
SRS Rank	Pearson correlation	1	0.806(**)
	Sig. (two-tailed)		0.000
	N	30	30

**significant at 0.01 level (2-tailed)

Table 5.3   Correlation of Sem and HCR

TCH		SEM Rank	HCR Rank
SEM Rank	Pearson correlation	1	0.919(**)
	Sig. (two-tailed)		0.000
	N	30	30

**significant at 0.01 level (2-tailed)

A t-statistic was also measured for Table 5.2 to test the hypothesis and with the r coefficient 0.806, t yielded 7.205 with the given degree of freedom of $n - 2 =$ 28; given $\alpha = 0.01$, the critical value of t was 2.7633. Since the t-statistic of 7.205 > 2.7633, this clearly rejected the null hypothesis (H_0) and the alternate (H_1) was accepted.

Table 5.3 illustrates a higher positive correlation between *Sem Rank* and *HCR Rank*. It shows a significant positive correlation between scores (r = 0.919 or 91.9%). The asterisks indicate significant correlation at 0.01, level (two-tailed). The significance value (p) for this two-tailed test is <0.05. Thus (r = 0.919; $p < 0.05$) also accepts the alternate hypothesis (H_1) earlier because *SRS Rank* is composed of *Sem Rank* and *Syn Rank*. This proves that achieving the Semantic Web dream means both syntactic and semantic matching must be given importance.

A t-statistic was also measured for Table 5.3 to test the hypothesis with the r coefficient = 0.919. Since the t-statistic of 12.334 >2.7633, it clearly rejected the null hypothesis (H_0) and the alternate hypothesis (H_1) was accepted. Figure 5.2 illustrates SRS, HCR, and SYN scores.

5.4.2.1 Reliability Test: SRS and HCR

Precision, recall, and the F-measures are currently standard tests for IR systems. However, only the precision measure is appropriate for this study. A new test called for reliability introduced in this chapter for validating SRS and HCR scores earlier. The reliability test in this context is a function of precision and relevance: Reliability (REL) = {precision and relevance}. Precision is denoted P_s and relevance

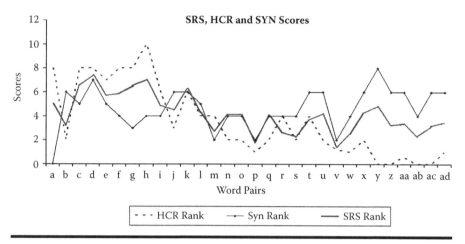

Figure 5.2 SRS, HCR, and SYN scores.

R_L; thus the function for reliability is REL = {P_s and R_L}. P_s and R_L are measured as:

P_s = number of correct responses

$$R_L = \frac{\text{number of relevant responses}}{\text{total number of responses}}$$

The two parts to reliability are precision and relevance. The semi-automated ontology mediation system is meant to reduce the workload of the ontologist, thus the ontologist must receive reliable information before he or she chooses data labels to be matched. The hypothesis here is that SRS scores that include syntactic and semantic measures are more reliable than SYN scores. The null and alternate hypotheses are stated as (H_0): SRS scores are less reliable than SYN scores and (H_1): SRS scores are more reliable than SYN scores.

Precision (P_s)—Considering 30 word pairs, to calculate precision (P_s) all the SRS scores were first normalized, after which the HCR responses were matched against them. The idea was to compare exact matches only. Of the 30 pairs, 12 were exact matches. Some were really close but they were not considered because they were not exact matches. The final precision score for the SRS score was 40% (P_s = 12/30); that is, based on the equation above, 12 correct responses were discovered in a total of 30. However, the precision score for *only syntactic* matches resulted in only 5 correct responses of the 30. The precision score for syntactic match was 16.67% (P_s = 5/30)—lower than the SRS scores. In summary, SRS scores provided greater precision.

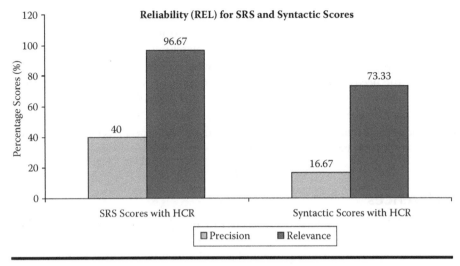

Figure 5.3   Reliability of SRS and syntactic scores.

Relevance (R_L)—The same number of word pairs was tested for R_L. The SRS scores and HCR scores were matched. The R_L for the SRS scores was 96.67% (29/30) or 29 relevant responses in a total 30. The (R_L) for *only syntactic* matches yielded 22 relevant responses of 30. Thus, a pure syntactic match resulted in only 73.33% (R_L =22/30). In summary, SRS measures provided better relevance scores.

Figure 5.3 illustrates the reliability of SRS and syntactic scores. The hypothesis test indicates that SRS scores composed of syntactic and semantic measures are more reliable to an ontologist compared to purely syntactic (SYN) scores. Thus the null hypothesis (H_0) is rejected and the alternate hypothesis (H_1) is accepted based on greater precision and relevance of SRS scores compared to purely syntactic match scores. This led to better reliability as well.

5.5 Conclusion

This chapter explains why semantic mediation should be included in ontology mediation systems. The hypothesis was that syntactic matches alone would not suffice as they are usually based on prefix, substring, and suffix matching. The importance of coupling semantics and syntactic matching was empirically tested to support this theory. New measures such as precision, reliability, and relevance were introduced and that step alone represents a significant contribution. Empirical tests were conducted to validate our approach including hypothesis tests, *t*-statistics, and reliability and relevance measurement. The main benefit of our approach is that erroneous data is filtered. Instead of reviewing 30,000 concepts, an ontologist must deal with only one tenth of that number. We are not trying to prove that our matching algorithm is superior; our intent is to introduce a cognitive or linguistic element that is significant for concept matching in ontologies. We believe that using the SRS measures will significantly reduce the workloads of ontologists based on the need to select from far fewer concepts. This should improve ontologist productivity drastically. This chapter provided a detailed matching algorithm along with new evaluation measures. We recognize that modification of context also modifies the semantic similarities of concepts. This aspect has not been covered and is a significant part of our future work.

References

Anderson, J.R. and P.L. Pirolli. 1984. Spread of activation. *Journal of Experimental Psychology: Learning, Memory, and Cognition, 10*: 791–798.

Budanitsky, A. and G. Hirst. 2006. Evaluating WordNet-based measures of lexical semantic relatedness. *Computational Linguistics 32*: 13–47.

Cilibrasi, R. and P. Vitanyi. 2007. Similarity of objects and the meaning of words. *IEEE Transactions Knowledge and Data Engineering, 19*: 370–383.

Doan, A., J. Madhavan, P. Domingos et al. 2002. Ontology matching: A machine learning approach. In *Proceedings of 11th International Conference on World Wide Web*. Honolulu.

Fowler, J., B. Perry, M. Nodine et al. 1999. Agent-based semantic interoperability in Infosleuth. *ACM SIGMOD Record 28*: 60–67.

Hirst, G. and D. St-Onge. 1998. Lexical chains as representations of context for the detection and correction of malapropisms. *WordNet: An Electronic Lexical database*, April: 305–332.

Jiang, J.J. and D.W. Conrath. 1997. Semantic similarity based on corpus statistics and lexical taxonomy. In: *International Conference Research on Computational Linguistics,* Taiwan, pp. 19–33.

Kalfoglou, Y. and M. Schorlemmer. 2003. IF Map: An ontology-mapping method based on information-flow theory. *Journal of Data Semantics 1*: 98–127.

Landauer, T.K. and S.T. Dumais. 1997. A solution to Plato's problem: The latent semantic analysis theory of acquisition, induction, and representation of knowledge. *Psychological Review* 104: 211–240.

Leacock, C. and M Chodorow. 1998. Combining local context and WordNet similarity for word sense identification. *WordNet: An Electronic Lexical Database*: pp. 265–283.

Lesk, Michael. 1986. Automatic Sense Disambiguation Using Machine Readable Dictionaries: How to Tell a Pine Cone from an Ice Cream Cone. In: *5th Annual International Conference on Systems Documentation*, 24-26. Toronto, Ontario, Canada.

Lin, D. 1998. An information-theoretic definition of similarity. In *Proceedings of 15th International Conference on Machine Learning*, Madison, WI, pp. 296–304.

Maedche, A., B. Motik, N. Silva et al. 2002. Mafra: A mapping framework for distributed ontologies. *Lecture Notes in Computer Science,* pp. 235–250.

Matveeva, I., G.A. Levow, A. Farahat et al. 2007. Term representation with generalized latent semantic analysis. *Amsterdam Studies in the Theory and History of Linguistic Science Series* 4, *292*: 45–54.

Miller, G.A. and W.G. Charles. 1991. Contextual correlates of semantic similarity. *Language and Cognitive Processes 6*: 1–28.

Missikoff, M., F. Schiappelli, and F. Taglino. 2003. A controlled language for semantic annotation and interoperability in e-business applications. In *Proceedings of Second International Semantic Web Conference,* Sanibel Island, FL, pp. 1–6.

Muthaiyah, S. and L. Kerschberg. 2007. Virtual organization security policies: An ontology-based mapping and integration approach. *Information Systems Frontiers,* Special Issue on Secure Knowledge Management, pp. 505–515.

Muthaiyah, S. and L. Kerschberg. 2006. Dynamic integration and semantic security policy ontology mapping for semantic web services (SWS). In *Proceedings of First International Conference on Digital Information Management,* pp. 116–120.

Noy, N.F. and M.A. Musen. 2000. PROMPT: Algorithm and tool for automated ontology merging and alignment. In *Proceedings of Twelfth Workshop on Knowledge Acquisition, Modeling and Management.* Austin, TX. MIT Press, Cambridge, MA.

Noy, N.F. and M.A. Musen. 1999. SMART: Automated support for ontology merging and alignment. In *Proceedings of 12th Workshop on Knowledge Acquisition, Modeling and Management,* Banff, BC, Canada, pp. 1–24.

Resnik, P. 1992. Wordnet and distributional analysis: A class-based approach to lexical discovery. In *Proceedings of AAAI Workshop on Statistically-Based Natural Language Processing Techniques,* pp. 56–64.

Resnik, P. 1995. Using information content to evaluate semantic similarity. In *Proceedings of 14th International Joint Conference on Artificial Intelligence,* Montreal, p. 1.

Resnik, P. 1998. Semantic similarity in a taxonomy: An information-based measure and its application to problems of ambiguity in natural language. *Journal of Artificial Intelligence Research, 11*: 95–130.

Turney, P.D. 2001. Mining the Web for synonyms: PMI-IR versus LSA on TOEFL. *Lecture Notes in Computer Science,* 491–502.

Weeds, J. and D. Weir. 2005. Co-occurrence retrieval: A general framework for lexical distributional similarity. *Computational Linguistics 31*: 439–476.

ONTOLOGY ENGINEERING AND EVALUATION

Chapter 6

An Ontology Engineering Tool for Enterprise 3.0

Elena Simperl
Karlsruhe Institute of Technology, Karlsruhe, Germany

Stephan Wölger, Katharina Siorpaes, Tobias Bürger, and Michael Luger
STI Innsbruck, University of Innsbruck, Innsbruck, Austria

Sung-Kook Han
Wan Kwang University Korea, Seoul, Korea

Contents

6.1 Introduction

Semantics promises to solve many challenging and cost-intensive problems of present day information and communication technologies. It provides representations and techniques for augmenting data and processes with machine-processable descriptions that form the basis for robust and scalable solutions for issues as diverse as interoperability, knowledge management, and e-commerce. These descriptions of data and processes reference ontologies that capture the most important concepts and relationships among them that can be covered in a system or context in a formal and explicit manner, and thus define the intended meanings of the descriptions.

With the appearance of the Semantic Web, ontologies are encoded in Web-suitable representation languages, are pervasively accessible, and are shared and reused across the Web. Correlated with the transition from the traditional Web to Web 2.0, this aspect of ontologies recently led to the study of ontology engineering as a collaborative process in which a potentially open and geographically distributed group of stakeholders or a community of practice agrees upon a common understanding of a domain of interest and methods to model their shared knowledge in terms of concepts, attributes, properties, relationships, and constraints.

Semantic wikis and other similar communication and collaboration platforms facilitating the exchange of ideas and discussion of modeling decisions are seen by many as the most important technologies supporting collaborative ontology engineering. This popularity is probably due to the user friendliness of wiki-based technology—a feature not necessarily a characteristic of semantically enabled applications—and to its focus on community aspects. Existing semantic wikis emphasize the creation of semantic (instance) data expressed in semantic web languages such as RDF(S) and OWL. The development of the underlying ontologies is also addressed but with some, we argue, important limitations.

As with native ontology development software, the focus of these approaches remains on typical modeling and knowledge representation issues, while the collaborative nature of wikis is assumed to inherently ease consensus building within an engineering team and encourage participation. The advantages that Web 2.0 offers in terms of easy-to-use technologies and incentives are not fully exploited, as most wiki-based ontology editors aim to provide a rich portfolio of development features comparative to those of their native counterparts, thus re-implementing much of their sophisticated functionality in an environment that claims to target lay users rather than ontology engineering experts.

A much more purposeful alternative would be, in our opinion, to design a collaborative platform that abstracts from the technical particulars of ontology engineering, possibly at the cost of reducing the expressivity of the resulting ontologies, but significantly lowering the entry barriers for nonexperts and truly leveraging the power of wiki-based technology. Such a platform would build on the positive experiences of massively collaborative Web 2.0-type knowledge articulation processes, whether tagging, Wikipedia-like content production, or blog-style content sharing. The power of such technologies stems from their massively collaborative natures and easy and intuitive handling characteristics while restricting them to resource annotation (tagging) and generation of interlinked, document-style content (wikis and blogs). These technologies could be extended to new levels of expressivity and computer processability via ontology-based semantics, while retaining intuitive and collaborative Web 2.0-style tools.

We have developed an extension of the Semantic MediaWiki (SMW) [14] that implements these ideas. Unlike other wiki-based ontology editors, our tool focuses on lightweight ontology modeling that can be carried out via appropriate interfaces by technically savvy users without knowledge engineering backgrounds. This is done by leveraging existing knowledge structures into ontologies and improving modeling results through knowledge repair techniques that identify potential problems and make suggestions to users. The intended meanings of ontological primitives are documented through lexical and multimedia resources that are more accessible to nonexperts than formal representations. The goal of this chapter is to introduce this tool. The chapter targets technology providers and potential adopters interested in becoming familiar with collaborative ontology engineering and also researchers who would like better overviews of the state of the art.

Section 6.2 reviews the key notions of collaborative ontology engineering and how they contribute to the realization of the so-called Enterprise 3.0. In Section 6.3 we describe our Semantic MediaWiki-based ontology engineering environment, followed by a walk-through example of how the tool can be used in Section 6.4. We evaluated our work in a case study, whose results are presented and discussed in Section 6.5. Finally, we summarize the main contributions and findings of our work and recommend future directions of research and development for the ontology engineering community in Section 6.7.

6.2 Collaborative Ontology Engineering for Enterprises

The next generation Web roadmap, as envisioned some years ago by industry analysts such as Gartner and the founders of the Semantic Web, predicts a natural evolution from controlled semantic environments into a global intelligent

Semantic Web. However, most initial products and services are seen as starting in controlled environments. A study by the Semantic Web Company of Vienna, the Know Center of Graz, and the Corporate Semantic Web Working Group of Freie Universität Berlin in April 2009 situated a corporate Semantic Web 5 years before mainstream market adoption. The late adoption of current state-of-the-art technologies in the Semantic Web field—even in controlled environments such as corporate intranets—is chiefly due to its high adoption barrier and underspecified potential return on investment.

Overcoming the adoption barrier problem is about creating semantically annotated content that is still considered prohibitive in corporate domains. Approaches for semantic content creation based on Web 2.0 principles promise to alleviate this situation by tapping the so-called wisdom of the crowds, combined with adequate incentives for participation to produce a critical mass of user contributions at the cost, however, of limited expressivity at the knowledge articulation level. Overcoming the current separation of the two paradigms by investigating means for bridging different levels of representation, e.g., to allow for seamless increasing of the expressiveness of semantic annotations ranging from shallow tags to expressive OWL axioms, would lead to the realization of the collaborative ontology engineering vision while tailoring the required ontology-related efforts to the promised positive return on investment.

We illustrate the benefits of this hybrid approach by means of a simple scenario applicable to every large organization that adopts Enterprise 3.0 practices and technology. Such an enterprise [19] "… is no longer one, monolithic organization. Customers, Partners, Suppliers, Outsourcers, Distributors, Resellers, … all kinds of entities extend and expand the boundaries of the enterprise, and make 'collaboration' and 'sharing' important. … Let's take some examples. The Sales force needs to share leads with distributors and resellers. The Product Design team needs to share CAD files with parts suppliers. Customers and Vendors need to share workspace often. Consultants, Contractors, Outsourcers often need to seamlessly participate in the workflow of a project, share files, upload information. All this, across a secure, seamlessly authenticated system."

In Enterprise 3.0, a user can tag any information item with any tag he or she wishes. The *tag* term as used here can include keywords used to describe files, folders, and bookmarks; items associated with information or processes; and metadata from semantic blogs, wikis, and others. Through various automatic techniques, one can determine equivalences between the tags used by different users, in fact transforming the underlying folksonomy in a more formal and structured, lightweight ontology. Using an ontology can considerably improve many knowledge management aspects, from knowledge sharing to information retrieval. It spans an informal knowledge repository distributed across users based on equivalence links between individually defined tags. Via automatic reasoning techniques, it also forms the basis for identifying further relationships between different user tags, and hence between different users' information and processes. This means that a user searching for information using his or her own particular tag naming convention will be presented with information tagged by another who imposed very different naming conventions. Additionally, analysis of user tags will enable communities of interest to arise naturally. The behaviors of users can be analyzed to determine the intensity of membership of such communities of interest, so that users can be advised of the experts on particular topics. In addition, reasoning can be used to compensate for inconsistencies among users.

Designing enterprise tools always raises high usability requirements. Our aim is to encourage users without background in knowledge engineering to contribute to the development of a shared knowledge model, i.e., an ontology capturing their understandings of their business domains. To lower the barriers of entry for nonexperts, the need is to develop user interfaces that provide a rich documentation of the ontology engineering process and also hide the technicalities of the process through appropriate natural language or multimedia elements.

To have a real chance of adoption within an enterprise, it is essential that the novel solutions optimally combining highly accessible Web 2.0 paradigms with computationally powerful ontology-based semantics build upon existing corporate technology, systems, and practices. Considering enterprise knowledge management trends in recent years, we can distinguish three broad phases: (1) the repository-centric view characterized by one or more central information repositories with a set of corporate contributors and reviewers; (2) a move to smaller, facilitated knowledge communities; and (3) social computing as a fast-advancing trend broadening and replacing previous knowledge management archetypes:

> "Front-line business people continue to tug at the fringes of hierarchical, bureaucratic, IT architectures by downloading and installing themselves productivity tools like desktop search, wikis and weblogs, and free online email. That one of the best old world KM tools of all, the water cooler conversation, now lives somewhere between your instant messaging network, email discussion threads, and the public blogosphere represents the near complete decentralization of KM. And it's not going to stop."
>
> **Enterprise 3.0 = (SaS + EE)" by Sramana Mitra,**
> **published for ReadWriteWeb on February 26, 2007, available**
> **at http://www.readwriteweb.com/archives/enterprise_30.php**

Following the same line of reasoning, it is equally important that the knowledge shared through communication and collaboration platforms and tools previously discussed, including wikis, weblogs, instant messaging, and email can be easily integrated and used in typical workflows relying on standard office automation tools such as text editors and spreadsheet applications. In addition, information produced via such tools should be utilized as input in ontology engineering tasks to increase the relevance and coverage of the developed ontologies, like the tagging example discussed earlier, and to make the overall process more efficient.

Creating and managing such lightweight ontologies by leveraging existing knowledge sources in an integrated enterprise IT landscape is the aim of our Semantic MediaWiki-based ontology editor presented in Section 6.3. Besides providing basic support for the creation of semantic content in a collaborative fashion, Semantic MediaWiki [14] includes various extensions and plug-ins allowing its use in combination with office tools as diverse as MS SharePoint, MS Word, MS Excel, and MS Project, and for many business-relevant tasks including process modeling, and project management [6].*

6.3 Semantic MediaWiki Ontology Editor

This section introduces the Semantic MediaWiki Ontology Editor implemented in the ACTIVE European research project.† Our work adheres to several design principles that will be introduced.

Large-scale participation—Following the wisdom-of-crowds paradigm, we believe that a diverse community consisting of domain experts and knowledge engineers is smarter and more agile than a small ontology development team alone. Instead of forcing one view of the world onto the user communities, we envision co-existence and interoperability of conflicting views to support the community in achieving consensus.

Lightweight ontologies—These ontologies represent prominent topics in ontology engineering, particularly for applying them to the corporate Semantic Web. The advantages are clear: the user community and domain experts can understand such models more easily and can be involved in their maintenance, while existing knowledge structures such as taxonomies can be translated into ontologies to allow for automatic reasoning tasks.

User-friendliness—Traditional ontology development environments usually impose high entrance barriers on users, while wikis allow many users to contribute easily with only basic Web editing skills. The culture of wikis is the underlying paradigm of this work. Also, we propose the use of multimedia elements to better convey the informal part of the intended meaning of a concept.

Combination of human and computational intelligence—Building ontologies is a task that depends on human intelligence as a source of domain expertise, for producing a consensual conceptualization, and to align ontologies and resolve inconsistencies. We aim to develop a functionality that combines human and computational power and thus supports users in achieving several ontology building

---

* http://semantic-mediawiki.org/
† http://www.active-project.eu/

tasks. This applies in particular to identifying potential inconsistencies and reusing external resources, such as the ones mentioned earlier, as baselines to automatically learn ontologies and components that can be evaluated and refined by humans.

Leveraging existing knowledge sources—With the Web growing daily, a wealth of available data can be reused to enrich ontologies. Examples include the W3C Linking Open Data (LOD) community project,[*] multimedia sharing platforms such as YouTube[†] and Flickr,[‡] Wikipedia,[§] Google,[⁵] Watson,[**] and data from OntoGame.[††]

Our SMW ontology editor is a platform for collaborative management of light-weight ontologies. It offers a rich user interface that allows inexperienced users to easily create and maintain ontology elements. The system is built atop the MediaWiki platform and the SemanticMediaWiki extension. It provides a metamodel that distinguishes between vocabularies, categories, properties, and elements. For the maintenance of evolving vocabularies, knowledge repair functionalities are provided to assist users with the discovery and mitigation of redundancies and inconsistencies in the knowledge base. A folksonomy import feature allows the import of external folksonomy data. Furthermore, the system supports the import and export of OWL ontologies.

6.3.1 Main Features

6.3.1.1 Rich Editing Interface

Users can add, edit, and delete categories using form-based interfaces. For example, while creating new categories, users can easily supply information such as the description of the category, synonyms of the preferred term used to denominate it, or related Web pages. They can also indicate a vocabulary to which an entity belongs, more general categories, and new and existing properties that apply to the category through dropdown menus. The form-based interface was built atop the SemanticForms MediaWiki extension.[‡‡] Thus it is possible for nonexpert users to build and maintain a Semantic Web knowledge base without having to learn the syntax of the Semantic MediaWiki and its extensions.

To support a user during this task, the tool automatically adds multimedia elements related to the category at hand through the Flickr API by searching for

---

[*] http://esw.w3.org/SweoIG/TaskForces/CommunityProjects/LinkingOpenData

[†] http://www.youtube.com

[‡] http://www.flickr.com

[§] http://www.wikipedia.org

[⁵] http://www.google.com

[**] http://kmi-web05.open.ac.uk/WatsonWUI/

[††] http://ontogame.sti2.at/

[‡‡] http://www.mediawiki.org/wiki/Extension:Semantic_Formshttp://www.mediawiki.org/wiki/Extension:Semantic Forms

images from the Flickr.com Web site* that are relevant to the labels of the category. The resulting images are displayed on the corresponding wiki page. Additional assistance is provided through context-dependent help menus and inline edits.

All these aspects can be edited directly by means of pop-up forms; this is a convenient way for a user to make minor changes and avoid the regular, richer edit form interface. Autocompletion is another powerful feature of the tool. It helps reduce redundancies and saves development effort by providing lists of similar, already existing entities to the project in process. Existing entities include those that are already stored in the system and external resources such as thesauri. The larger a knowledge base grows, the harder it can be for a user to find specific content. Therefore, the ontology editor implements several features for navigating the content, rearranging hierarchies of categories and properties, and emphasizing frequently used or prominent content.

One way to ease navigation is by utilizing "tag clouds." An individual wiki page is accompanied by a tag cloud that displays a group of associated categories, properties, and elements. The entities of the tag cloud are displayed in different colors and font sizes according to their significance. Entities that exhibit a higher number of page accesses and links to other pages are displayed with larger fonts. The main overview page of the tool displays a tag cloud representing the entire knowledge base. To navigate through categories, we implemented a tree-based visualization of category hierarchies via the CategoryTree extension of MediaWiki.[†] This interface also allows easy rearrangement of hierarchies by offering drag-and-drop functionality.

6.3.1.2 Knowledge Repair

A knowledge base created and managed collaboratively by lay users may contain inconsistencies and other modeling errors. Such issues are identified by the knowledge repair mechanisms implemented in the editor. A first category of issues is related to similar entities (categories, properties, elements). The ontology editor identifies entities with similar labels according to the Levenshtein distance, potentially similar categories based on overlapping property sets, and equivalent categories based on cyclic category hierarchies. A second category refers to misclassified categories and elements, e.g., specialization and generalization relationships between categories along with instantiation relationships between elements and categories.

To avoid such issues, the system provides a list of categories that have no subcategories. The user must then decide whether the entity is indeed a category or is actually an element. The editor displays knowledge repair information in several ways, including an overview of all suggested issues for each entity or for an entire vocabulary, or statistical overviews for all vocabularies managed by the tool. The

---

* http://www.flickr.com/
† http://www.mediawiki.org/wiki/Extension:CategoryTree

user has access to information about the minimum, average, and maximum values of a specific knowledge repair issue at every level, and these values can be compared to the values of the entity at hand. Issues can be ordered based on various criteria and are further highlighted using different colors based on severity.

6.3.1.3 Versioning

Since ontologies change over time (because the domain to model changes or because users add, delete, or change parts of the ontology), it may be useful to track such changes and provide means to restore prior versions. The versioning special page allows a user to display and restore the history of changes of vocabularies and/or categories. He/she can restore the structure of a vocabulary and the field information of categories independently.

6.3.1.4 Knowledge Import and Export

The ontology editor provides import functionality for externally developed ontologies, and for translating folksonomies into lightweight ontologies. The latter function is carried out according to the FolksOntology method introduced in [2], consisting of the following steps applied to a particular set of tags. The underlying idea is to infer lightweight ontologies in SKOS from folksonomies by exploiting the full spectrum of existing knowledge resources available online and heuristics:

- Compute similarly labeled tags using the Levenshtein distance.
- Search the WordNet thesaurus to identify additional similar tags.
- Search tags in Wikipedia to discover wiki pages under the same name and redirects.
- Check spelling and translations.
- Group tags based on results of previous steps.
- Compute co-occurrence and co-actoring matrices.
- Build tag clusters that map into ontological primitives.
- Translate output to SKOS.
- Import SKOS into SMW ontology editor metamodel.

Besides folksonomies, it is also possible to import OWL ontologies through a form-based interface. The ontological entities are mapped to the SMW ontology editor metamodel consisting of categories, properties, and entities. If clashes exist with already existing entities (e.g., if an entity with the same title already exists), the user is informed and can resolve conflicts by deciding which entity to keep. The supported import syntax is OWL/XML. Each vocabulary page contains an export tab that leads to an interface to export the vocabulary and its associated categories, properties, and elements in the form of an ontology. The export format is OWL/XML. We now turn to implementation of these features.

6.3.2 Implementation Details

MediaWiki is probably the "wiki software of the day," used by prominent initiatives such as Wikipedia to enable communication and collaboration within communities of interest. Topics in Wikipedia are described on wiki pages that may be assigned to categories. In addition, MediaWiki also provides so-called special pages. Some of these gather general information that enhances the usability of the wiki, while others list potential inconsistencies in content, structure, and interlinking issues. Semantic MediaWiki introduces concepts and properties to this simple wiki model, and thus enhances the way information in a wiki can be managed, searched, and organized. Our editor, in turn, is an extension of Semantic MediaWiki toward user-friendly, form-based ontology development with a focus on lightweight design, knowledge repair, and knowledge leverage.

We use the same ontological entities (categories, properties, elements) as Semantic MediaWiki, with new namespace for vocabularies and special pages providing comfortable access to vocabularies. In addition to the SemanticForms and CategoryTree components, we resort to several other libraries to improve the usability of the editor:

- GoogieSpell for spell checking of input fields[*]
- phpFlickr to automatically annotate categories with corresponding images from Flickr[†]
- facebox for inline edits, displaying images and divs[‡]
- silkicons from famfamfam to focus user attention on important parts of a form[§]
- jQuery to manage all the jQuery project libraries[¶]
- AutoSuggest for auto-completion[**]

The algorithms underlying the knowledge repair approaches are embedded in special pages. This is convenient because the pages are in a separate namespace and therefore easily distinguishable from the ontological entities, and also may be collected in a knowledge repair section among all the other special pages.

6.4 Using Editing Tool

Since the SMW ontology editor is an extension of Semantic MediaWiki (and thus also an extension of MediaWiki), use of the editor is straightforward for users

---

[*] http://orangoo.com/labs/Main/

[†] http://phpflickr.com/

[‡] http://famspam.com/facebox

[§] http://www.famfamfam.com/

[¶] http://jquery.org/

[**] http://www.brandspankingnew.net/archive/2006/08/ajax_auto-suggest_auto-complete.html

familiar with the base technology. However, one does not need to be an expert in using wikis to be able to use the editor because most of the user inputs are collected through forms and the editor is documented in detail.

Main page—This is the entry point of the SMW ontology editor (see Figure 6.1). The primary navigation can be found on the left side containing links to the most important functionalities, including those for vocabulary, category and property creation, import functionalities for folksonomies, and external OWL ontologies. Furthermore the primary navigation includes links to the most important knowledge repair functions such as category statistics, cyclic hierarchy checks, and reviews for redundant links, naming conflicts, and versioning. Finally it includes some popular links from the original MediaWiki software. The main page also gives a short introduction to the tool and an overview of wiki content including namespaces and a tag cloud. We will now illustrate the functionality of the editor using an example in which a vocabulary about vehicles is created.

Entity creation—To create a new vocabulary, one can use the corresponding link in the primary navigation that leads to the *Create Vocabulary* form (see Figure 6.2) on which the user can enter a vocabulary name and description and also create corresponding categories and properties. After saving the created vocabulary about *Vehicles,* the user is directed to the vocabulary overview displaying the

Figure 6.1　Main page.

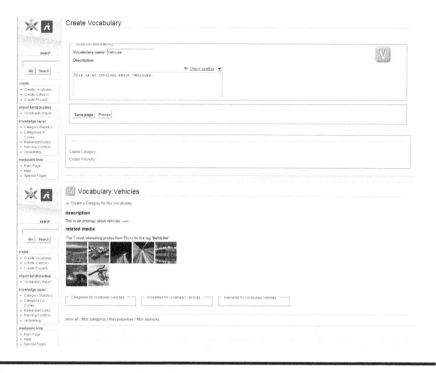

Figure 6.2   Create vocabulary form and overview page.

entered vocabulary name, description, and automatically added metadata such as Flickr images. Moreover, the vocabulary overview links to the *Create Category* form that can be used to create categories for existing vocabularies (Figure 6.3). This form may be used, for example, to create a *Car* category for the *Vehicles* vocabulary.

Upon entry of the category name, the autocompletion feature displays already existing entities with similar names to the one just entered, along with drop-down menus to support the user. The category creation form offers subforms for entering a name for the category, a corresponding vocabulary (which is, by default, preselected to the currently created vocabulary), related links, synonyms, a sample sentence, and a description.

In the next step, the user can create new properties (such as *has_Designer*) that correspond to the category, or he can choose among the already available ones (such as *Horsepower*). Moreover the user can choose a supercategory for this property and finally can check the category for name similarities with other categories. After saving the category, the system displays the category overview page that shows the just entered information (see Figure 6.4). Additionally the system provides a tag cloud to easily access the entities and the most interesting images on Flickr related to the category. To support the user, a tree-based visualization of taxonomies can be used for navigation, to create corresponding elements, and to edit the entered information.

Figure 6.3   Create category form.

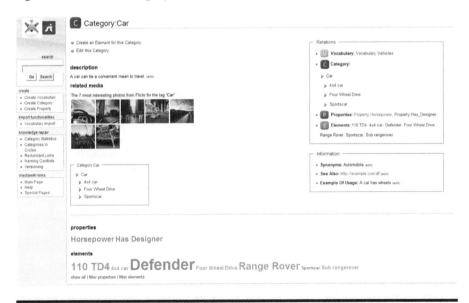

Figure 6.4   Category overview.

This can be done by clicking on the *Edit* links that open pop-ups for inline edit (see Figure 6.5 in which the *Automobile* synonym is changed to the *Auto* synonym).

Knowledge repair —These algorithms can be accessed by clicking on the special page corresponding to the algorithm under consideration. After clicking on *Category Statistics*, the system provides a comprehensive overview of wiki categories,

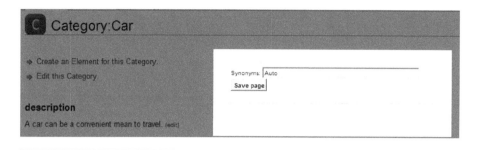

Figure 6.5 Changing parameters with inline edit.

special

Category Statistics

This page displays certain figures regarding all the categories in the wiki. The first table provides some explanations to the values calculated. The second table shows the minimum, average and maximum of the calculations using all categories. The third table shows the calculations for each single category. Orange cells indicate that there might be something wrong, e.g. the value equals the minimum or maximum value. Red cells indicate that there is indeed a problem, like a redundant link.

Subcategories	Subcategories are categories, which are a specialization of another category.
Supercategories	Supercategories are categories, which are a generalization of other categories.
Elements	Elements are individuals of a category; however, there also might be elements which are not type of a certain category
Siblings	Siblings are categories, which have a common supercategory
Properties	The value 'Properties' indicates the number of properties of a category
Element properties	The value 'Element properties' indicates the number of properties of all the elements, which are type of a certain category
Redundant links	This column shows how many redundant links a category has. If there is a cylce this value cannot be calculated until the cycle has been resolved.
Path length to top	This column shows the number of supercategories in a row until reaching the top. If there is a cylce this value cannot be calculated until the cycle has been resolved.
Path length to bottom	This column shows the number of subcategories in a row until reaching the bottom. If there is a cylce this value cannot be calculated until the cycle has been resolved.

All categories	Subcategories	Supercategories	Elements	Siblings	Element properties	Min path length to top	Max path length to top	Min path length to bottom	Max path length to bottom
min	0	0	0	0	0	0	0	0	0
avg	0.773	0.482	0.291	0.864	0.027	0.718	0.727	0.364	0.473
max	18	2	3	17	2	4	4	2	4

Category name	Subcategories	Supercategories	Elements	Siblings	Properties	Element properties	Redundant links	Path length to top min-max	Path length to bottom min-max
110_TD4	0	0	0	0	1	No elements!	0	2-2	0-0
4x4_car	2	0	1	0	2	1	0	1-1	1-2
Activity	2	1	0	0	1	No elements!	0	3-3	1-1
Animal	18	1	0	3	1	No elements!	0	1-1	1-2
Architecture	0	0	0	0	1	No elements!	0	0-0	0-0
Assistant	0	1	0	0	1	No elements!	0	2-2	0-0
Attack	0	0	0	0	1	No elements!	0	0-0	0-0
Authority	0	1	0	1	1	No elements!	0	2-2	0-0
Auto	0	2	0	7	1	No elements!	0	2-2	0-0
Automobile	2	0	0	0	1	No elements!	0	0-0	1-1
BigStack	0	1	0	0	0	No elements!	0	1-1	0-0
Bleistift	1	1	0	1	1	No elements!	↻	↻	↻

Figure 6.6 Category statistics.

probable issues with them, and helpful information for error detection directing the user's focus to potential problems (see Figure 6.6 displaying general issues with *Car* and the specific information that *Car* is part of a cycle). The big table then displays values for all the categories. If the user is interested in a specific category instead of all of them, he or she can click on tab repair on the category page (*Car*) to reach an overview page of the specific category displaying potential issues (see Figure 6.7 displaying name similarities to other categories, general issues, and a cycle).

The *Categories* special page in cycles displays categories that are parts of other cycles or parts of a taxonomy containing a cycle (see Figure 6.8, showing the accidentally introduced cycle with respect to the *Car* category). The user may then decide whether the specific cycle will be accepted.

The special page titled *Categories with Redundant Subclass Relations* displays categories with links to two or more predecessors (Figure 6.8). The user can then decide which link is redundant and delete the specific one "on the fly." However, this is possible only if the category is not part of a cycle. Obviously there are no issues with respect to *Car*.

The special page called *Entities with Similar Names* provides information about entities with similar names (see Figure 6.8; *Car* has a name similar to the names of other categories in the knowledge base). For each entity, the system calculates the Levenshtein distance to other categories and displays the results. Each type of entity has one list in order to limit redundancies when two or more entities with similar names representing the same concept are created.

In the *Knowledge Repair* section of the special pages, a user can find other means to repair knowledge, for example, the *Category Histogram, Property Histogram, Categories with Similar Property* sets, and *Unsubcategorized categories*. Each component addresses a specific type of problem or provides a comprehensive view on

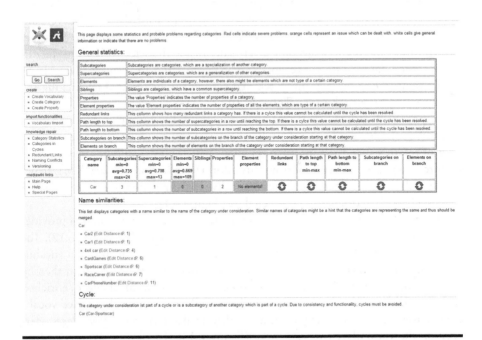

Figure 6.7   Category knowledge repair.

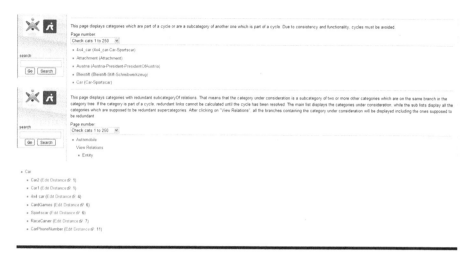

Figure 6.8 **Categories in cycles, categories with redundant subclass relations, and entities with similar names.**

a certain aspect of the wiki (see Figure 6.9). The versioning special page makes it possible to display and restore the history of changes of vocabularies and/or categories. Furthermore, it is possible to restore the structure of a vocabulary and the field information of categories independently on the versioning page by selecting a vocabulary or category (by clicking on the picture beside the name on the list). When a vocabulary or category is selected, a pop-up with the detailed versioning information is displayed. It is possible to choose between *Vocabulary Structure Changes* and *Category Changes* on the left side. Inside the selected box are the different version dates. Different versions can be selected and are displayed (via AJAX) on the right side of the pop-up. A selected version can be restored by clicking the *Restore Selected Version* button (Figure 6.10).

Import and export—This tool offers the possibility to import functionalities and OWL ontologies. To use the folksonomy import functionality, a set of tags, a set of resources, and the information about which tags should be used for each resource are needed. After importing this information in a proprietary XML structure, vocabularies are generated automatically. In a final step, the best choice of suggested vocabularies has to be selected (see Figure 6.11).

To import an OWL ontology, one can use the corresponding form that provides input fields for vocabulary name, description, and source file (see Figure 6.12). The system uploads the OWL file, extracts the entities, and maps them into a vocabulary based on the SMW ontology editor metamodel. This vocabulary can then be used like any other vocabulary created online; it can be browsed, changed, enriched with new data, and exported. Moreover, the tool allows export of the created vocabularies using the ontology export functionality available via the *Export Pages* reference on the vocabulary overview page (Figure 6.13). The feature exports a given vocabulary into an OWL file that can then be used offline.

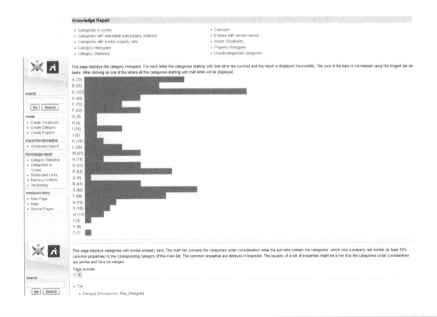

Figure 6.9 Section knowledge repair category histogram and categories with similar property sets.

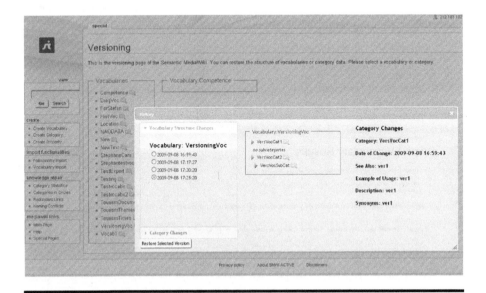

Figure 6.10 Versioning.

Figure 6.11   Folksonomy import.

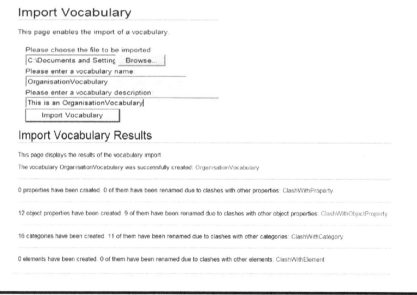

Figure 6.12   OWL import.

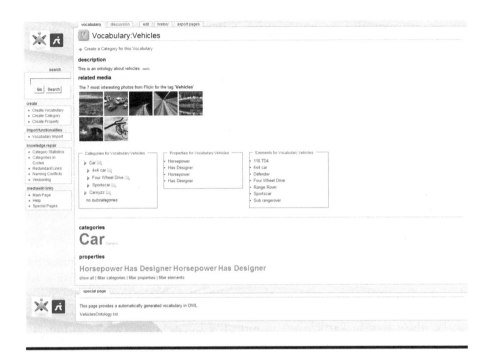

Figure 6.13   OWL export.

6.5 Evaluation

We now present a preliminary evaluation of the core features of the ontology editor in two steps: (1) in early experiments, we evaluated the usability of the tool with design experts; (2) in a second step, we performed a usability study with 20 representative end users.

6.5.1 Methodology

In order to evaluate the usability of the editor, we used the ISO 9241-110 standard [10]. The standard defines usability as "the extent to which a product can be used by specified users to achieve specified goals with effectiveness, efficiency and satisfaction in a specified context of use."

Nielsen [16] describes methods for evaluating usability and distinguish between summative and formative questionnaires. Summative questionnaires are usually applied to a completed product to determine whether it fulfills the requirements; they use numeric values. Formative questionnaires aim to detect weaknesses at design time. In this evaluation, we make use of the isometrics questionnaire

[8] evaluating whether a software system fulfills ISO-U comprising seven dialog principles:

1. Suitability for the task; the dialog should be suitable for a user's task and skill level.
2. Self-descriptiveness; the dialog should make clear what the user should do next.
3. Controllability; the user should be able to pace and sequence the interaction.
4. Conformity with user expectation; the dialog should be consistent.
5. Error tolerance; the dialog should be forgiving.
6. Suitability for individualization; the dialog should be able to be customized to suit a user.
7. Suitability for learning; the dialog should support learning.

Isometrics distinguishes between two kinds of questionnaires: one for summative (IsoMetrics-short) and one for formative (IsoMetrics-long) evaluations. We used the formative version that contains the same questions as the short version, but a participant additionally has the ability to rank the importance of each question to the whole system. Participants in formative questionnaires can also provide qualitative feedback to improve the prototype. Each question consists of three subquestions: (1) a numeric value ranging from 1 (predominantly disagree) to 5 (predominantly agree) must be chosen; (2) the importance of the question must be rated; and (3) participants are asked for feedback. Our survey focused only on the numerical ratings (1).

We carried out the experiment in the following fashion. The prepared survey was sent to previously selected users with no knowledge about the editor, but with basic knowledge of ontologies. Each participant was asked to create a small vocabulary using the editor and use the knowledge repair features offered by the editor. The email contained a detailed procedure on use of the editor to perform the experiment. After completing work on the vocabulary, users were asked to answer questions in an online questionnaire.

6.5.2 Results and Discussion

This section summarizes results of the usability evaluation. Table 6.1 presents our findings from the isometrics questionnaire; participants rated questions from 1 (predominantly disagree) to 5 (predominantly agree). The table indicates the mean of user replies. Each entry is an aggregate of multiple questions in a respective category.

The results from the isometrics questionnaire were entirely positive. The participants found the suitability of the tool for learning very satisfying (4.28). The next issue addressed by the questionnaire was suitability for individualization (the system is constructed to allow for adaptation to users' individual needs and skills

Table 6.1   Isometrics Questionnaire Results

Category	Mean
Suitability for task	4.11
Self-descriptiveness	4.23
Controllability	4.23
Conformity with user expectations	4.01
Error tolerance	4.09
Suitability for individualization	n/a
Suitability for learning	4.28

for a given task) [8]. This issue was not addressed in SMW editor development, and therefore was not tested. Error tolerance related mainly to the ability to undo actions that produced unwanted consequences. This was realized by the system in a satisfying manner. The issue of conformity to user expectations scored high with a mean of 4.01—the behavior of the system was consistent. Controlability of the system also rated high (4.23), indicating that users were able to control the pace and sequence of interaction. Results for self-descriptiveness and suitability for the task were also rated high (4.23 and 4.11, respectively). Furthermore, users found the overall suitability for the task of collaborative ontology building of the system more than good.

6.5.3 NeOn Questionnaire

We used the NeOn questionnaire aimed at evaluating ontology engineering environments to examine the ontology engineering-specific features of the SMW ontology editor [19]. In the course of evaluating the editor, we selected questions that corresponded to the functionality covered by the SMW editor. In Table 6.2, we outline the selected questions and respective results. Participants had to answer questions using the same scale used for the isometrics questionnaire (1 means fully disagree, 5 means fully agree). We concluded that most questions from the NeOn questionnaire received very positive feedback with the exception of the third question whose answers indicated room for improvement for the tool tips provided.

6.6 Related Work

Various semantic wikis have been proposed in recent years. Most focus on the creation of RDF data [4,14,20] but issues specific to ontology design are also explicitly

Table 6.2   Results of NeOn Questionnaire

Question	Mean
I like the software support very much	4.17
I think provided explanations are useful	4.55
Provided tool tips for software are sufficient	3.56
User interface is designed well	4.05
Graphic elements (icons, etc.) are clear and legible	4.45
I am satisfied with the interface design of the editor	4.10
I liked the overall behavior of the editor and tools	4.10

addressed [5,18,22]. This second group of approaches uses the wiki paradigm to facilitate consensus building among the stakeholders participating in an ontology engineering process. Our ontology editor implements a similar functionality for ontology design, but does not consider discussions or argumentation support; instead, it offers user-friendly features for knowledge leverage and repair along with interlinking to external resources. These features, arguably more than the systematic decision making mechanisms provided elsewhere, are essentially required in ontology engineering processes that are openly operated by nonexperts.

A more structured approach [22] has benefits, in particular in ontology engineering scenarios in decentralized, closed environments, while features as those implemented in our work are probably meaningful add-ons. In parallel to semantic wikis, the ontology engineering community has developed native ontology editors with communication and collaboration support. OntoSaurus, for instance, is a Web-based tool for editing and browsing ontologies [21]; however, it has no explicit support for collaborative work, although online access allows a number of different stakeholders to contribute to the ontology engineering process.

Domingue describes Tadzebao and WebOnto in [7]: Tadzebao supports asynchronous and synchronous discussions on ontologies, while WebOnto complements it with collaborative browsing, creation, and editing of ontologies. Vrandecic and colleagues [23] describe the DILIGENT process model, according to which ontology evolution and collaborative ontology alignment are applied to deal with the conceptual dynamics of a domain of interest. OntoEdit is another example of a collaborative ontology development environment but targets expert-driven scenarios.

Kotis and Vouros describe the HCOME methodology in [13]. Similar to DILIGENT, the focus is on ontology evolution and alignment, while also taking into account external ontology-like sources that may aid domain analysis and conceptualization. HCOME is a decentralized engineering model; each participant first formalizes his or her own ontology and shares it with the community in a further step. This is different from our approach because the ontology is not open to the community at all times. SharedHCOME is a framework that provides a working implementation of the ontology-based argumentation, exploitation, and inspection methodology HCOME in a semantic wiki.* Like our editor, the SharedHCOME tool supports collaborative editing of vocabularies. Its focus on argumentation support allows the attachment of comments and voting on ontology elements and versions [11,12,17].

Braun and colleagues [1] present an ontology evolution process consisting of four steps: emergence of ideas, consolidation in communities, formalization, and axiomatization. They understand the evolution of an ontology as maturing from tags to formal ontologies via the community. This model is compatible to a large extent with our ontology editor. Finally, De Moor, De Leenheer and colleagues describe the DOGMA ontology engineering approach [3] focusing on community-grounded ontology evolution in interorganizational settings based on lexical resources. Our tool could form a user-friendly basis for a development environment with integrated DOGMA-MESS support.

Besides these approaches, more traditional ontology engineering environments exist. Protégé and Topbraid Composer are, for instance, summarized and compared in [9]. Newer ontology engineering environments include the Neon toolkit.†

6.7 Conclusions

In addition to continuing the evaluation of our editor with more extensive user studies, and implementing the results of such studies, we plan to extend the tool to accommodate recent technology trends such as Linked Open Data. As more (RDF) data will be published online, the need for shared ontologies describing the meanings and structures of this data will become essential for effective usage.

The collaborative ontology engineering community must adjust its methods and techniques to the particularities of this new setting and leverage the huge volume of data on the Web as a valuable input for the machine-supported creation of joint ontologies. Such methods and techniques will be data- rather than human-driven, and user contributions will be optimally leveraged to resolve issues that cannot be feasibly automated; ontology engineering tools, including our editor, will have to be adapted to reflect this shift. Another interesting development direction is in folksonomy management. Our editor can translate sets of tags into lightweight OWL-based vocabularies.

As a pretranslation step, we are considering form-based features for creating and managing tags, thus bringing more conceptual structure into the underlying

---

* http://icsd-ai.aegean.gr/sharedhcone
† http://neon-toolkit.org/

folksonomy. Such folksomies would lead to richer ontologies to capture more meanings of the corresponding domain of interest. In terms of deployment, our editor will be utilized in two case studies in the context of the ACTIVE European research project, at a global telecommunication operator and a large consulting company, respectively.

References

1. S. Braun, A. Schmidt, A. Walter, G. Nagypal, and V. Zacharias. *Ontology maturing: A collaborative web 2.0 approach to ontology engineering.* In *Proceedings of the Workshop on Social and Collaborative Construction of Structured Knowledge (CKC 2007)* at the 16th International World Wide Web Conference (WWW2007).

2. C. Van Damme, M. Hepp, and K. Siorpaes. 2007. Folksontology: An integrated approach for turning folksonomies into ontologies. In *Proceedings of the ESWC Workshop Bridging the Gap between Semantic Web and Web 2.0*, pp. 71–84.

3. A. De Moor, P. De Leenheer, and R. Meersmann. *DOGMA-MESS: A meaning evolution support system for interorganizational ontology engineering*, In *Proceedings of the 14th International Conference on Conceptual Structures (ICCS 2006)*, pp. 189–203, Springer, 2006.

4. C. Dello, E. Paslaru Bontas Simperl, and R. Tolksdorf. Creating and using semantic content with makna. In *Proceedings of the Workshop on Semantic Wikis at the 3rd European Semantic Web Conference (ESWC2006)* 2006.

5. K. Dellschaft, H. Engelbrecht, J. Monte Barreto, S. Rutenbeck, and S. Staab. Cicero: Tracking Design Rationale in Collaborative Ontology Engineering. In *Proceedings of the 5th European Semantic Web Conference (ESWC 2008)*, pp. 782–786, Springer LNCS, 2008.

6. F. Dengler, S. Lamparter, M. Hefke, et al. Collaborative process development using Semantic MediaWiki. In *Proceedings of the 5th Conference on Professional Knowledge Management Wissensmanagement 2009*, pp. 97–107, GI, 2009.

7. J. Domingue. Tadzebao and WebOnto: Discussing, Browsing, and Editing Ontologies on the Web. In *Proceedings of the 11th Knowledge Acquisition for Knowledge-Based Systems Workshop*, 1998.

8. G. Gediga and K.-C. Hamborg. Isometrics: An usability inventory supporting summative and formative evaluation of software systems. In *Proceedings of the Conference on Human Computer Interaction (HCI 1999)*, pp. 1018–1022, Lawrence Erlbaum, 1999.

9. A. Gomez-Perez, M. Fernandez-Lopez, and O. Corcho. 2004. *Ontological Engineering: Advanced Information and Knowledge Processing*, Springer Verlag, Berlin.

10. ISO. Ergonomics of human-system interaction - Part 110: Dialogue principles. ISO: 9241-110, available at http://www.iso.org/iso/iso_catalogue/catalogue_tc/catalogue_detail.htm?csnumber=38009, 1996.

11. Konstantinos Kotis: On Supporting HCOME-3O Ontology Argumentation Using Semantic Wiki Technology. OTM Workshops 2008, pages 193–199, Springer LNCS, 2008.

12. K. Kotis, A. Papasalouros, N. Pappas et al. 2009. E-class in ontology engineering: Integrating ontologies to argumentation and semantic wiki technology. In *Proceedings of Workshop on Intelligent and Innovative Support for Collaborative Learning Activities*.

13. K. Kotis and G.A. Vouros. 2005. Human-centered ontology engineering: The HCOME methodology. *Knowledge and Information Systems, 10*: 109–131.

14. M. Krötzsch, D. Vrandecic, M. Völkel et al. 2007. Semantic Wikipedia. *Journal of Web Semantics, 5*: 251–261.

15. B. Swartout, R. Patil, K. Knight, and T. Russ. Ontosaurus: a tool for browsing and editing ontologies. In: *Proceedings of the 9th Banff Knowledge Aquisition for Knowledge-based systems Workshop, 1996*.

16. J. Nielsen. 1993. *Usability Engineering*. Morgan Kaufmann.

17. N. Pappas and K. Zoumpatianos. 2009. Sharedhcone: A semantic wiki-based argumentation system. Diploma thesis, University of the Aegean.

18. S. Schaffert. Ikewiki: *A semantic wiki for collaborative knowledge management*. In WETICE, pp. 388–396, IEEE Computer Society, 2006.

19. S. Mitra. 2007. Enterprise 3.0 = (SaaS + EE). http://www.readwriteweb.com/archives/enterprise_30.php

20. A. Souzis. 2005. Building a semantic wiki. *IEEE Intelligent Systems, 20*: 87–91.

21. B. Swartout, R. Patil, K. Knight et al. 1996. Ontosaurus: A tool for browsing and editing ontologies.

22. C. Tempich, E. Simperl, M. Luczak et al. 2007. Argumentation-based ontology engineering. *IEEE Intelligent Systems, 22*: 52–59.

23. D. Vrandecic, S. Pinto, C. Tempich et al. 2005. The diligent knowledge process. *Journal of Knowledge Management, 9*: 85–96.

Chapter 7

Learning of Social Ontologies in WWW: Key Issues, Experiences, Lessons Learned, and Future Directions

Konstantinos Kotis and Andreas Papasalouros

University of the Aegean, Samos, Greece

Contents

7.1 Introduction

Web, Social Web, and even Semantic Web content can be reused for the creation of semantic content, shaping information (or existing knowledge) into ontologies. Ontologies play a key role in the realization of the Semantic Web. However, a critical mass of *useful* semantic content is missing. Web users can find only a few well-maintained and up-to-date domain ontologies and the amount of RDF data publicly available is limited compared to the size of the unstructured Web information. Only a small number of Web users, typically members of the Semantic Web community, build and publish ontologies. To assist and motivate humans to participate in the Semantic Web movement and contribute their knowledge and time to create, refine, and enrich useful ontologies, we must boost semantic content creation by providing Web users with "starting points of assistance"—automatically learned ontologies.

Traditionally, the learning of ontologies involved the identification of domain-specific conceptualizations extracted from text documents or other semi-structured information sources such as lexicons and thesauri. Such learned ontologies do not utilize available social data that may be related to the domain ontology, e.g., information ownership details (contributor, annotator, end user); tags or argument and dialogue items that comment, organize, or disambiguate domain-specific information; querying information related to user clicks on retrieved information. Recently, the learning of ontologies has included social content generated mainly within Web 2.0 applications. Social content encompasses various types of publicly available media matter produced by Web users in a collaborative and communicative manner. Such content is associated to some social data produced as a result of *social fermentation*. The most popular social data in Web 2.0 content appears as *tags* that are (often) single words listed alphabetically and with a different font size or color (to capture their importance). Tags are usually hyperlinks that lead to a collection of associated items. Such social data can be processed in an intelligent way for shaping social content into ontologies. Since social data is produced in the course of social fermentation (tags are introduced in a collaborative and communicative manner), it can be claimed that the learned ontologies produced from such a process encapsulate some degree of agreement and trust of the learned conceptualizations.

Social content generation (SCG) refers to a conversational, distributed mode of content generation, dissemination, and communication among communities. Social intelligence (SI) aims to derive actionable information from social content in context-rich application settings and provide solution frameworks for applications that can benefit from the "wisdom of crowds" through the Web. Within this setting, a social ontology can be defined as an explicit, formal, and commonly agreed-upon representation of knowledge that is derived from both domain-specific and social data. In the context of this chapter, the meaning of *social ontology* must be clearly distinguished from the meaning used in social sciences. A representative social science definition was given by T. Lawson of the Cambridge Social Ontology Group in 2004*: "...the study of what is, or what exists, in the social domain; the study of social entities or social things; and the study of what all the social entities or things that are have in common."

Formally, an ontology is considered a pair $O = (S, A)$ where S is the ontological signature describing the vocabulary (terms that lexicalize concepts and relations between concepts), and A is a set of ontological axioms restricting the intended interpretations of the terms included in the signature (Kotis et al. 2006). In other words, A includes the formal definitions of concepts and relations that are lexicalized by natural language terms in S. In this chapter, the model is extended by a social dimension (equal to social semantics) influenced by the definition of the actor–concept–instance model of ontologies (Mika 2007) formulated as a generic abstract model of semantic–social networks. The extended model is built on an implicit realization of emergent semantics, i.e., meaning must rely on a community of agents. According to the extended model, a social ontology can be considered a triple $O=(C, S, A)$ where C is the set of collaborated contributors that participated in a task of social content generation (SCG) from which S and A (signature and axiom sets of the ontology) were derived using the social intelligence (SI) of C. The range, however, of C over both S and A at the same time is not guaranteed; S may have been derived from C, but not A (which may have been automatically derived from external information sources such as a general ontology or lexicon from WordNet).

The automated learning of social ontologies can be seen as a two-dimensional problem. The first dimension concerns the automated creation of ontologies from content (social and domain-specific), and the second or social dimension concerns collaboration and communication aspects (social fermentation) involved during the creation of the content. Since automation is involved, and humans cannot be also involved in the agreement process, a key issue here is the trust on the extracted ontological agreement from social data to assure that contributors of shared conceptualizations about a specific domain have agreed on a common understanding about the domain, and that such agreement is successfully extracted in an automated fashion from social data (in an open Web agents' world where agents

---

* http://www.csog.group.cam.ac.uk/A_Conception_of_Ontology.pdf

must trust each others' conceptualizations about the domain of discourse to be able to collaborate within an agreed context). In terms of the "trusting of content" problem, this chapter assumes that the content used as input in the ontology learning process is social (or involved in social fermentation), and thus at least to some degree, agreed and trusted. Blogs, (semantic) wikis, folksonomies, and other more sophisticated Web 2.0 applications such as Yahoo!Answers or Fixya provide reputation-based trust (using personal experience or the experiences of others, possibly combined) to make trust decisions about entities or voting mechanisms for their content. Other types of content such as Web users' query logs provide a form of trust in their content based on the majority vote of user clicks on Web search results.

Although trust is a major issue in automated learning of social ontologies, this chapter focuses rather on the learning of *useful* social ontologies. A useful ontology plays a significant role mainly in the ontology development lifecycle of a collaborative and human-centered ontology engineering methodology for devising evolving ontologies. The importance of a useful ontology (usefulness) can be shaped in the following tasks:

- Consultation of a kick-off ontology during a process of improvising an ontology "from scratch"
- Reuse of a kick-off ontology in a process of developing an ontology (merger with another ontology)
- Comparison of a kick-off ontology with an improvised ontology and reusing (copying) parts of it

Furthermore, the importance of a useful ontology (usefulness) in terms of its use in applications can be shaped in the following tasks:

- View or browse knowledge that users want to retrieve in a formal and structured form that the learned ontology provides.
- Annotate documents and data that users want to query using the semantics of the learned ontology.
- Use the learned ontology to reformulate and/or enrich NL queries toward retrieving unstructured information.
- Use the learned ontology as a formal query to retrieve Semantic Web documents using ontology matching methods.

This chapter reports experiences and challenges related to automated learning of useful social ontologies, following a holistic approach related to the different types of content that may be involved in the learning process, i.e., Web, Web 2.0, and even Semantic Web content, and discusses recently proposed methods as first steps to meet a few of these challenges for tackling the Semantic Web content creation bottleneck.

7.2 Background and Key Issues

Ontology learning is an important research area for Semantic Web realization. Many research efforts over recent years focused on the extraction of concepts and simple relations (mainly hierarchical) from text, especially from large collections of text documents. An early work (Maedche and Staab 2001) proposes an ontology learning framework that integrates data mining approaches (such as hierarchical cluster and association rule) and some background knowledge to learn concepts, hierarchical relations, and associative relations from text. An alternative approach (Han and Elmasri 2003) proposed the extraction of domain ontologies from Web pages based on HTML tags, lemmatization tags, and conceptual tags. Other efforts targeted measurement of the accuracy of the learned ontologies [evaluation problem of learning ontologies, e.g., OntoEval systems (Dellschaft and Staab 2006)].

Recently, several researchers proposed methods to learn ontologies from user-created social data, e.g., folksonomies, in collaborative social tagging. Such methods propose the learning of a domain ontology using tag clouds generated during the tagging of Web content in social networking authoring environments. The learned ontology is, or at least should be, a compromise between a formal ontology and freely created folksonomies (Gruber 2007).

A few algorithms have been proposed for learning synonym and hypernym relations between tags. Other efforts attempted to generate clusters of highly related tags and associate each cluster to a concept of an existing ontology. Still others propose unsupervised methods for exploring the hierarchical relations between tags but without considering the different types of relations (hypernyms, synonyms) between tags. A recent method (Tang et al. 2009) is capable of both discovering synonym relations and finding hypernyms and other semantic relations between tags without requiring prior knowledge about the domain. Such an approach can learn an ontology hierarchy from any social tagging application. In any case, the methods proposed to date for learning ontologies from tags integrate social data in a direct way (social data is not implied, it is there and is associated to the generated content). Such integration is important since it "moves" an already agreed-upon organization of information (folksonomy) into a new formal organization (ontology) that works (in applications) well only if this organization represents common agreement.

This chapter was motivated by recent research on ontology learning, collaborative ontology engineering, and Web 2.0 technologies, and covers specific key research issues related to learning of useful social ontologies. It is conjectured that the research community, in dealing with such issues, will be able to contribute to the forthcoming Web 3.0 infrastructure in which the technological fusion of Web, Web 2.0, and Semantic Web will be achieved. As Halevy et al. (2009) stated, "building Semantic Web (services in particular) is both engineering and a sociological challenge." A semantic interpretation problem exists even if one uses a Semantic

Web framework. It is a scientific problem of interpreting content: learning as much as possible about the context of the content to correctly disambiguate it (Halevy et al. 2009) and trust it.

Due to the nature of the social ontology learning problem, this chapter discusses three key research issues: dependency, automation of process, and type of input content.

The dependency issue concerns the identification of two different types of ontology learning methods: (1a) those developed to handle the problem of ontology learning in a direct way and (2) those that depend on the efficiency of methods developed to tackle other problems of ontology engineering. Such an example is an ontology learning method that produces a learned (target) ontology indirectly from the alignment and/or merger of two source ontologies. Human involvement is needed to validate (and disambiguate where needed) the input information prior to the execution of the learning process. The challenge is to reuse already learned ontologies produced from both methods as inputs (background knowledge) to a new ontology learning task. Although such an approach of reusing ontologies as background knowledge has been lately incorporated successfully in ontology alignment (Lanzenberger et al. 2008), we know of no report concerning its integration into the ontology learning problem.

The automation issue concerns the different approaches used to develop social ontologies: fully automated, semi-automated, or human-guided. A trade-off (gold approach), balancing automation with precision and recall of the learned conceptualizations is of course the most challenging. Based on our latest research observations, the following types of approaches exist.

Fully automated social ontology learning—This method in its general dimension is also known as "ontologies on demand" since it is assumed that the learning process is not assisted in any way by humans (unsupervised approach). Data mining, natural language processing, machine learning, and information retrieval techniques, separately or in combination, must be integrated in methods (stand-alone or in ontology learning frameworks) to process domain-specific and social data and generate the learned social ontology in an automated manner. The challenge is to identify social data related to the domain-specific one, then provide automated analysis (mining) of such data (first step) and find suitable and machine-processable forms to represent it (second step). The automated instantiation (population) of formal representations of the interlinking of domain and social data (since such representations already exist) is another challenge.

Semi-automated social ontology learning—This approach is concerned with human intervention (supervision) during the learning process. The tune-up of such involvement (trade-off among human involvement, time, cost, and accuracy of learned conceptualizations) is a real challenge because it has not been studied extensively. Placing human involvement in the early stages of an ontology learning task (i.e., in the disambiguation stage of terms via discussion, voting, argumentation, or other form of social fermentation) may be a solution to the problem of accuracy of the learned conceptualizations at minimum cost, as proposed and achieved in the ontology alignment–merging problem (Lanzenberger et al. 2008*).* Human involvement in the learning processes of social ontologies contributes to the validation of the learned conceptualizations and also to the indirect integration of social data (human understanding, opinion, trust, agreement).

Guided-by-tutor ontology learning—This approach concerns agreement upon proposed conceptualizations achieved within a social learning network following specific learning on how to develop an ontology. Such a process can be described as ontology engineering learning supported by intelligent collaborative learning platforms based on semantic wikis and argumentation and agreement technologies (Kotis et al. 2009b). Although first outcomes of related approaches show the ability in collaborative ontology engineering to interlink domain ontologies and their components with social data (agreement details, voting, human logic behind changes and evolution), the challenge is to advance the approach in new directions such as automated analysis of recorded social information (arguments, voting) to assess contributors (expertise identification) or contributions (automated trust and reputation generation); see Artz and Gil (2007).

The type of input is also an important issue related to learning of social ontologies. This chapter reports on efforts that learn ontologies from content that has direct or indirect relations to social data. Based on latest research observations, it is a challenge to use different types of input to solve the problem of learning social ontology.

Web content is shaped usually by following simple natural language grammar and syntax rules. However, specific content of Web applications such as domain-specific queries (clustered on demand using click information on preferred-by-users documents returned from search engines) can be used as inputs to a social ontology learning process. Such content "hides" social data (humans search interests, humans preferences for domain information, implied term disambiguation), which is eventually indirectly modeled in the learned ontology as agreement. Domain-specific query logs of Web users can be analyzed in a synthesized way, capturing their authors' collective intelligence.

Social content from Web 2.0 applications is shaped usually in a semi-structured manner using topics hierarchies and/or organized/structured discussion or collaborative authoring systems. Folksonomies have been already discussed related to current research status of the problem of ontology learning. The challenge is the integration of other Web 2.0 content such as content that facilitates semi-structured discussion and/or argumentation on specific topics. A representative example is Yahoo!Answers, a Web 2.0 application that facilitates agreement on discussed topics (already preorganized in a suggested topic hierarchy) in the form of questions and answers, also providing a mechanism for voting for the best answer. Semantic Web content has been shaped already in a structured (and formal) manner, and existing generic or domain ontologies can be used to learn other ontologies. This challenge was discussed from the dependency view in an earlier paragraph.

Web 3.0 content is shaped in a structured (and formal) manner (existing domain ontologies used in social networking applications to organize and share information and allow its retrieval in an intelligent way). Although such input is not yet widely available (semantic wikis, for example), at least one case study exists that can be used as an example in future social ontology learning methods (Kotis et al. 2009a). The challenge is to use social and semantic content as inputs to learn social ontologies. Although content is already organized and formalized in a machine-processable form (RDF classes and properties), and the relation of social content to the domain knowledge is formally recorded (meta-information models that inter-link social and domain information in a harmonic manner), their transformation into new knowledge could be achieved by devising ways to support its reasoning with social semantics and with interlinked domain knowledge.

In addition to the research issues and challenges cited above, this chapter also acknowledges the key issue of evaluating learned ontologies. Such evaluations have always represented challenges for the research community, and the learning methods proposed to date usually relate to a specific evaluation that works in favor (in a fair way) of the ontology learning method.

This chapter targets the conjecture that an effective way to evaluate a learned ontology is by allowing stakeholders to discuss it in an open but guided manner, allowing them to (indirectly) integrate new social data (agreement, voting, human logic on changes) to the domain-specific ontology as presented by Kotis et al. (2009a). The real need is to balance automation with guided agreement on the validation of learned conceptualizations. One approach is to provide a new framework for evaluating learned ontologies in which validation will be executed in two phases: (1) automatic validation of learned ontology against a gold ontology and (2) guided agreement on the results of the automated validation, that is, agreement on the alignments provided in the first step. In this way, the ontology evaluation is assisted by automation and the automated validation is complemented in the sense that any social data that have been integrated in the learned social ontology can now be also evaluated by the members of the social network.

7.3 Experiences with Useful and Social Ontology Learning

We now report on recent experiences of the authors and their colleagues during their research on learning social ontologies. The methods presented and initially introduced in their early work on semantic search (Kotis and Vouros 2006; Kotis 2008) explore the automated learning of ontologies from query logs. As to the key research issues covered in the previous section, the methods we present are not dependent on any other ontology engineering task; they are fully automated and analyze and utilize unstructured information with *no social data directly associated* to the domain-specific one. The social dimension of the learning process is "hidden" in the type of input content (query logs) and by its organization into domain-specific clusters prior to the execution of the ontology learning process (majority vote of user clicks).

The next section presents the method of learning useful and social ontology from the disambiguation, reformulation, and structure of a single query, using external knowledge from the WordNet lexicon, with the aim of advancing semantic search in related applications. We then discuss extension of the method for learning richer and consistent kick-off (starting) ontologies with the aim of aiding workers and engineers in creating semantic content (ontologies) for the Semantic Web. Finally, we present evaluation methods applied to these experimental learning methods with the obvious aim to assess the usefulness of the learned ontologies in ontology-based application and ontology engineering environments.

7.3.1 Ontology Learning in Ontology- Based Search Applications

Based on the inabilities of most Web users to express formal queries to retrieve Semantic Web documents (SWDs), the proposed method (Spiliopoulos et al. 2008) is a two-step approach for learning a formal lightweight ontology from a single free-form query. The aim is to support users' ability to place queries without requiring them to have knowledge and skills for expressing queries in a formal language. The two implementations based on this method were evaluated using Swoogle's search engine by retrieving and semantically (re)ranking SWDs (OWL ontologies).

The method was implemented as part of the SAMOS (semantics and automated matching of ontologies system) developed for experimental purposes in the semantic search domain. SAMOS combines several technologies for delivering a metaengine for filtering SWDs returned by the Swoogle search engine. Swoogle (Ding et al. 2004) is a crawler-based indexing and retrieval system for SWDs in RDF(S), DAML, or OWL syntax and provides techniques for semantically relating SWDs prior to the execution of queries. It extracts metadata and computes relations between documents. Although Swoogle presently serves as an SWD indexing system, its retrieval technology is based on lexical matching of query terms and the indexed labels of ontology classes and properties. By using Swoogle, the aim is to prove that the precision of retrieval for a simple query can be improved if the proposed semantic search method is applied.

SAMOS (Figure 7.1) implements the automatic construction of formal queries, namely query ontologies, from free-form queries to achieve ontology matching-based retrieval and/or ranking of SWDs. Other systems and approaches use formal languages to construct queries, an existing domain ontology as a prebuilt query, or a preexisting reference ontology in addition to a free-form query for on-the-fly meaning disambiguation. SAMOS implementation falls in the third

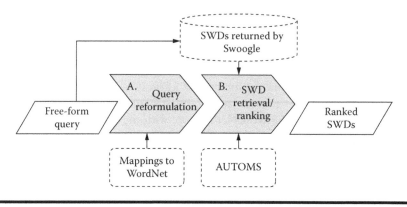

Figure 7.1 SAMOS overall architecture based on a two-step approach (steps depicted as shaded arrows).

case—external resources (lexicon) are used to disambiguate the meaning of the free-form query.

This implementation does not require a reference ontology. The external resources are embedded in the disambiguation method by means of the WordNet generic lexicon. This presents an advantage over other solutions since it is not always the case (in fact it is very rare) that a reference ontology will exist for every domain to be queried. The proposed basic method uses the WordNet generic lexicon to disambiguate query terms by automatically mapping them into WordNet senses. Any other lexicon or thesaurus that can provide semantic relations between the query terms such as subsumption, equivalence, part-of, etc. can be used for this implementation. An enhanced SAMOS approach, presented also in Spiliopoulos et al. (2008), does not require external resources.

In addition to the automatic construction of the query ontology, SAMOS implements the retrieval of SWDs using the AUTOMS automated ontology matching tool (Kotis et al. 2006a). For the effective retrieval of SWDs, AUTOMS computes the similarity between the SWDs and the reformulated query (query ontology). Such functionality is beyond the scope of this chapter. For a detailed description, readers are encouraged to read the related paper (Spiliopoulos et al. 2008).

Finally, SAMOS implements the ranking of retrieved SWDs based on how well they match the query ontology as determined by the number of mappings computed between the query ontology and SWDs. The more mappings there are between the query ontology and an SWD, the higher the position of the SWD in the final ranking. Actually the set of SWDs participating in the ranking algorithm is the set of documents retrieved by the submission of the free-form query to Swoogle. Thus, the ranking can be seen as a filtering of SWDs returned by a keyword-based search. We now present a detailed description of SAMOS implementation, outlining technological issues only for the individual steps related to the query ontology construction.

7.3.1.1 Query Disambiguation

In this step, each term of a free-form query is disambiguated, assessing its user-intended meaning specified by a WordNet sense. Although in other lines of research this process is accomplished by Latent Semantic Indexing (LSI) technology (Kotis et al. 2006a), this implementation uses Vector Space Model (VSM) technology (Raghavan and Wong 1986) due to the nature of available data (very few terms in queries) and the need to reduce SAMOS response time. Specific VSM implementation will be presented in detail along with use of its outputs to construct triples in the form of a query ontology; reformulating the initial free-form query into a formal one is also outlined.

To map a query term to its intended meaning, its semantic similarity to a set of WordNet senses is computed. The set is obtained by lexical matching of the term with a WordNet term entry. The algorithm takes into account the vicinity V_t of each query term t. Since this computation is based on the hypothesis that query terms are related to each other, the vicinity of a query term includes all the other terms in the query. In the next paragraph we describe in detail how VSM is exploited to disambiguate a free-form query using the WordNet lexicon.

A query term t is represented as a document ("bag of words" representation). Since a t term is related to all terms in its vicinity (V_t), the document representing t includes all terms in V_t. Similarly, each WordNet sense $S_1, S_2 \ldots S_m$ representing the m possible meanings of t is represented as a document. The most common document representation in information retrieval is adopted—a weighted vector of the form $(w_1, w_2, \ldots, w_N)$, where w_i ($i = 1$) and t is the *tf-idf* value (Raghavan and Wong 1986) of the corresponding word i (of the distinct t terms extracted from all the WordNet senses plus all query terms in the vicinity V_t of t), extracted from the related WordNet senses or a query term in the V_t of t. The calculation of w_i of a term i is:

$$w_i = tf_i * idf_i$$

$$idf_i = \log_2 \frac{N}{n_i}$$

where tf_i (term frequency) is the number of times that term i appears in a particular document (query or WordNet sense), idf_i (inverse document frequency) is the inverse of the percentage of documents that contain the word i, N is the total number of documents, and n_i is the number of documents that contain the word i at least once. The major advantage of using the *tf-idf* technique is that it identifies and promotes terms that are discriminative for documents in the corpus. The word weight gives prominence to the words closely related to the specific documents.

It must be pointed out that in WordNet utilization, the intended meaning of a term *t* is computed using VSM against all available senses (S_1, S_2,..., S_m) of the corresponding WordNet entry. Terms are extracted from a WordNet sense *S* using (1) words that label the sense, (2) a natural language description of the sense (the "gloss"), and (3) all direct hypernyms and hyponyms of *S*.

Tokenization, stemming, and elimination of stop words are performed on the set of extracted terms. The mapping of a query term to a document (sense in WordNet or a set of concept names, labels, or comments in a reference ontology) is computed by measuring the distance between the query vector *q* and each document vector. The result is a ranked list of documents. The document with the highest cosine coefficient similarity (Salton and McGill 1983) represents the user-intended meaning of term *t*. The cosine coefficient similarity between two vectors $w_i = (w_{i1}, w_{i2}, ..., w_{iT})$ and $w_j = (w_{j1}, w_{j2}, ..., w_{jT})$ is defined as follows:

$$Sim\left(w_i, w_j\right) = \frac{\sum_{k=1}^{T} w_{ik} w_{jk}}{\sqrt{\sum_{k=1}^{T} (w_{ik})^2 * \sum_{k=1}^{T} (w_{jk})^2}}$$

The steps for mapping a query term to a WordNet sense using VSM are shown in Figure 7.2.

Consider the following example query: *play theater mystery*. A human could guess that the user-intended meaning of *play* is captured by the WordNet sense as *play, drama, dramatic play—(a dramatic work intended for performance by actors on a stage; he wrote several plays but only one was produced on Broadway)*. The VSM-based disambiguation method can also guess the intended meaning of *play* by automatically generating the mapping of the term to the corresponding WordNet sense. The remaining terms are also correctly mapped to the appropriate WordNet senses. *Theater* is mapped to *dramaturgy, dramatic art, dramatics, theater, theatre—(the art of writing and producing plays* and *mystery* to *mystery, mystery story, whodunit—(a story about a crime (usually murder) presented as a novel or play or movie)*. The

---

1. Choose a term for query string. Let *t* be the term name.
2. Lexicalize all WordNet senses S_1, S_2, ... S_m, by *t*.
3. Compile direct hyperonyms and hyponyms of all *t* senses.
4. For each WordNet sense S_1, S_2 ... S_m, create a corresponding document based on the *VSM*.
5. Build a document for query term *t* using all terms in the query string (*t* and its *vicinity* V_t) based on the *VSM*.
6. Find the ranked associations between the query document of term *t* and documents representing WordNet senses of *t*. Consider the association with the highest cosine coefficient similarity.

Figure 7.2   The steps for computing the mapping of a term to a WordNet sense.

WordNet 2.0 version exploited in this experiment provided 57 senses for *play*, 2 for *mystery*, and 3 for *theater*.

For a *play a role in theatre* query, for instance, the *play* term has a different meaning from the example above—*playing a role in a theatrical play*. The newly introduced *role* term in the freely formed string has four different senses in WordNet. The system correctly uncovers the intended meaning of this term and maps the *play* term to the WordNet sense: *act, play, represent—(play a role or part; Gielgud played Hamlet; She wants to act Lady Macbeth, but she is too young for the role; She played the servant to her husband's master)*. The *theatre* term has the same meaning as in the previous example, while *role* is correctly mapped to *character, role, theatrical role, part, persona—(an actor's portrayal of someone in a play; She played the part of Desdemona)*.

7.3.1.2 Construction of Query Ontology

After terms are mapped to WordNet senses (their intended meanings), RDF triples that comprise concepts and relations between them can be generated. For each query term of the *play a role in theatre* query mapped to a WordNet sense, the following constructing rules are applied:

■ A concept lexicalized by the word that labels the corresponding WordNet sense is created. For instance, the assessed sense of the *theatre* term is labeled as *dramaturgy*. As a result, a concept labeled *dramaturgy* is created (Figure 7.3).
■ If more than one word labels the lexicon entry, a new concept, lexicalized by the corresponding word, is created for each word. All generated concepts are marked as equivalent because all the terms labeling the corresponding WordNet senses are synonyms. The mapped sense of the *theater* term contains

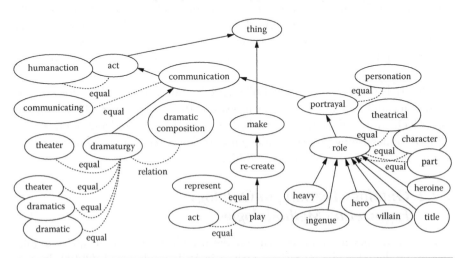

Figure 7.3 Part of the query-ontology for "play a role in theater" query.

four synonyms, namely *dramaturgy, dramatic art, dramatics,* and *theatre.* As depicted in Figure 7.3, four equivalent concepts are introduced.

■ For all WordNet hyperonyms (hyponyms), super-concepts (respectively, sub-concepts) of the corresponding concept that represents this particular sense are created, according to the previous rules. The resulting taxonomy for the *play a role in theatre* query is depicted in Figure 7.3. In this implementation, two levels of hypernyms and hyponyms are exploited—not only the direct ones. Thus, constructed ontology includes more concepts and as a result leads to better performance of the implemented system.

■ If two different query terms are mapped to the same WordNet sense, the sense constitutes their common intended meaning and is represented in the query ontology by a single concept. Moreover, if hypernyms (or hyponyms) of two different query terms happen to be the same, the concept created for this sense corresponds to the same concept in the created taxonomy. For example, as in Figure 7.3, *communication* is the hypernym of both *dramaturgy* (representing *theater*) and *character* (representing *role*) in the WordNet taxonomy. As a result, this is a super-concept of both corresponding concepts in the generated ontology.

■ Other kinds of semantic relations between WordNet senses (meronyms and holonyms) are represented by means of a generic property lexicalized by *relation.* For example, the assessed sense of the *theater* term has a single direct meronym: *dramatic composition, dramatic work(a play for performance on the stage or television or in a movie, etc.).* In this case, a concept representing this sense is created based on the previous rules. This sense is related with *theater* through a *relation* as depicted in Figure 7.3. In this example, the *theater* term has no holonyms.

The output of this step is a set of concepts and their relations in the form of triples following the RDF(S) specifications. For the *play a role in theatre* example query, a fragment of the output triples is shown (using space as separator between triple elements) in Table 7.1. Figure 7.4 illustrates part of the query ontology for a *play theatre mystery* query.

The triple syntax follows the RDF(S) specification (Beckett 2004) for transformation into an OWL query ontology in a straightforward manner. OWL builds on top of RDF and RDF Schema (Patel-Schneider et al. 2004) and adds more expressiveness for describing properties and concepts. For a detailed presentation, see the related article by Spiliopoulos et al. (2008).

7.3.2 Ontology Learning in Ontology Engineering Methodologies

This method does not aim to focus on the usefulness of kick-off query ontologies in ontology-based applications such as in Spiliopoulos et al. (2008). In contrast to related approaches, our method is intended show that query logs, when

Table 7.1   RDF Triples Representation of Constructed Query Ontology for *Play a Role in Theater* Query

<dramaturgy rdf:type owl:Class>

<dramatic_art rdf:type owl:Class>

<dramaturgy owl:equivalentClass dramatic_art>

<dramaturgy owl:equivalentClass dramatics >

<communication rdf:type owl:Class>

<dramaturgy rdfs:subclassOf communication>

<stage rdfs:subclassOf dramaturgy>

<relation rdf:type owl:objectProperty>

<relation rdfs:domain dramaturgy>

<relation rdfs:range dramatic_composition>

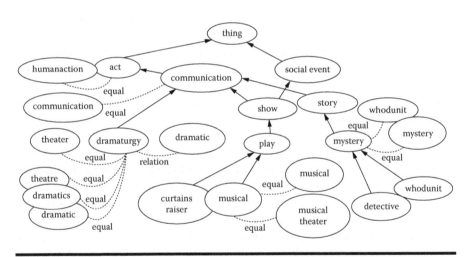

Figure 7.4   Part of the query-ontology for "play theater mystery" query.

combined with general lexicons or other external knowledge resources, can be used to automatically learn both lightweight ontologies and rich ontologies that are useful in the kick-off phase of the development lifecycle of a collaborative and human-centered ontology engineering methodology for devising evolving ontologies. An empirical evaluation (user interviews, questionnaires, usability testing) of the approach that engages end users provides preliminary evidence. This section presents a method that learns kick-off ontologies with richer semantics and vocabulary than the lightweight versions of related approaches (disjoint axioms, equivalent classes and individuals) and extends the method of Spiliopoulos et al. (2008) in the following ways:

1. It deals with the mining of a set of queries, not of a single one, that is automatically clustered from a query log to develop a single kick-off query-ontology.
2. The learned ontology is richer in terms of semantics (disjoint classes, individuals, synonyms).
3. A different vector-based space model method is used in the disambiguation of query terms, due to the utilization of more than one query in the computation of the vicinity of query terms ("bag of words" used with latent semantic indexing to map query terms to WordNet senses).

An approach for mining domain-specific queries for learning useful kick-off query ontologies is presented. The approach meets the following specific requirements:

■ Learn kick-off domain ontologies to advance Semantic Web content creation, integrating ontology-learning-related tasks in HCOME O.E methodology.
■ Learn such ontologies from domain-specific query logs. The approach can take input of query logs from the open Web, e.g., search engine query logs because a preprocessing step is performed to classify queries in domain-specific query sets (clustering method).
■ Learn semantically rich ontologies using semantics extracted from external sources such as lexicons.
■ Automate the learning process.

Query logs reflect knowledge workers' domain-specific search interests. Knowledge workers query information spaces, searching for domain-related information. Such queries are recorded in logs, usually without linking them to meta information concerning the precision and recall of the returned information. A query log may contain queries made in different forms in the past and also may contain queries from different knowledge workers.

The first step of the proposed method is to analyze the query set and identify the terms that occur more than once. In addition, the neighbors of each term (the *vicinity*) of every query are identified. Stop words are excluded from the vicinities of the terms. Such information is needed for the disambiguation of terms using latent semantic indexing to map key terms to WordNet senses (Kotis et al. 2006). The analysis of a domain-specific query log is based on the assumption that all queries are related to a unique domain and thus their terms should be somehow related to each other. We conjecture that such a domain-related relation is present between terms of an individual query and also between terms of every query of a particular domain-specific query log. Formally, the vicinity of each query term is computed as follows:

For a term t_i that occurs only in one query $q_j = \{t_1, t_2, ..., t_k\}$ of the query set $Q = \{q_1, q_2, ..., q_n\}$, the vicinity V_{ti} of t_i comprises the remaining terms of q_j, i.e., $V_{t_i} = q_j \setminus \{t_i\}$.

For a term t that occurs in more than one query (an *important* term), its vicinity V_t comprises the remaining terms of all queries in which the important term is contained, i.e., $V_t = \bigcup_{t \in q_j} q_j \setminus \{t\}$.

LSI maps bags of query terms to WordNet synsets, thus computing a mapping between each term and a "hidden intermediate" ontology (Kotis et al. 2006b). This mapping by LSI assumes an underlying latent semantic space that it estimates by means of statistical techniques using an association matrix ($n \times m$) of terms and documents: Documents in our case correspond to WordNet senses. The use of a latent semantic space helps deal with problems of imprecise and vague query descriptions, as well as cases of polysymy and synonymy that other traditional techniques such as vector space models (VSMs) cannot handle.

LSI is implemented via latent semantic analysis (LSA) that computes the arrangement of a k-dimensional semantic space to reflect the major associative patterns in the data by deriving a set of k uncorrelated indexing factors. Then each term and document is represented by its vector of factor values, indicating its strength of association with each of the underlying latent concepts. By virtue of dimension reduction from the N terms space to the k factors space, where $k < N$, terms that did not appear in a document may still end up near the document, if this is consistent with the major patterns of association in the data.

The second step of the proposed ontology learning is to identify the part of speech (POS) for each query term of each query, using a general POS tagging algorithm such as the Stanford tagger.* Future work on this step will focus on alternative techniques to POS identification to avoid incorrect tagging due to tagger inability to perform well with very small queries (information absence). This step identifies mainly nouns, verbs, and adjectives in order to apply simple heuristics, e.g., for the identification of object properties.

The third step is the core of the proposed approach, since it takes as input the first and second step and a mapping method to assign WordNet senses to query terms, and returns in the output a set of semantically related query terms. The output of this step is used by an ontology construction module to transform such information into a W3C standard formalism such as OWL (Web Ontology Language). Figure 7.5 presents the algorithm for the main (WordNet-based) functionality of the proposed approach. The algorithm currently discovers subsumption, synonym, and disjoint relations among query terms (using WordNet Hypernym/Hyponym, Synonym and Antonym relative semantic relations between senses). Individual objects are also discovered using WordNet API† provided functionality.

---

* http://nlp.stanford.edu/software/tagger.shtml
† http://lyle.smu.edu/cse/dbgroup/sw/jaws.htm

```
 1. Perform query set pre-processing
 2. For each query q
 3.  For each query term t
 4.  POS tag t
 5.   Disambiguate t using neighbor terms of queries that include t
 6.    Occurrence: return the mapped WordNet sense s
 7. If t POS is Noun
 8. If s is Instance
 9.  Find WordNet hypernym ch for concept
10.  Add ch in ontology
11.   Add s in ontology as individual of class ch
12. End if
13. Else (*s is a class*)
14.  Add s in ontology as a class
15.  Add synonyms of s as label of class
16.  Add hypernyms up to depth UPPER_DEPTH (> = 0)
17.  Add hyponyms up to depth LOWER_DEPTH (> = 0)
18. Else if t.POS is Verb
19. Add s in ontology as class
20.  Add synonyms s as label of class
21.  Add antonyms of s as disjoint class
22.  Add hypernyms up to depth UPPER_DEPTH (> = 0)
23. End if
24. End for
25. End for
```

Figure 7.5 Algorithm for the main (WordNet-based) functionality of the proposed approach.

Note that the learned ontology is not just a projection of a WordNet terminological subset, although it is heavily dependent on it since non-WordNet terms are also handled by the method (not depicted in the Figure 7.5 algorithm). Such terms may be single (no entries in WordNet) and compound. For instance, a query term lexicalized by the *ecology-car* is transformed by the proposed algorithm to an *ecology-car* class under an introduced *car* class. Furthermore, an introduced *ecology* class will be related with the *ecology-car* class via a *related_to* generic role. Different forms of compound terms are also handled by the algorithm, using heuristic rules. For instance, terms *ecology car, ecology-car,* and *ecologyCar* are also identified equally as compound terms.

Finally, in extension to other approaches (Spiliopoulos et al. 2008; Cimiano et al. 2007), the constructed ontology utilizes a set of queries (a domain-specific subset of a query log) and the interrelation of their terms to learn a single ontology (many queries to one ontology mapping, *m*:1). Another extension for future work is learning of a kick-off ontology for a single query (one query to one ontology mapping, 1:1) using *however* terms from other *related* queries of the domain-specific subset of the log to which the query belongs. For a detailed presentation of the method, the reader should obtain a copy of the related articles (Kotis and Papasalouros 2010; Kotis et al. forthcoming).

7.3.3 Ontology Learning and HCOME

This section presents an ontology learning approach that tackles the bottleneck in semantic content creation by integrating tasks related to ontology learning in the ontology development lifecycle of HCOME methodology. Viewing the approach in the context of the specific ontology engineering (OE) methodology, it should advance the potential of consulting or reusing automatically learned formal conceptualizations of domain knowledge. Specifically, the aim is to expand the HCOME methodology by incorporating an ontology learning task to boost the human-centered collaborative ontology engineering. The ontology learning-related tasks that extend HCOME methodology are presented below.

During the HCOME specification phase, knowledge workers and engineers join groups concerned with developing agreed-upon ontologies. As a group of collaborators during this initial phase, they discuss requirements, produce specification documents, and agree on the aim and the scope of the new ontology. (Note: learning tasks are presented in the lists of tasks using italics). Such tasks are integrated in the corresponding phases of the ontology engineering lifecycle, from specification to exploitation.

The specification phase of the ontology lifecycle is performed conversationally in a shared space and includes:

1. Specifying the scope and aim(s) of the ontology. This is essential to give participants an agreed initial reference of the way they understand the domain and the way they want initially to model it according to their information needs.
2. Argumentation dialogue among members of the group to determine commonly agreed-upon specification requirements.
3. Recording the agreed specifications in appropriate forms and/or documents.
4. *Specification of the information sources that will be used to learn a kick-off ontology (e.g., a set of queries).*

After agreeing on the scope and aim of the ontology to be developed, workers and engineers in their personal spaces can follow any approach or combination of approaches to ontology development. They may improvise by integrating new concepts, learn a kick-off ontology from their queries, provide concepts with informal definitions, and compare, merge and refine, and/or generalize existing ontologies. Since the consultation of other well known or widely acknowledged resources is critical to ontology development, the collaborators may perform this task before sharing their conceptualizations. Collaborators should be able to create, store, maintain, compare, merge, and manage different versions of ontologies or the learned kick-off ontology. The conceptualization phase includes the following tasks:

1. Importing existing ontologies for the reuse of conceptualizations.
2. Consultation of generic top ontologies, thesauri, and domain resources for better understanding and clarification of the domain conceptualizations.

3. From-scratch development of formal ontologies based on participants' perceptions of the domain.
4. Mapping, merging, and management of multiple versions of ontologies, supporting reuse and evolution.
5. Comparison of different versions of an ontology for inspecting their evolutions and identifying ontologies that can possibly be merged.
6. Attaching information items with further comments, examples, and specification details to ontology class and property information.
7. *The learning of kick-off ontologies from information sources (e.g. queries).*
8. The consultation of a kick-off ontology during a process of improvising an ontology from scratch.
9. The reuse of a kick-off ontology in a process of developing an ontology (merger with another ontology).
10. The comparison of a kick-off ontology with an improvised ontology, reusing (copying) parts of it.

According to HCOME, the need to achieve a common understanding of a domain inevitably pushes ontologies developed in personal spaces to the shared space. Shared ontologies can be used within participants' settings, in the context of specific ontology-driven applications and tasks to be exploited and evaluated conversationally. The exploitation and assessment of an ontology version developed by colleagues is seen as part of the ontology lifecycle, since it may provide feedback on the conceptualizations developed. The evaluation and further development of personal ontologies and a kick-off ontology is achieved via structured conversation and criticism of ontology versions posted in the shared space. The recording of such conversations enables the tracking of changes and rationales behind ontology versions, supporting the decisions on conceptualizing the domain in the final ontology. The exploitation phase includes:

1. Inspection of agreed-upon or shared ontologies by individuals in their personal spaces or by collaborators in the shared space for reviewing, evaluating, and criticizing the specified conceptualizations.
2. Comparison of shared versions of an ontology, for identifying their differences or comparing the kick-off ontology with its revisions.
3. Posting of arguments about versions of ontologies to support decisions for or against specifications.
4. *Browsing and exploitation of the learned ontology, bringing forward kick-off conceptualizations for evaluation.*

In conclusion, HCOME has been extended by new tasks related to the learning of kick-off ontologies from information sources. The approach effectively supports the active and extensive involvement of humans in the development of domain ontologies by automatically learning kick-off ontologies within an ontology development lifecycle. The approach extends the HCOME ontology engineering methodology (and any other OE methodology that lacks such a task) by adding ontology-learning-related tasks. This approach can be used in large-scale and open environments such as the Web, with an unsupervised and automated process of learning domain ontologies. The learned ontologies can represent rich conceptualizations of a domain, forming expressive and consistent OWL ontologies. Ontologies created from such an approach should be further evaluated and evolved, placing them in an OE methodology, before they can be used in real Web applications.

7.3.4 Related Work

In Sekine and Suzuki (2007), a list of predefined name entities (NEs) is matched against the query logs and frequencies are counted to identify typical contexts of NE categories. For instance, typical contexts identified for an *awards* category include *winners, history,* and *nominations* since *academic + awards + winners, academic + awards + history,* and *academic + awards + nominations* queries appeared in the query logs 86, 76, and 74 times, respectively. A co-occurrence normalization formula is used to penalize frequent contexts for each category appearing very often. The approach, although proposed for the acquisition of ontological knowledge, does not focus on issues related to the automatic learning of ontologies. Evaluation of the approach was extensive, but the usefulness of the learned ontologies in an ontology development lifecycle or in ontology-based applications was not reported; no evaluations of the learned ontology against a gold ontology were reported.

Another related work concerns the mining of query logs to assist ontology learning from relational databases (Zhang et al. 2006). The novelty is that this approach expands the ontology to a lower level by exploiting data dimensions. Consider an example database. If a query to the *person* table with a *where* clause *equals age > 60 and gender = male* is frequently executed by a user, one may agree that an *elder man* concept should become a subconcept of *person*. Additionally, the approach proposes a set of rules for schema extraction that provides initial input. Formal concept analysis (FCA) is used to build the concept hierarchy semi-automatically. The approach depends heavily on schema extracted from the database since it is used as input in the mining of the query log. Constructed hierarchies are evaluated manually. More importantly, the usefulness of the learned ontologies is not measured in terms of evaluating them in an ontology development lifecycle or in an ontology-based application.

In Gulla et al. (2007), an unsupervised key phrase extraction system is used to accelerate the construction of search ontologies. The extracted key phrases serve as concept candidates in the ontology and indicate how hierarchical relations should be defined. The candidate phrases were weighted using the term frequency *tf.idf* measure used in information retrieval. This is a lightweight ontology learning approach, addressing the problem of searching in an adequate manner. The learned ontologies are verified manually by domain experts and concepts are related to each other with various hierarchical and associative relationships appropriately (manual work is needed to complete the hierarchies and possibly add more abstract concepts that link components in complete ontologies). Evaluation of the usefulness of the learned ontologies in an ontology development lifecycle or in ontology-based applications is not reported.

Park et al. (2003) reported a method for building ontologies on demand from scientific queries by applying text mining technologies. The method induces ontological concepts and relationships relevant to queries by analyzing search result documents and domain-specific knowledge sources on the Web. The system processes documents returned by a search engine to find terms semantically related to the target query. It also identifies the relationships in which they participate. The ontology constructed is lightweight because it defines only the concepts represented by the query terms. The approach is heavily based on the analysis of the returned documents, even if they are returned incorrectly by the search engine. Furthermore, the constructed ontology does not utilize a set of queries and the interrelation of their terms; it formalizes a single query using information only from the query (not from the query set).

In ORAKEL, Cimiano et al. (2007) followed a similar approach. However, a target corpus must be available to construct custom lexicons to assist the learning methods of lightweight ontologies. Furthermore, the constructed ontology does not utilize a set of queries and the interrelation of their terms.

Finally, related work concerning the learning of ontologies directly from text corpora (Cimiano et al. 2006; Zavitsanos et al. 2008) and semantically enriching tag clouds of Web 2.0 information resources (Angeletou 2008) is acknowledged. Such efforts, although related to the ontology learning problem, do not report on the utilization (mining) of query logs, and the learned ontologies do not include additional input data semantics (semantics extracted from external knowledge sources such as lexicons, e.g., synonyms, antonyms, meronyms). Thus they cannot be considered as rich as the kick-off query-ontologies learned from the proposed approach.

7.3.5 Evaluation of Learning Methods

7.3.5.1 Evaluation of Learning Ontologies in Ontology Development Lifecycle

An empirical method to evaluate ontologies learned from a learning method that aims to advance the development of ontologies by assisting ontology developers in the kick-off phase of an ontology development lifecycle means putting these learned kick-off ontologies into the ontology development lifecycles of selected users. Users with different experiences and roles (knowledge workers and knowledge engineers) should be asked to assess the qualities of the ontologies—how well they reflect the domain of the query set and how consistent the formal conceptualizations are. More important, they should be asked to assess the usability of the learned kick-off ontologies. To do so, they should be provided with both the learned ontology and the data (query set in this case) from which the ontologies have learned.

Our recent work (Kotis and Papasalouros 2010; Kotis et al. forthcoming) involved two domains (Automobile and Movies)—we had no particular reason for selecting them. Four ontology–query set pairs with a variety of lengths (query numbers and numbers of learned ontology elements or axioms) were put in the HCOME ontology development lifecycle as kick-off ontologies. The feedback from this evaluation process was obtained by personal interviews and via questionnaires. The evaluators were Web users who had academic training in ontology engineering and were familiar with the HCOME methodology and with ontology development tools such as Protégé and HCONE. The evaluators received questionnaires and related materials (learned ontologies and query sets of Yahoo! and Google). Questions were in three-level Likert scale form with high, medium, and low options. Qualitative and quantitative examinations of the completed questionnaires can be summarized as follows.

- All evaluators considered the contribution of a kick-off ontology of high (four of eight users) or medium (four of eight users) importance. Furthermore, 75% (6) of the evaluators usually use a kick-off ontology mainly to compare it with their own ontologies, copy parts of it in their own ontologies, and use it as a consultation for constructing their own ontologies; they find kick-off ontologies useful in the ontology development process.
- When questioned about the usefulness of query ontologies in ontology-based applications, five of eight evaluators reported that using these ontologies to annotate documents to be queried was of high usefulness; five of eight (62.5%) reported that using ontologies to reformulate and/or enrich queries to retrieve information was also highly useful. In aggregate, 47% found query kick-off ontologies of high usefulness; 44% considered them of medium usefulness; only 11% did not find them useful.
- Most evaluators found medium utility in a large a kick-off ontology based on queries. This implies a trade-off between the extent and depth of a kick-off ontology and the capability of the knowledge engineer to handle the volume of an extended ontology. Concerning sample ontologies in the domains of Automobiles and Movies, most evaluators found them highly useful for comparison with the ontologies they were developing and for copying parts into their own ontologies. To summarize, evaluators, playing the roles of both knowledge engineer and knowledge worker found kick-off ontologies useful in principle. They also found the particular ontologies created by query logs useful to the same extent. Large sizes of kick-off ontologies seemed to obstruct ease of use.

7.3.5.2 Evaluation of Learned Ontologies with Gold Ontology

A popular way to evaluate learned ontologies is to compare their similarities with those of gold ontologies. Several evaluation approaches have been proposed to achieve this goal (Dellschaft and Staab 2006; Zavitsanos et al. 2008). This section covers the method used by Kotis and Papasalouros (2010) and (Kotis et al. (forthcoming) to evaluate learned ontologies by using Dellschaft and Staab's approach (2006) and reusing OntoEval* due to its simplicity.

The approach takes two ontologies defined in OWL formats as inputs, one of which is assumed the gold standard (reference) ontology and the other as the machine-computed ontology; evaluation is performed by computing measures such as Lexical Precision (LP), Lexical Recall (LR), Taxonomic Precision (TP), Taxonomic Recall (TR), and F-Measure (TF). We conjecture that any other state-of-the-art automated evaluation method could be used if the inputs of the method are a gold ontology and a learned one. Also, any automated ontology mapping method could likely be used to discover alignments between the learned and gold ontologies, uncovering lexical and semantic similarities between the two ontologies.

7.3.5.3 Evaluation of Learned Ontologies in Application Setting

A more concrete way to evaluate learned ontologies is to actually use them in the application in which they were to be used and examine their effectiveness in the application setting. Examples of such application settings include ontology-based search, Semantic Web search, and semantic annotation of data. The next section discusses the evaluation of learned ontologies from free-form queries with the aim of retrieving Semantic Web documents in a more accurate manner.

A number of versions of the ontology learning method presented in Spiliopoulos et al. (2008) were evaluated in an application setting. More specifically, the ontologies learned from free-form queries ("query ontologies") were used to retrieve Semantic Web documents (SWDs or OWL ontologies) indexed by the Swoogle semantic search engine. An OAEI contest-evaluated ontology mapping tool known as AUTOMS[†] was used to match the query ontologies with the SWDs. The retrieved and ranked SWDs used in the experiments indicated that a high percentage of the intended meanings of the initial NL queries were uncovered correctly and reflected in the query ontologies. However, such an evaluation was influenced by the precision performance of the ontology mapping tool and also by the expressiveness of the SWDs. The evaluated approach was tested for single queries, one at a time. Further experimentation must be conducted, for example, learning a kick-off ontology for a single query, using for disambiguation purposes terms from other related queries of the domain-specific subset of the log to which the query belongs. Finally, since the latest tools discover mappings between subsumed and/or disjoint classes of two ontologies, and such semantic relations are learned in the kick-off ontologies of the presented approach, additional experiments must be conducted with alternatives to AUTOMS tools.

---

* http://nlp.shef.ac.uk/abraxas/onteval.html
† www.dit.unitn.it/~p2p/OM-2006/8-automs-OAEI'06.pdf

The application-based evaluation method and the effectiveness of the presented ontology learning method have proven highly effective (Spiliopoulos et al. 2008). The re-ranking of the Swoogle* search engine's returned SWDs due to semantic mappings between the query ontology and classes of SWDs was closer to the intended meaning of the NL query.

7.4 Lessons Learned

The tight integration of an ontology learning task to OE methodologies is recognized by the research community as a very important challenge for ontology engineering and evaluation. Investment is crucial for the development of new ontology engineering methodologies able to integrate the results of ontology learning systems in the OE process, keeping user involvement at a minimum level while maximizing ontology quality with respect to a particular domain (Cimiano et al. 2006). The integration of an ontology learning task with OE methodologies serves as a mean for manually evaluating the ontology learning results (iteratively or stage by stage) and avoiding propagation of errors.

Based on the knowledge captured to date in the ontology learning field, to create ontologies of sufficient conceptual precision and rich semantics, ontology learning results should be further engineered by other OE methodology phases (development, evaluation, maintenance) and should consider various requirement specifications. Learned ontologies may also be used within the development and maintenance phase for extending existing domain ontologies (consulting, comparing, merging tasks).

We suggest that the effectiveness of an ontology learning method, and consequently the quality of learned ontologies, is influenced by the nature of the queries. Querying is about following syntactic rules to form a query and also about following logical rules related to the way humans express the intended meaning of a query and the disambiguation of vague meanings. For instance, the query *brakes auto repair instructions* follows some syntactic method allowing automated taggers to identify POS, the *auto* term is ambiguous (especially when used just before *repair*) since it may not be automatically related to the intended meaning of *car brakes repair instructions*. Another logical interpretation could be *instructions for automatic repair of brakes* where *brakes* can be intentionally related to *airplane brakes* instead of *car brakes*. Although the methods presented here are aware of this problem, certain limitations remain to be overcome.

Incorrect POS tagging is frequent due to the inability of taggers to perform well with very weak input data (few-terms queries) due to lack of information. This problem arises from both tagger performance and tagging strategy in general.

---

* http://swoogle.umbc.edu/

Future work should involve the experimentation with alternative algorithms that utilize information externally—not in queries but in corpora related to them.

WordNet-based disambiguation of terms using vector-based analysis methods (VSM, LSI) is a promising method used recently in many lines of related research. However, its dependence on a specific lexicon may lead to incorrect results due to absence of information. Although non-WordNet terms may be handled by the proposed approaches via specifications in the learned ontology, the validation of the intended meanings of these terms is left to humans.

Other limitations of the proposed approach relate to the general strategy of the learning method. Learning conceptualizations must not depend heavily on a single external source (currently WordNet). A combination of sources must be utilized and the union of the learned conceptualizations must be eventually specified in the ontology. Such sources are existing ontology repositories or Web thesauri and lexicon documents.

Finally, an open issue in social ontology learning is trust of the learning method. As noted earlier, the automatic learning of social ontologies is a two-dimensional task. The first dimension concerns the automatic creation of ontologies from content (social or domain-specific), and the second or social dimension concerns collaboration and communication aspects (*social fermentation*) arising during the creation of the content. Since automation is involved and humans cannot be involved in the agreement process, the key issue is how much to trust or not trust the ontological agreement extracted from social data to ensure that contributors of shared conceptualizations about a specific domain have already agreed on a common understanding about the domain and that such agreement is successfully extracted in an automated fashion from social data (in an open Web agents' world where agents must trust each others' conceptualizations about the domain of discourse in order to collaborate within an agreed context). Blogs, wikis, folksonomies, and other sophisticated Web 2.0 applications such as Yahoo!Answers* and Fixya[†] provide reputation-based trust (using personal experience or the experiences of others, possibly combined, to make a trusted decision about an entity) or voting mechanisms for their content. Other types of content such as Web users' query logs provide a measure of trust of content based on majority votes of user clicks on Web search results.

7.5 Future Directions

Future research work on social ontology learning methods should integrate new or extended techniques for overcoming the limitations discussed above. In addition, research should be directed toward implementing methods that utilize the theory

---

* http://answers.yahoo.com/
[†] http://www.fixya.com/

of Hearst patterns applied on Wikipedia and Wiktionary information resources to extract semantics that will eventually enrich kick-off ontologies. The unions or other kinds of operators (e.g., geometric mean) of WordNet-extracted semantics and semantics extracted from this future implementation should be also examined.

Furthermore, experimentation with other types of input data as alternatives to the approaches presented in this chapter should be conducted. Extending the work conducted using query logs as inputs to an ontology learning process as a future direction is proposed in this chapter, with the aim of learning social ontologies from Web 2.0 content. Such social content was created by the Yahoo!Answers community. Yahoo!Answers (http://answers.yahoo.com/) is a shared place where people collaborate and communicate by asking and answering questions on any topic. The aim of such social fermentation is to build an open and commonly agreed knowledge base for the benefit of the community. Organized in topics (simple thematic category hierarchy), questions are posted by the users of the social network who expect several answers that will eventually satisfy their knowledge acquisition needs. A voting for the best answer mechanism ensures that agreed-upon (by the majority) and trusted (by the number of "for" voters) answers relate to their questions.

Professional knowledge can also be shared within the community by knowledge partners. Such knowledge supplements the answers received from the community by answering questions in a specialized field, drawing on partners' training, their professional experiences, and other appropriate resources. As a benefit, knowledge partners may mention their products or services if relevant in answers, for advertisement reasons. This mutual benefit (for partners and community users) can guarantee a live social network that is viable and can guarantee building of a strong trust of the content shared by both stakeholders. The proposed method, which is still at the design stage, requires two inputs.

Question and answer document—The following information is contained in this document:

1. The topic (and more general categories of the hierarchy) of the question. Topics are predefined by Yahoo!Answers application.
2. User information. Who posted the question? Who posted an answer? Who voted against or for answer mechanisms? As to the question and associated answers in natural language, users can post a title and comment for the question and post only comments for their answers. Other parameters are (a) the best answer and the votes for it; (b) the votes for all other answers; and (c) other resolved or open questions on the same topic.

WordNet lexicon—The lexicon is used to enrich the ontology with additional semantics (entities, semantic relations, individuals). The processing of the method is outlined below. The method builds kick-off RDF triples from the hierarchy of concepts of the predefined hierarchy under which the topic of the posted question is classified.

1. The posted question (both title and comment) is analyzed using an NLP API (GATE* is a first choice) to identify POS and perform tokenization.
2. Since context is known (from Step 1) and text analysis is complete to an extent, important terms can be identified and semantic relations between them can be recognized. Further disambiguation of terms is not needed. Two techniques can be used in combination (a) Hearst patterns and (2) simple heuristic rules that utilize knowledge from the POS tagging.
3. Semantics is enriched using WordNet. Mapping of terms to WordNet senses is performed automatically using statistical techniques from information retrieval to compute latency of terms in term–document spaces (LSI method). To be able to perform this step, an entry of the term must exist in WordNet (latest version for the experiments is 3.0). Mapped senses can be validated automatically since the context of the mapped terms is known from Step 1.
4. Steps 2 to 4 are repeated for the best posted answer. The ontology elements extracted from this step (classes, properties, instances) are assigned an uncertainty value of 1.0 (representing the uncertainty of this element in respect to the community trust of the commonly agreed-upon best answer).
5. Steps 2 to 4 are repeated for the remaining posted answers. To keep the size of the learned ontology small and avoid noise, only important terms must be introduced as classes. The importance of terms is a threshold value that can be empirically set at 2. However, in large-sized answers (more than a single paragraph of text), the threshold must be set higher. Other techniques should be also tested to avoid noise of large answers (to first locate important partitions of the text, applying n-gram analysis for instance, and then extracting important terms). The ontology elements extracted from this step (classes, properties, instances) are assigned uncertainty values between 0 and 0.9.
6. The generated RDF triples from Steps 2 to 6 are transformed into an OWL model. Classification and consistency checking are performed by an OWL reasoner. The development proposed is based on Jena API and Pellet.

The output of the method is a learned ontology with uncertainty weights attached to its elements (classes, properties, instances).

The voting mechanism integrated in Yahoo!Answers and in other Web 2.0 related applications provides social data that can relate content such as a posted answer to other content such as a posted question. This relation can be interpreted as agreement or disagreement based on users' opinions and eventually as a trust value of the shared knowledge is encapsulated in the most agreed-upon opinion (best voted answer). Based on (more or less) trust, the related-to-a-topic knowledge is shaped into a domain ontology in which each element is eventually

---

* http://gate.ac.uk/

associated with an uncertainty value computed directly from social data associated with the represented content. Professional knowledge can also be shared within the community by knowledge partners. Their knowledge supplements the answers received from the community. Since this kind of knowledge is contributed by experts, it can be considered highly trusted. Furthermore, the mutual benefit of knowledge partners and community users (advertisement and expertise knowledge contributions) plays a key role to truth telling in partners' answers in community users' posts. This can guarantee a live social network with strong roots of trust for the content shared by all stakeholders. As to ontology learning from query logs, the proposed ontology learning method can be trusted to a higher degree because its social data is both directly and indirectly associated with that represented in the ontology content.

The content of Yahoo!Answers is similar to the content of query logs in one aspect. Question posts in Yahoo!Answers have a correspondence to Web queries and answer posts correspond to search engine Web pages returned as results. Based on this, the Yahoo!Answers-learned ontologies, reflecting domain-specific search interests as they do in the query logs-based ontology learning method, are good candidates for use in semantic search applications.

In future research work, the definition of $O = \{C, S, A\}$ will be extended by introducing trust T for S and A such as $T = \{u, v_a, v_f\}$ where u is the uncertainty value computed for a given instance of S or A, v_a is the number of votes that do not trust an instance of S or A, and v_f represents the number of votes that do trust an instance of S or A. Contributors C trust or do not trust the learning (and eventually the conceptualization) of a certain class, property, instance (an instance of S is ontology signature), or axiom (an instance of A is ontology axioms) extracted from the contributed content. Although the computation of u (uncertainty value) reflects the trust of S and A for a social network of C contributors, v_a and v_f values reflect the absolute number of agreements between Cs for given S and A. Based on this, the definition of the social ontology is reformulated as $O = \{T, C, S, A\}$ where $T = \{u, v_a, v_f\}$ is the trust function (uncertainty, votes against, votes for) for ontological signature S and axioms A for which a set of collaborated contributors C participated in a task of social content generation (SCG) derived using social intelligence (SI).

7.6 Conclusions

This chapter reports on recently proposed methods for the automated learning of social ontologies—an important ontology engineering task that contributes to the Semantic Web incentive of semantic content creation. Specifically, it discusses automatically learning ontologies from content that is directly or indirectly related to social data, considered as products of social fermentation among users in open, collaborative, and communicative environments. Social fermentation ensures automatic encapsulation of agreement and trust on the shared knowledge of participating stakeholders in the learning process.

The chapter covered recent experiences related to the automated learning of *useful* social ontologies and accentuates the impacts of recently proposed ontology learning methods from queries for dealing with the bottleneck of semantic content creation from an ontology engineering methodological view. It also presented important lessons learned from experimentation with the presented methods and proposes key directions for future research, focusing on the design of new methods that will mainly deal with trust of social ontology learning methods and representing such trust in the learned conceptualizations.

References

Angeletou, S. 2008. Semantic enrichment of folksonomy tag spaces. In *Proceedings of International Semantic Web Conference*, Springer Verlag, Berlin, pp. 889–894.

Beckett, D. 2004. RDF/XML Syntax Specification (Revised), W3C Recommendation. http://www.w3.org/TR/rdf-syntax-grammar/

Cimiano, P., P. Haase, and J. Heizmann. 2007. Porting natural language interfaces between domains: A case study with the ORAKEL system. In *Proceedings of 12th International Conference on Intelligent User Iinterfaces*, ACM Press, New York, pp. 180–189.

Cimiano, P., J. Völker, and R. Studer. 2006. Ontologies on demand: A description of state-of-the-art applications, challenges and trends for ontology learning from text. *Information, Wissenschaft und Praxis*, 57: 315–320.

Dellschaft, K. and S. Staab. 2006. On how to perform a gold standard-based evaluation of ontology learning. In *Proceedings of International Semantic Web Conference*, Springer Verlag, Berlin, pp. 228–241.

Ding L., T. Finin, A. Joshi et al. 2004. Swoogle: A search and metadata engine for the Semantic Web. In *Proceedings of International Conference on Information and Knowledge Management*, ACM Press, New York, pp. 652–659.

Donovan, A. and Y. Gil. 2007. A survey of trust in computer science and the Semantic Web. *Journal of Web Semantics*, 5: 58–71.

Gruber, T. 2007. Ontology of folksonomy: A mash-up of apples and oranges. *International Journal on Semantic Web and Information Systems*, 3: 1–11.

Gulla, J., H. Borch, and J. Ingvaldsen. 2007. Ontology learning for search applications. In *On the Move to Meaningful Internet Systems*, Springer Verlag, Berlin, pp. 1050–1062.

Halevy, A., P. Norvig, and F. Pereira. 2009. The unreasonable effectiveness of data. *IEEE Intelligent Systems*, 24: 8–12.

Han, H. and R. Elmasri. 2003. Ontology extraction and conceptual modeling for web information. *Information Modeling for Internet Applications*, IGI Global, Hershey, PA, pp. 174–188.

Kotis, K., A. Papasalouros, and M. Maragoudakis. 2009a. Mining Web queries to boost semantic content creation. In *Proceedings of IADIS Conference on WWW/Internet*, IADIS Press, pp. 158–162.

Kotis, K., A. Papasalouros, and M. Maragoudakis. 2011. Mining query logs for learning useful ontologies: An incentive to SW content creation. *International Journal for Knowledge Engineering and Data Mining*.

Kotis, K., A. Papasalouros, G. Vouros et al. 2009b. e-Class in ontology engineering: Integrating ontologies to argumentation and semantic wiki technology. Paper presented at Workshop on Intelligent and Innovative Support for Collaborative Learning Activities, May 30, Rhodes, Greece. http://chocolato.org/wiiscola/wp-content/uploads/2009/05/2-e-class-in-ontology-engineering.pdf.

Kotis, K., A. Valarakos, and G. Vouros. 2006a. AUTOMS: Automating ontology mapping through synthesis of methods. In *Ontology Alignment Evaluation Initiative, Ontology Matching International Workshop*, Atlanta, GA.

Kotis, K., G. Vouros, and K. Stergiou. 2006b. Towards automatic merging of domain ontologies: The HCONE merge approach, *Journal of Web Semantics*, 4: 60–79.

Kotis, K. and A. Papasalouros. 2010. Learning useful kick-off ontologies from query logs: HCOME revised. In *Proceedings of Fourth International Conference on Complex, Intelligent and Software Intensive Systems*, IEEE Computer Society, New York, pp. 345–351.

Kotis, K. and G. Vouros. 2006. Towards semantic web document retrieval through ontology mapping: Preliminary results. Paper presented at Workshop on Web Search Technology: from Search to Semantic Search, September 4, Beijing.

Kotis, K. 2008. Semantic Web Search: Perspectives and key technologies. In *Encyclopedia of Data Warehousing and Mining*, Idea Group, pp. 1532–1537.

Lanzenberger, M. et al. 2008. Making ontologies talk: Knowledge interoperability in the Semantic Web. *IEEE Intelligent Systems* 23: 72–85.

Maedche A. and S. Staab. 2001. Ontology learning for the semantic web. *IEEE Intelligent Systems*, 16: 72–79.

Mika P. 2007. Ontologies are us: A unified model of social networks and semantics. *Journal of Web Semantics*, 5: 5–15.

Park, Y., R. Byrd, and B. Boguraev. 2003. Towards ontologies on demand. In *Proceedings of Workshop on Semantic Web Technologies for Scientific Search and Information Retrieval, Second International Semantic Web Conference*. http://sunsite.informatik.rwth-aachen.de/Publications/CEUR-WS//Vol-83/int_3.pdf

Patel-Schneider, P.F., P. Hayes, and I. Horrocks. 2004. OWL Web Ontology Language Semantics and Abstract Syntax. W3C Recommendation. http://www.w3.org/TR/owl-semantics/

Raghavan, V.V. and S.K.M. Wong. 1986. A critical analysis of vector space model for information retrieval. *JASIS*, 37: 279–287.

Salton, G. and M.H. McGill. 1983. *Introduction to Modern Information Retrieval*. McGraw-Hill, New York.

Sekine, S. and H. Suzuki. 2007. Acquiring ontological knowledge from query logs. In *Proceedings of 16th International Conference on World Wide Web*, ACM Press, New York, pp. 1223–1224.

Spiliopoulos, V., K. Kotis, and G. Vouros. 2008. Semantic retrieval and ranking of SW documents using free-form queries. *International Journal of Metadata, Semantics and Ontologies*, 3: 95–108.

Tang J., H. Leung, Q. Luo et al. 2009. Towards ontology learning from folksonomies. In *Proceedings of 21st International Joint Conference on Artificial intelligence*, Morgan Kaufmann, Pasadena, CA, pp. 2089–2094.

Zavitsanos, E., G. Paliouras, and G. Vouros. 2008. A distributional approach to evaluating ontology learning methods using a gold standard. Paper presented at Ontology Learning and Population Workshop, July 22, Patras, Greece.

Zhang, J., M. Xiong, and Y. Yu. 2006. Mining query logs to assist ontology learning from relational database. In *Frontiers of WWW Research and Development*, Springer Verlag, Berlin, pp. 437–448.

Chapter 8

Relation Extraction for Semantic Web with Taxonomic Sequential Patterns

Sebastian Blohm
Universität Karlsruhe, Karlsruhe, Germany

Krisztian Buza and Lars Schmidt-Thieme
Universität Hildesheim, Hildesheim, Germany

Philipp Cimiano
Universität Bielefeld, Bielefeld, Germany

Contents

185

8.1 Introduction

The Semantic Web relies on explicit content captured by means of the RDF(S) and OWL Semantic Web languages. As most of the content (text in particular) available on the Web is still unstructured, effective and efficient techniques are needed to extract and capture the relevant information so that it can be formalized in RDF and/or OWL, thus becoming accessible to the Semantic Web. The data models of the Semantic Web (especially RDF) build on the central notion of a triple of the form (s, p, o) where s is the so-called subject, p the predicate, and o the object. The extraction of binary relations or tuples (s, o) standing in a relation (predicate or property) p is thus a crucial task from a Semantic Web perspective. In this chapter we are concerned with extracting binary relations or tuples from large bodies of textual data.

Many approaches have been presented to deal with this task. On the one hand, we can distinguish discriminative techniques that train a statistical classifier using machine learning techniques to spot mentions of the relation of interest [5,21,22,23,24]. On the other hand, pattern-based approaches that induce and match explicit patterns have also been proposed [4,6,8,15,16,18,10].

Patterns can be understood as constraints on the surface form of a text fragment. We say that a pattern matches a textual fragment if the fragment fulfills all the constraints defined by the pattern. In this work, we follow the pattern-based approach and present a new class Taxonomic Sequential Patterns (TSPs). Patterns can be thought of as simple crisp classifiers that match or do not match a given text fragment. If they match, we can extract the corresponding tuple by way of marked argument positions in the pattern. Clearly, the expressiveness of the pattern class considered determines the performance of a pattern-based approach to relation extraction.

Many pattern-based approaches to relation extraction incorporate some sort of morpho-syntactic or semantic types into the pattern class to yield more general patterns. However, the impact of these features on extraction quality is typically not assessed. We can expect that at least two dimensions of pattern classes have a major impact on extraction performance: (1) the pattern language elements that allow for under-specification (wild card, skip, disjunction) and (2) the set of features (morpho-syntactic, semantic types, etc.) taken into account during pattern matching.

*	*	*	*	*	*	*	*
		noun		*noun*			*noun*
quantifier	*adjective*	*living being*	*other*	*location*	*verb*	*other*	*location*
determiner	*superlative*	*person*	*preposition*	*country*	*stative*	*preposition*	*city*
The	happiest	people	in	Germany	live	in	Osnabrück

Figure 8.1 Example sentence with morpho-syntactic token features. The features for each token are ordered by generality. * denotes the most general constraint, matching everything.

This work constitutes a generalization of approaches that allow integration of a taxonomy of morpho-syntactic and lexico-semantic features directly into the pattern mining process. Figure 8.1 gives an example of a sentence that is indicative of an instance of the *locatedIn* relation along with linguistic information available for each token. The features for each token are ordered by generality, i.e., each column above the surface string of a token corresponds to the token's path in a taxonomy. The topmost row contains for each token the * wild card !!! feature that matches any token. It constitutes the top concept of the taxonomy or, in a constraint view, is the constraint that does not exclude any token.

The goal is to identify for each token in the pattern the right level of detail at which a constraint is added to the pattern. Figure 8.2 illustrates this for the example sentence. The greyed token information will not be part of the pattern. To identify patterns, we present a principled and uniform mining approach based on sound techniques from the area of knowledge discovery and, in particular, frequent sequence mining. More specifically, this chapter makes the following contributions:

■ We introduce Taxonomic Sequential Patterns (TSPs) as generalizations of many pattern classes adopted in the literature. Through this pattern class we can study the effect of taxonomic knowledge on the information extraction task and reproduce many other pattern classes from the literature with which to compare the TSP pattern class. The main question we address in this chapter is whether TSPs are superior to other types of patterns by looking in particular at the precision–recall trade-off.

■ We present a principled mining algorithm as an extension of the well known ECLAT algorithm [13] that allows us to mine taxonomic sequential patterns and all the pattern classes that we directly compare with, e.g., the patterns used in the URES system [18] and a few baseline pattern classes. Such comparisons of performance across different classes do not exist, probably because most mining algorithms are somewhat ad hoc and cannot be directly extended to mine other types of patterns. The mining algorithm we present is principled in the sense that it is complete (guaranteed to find all patterns with a given frequency threshold of occurrence, called *minimum support*)

quantifier determiner	adjective superlative	noun living being person	other preposition	noun location country	verb stative	other preposition	noun location city
*	*	*	*	*	*	*	*
The	happiest	people	in	Germany	live	in	Osnabrück

Figure 8.2 Possible choice of features for pattern from example sentence.

and extensible by making minimal assumptions on the patterns (an order of specificity defined on them).

■ We present results of experiments on four relations for five pattern classes, showing that TSPs perform generally better compared to the URES and other baseline pattern classes.

The chapter is structured as follows. After defining the task addressed in more detail in the following section, we describe the overall settings and workflow of our approach in the process section. We then introduce the pattern class of TSPs. In the section on pattern mining, we describe a novel extension of the well-known ECLAT algorithm that allows efficient mining of TSPs and many of the other pattern classes suggested in the literature. We then present our experimental results, showing the superiority of TSPs in relation to three other pattern classes as baselines. Before concluding, we discuss related work.

8.2 Problem Statement

As noted in the introduction, the basic data units in the Semantic Web are triples of the form $(s, p\ o)$ where s is the so-called subject, p the predicate, and o the object. The extraction of binary relations or tuples (s, o) standing in a relation (predicate or property) p is crucial from a Semantic Web perspective. This chapter is concerned with extracting binary relations or tuples from large bodies of textual data. For example, we want to extract information like *Osnabrück* is located in *Germany* or *Paris* is the capital of *France*. More formally, we can say, that the tuple *(Osnabrück, Germany)* belongs to the extension of the binary relation *locatedIn*. The second tuple *(Paris, France)* is an instance of the relation *capitalOf*. For given relations, we aim to extract all their tuples from large collections of texts.

We define the text formally as follows: given (1) a large collection of texts (e.g., the Web as a whole), (2) a binary relation R between entities mentioned in the texts, and (3) a few given tuples belonging to R (the so-called seeds), the goal is to extract all the tuples of R that occur somewhere in the given collection of texts.

The relation R can be, e.g., *locatedIn* (Figure 8.1), *productOf* (a company), *bornInYear*, etc. We assume that some (few) tuples of R are already known and we want to extract all additional tuples mentioned in a large collection of texts. The goal of our work is not to develop a completely new system, but to analyze the impact of a crucial design choice on pattern-based relation extraction: the pattern class or pattern language that defines which patterns can be expressed. The choice of the pattern class directly determines the search space for patterns and thus clearly has the potential of affecting performance.

We explore one particular type of design choice by analyzing the impact of factoring taxonomic information into the pattern class. We do so by designing a generic pattern class (TSPs) that subsumes many of the pattern classes discussed in the literature and allows us to explore the impact of taxonomic versus non-taxonomic patterns from a general view. While many pattern classes incorporate type information (sense information, semantic or named entity tags, etc.) into the patterns, the positive effects have not been empirically demonstrated. For the sake of simplicity, we assume that all information can be encoded into a single hierarchy—clearly an over-simplification because the hierarchy will then contain classes corresponding to different linguistic levels. This assumption may lead to ad hoc modeling decisions, such as putting the *person* class under the *noun* part of speech in the hierarchy. Nevertheless, this assumption eases the task of mining patterns, as the algorithm must deal with a single taxonomy instead of many.

In many approaches in the literature, the description of the pattern class or language is mixed with the description of the way the patterns are matched and thus takes on a somewhat procedural nature. A declarative description such as we attempt here makes systematic comparison of the features used in different pattern languages easier.

Overall, we are re-examining and substantiating with experimental evidence an assumption that many systems have made: that abstraction with respect to a type system or taxonomy can have a positive effect on extraction performance. In this sense we are contributing to clarification of a fundamental issue that will help designers make more informed decisions about the designs of pattern classes in future work on relation extraction.

While it sounds straightforward that additional information (part of speech or semantic tags) can improve extraction, the result is far from obvious as an adverse effect is possible (compare Figure 8.3). Suppose we are given a simple pattern class that only includes words and (untyped) wild cards. The introduction of a taxonomy could have at least three effects:

1. The integration of type information (by way of a taxonomy of concepts) increases recall (and potentially decreases precision) as concrete tokens in the pattern may be replaced by more generic "types" (*generalization effect*).
2. Gaps or untyped wild cards (tokens in patterns that match arbitrary input tokens) may be replaced by typed gaps or wild cards, thus restricting the

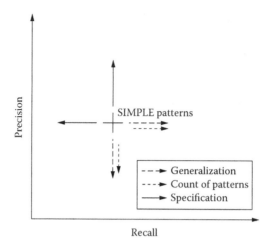

Figure 8.3 **Effects of introduction of a taxonomy into a simple pattern class: concrete words in patterns may be generalized, the count of patterns may increase, wild cards in patterns may be replaced by more specific taxonomical concepts.**

sequences that the pattern matches and potentially increasing precision, but possibly at the expense of a decrease in recall (*specification effect*).

3. The count of patterns (frequent sequences) may change as occurrences that are not frequent per se may become frequent via taxonomic generalization. Recall may yield more patterns at the cost of a possible decrease in precision. (We show an example of this effect in Section 8.6.4.)

Figure 8.3 illustrates case 1 with dashed arrows, case 2 with solid arrows, and case 3 with dotted arrows. These cases constitute classical precision–recall trade-offs, but the crucial question is whether the three effects add up to yield an overall improvement. In particular, as all the three effects produce both positive and negative side-effects, it would certainly be desirable to balance the effects in such a way as to increase both precision and recall. However, whether both precision and recall really improve is not obvious. In fact, this is the question we address in this study.

8.3 Process

In this section, we focus on the pattern mining step, adopting the iterative pipeline depicted in Figure 8.4 that may be considered a generalization of the processing

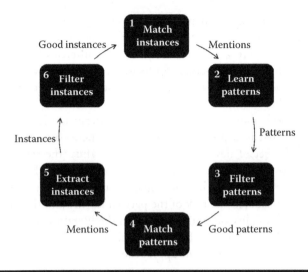

Figure 8.4   Sequence of steps in induction cycle.

adopted in many systems [3,8,15,18]. Intuitively, the iterative induction of extraction patterns can be described as follows:

The process starts with a set of *seed instances* that are known to be correct [*(Hollywood, U.S.),(Osnabrück,Germany),(Nice,France)*] for the *locatedIn* relation. Mentions of these seed instances are detected in the corpus, yielding occurrences such as: *The richest people in the U.S. live in Hollywood, The happiest people in Germany live in Osnabrück*, and *The luckiest people in France work in Nice*, …

The process generalizes these occurrences to patterns that can be matched in text.

The most valuable patterns are filtered based on various performance metrics and will be used later in the process.

The fragments of the texts that match the patterns are found. For example, *The hardest-working researchers in the UK live in Sheffield* fragment is matched by the pattern * * * * * *<country> live in <city>*.

The process finds tuples by matching the patterns, extracting *Sheffield,UK* from *The hardest-working researchers in the UK live in Sheffield*, for example.

Finally, extracted instances are filtered and the process is repeated with the most promising instances.

Figure 8.4 gives an overview of this process divided into six steps. First, the instances are matched in the corpus (1) that as a step produces a set of *instance mentions*. Pattern learning is then applied to yield generic patterns abstracting from single occurrences (2). Patterns, i.e., underspecified generalized descriptions of the mentions, are generated. They are then filtered (3) to yield only patterns that are likely to produce good results when subsequently matched (4). The occurrences matched by the new patterns are processed to extract new tuples (5) that are in turn filtered (6).

According to the above cycle, in each step patterns are learned on the basis of mentions extracted in a previous step. In turn, these patterns are filtered and matched to yield a set of new instance mentions. Thus, the set of patterns and instances co-evolve. This was called *pattern–relation duality* by Brin [4].

It may seem unnecessary to list filtering of patterns and instances as a separate step. It could be considered the task of the pattern learner and the instance extractor to produce high-quality output. However, in the literature, these steps are usually separated as they build on different assumptions and inputs. The separation thus facilitates the comparison of the approaches.

8.4 Taxonomic Sequential Patterns

We introduced TSPs as a generic pattern class allowing the introduction of taxonomic knowledge into patterns. A pattern class in our sense consists of a repertoire of pattern features used to express constraints on the set of sequences the pattern matches. TSPs are sequences consisting of standard tokens together with a *t* set of pattern features that we transfer to frequent sequence mining.

- *Wild cards (ANY)*: A token in the pattern that matches an arbitrary single token in the input sequence.
- *Typed wild cards (ANY[type])*: A token in the pattern that matches any single token of *type* in the input sequence. Most systems use typed wild cards as a way to introduce additional external linguistic knowledge into the mining process, such as part-of-speech (POS) information, named-entity tags, word-sense information, and (shallow) parses. We use typed wild cards to factor in taxonomic information that may be used to constrain the tokens allowed at a certain position via these taxonomic types. As an example, the third column in Figure 8.2 corresponds to *ANY[living being]*.
- *Gaps*: Our patterns allow gaps while matching. Gaps are not specific to a certain position in patterns, but a global property that may or may not be active. Gaps are implemented in our approach through "semi-continuous" patterns allowing drop (leaving unmatched) tokens in the input sequence at arbitrary positions. Semi-continuous patterns may have the same concrete syntax as others but differ in the matching process. We define the class of (d, n)-semi-continuous patterns as those that allow at most during their matching n drop operations, each of them having a maximal length of d

tokens. In its (3, 2)-semi-continuous version, the pattern from Figure 8.2 would also match "The happiest people from Asia in Europe live in big cities like Paris," where the underlined parts represent two gaps with at most three tokens to be left unmatched. This mention would not be matched by the (2, 2) or (3, 1)-semi-continuous version of our pattern class incorporating gaps.

■ *Argument slots* ($ANY[type]_{argn}$): Many systems use special argument slots to actually mark the position where a specific argument of a tuple occurs. We also allow restriction of argument slots to a specific taxonomic type. In the example from Figure 8.2, the fifth column translates into $ANY[country]_{arg2}$. Note that the type for the argument slots, as with typed wild cards, constitutes a constraint on the tokens that can "fill" the respective position. For example, the last token in the example pattern only matches tokens previously recognized as *location*.

■ The line-up of pattern classes we investigated experimentally is depicted in Figure 8.5. Our novel TSP class is tested by way of the two variants designated TAX and TAX-GAP. They both support typed wild cards and typed argument slots. While TAX-GAP allows semi-continuity (we set $d = 1$ and $n = 2$), TAX patterns are continuous in the sense that they do not allow for gaps (but nonetheless do so for typed wild cards). Apart from that, we investigate a SIMPLE pattern class as a baseline, allowing only argument slots and untyped wild cards. We also use the above repertoire of pattern features to reproduce the URES pattern class.* URES patterns feature (typed) argument slots and can contain skips that are marked in the pattern but differ from wild cards in the sense that they consume arbitrary numbers of consecutive tokens.

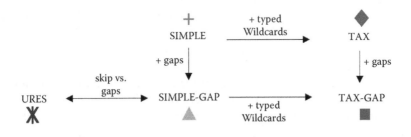

Figure 8.5   Pattern classes considered and their features that differ.

---

* For the sake of generality we do not implement the very specific heuristics implemented in URES (e.g., providing a list of relation-specific and manually selected keywords that increase the probability that a text fragment considered already contains the relation in question) to ensure the generality of our results. We do thus implement the patterns used in URES but do not compare our results with the URES system as a whole with its very proprietary settings.

The taxonomy used for the TAX-GAP class incorporates linguistic information at several levels of abstraction (syntactic and semantic). It comprises information on the part-of-speech level as well as on the named-entity-tag level (assuming that each entity type can be identified with one part of speech which is a slight simplification), and allows for subclass relationships between entity tags (*city* is-a *location*). The taxonomy was constructed specifically for the work described here. The top level consists of generic classes of part-of-speech tags (noun, verb, etc.). Below that, more specific POS tags, WordNet supersense tags, and WSJ tags were manually included (see the section on datasets for more details).

Taxonomic sequential patterns constitute a generalization of various approaches from the literature discussed in the section on related work (in particular *RAPIER* [20], *ExDisco* [25], *Pronto* [3], *KnowItNow* [8], *Espresso* [15], and those used by Ravichandran and Hovy [16]) because they take a more general approach to the integration of background knowledge by using a taxonomy. In this sense, the empirical investigation of TSPs allows us to re-examine the assumption in all of the above works that generalized patterns are useful, grounding it in a series of experiments.

8.5 Pattern Mining

The task of pattern induction is non-trivial from a computational view. By way of example, suppose we are given a dictionary of 5,000 words, and want to explore textual patterns consisting of maximal 10 words. The count of possible simple sequential patterns (without considering wild cards, gaps, etc.) is $\sum_{i=1}^{10} 5000^i \approx 9.76 \times 10^{36}$. In cases of longer or more sophisticated patterns where gaps and taxonomical concepts are allowed, the complexity obviously increases.

Consequently, due to the size of the pattern space, all possible patterns cannot be examined individually. A naive pattern induction strategy (such as that in the URES system) combines pairs of text segments to derive patterns. As a result, it is easy to miss the most valuable patterns, especially in case of more complex patterns, for example, those with taxonomical wild cards and/or gaps, etc. Suppose that we want to induce patterns to learn the relation between persons and the years they were born (*bornInYear*) and are given the following sequences:

i) *J.S.Bach, the famous composer in Europe, was born in March 1685.*
ii) *King Frederick V of Denmark was born in March 1723.*
iii) *King August II of Poland (Europe) was born in 1733.*

Denoting wild cards with *, the possible pair-wise combinations lead to the following patterns:

i + ii) * <arg1> * was born in * March <arg2>
ii + iii)   King <arg1> * of * was born in * <arg2>
i + iii)   * <arg1> * Europe * was born in * <arg2>.

However, if we want to learn the birth years of kings, Europeans, and people born in March, we would need a pattern like *<arg1> * was born in * <arg2>*. This pattern can be induced by taking all the three sentences into account, but not by generalizing occurrences only pair-wise as in URES [18]. In this sense, the mining algorithm implemented in URES is not complete and may miss many useful patterns, thus resulting in lower recall (recall is, however, not reported for URES). In contrast, our approach is complete in the sense that it is guaranteed to find all patterns that match at least m input sequences. It is important to emphasize that our aim is a comparison to the URES pattern class (described by its pattern features cited in the previous section), not to compare the naive pattern mining strategy in URES against complete mining. Thus we mine all pattern classes, including URES, with a complete algorithm.

The basic idea of complete pattern mining algorithms is to organize searches efficiently by exploiting the anti-monotonicity of patterns. On the basis of patterns already found nonfrequent, one infers that all other patterns subsuming these are not frequent either, excluding them from further investigation and thus pruning search space.

In our case, a collection of textual sequences and a minimum support threshold m are inputs, and p is a frequent pattern if the support of p is at least m, i.e., at least m input sequences match p. The task is to find all frequent patterns. Note that the presence of a frequency threshold (support) does not imply that we ignore rare cases. Generalized patterns (such as URES, SIMPLE-GAP, TAX, and TAX-GAP) can be frequent if the identical textual fragment occurs several times and also if similar textual fragments occur several times and can be generalized into a single pattern using the repertoire of the pattern class (wild card, gaps, taxonomic abstraction, etc.).

Although pattern mining, particularly frequent item set mining, is well studied, the mining of taxonomical sequential semicontinuous patterns is almost unstudied. One exception is the work of Buza and Schmidt-Thieme [7], who apply a breadth-first search-like implementation (known as APRIORI). In case of textual data, a depth-first search (DFS) strategy is more efficient compared to APRIORI due to specific characteristics of text extraction that may involve very long patterns. We therefore build on the well-known DFS-based ECLAT [14] and extend it appropriately to mine all the different pattern classes we consider.

Algorithm 1 (below) shows the extended ECLAT in pseudocode. As input, textual sequences (S) and a minimum support threshold (m) are given. Each textual sequence has a unique integer identification (ID). A dictionary D (line 1) contains all the items necessary for the current pattern class (words, argument slots,* taxo-nomical concepts, gaps, etc.). Each item $i \hat{I} D$ is associated with a so called TID-list[†] showing the identifiers of sequences that contain i (line 2). After calling *eclat* initially (line 3) with the empty string as prefix and the list of IDs of all input sequences as TID-list of that prefix, patterns are recursively expanded (lines 5 to 40), as long as their support is not less than m. For p patterns, there are two types of expansion:

- One of the root items in D is concatenated to p (lines 5 to 22). This is justified by the so called antimonotone property of support: if a pattern p is a substring of p', then the support of p is not greater than the support of p', because every sequence matching (containing) p' matches its substring p as well. Thus if p is not frequent, p' can also not be frequent. However, if p is frequent, it is worth checking whether p' is also frequent.
- The last element of p is replaced by one of its direct taxonomic descendants (lines 23 to 40). The rationale behind this expansion is the taxonomic anti-monotone property of support: the support of a pattern $p = (z_1, z_2, ..., z_k, x)$ cannot be less than the support of $p'' = (z_1, z_2, ..., z_k, y)$, where y is a taxo-nomic descendant of x. As in the previous case, if p is frequent, it is worth checking whether p'' is also frequent.

If non-taxonomic patterns are mined, as for URES, SIMPLE, and SIMPLE-GAP, all items in D are considered roots, i.e., only the first type of expansion is performed and it is performed for all items.

When mining set patterns (like bag-of-words patterns), the support of patterns can be determined based on the intersection of TID lists (lines 10 and 27).[‡] This is one of the keys to the efficiency of ECLAT. However, in case of sequential pat-terns, the intersection of TID lists is not sufficient. As the intersection does not consider order, only a superset of the IDs of the sequences matching the pattern is determined. In this sense, the intersection over-generates and some members must be eliminated again later. Thus, an additional support check is necessary (lines 12 to 16 and 29 to 33), but only in the case that the cardinality of the intersection is not less than m.

We measured the time necessary for mining the patterns. For example, on a 2.4 GHz machine for the *productOf* relation (100 mentions) at a minimum support of 5, it took 27 seconds to find all 270,475 patterns using the algorithm in Figure 8.5. Before using the patterns for the extraction of new instances of a relation, they will

---

* As in cases of taxonomic patterns, arguments are taxonomic concepts; for extracting k-ary relations in cases of t taxonomical concepts, there are kt words for argument slots.
† Database records are often called transactions in the frequent item set mining literature. In our case a transaction is an input sequence $s \in S$; TID = transaction identifier.
‡ Support of a set I is determined by the size of the intersection of TID lists of all items $i \in I$.

be filtered according to their scores (see subsection on the experimental setup) and specificities. As in URES, we use specificity as a criterion for pattern evaluation: if pattern p_1 can be derived from p_2 by removing a token or replacing a concrete token, gap, or wild card by a more general one, p_1 will be removed, thus keeping only the most specific patterns.

Algorithm 1 Generalized Eclat Algorithm

Require: InputSequences S, minSupport m
Ensure: Set of induced patterns PATTERNS

1: Dictionary D = { words, taxonomic concepts, argument slots, etc. }
2: TID_Lists TL = initItemTIDLists() // TID-Lists for $\forall$ w $\in$ D
3: CALL eclat(empty prefix,list of all transaction IDs)
4: **return** PATTERNS

5: **METHOD** eclat(Prefix p, TID_List_of_Prefix tid)
6: PATTERNS.add(p)
7: **for** $\forall$ w $\in$ D **do**
8:   **if** w is root **then**
9:     p1 = concat(p,w)
10:    tid1 = intersect(tid,TL.getTIDList(w))
11:    **if** tid1.size() $\geq$ m **then**
12:      **for** $\forall$ id $\in$ tid1 **do**
13:        **if** p1 does not match S.getInputSequence(id) **then**
14:          tid1.delete(id)
15:        **end if**
16:      **end for**
17:      **if** tid1.size() $\geq$ m **then**
18:        CALL eclat(p1,tid1)
19:      **end if**
20:    **end if**
21: **end if**
22: **end for**
23: **if** length(p) $>$ 0 **then**
24:   **for** $\forall$ w $\in$ D **do**
25:     **if** w is direct descendant of lastItem(p) **then**
26:       p1 = replaceLast(p,w)
27:       tid1 = intersect(tid,TL.getTIDList(w))
28:       **if** tid1.size() $\geq$ m **then**
29:         **for** $\forall$ id $\in$ tid1 **do**
30:           **if** p1 does not match S.getInputSequence(id) **then**
31:             tid1.delete(id)
32:           **end if**
33:         **end for**
34:         **if** tid1.size() $\geq$ m **then**
35:           CALL eclat(p1,tid1)
36:         **end if**
37:       **end if**
38:     **end if**
39:   **end for**
40: **end if**

8.6 Experiments

The goal of our experiments was to assess the performance of taxonomic patterns in comparison to patterns not incorporating taxonomic information. We performed our experiments on a large, publicly available corpus (thus making our results reproducible) with the aim of extracting four non-taxonomic relations for which the full extension is assumed to be given for evaluation purposes. Furthermore, we isolated the task of relation extraction from lower-level preprocessing by using a corpus preprocessed with standard tagging tools (sentence splitting, tokenization, part-of-speech tagging, named-entity tagging). We performed relation extraction with different pattern variants and compared the extraction quality.

8.6.1 Evaluation Protocol

Our goal was to investigate the designs of pattern languages and the uses of taxonomic sequential patterns. Therefore, we designed our experiments to maximize the generality of our results rather than optimizing the performance for a given setup. In this sense, we avoid tuning our system in two ways:

- As far as possible, parameters were avoided. The mining algorithm takes only one parameter (support m), and a threshold t on the score of each pattern (see section on experimental setup). The values of these parameters were determined measuring system performance on the training set as described below. This avoids tuning the parameters in an informed way (e.g., on the test data). In particular, for each pattern language and each relation we determined the best parameter settings on the training data. We report results on test data using these parameter settings.
- For the parameters of the evaluation configuration and linguistic processing, parameters were chosen based on previous systems (see section on datasets for details).

The evaluation protocol was designed following those used with other recent Web-oriented relation extraction systems like KnowItNow [8], Espresso [15], and URES [18]. We identified a set of relations for which the extension of the relation was known. A small subset was taken as training data, while the remaining examples served as a test set against which the output was compared. The datasets for each relation were obtained from hand-compiled Wikipedia category membership assignments.

We then identified four non-taxonomic relations (described below) for which the full extension is assumed to be given for evaluation purposes. The extracted tuples were evaluated for precision, recall, and F-measure with respect to the gold standard as follows. Assume E is the set of extracted tuples (normalized wrt. synonymy) and R is the set of the known correct relation instances present in the text, precision = $|E \cap R| / |E|$ and recall = $|E \cap R| / |R|$. We report their harmonic mean, the F_1 measure, as a canonical way to aggregate these two scores $F_1 = 2 \cdot precision \cdot recall \, / \, precision + recall$. The F_1 measure is commonly used as a quality measure in information extraction, as it integrates both missed and erroneous output errors, and thereby penalizes weak performance on one error type stronger than the arithmetic mean would.

Compared to the other systems, we used a similar number of relations as test setups (KnowItNow uses four, Espresso and URES both use five). These studies, however, do not report recall numbers but resort to stating recall relative to previous systems (Espresso) or only absolute extraction counts (KnowItNow and URES). Clearly, a set of four relations does not allow a conclusive statement on whether taxonomic patterns are always or at least on average superior to other types of patterns. However, the set of four relations clearly suffices to show that using taxonomic information in the pattern language has the potential of increasing the performance of a pattern-based information extraction system—not shown earlier.

We varied the minimum support m between 2, 5, 10, 15, and 20 and the cutoff percentile t_{score} for URES scores of patterns from 0 to 100% in steps of 10%. After measuring precision and recall for each configuration on the training data, we chose the best performing support and pattern score cut-off values for each setup in order to evaluate test data.* The configurations were chosen based on the F_1 measure on P (the set of given positive training examples) and N (the set of automatically generated negative training examples). The strategy to generate negative examples from the provided seed set (including only positive examples) is explained in detail below.

8.6.2 Dataset and Preprocessing

The textual dataset used for our experiments consisted of the Semantically Annotated Snapshot of the English Wikipedia, a publicly available dataset for hypertext mining provided by Hugo Zaragoza et al. [26]. It contains all 1,490,688 articles of a December 2007 version of the English Wikipedia.

Our evaluation involved four semantic relations from different domains: 172,696 (61,476)[†] famous persons and their years of birth, 14,762 (757) companies and the locations of their headquarters, 34,047 (2,561) geographic entities and their locations, and 2,650 (406) products from the automotive domain and their

---

* Due to the combinatoric number of possible frequent patterns through abstractions at different levels in the taxonomy, operating with a minimum support of two or five became computationally intractable for some relations so these settings were skipped. However, a good set of patterns was generated with higher minimum support due to the better ability to generalize by incorporation of taxonomic knowledge. For URES and the other baseline pattern languages, all support values were used.

[†] Numbers in brackets indicate actual occurrences of complete extension within our chosen window size in the corpus. We will refer to this as the corpus-pruned extension or gold standard for simplicity.

makers. This is a subset of the publicly available dataset used by Blöhm et al. [3]*
from which we excluded those relations for which no proper entity tagging was
available in the corpus (albums and soccer teams) and which were too small for our
setup (currencies).

The Wikipedia corpus was in turn restricted for each relation to contexts
containing entities of the appropriate type, i.e., *[Mozart]*$_{person}$ *was born in [1756]*$_{Year}$
would be retained as context for the *bornInYear* relation (as would also *[Mozart]*$_{person}$
died in [1791]$_{Year}$) but not *[Mozart]*$_{person}$ *was born in [Salzburg]*$_{city}$ as it does not
contain entities of the appropriate type. For this, we also simulate a perfect named-
entity tagging by restricting ourselves to co-occurrences of entities mentioned in at
least one tuple in the gold standard of the target relation (obviously not necessarily
in the same tuple). It is important to note that perfect tagging has been introduced
to create a solid basis for comparison and does not favor any pattern language
because perfect tags are taken into account only during co-occurrence selection,
uniformly performed prior to the matching of all patterns. We take into account
occurrences of the corpus for which the arguments of a tuple are at most 10 tokens
apart. We used WordNet and Wikipedia redirects as sources for (approximate) synonyms during both matching and evaluation.

To incorporate taxonomic knowledge, we relied on the Semantically Annotated
Snapshot of the English Wikipedia that has been preannotated with coarse semantic categories including a word's part of speech (e.g., noun, infinite verb, pronoun,
or punctuation), and named-entity tags from the WSJ tag set. In total, the taxonomy contained 135 concepts. An excerpt of the taxonomy corresponding to the
location subhierarchy is displayed in Figure 8.6 (see [26] for a documentation of the
categories for verbs, nouns, and the tag set). We relied on a gazetteer, not WSJ tags,
for marking vehicle models because the entity tagger recognized vehicle models
with very poor precision.

8.6.3 Experimental Setup

Our processing started with a set of 100 frequently mentioned sample relation
instances for each relation. This number is larger than those of most Web-oriented
studies. We opted for a larger sample because, as shown in [2], Wikipedia pattern
mining requires a larger seed set due to the low redundancy of the corpus. We ran
all experiments over the five pattern languages described in the previous sections.
Overall, our setup was similar to that used by [18], but we chose Wikipedia in order
to have a freely available, reproducible, and closed corpus instead of Web search
results that are subject to continuous change. We did not require a set of additional
keywords for each relation to be present in the contexts (as in URES); we considered this condition too strict (with a bias toward precision) and wanted to keep our
settings fairly general.

---

* http://www.aifb.uni-karlsruhe.de/WBS/seb/datasets/

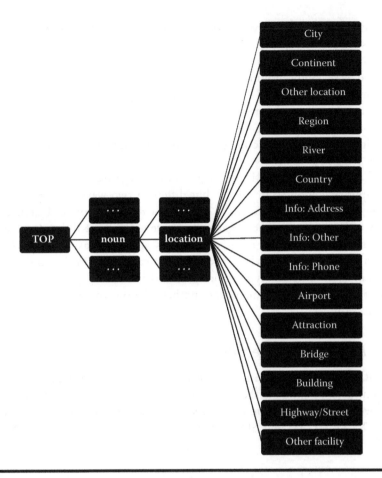

Figure 8.6 Excerpt from taxonomy showing noun subhierarchy for location along with its root path.

As noted earlier, the relevant parameters of our system are the minimum support *m* and threshold t_{score} on the scores of the patterns. Since we directly compared to URES, we used the same score:

$$score_p = \frac{|\bigcup_{o \in P} ex(p,o)|}{|\bigcup_{o \in N} ex(p,o)| + 1}$$

where *ex(p, o)* denotes the tuple (as singleton set) that can be extracted by pattern *p* in candidate occurrence *o*. Here, a candidate occurrence is a text fragment with entities of the appropriate types. So *ex(p, o)* is equal to the tuple in *o* pointed out by *p*'s argument positions if the pattern matches, or to Ø if the pattern does not match. This is a way of assessing the precision of the pattern.

We differ slightly, however, in the strategy adopted to generate the negative examples *N*. Essentially, we consider as negative all occurrences that do not correspond to tuples in the training set of the gold standard but contain tuples that can be created by swapping arguments between different tuples from the gold standard. For example, given that BMW and Yaris appear in our gold standard as the first and second arguments of some tuple (but not in the same tuple), the (Yaris,BMW) tuple would constitute a negative example, such that every pattern matching the following sentence and extracting (Yaris,BMW) should be penalized, e.g., *I bought my Yaris at a BMW dealer.*

Our version of the algorithm for generating negative examples was inspired by the approach adopted in URES, but differs in two ways: (1) we were able to generate more negative examples as we did not require a correct instance of the relation to be present in the negative sentence and (2) we did not use positive examples of one relation as negative examples of another as in the URES. This is due to the fact that our relations differ from each other in the sense that they have completely different type signatures, and thus using positive examples of one relation as negative examples for another relation would not generate useful negative examples.

8.6.4 Experimental Results

Figure 8.7 shows F_1 measure results for each pattern class averaged over all relations considered. Figure 8.8 shows precision and recall averaged over the four relations investigated, and Figure 8.9 shows the results for individual relations. Note that TAX, TAX-GAP, and SIMPLE-GAP outperform our URES and SIMPLE

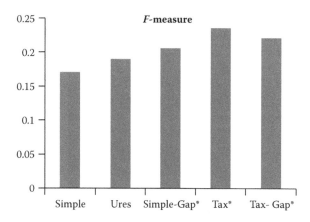

Figure 8.7 *F*-measure achieved with the different pattern languages averaged over four relations. The strategies marked with an asterisk perform statistically significantly better than the remaining ones.

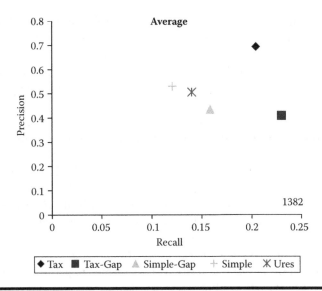

Figure 8.8 Precision over recall achieved with the different pattern languages averaged over all four relations. The scale on the X-axis also gives absolute result counts.

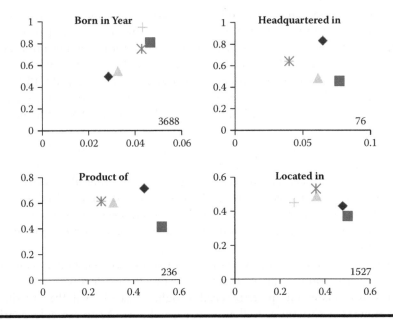

Figure 8.9 Precision over recall achieved with the different pattern languages for each of the four relations. The scale on the X-axis also gives absolute result counts.

baselines in a statistically significant manner (based on a two-sided pair-wise Student's *t*-test with an α level of 0.01, shown in Figure 8.7 by an asterisk). The conclusions to be drawn from our results are the following.

As shown in Figure 8.7, Taxonomic Sequential Patterns (TAX and TAX-GAP) outperformed state-of-the-art patterns used in URES as well as simple sequential patterns (SIMPLE) in terms of F_1 measure. This clearly demonstrates the benefit of integrating taxonomic information into patterns and shows that the different effects (generalization and specialization) play together in an optimal way to increase overall performance.

As Figure 8.8 indicates, TAX in particular increases both precision and recall at the same time. The increased recall is due to the higher number of patterns that can be found, and also because more general nontrivial patterns can be found when mining with typed wild cards. The higher precision is caused by the use of wild cards with type information; they are more selective than general wild cards. This can be seen in particular for the *productOf, headquarteredIn,* and *locatedIn relations*, while on the *bornInYear* relation, TAX seemed to perform worst (see comments below). On the averaged precision–recall diagram, one can clearly see that TAX increased both precision and recall compared to the other configurations we considered. TAX-GAP seemed to increase recall at the expense of a reduction in precision, such that the introduction of gaps can be clearly considered as leading to over-generalization.

The better performance of taxonomic patterns (in particular of TAX-GAP) does certainly not stem from the allowed GAPs only, as the comparison with SIMPLE-GAP shows, so that we can indeed claim that the taxonomic information is mainly responsible for the increase in performance. In fact, the semicontinuity seems to increase recall while reducing precision. For instance, SIMPLE-GAP has a higher recall but lower precision than SIMPLE (except for *bornInYear*) and TAX-GAP showed higher recall but lower precision than TAX (with the same exception).

For the *bornInYear* relation, TAX patterns performed worst. In fact, all relations produced very low recall due to the large extension of the relation. As all pattern classes performed poorly on this relation, no meaningful conclusions can be drawn. The main problem with TAX is that the parameter selection on the training dataset led to suboptimal configuration of the system. This also shows that more advanced strategies to determine parameters beyond *F*-score are needed on the training data set.

Note that due to the stricter evaluation protocol, our scores cannot be compared directly to other results in the literature (see Section 8.7 for details).

The reason taxonomic patterns yield a higher recall is that they produce a higher number of patterns as well as more general ones. As an example, consider the following pattern for the locatedIn relation: *NT-verb.state in <city>, <country>*, where *NT-verb.state* matches any state verb such as *born, built,* etc. This is obviously a reasonable pattern that might not be found as a sequential pattern without taxonomic knowledge, as each individual state verb might occur too rarely. By referring to the class of state verbs rather than to single verbs, the pattern might suddenly become frequent. On the other hand, a system merely inserting a wild card as * *in* <city>, <country> would be likely to over-generate.

The observation that taxonomic pattern classes may increase recall arises from the fact that more general but still frequent patterns can be formulated. As an example, for the headquarteredIn relation, a frequent pattern is <company> PUNCT <country>. There is no corresponding pattern in the non-taxonomic case because this pattern is only frequent when considering all sentence punctuation characters matched by the taxonomy concept PUNCT, while each individual one does not occur frequently enough between <company> name and <country>. One of the best performing patterns for the locatedIn relation is verb.creation in <city>, <country>. Note that the colon is kept concrete while a multitude of verbs (born, built, ...) is matched by NT-verb.state. This example illustrates how the different effects of taxonomic generalization play together: the taxonomy is used to generalize patterns and thus increase recall (i.e., using verb.creation instead of specific verbs such as *build* for instance), while making sure that no other verbs match the given position, thus keeping precision at reasonable levels at the same time.

8.7 Related Work

Most pattern-based information extraction systems aimed at large-scale processing employ some sort of abstraction over the textual surface in the form of wild cards [3, 25], typed wild cards, or gaps [18]. Various morpho-syntactic and lexical types have been used for typed wild cards, in particular, part-of-speech information [7,15,19]), named entity tags [1,16,18]), word-sense information [25], and (shallow) parses [8,20]. None of these systems, however, is general enough to allow for several types of taxonomic information at the same time and they have not empirically compared the performance of their approaches with and without the incorporation of additional background knowledge. Furthermore, taxonomic information has not been demonstrated to have a positive effect.

For pattern induction, various ad hoc solutions have been found, for example, pair-wise sequence comparison [18], grouping based on infixes [4], and bottom-up testing of abstractions [10]. We have provided a uniform pattern mining approach that is versatile enough to mine and compare different pattern classes while allowing for efficient exhaustive mining. Another efficient approach is the use of suffix trees [15,16]; this method, however, does not extend to taxonomic patterns and merely counts the frequencies of substrings.

It is important to emphasize that two different tasks can be distinguished in relation extraction: (1) a Boolean classification of the sentence w.r.t. whether it mentions the given relation or not, but without extracting the arguments of the tuple as in [6], and (2) extracting the tuples standing in a given relation from a given sentence or corpus.

Interestingly, most supervised and discriminative approaches to relation extraction were developed for and evaluated on the first task. For example, Bunescu and Mooney [6] report an area under the precision–recall curve of 81.1% for the sentence classification task. However, the task of classifying a sentence as expressing or not expressing the relation in question is inherently easier than the task we consider here (it is actually a subtask of our task), so that we cannot compare directly to these types of approaches.

Concerning the second task, mainly pattern-based approaches have been applied. The main reason is that patterns can accomplish the two tasks in one step, i.e., they classify the matched fragment as expressing an instance of the relation type considered and can extract the correct arguments of the tuple at the same time. For this purpose, patterns typically use special machinery to explicitly mark the arguments of the relation. However, supervised and discriminative approaches have trouble spotting the arguments of the relation if they cannot be clearly determined from the named entity types. In the sentence *Yaris is produced by Toyota, but not by BMW*, for example, two car makers (Toyota and BMW) are named. An approach only classifying the whole sentence as merely mentioning an instance of the relation type in question will certainly have trouble assigning the named entities to the right argument of the tuple, i.e., which is the maker: BMW or Toyota? An exception is [24], where two classifiers are used, one for sentence classification and one to spot the arguments.

Approaches have been evaluated in very different ways and using different corpora so that results are not directly comparable. Some approaches evaluate only precision by manual inspection of sampled results (a posteriori) without measuring recall, yielding high precision rates as with URES (0.7 to 0.98). However, the URES system was developed in such a way that it is biased towards higher precision by incorporating manually defined relation-dependent keywords both into the mining process and in corpus generation.

The recall of URES has not been evaluated, so its results are not comparable to ours. In some approaches "relations have not been pre-determined in any way", but they are identified a posteriori (Davidov et al. [11]). The latter achieves precision between 0.77 and 0.98 and recall–coverage between 0.51 and 0.95, depending on the relation considered. Recall–coverage is not measured as strictly as in our approach (see end of Section 6.1 in [11]). Further, the possibility of defining relations a posteriori results in a less strict evaluation protocol compared to the case when relations are given a priori. Davidov et al. [11] evaluated only 25 of the 31 binary relations that their system learns—the "clearly identifiable" ones. Our approach aims to extract the full extension of a predefined relation from a given corpus. This is the hardest type of evaluation and led to low recall values as we reported. This result is not a low quality indicator of the approach, but an indication of the difficulty of reproducing the complete extension of a relation, even if it is restricted to occurrences in the corpus.

8.8 Conclusions

The extraction of factual information from text is an important task for building semantics-aware applications. An approach like the one we presented here has important applications in biochemistry where information extraction techniques are typically applied to extract relevant relations (e.g., interacting proteins) and even complete regulatory networks or pathways from scientific literature [19]. It also has strong application in business analytics, as it can extract relevant relations between companies to support tasks such as competitor analysis and risk assessment [12].

We introduced TSPs for relation extraction, together with a principled and exhaustive mining algorithm that allows efficient mining across a variety of pattern classes. We have shown that TSPs are generally and significantly superior with respect to the precision–recall trade-off compared to a simple baseline and state-of-the-art pattern-based approach such as URES.

The superiority can be explained with the help of three effects discussed in the Section 8.2 problem statement. On one hand, taxonomic generalization yields more general patterns, effectively increasing recall (generalization effect) while increasing precision by replacing untyped wild cards by typed wild cards, thus adding stronger constraints (specification effect). On the other hand, by way of generalizing along a hierarchy, more patterns above the minimum support can be found, again increasing recall. The main contribution of our work is to show that the above effects complement each other, yielding overall improved performance with respect to approaches based on non-taxonomic patterns.

In general, our work shows that the choice of pattern class is crucial and investigations to determine which pattern classes perform better are important. We provided a first investigation of the impact of factoring taxonomic information into pattern language, showing that it can indeed have a positive effect.

Future work should definitely consider increasing the recall of our approach (e.g., by means of iterative induction) and also investigate more advanced strategies for pattern scoring. A comparison and combination of pattern-based approaches with those relying on discrimination would be another important research avenue. To date, these approaches have been applied to different tasks.

From a more general perspective, we have shown that extracting binary relations is a nontrivial task. For some relations, the results are indeed acceptable, while for other relations they are far from satisfactory. However, the Semantic Web builds on triple-centered data models so that the extraction of binary relations from text and other unstructured resources is crucial. In this sense, much more work on extracting high-quality relations from unstructured data is needed.

Acknowledgement

This work was funded by the DFG under grant number 38457858 (MULTIPLA Project).

References

1. E. Agichtein and L. Gravano. 2000. Snowball: Extracting relations from large plain-text collections. In *Proceedings of Fifth ACM conference on Digital Libraries*, pp. 85–94.
2. S. Blohm and P. Cimiano. 2007. Using the web to reduce data sparseness in pattern-based information extraction. In *Proceedings of 11th European Conference on Principles and Practice of Knowledge Discovery in Databases*, pp. 18–29.
3. S. Blohm, P. Cimiano, and E. Stemle. 2007. Harvesting relations from the web: Quantifying the impact of filtering functions. In *Proceedings of 22nd Conference on Artificial Intelligence*, pp. 1316–1323.
4. S. Brin. 1998. Extracting patterns and relations from the world wide web. In *Proceedings of WebDB Workshop, Sixth International Conference on Extending Database Technology*.
5. R. Bunescu and R. Mooney. Subsequence kernels for relation extraction. In *Advances in Neural Information Processing Systems (NIPS) 18*, pp. 171–178, 2006.
6. R. Bunescu and R. Mooney. 2007. Learning to extract relations from the web using minimal supervision. In *Proceedings of 45th Annual Meeting of Association for Computational Linguistics*, pp. 576–583.
7. K. Buza and L. Schmidt-Thieme. 2009. Motif-based classification of time series with Bayesian networks and SVMS. In *Proceedings of 32nd Annual Conference of Gesellschaft f'ur Klassifikation*.
8. M. J. Cafarella, D. Downey, S. Soderland et al. 2005. KnowItNow: Fast, scalable information extraction from the web. In *Proceedings of Human Language Technology Conference and Conference on Empirical Methods in Natural Language Processing*, pp. 563–570.
9. M. Califf and R. Mooney. 1997. Relational learning of pattern match rules for information extraction. In *Proceedings of ACL Workshop on Natural Language Learning*, pp. 9–15.
10. F. Ciravegna. 2001. Adaptive information extraction from text by rule induction and generalisation. In *Proceedings of International Joint Conference on Artificial Intelligence*, pp. 1251–1256.
11. D. Davidov, A. Rappoport, and M. Koppel. 2007. Fully unsupervised discovery of concept-specific relationships by web mining. In *Proceedings of Annual Meeting of Association for Computational Linguistics*, pp. 232–239.
12. R. Feldman. 2005. Managing risk for the financial services market in a world of uncertainty, unified business intelligence in action. *Information Management Online*.
13. J. Han, J.Pei, Y. Yin et al. 2004. Mining frequent patterns without candidate generation. *Data Mining and Knowledge Discovery*, 8: 53–87.
14. J. Han, J. Pei, and Y. Yin. 2000. Mining frequent patterns without candidate generation. In *Proceedings of International Conference on Management of Data*, pp. 1–12.

15. P. Pantel and M. Pennacchiotti. 2006. Espresso: Leveraging generic patterns for automatically harvesting semantic relations. In *Proceedings of 21st International Conference on Computational Linguistics and 44th Annual Meeting of Association for Computational Linguistics (ACL)*, pp. 113–120.
16. D. Ravichandran and E. Hovy. 2001. Learning surface text patterns for a question answering system. In *Proceedings of 40th Annual Meeting of Association for Computational Linguistics*, pp. 41–47.
17. B. Rosenfeld and R. Feldman. 2006. High-performance unsupervised relation extraction from large corpora. In *Proceedings of Sixth IEEE International Conference on Data Mining*, pp. 1032–1037.
18. B. Rosenfeld and R. Feldman. 2006. URES: An unsupervised web relation extraction system. In *Proceedings of 21st International Conference on Computational Linguistics and 44th Annual Meeting of Association for Computational Linguistics*.
19. J. Saric, L.J. Jensen, R. Ouzounova et al. 2004. Extraction of regulatory gene expression networks from PubMed. In *Proceedings of Annual Meeting of Association for Computational Linguistics*, pp. 191–198.
20. R. Snow, D. Jurafsky, and A.Y. Ng. 2005. Learning syntactic patterns for automatic hypernym discovery. In *Proceedings of 17th Conference on Advances in Neural Information Processing Systems*.
21. F. Suchanek, G. Ifrim, and G. Weikum. 2006. LEILA: Learning to extract information by linguistic analysis. In *Proceedings of Second Workshop on Ontology Learning and Population: Bridging the Gap between Text and Knowledge*, Sydney, pp. 18–25.
22. J. Tomita, S. Soderland, and O. Etzioni. 2006. Expanding the recall of relation extraction by bootstrapping. In *Proceedings of EACL Workshop on Adaptive Text Extraction and Mining*.
23. G. Wang, Y. Yu, and H. Zhu. 2007. PORE: Positive-only relation extraction from Wikipedia text. In *Proceedings of Sixth International Semantic Web Conference and Second Asian Semantic Web Conference*, Springer Verlag, Berlin, pp. 575–588.
24. F. Wu and D. S. Weld. 2007. Autonomously semantifying Wikipedia. In *Proceedings of 16th International Conference on Information and Knowledge Management*, pp. 41–50.
25. R. Yangarber. 2003. Acquisition of domain knowledge. In *Extraction in the Web Era*, Springer Verlag, Berlin, pp. 1–28.
26. H. Zaragoza, J. Atserias, M. Ciaramita, et al. 2007. Semantically annotated snapshot of the English Wikipedia, Version 1 (sw!). http://www.yr-bcn.es/semanticWikipedia.

Chapter 9

Data-Driven Evaluation of Ontologies Using Machine Learning Algorithms

Dae-Ki Kang
Dongseo University, Busan, Korea

Contents

9.1 Introduction

Ontology evaluation is an assessment based on certain criteria of application. Generally, ontology evaluation involves choosing which of several ontologies would best suit a particular purpose. Several categorizations have been made to evaluate ontologies (Brank et al., 2005). The approach depends on the type of ontology to be evaluated and for what purpose. Some common categorizations are as follows:

1. Task-based approach (Cimiano et al., 2003; Porzel and Malaka, 2004; Kang et al., 2004, 2005; Kang and Sohn, 2009) utilizing ontologies in a certain application and evaluating the results
2. Comparison or assessment using formally defined measures (Maedche and Staab, 2002; Grefenstette, 1994; Welty and Guarino, 2001; Gangemi et al., 2006; Kohler et al., 2006) such as similarities

3. Comparison of an ontology with a source of data (Brewster et al., 2004) about the domain to be covered by the ontology

4. Evaluation by human experts (Lozano-Tello and Gómez-Pérez, 2004; Noy et al., 2005; Smith et al., 2004; Gulla and Sugumaran, 2008) to determine how ontologies meet prespecified criteria

This chapter describes data-driven evaluations of ontologies using machine learning algorithms—one of task-based approaches for evaluation. Before we describe our approach in brief, it is helpful to explain the structure and the logic path of this chapter. The task we consider is measuring the performances of machine learning algorithms that can use ontologies (Dhar and Tuzhilin, 1993; Han and Fu, 1996; Hendler et al., 1996; Taylor et al., 1997; Zhang et al., 2002; Zhang and Honavar, 2003; Kang et al., 2004; Zhang and Honavar, 2004; Kang et al., 2005; Wu et al., 2005; Kang and Sohn, 2009). We then assess the quality of the ontologies based on the performance results of the machine learning algorithms.

We first discuss different types of ontologies, ontology learning algorithms, and ontology-aware machine learning algorithms. The ontologies we will introduce are attribute value taxonomy (AVT; Zhang and Honavar, 2003, 2004; Kang et al., 2004; desJardins et al., 2000), word taxonomy (WT; Kang et al., 2005), and propositionalized attribute taxonomy (PAT; Kang and Sohn, 2009). The ontology learning algorithms we propose are AVT learner (Kang et al., 2004), word taxonomy learner (WTL; Kang et al., 2005), and PAT learner (Kang and Sohn, 2009). The ontology-aware machine learning algorithms discussed are AVT-guided naive Bayes learner (AVT-NBL; Zhang and Honavar, 2004), word taxonomy-guided naive Bayes learner for the multinomial event model (WTNBL-MN; Kang et al., 2005), propositionalized attribute taxonomy guided decision tree learner (PAT-DTL; Kang and Sohn, 2009), and propositionalized attribute taxonomy-guided naive Bayes learner (PAT-NBL). For each triple (ontology, ontology learning algorithm, ontology-aware machine learning algorithm), we will present corresponding experimental results on a broad range of benchmark data sets that allow us to assess the quality of ontologies: how effective they are for machine learning tasks.

We introduce the basics of ontology-aware machine learning algorithms. For these algorithms to use ontologies, the ontologies must be represented and stored in a format that the algorithms can recognize and manage. We usually represent ontologies in various data structures (list, tree or directed acyclic graph, and directed or undirected graph). Graphs are very powerful data structures to express ontology for machine learning algorithms, but inference with graphs is widely believed to be intractable. Taxonomy is one widely used form of ontology and has proven useful in constructing compact, robust, and comprehensible classifiers, although in many application domains, human-designed taxonomies are unavailable.

Because of these issues, we introduce algorithms for automated construction of taxonomies inductively from both structured (UCI Repository) and unstructured (text and biological sequences) data. More precisely, the following algorithms we consider are based on the taxonomy they use.

9.1.1 Attribute Value Taxonomy (AVT) and Attribute Value Taxonomy Learner (AVT Learner)

An attribute value taxonomy is generated by grouping attribute values to yield a more abstract attribute value (Zhang and Honavar, 2003, 2004; Kang et al., 2004; des Jardins et al., 2000) when a data instance is represented as an ordered tuple of a fixed number of attribute values. The instance is generated from a multivariate model, and since one taxonomy is generated for one attribute, attribute value taxonomies are generated from a data set. Attribute value taxonomy learner (AVT learner; Kang et al., 2004) is an algorithm for automated construction of AVTs from multivariate data.

9.1.2 Word Taxonomy (WT) and Word Taxonomy Learner (WTL)

A word taxonomy is generated by grouping words (or values) to generate a more abstract word (Kang et al., 2005) when a data instance is represented from a univariate model. Contrary to the first approach, in inductive learning scenarios of sequences such as text documents and biological sequences, an instance is usually represented as a set or bag of values, that is, one instance is an unordered tuple of value frequencies or binary values to denote the presence of the value. Again, these words can be grouped together to reflect similarities among the vales in the context. Such hierarchical grouping of words yields word taxonomy (WT; Kang et al., 2005). Word taxonomy learner (WTL; Kang et al., 2005) is an algorithm for automated construction of a WT from the vocabulary or alphabet of text and sequence data.

9.1.3 Propositionalized Attribute Taxonomy (PAT) and PAT Learner

An attribute is propositionalized to generate multiple attributes with binary attribute values. A propositionalized attribute taxonomy (PAT) is generated from all the generated attributes (Kang and Sohn, 2009). The propositionalized attribute taxonomy learner (PAT learner) of Kang and Sohn (2009) is an algorithm to propositionalize attributes and construct a taxonomy from the propositionalized attributes. In short, these algorithms basically use hierarchical agglomerative clustering (HAC) to group attribute values based on the distribution of classes that co-occur with the values.

9.1.4 Taxonomy-Aware Machine Learning Algorithms

To evaluate the generated taxonomies from AVT learner, WTL, and PAT learner, we used appropriate taxonomy-aware machine learning algorithms.

AVT learner—We used AVT-NBL (Zhang and Honavar, 2004), an extension of naive Bayes learner for learning with AVTs. AVT-NBL is a generalization of the naive Bayes learner for multivariate data using AVTs.

WTL—We used WT-guided naive Bayes learner for the multinomial event model (WTNBL-MN; Kang et al., 2005) because it exploits word taxonomy to generate compact classifiers; it is a generalization of the naive Bayes learner for the multinomial event model for learning classifiers from data using word taxonomy.

PAT learner—We used propositionalized attribute taxonomy-guided decision tree learner (PAT-DTL; Kang and Sohn, 2009) and propositionalized attribute taxonomy-guided naive Bayes learner (PAT-NBL). PAT-DTL is a generalization of the DTS for exploiting propositionalized attribute taxonomy (PAT). PAT-NBL is a generalization of the naive Bayes learner to exploit propositionalized attribute taxonomy (PAT).

9.1.5 Value of Taxonomy in Machine Learning

Before we describe the algorithms and experimental results, we explain why taxonomy is useful in machine learning tasks. An important goal of inductive learning is to generate accurate and compact classifiers from data. In a typical inductive learning scenario, instances to be classified are represented as ordered tuples of attribute values as shown in Figure 9.1.

However, attribute values can be grouped together to reflect their assumed or actual similarities in a domain of interest or in the context of a specific application. Such a hierarchical grouping of attribute values yields an attribute value taxonomy (AVT). For example, Figure 9.2 shows a human-made taxonomy associated with

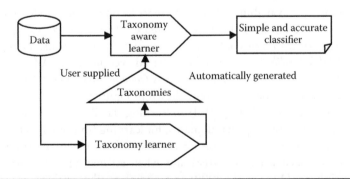

Figure 9.1   Machine learning scenarios.

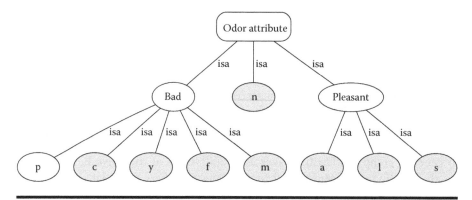

Figure 9.2   Human-made AVT from *odor* attribute of UCI AGARICUS-LEPIOTA mushroom data set.

a nominal *odor* attribute of the AGARICUS-LEPIOTA mushroom data set of the University of California at Irvine (UCI; Blake and Merz, 1998).

Hierarchical groupings of attribute values (AVTs) are common in the biological sciences. For example, the Gene Ontology Consortium is developing hierarchical taxonomies for describing many aspects of macromolecular sequences, structures, and functions (Ashburner et al., 2000). Undercoffer et al. (2003) developed a hierarchical taxonomy that captures features that are observable or measurable by the target of an attack or by a system of sensors acting on behalf of a target. Several ontologies under development as part of the Semantic Web-related efforts (Shadbolt et al., 2006; Berners-Lee et al., 2001) also capture hierarchical groupings of attribute values. Kohavi and Provost (2001) cited the need to incorporate background knowledge in the form of hierarchies over data attributes in electronic commerce applications of data mining.

Among the several reasons for exploiting AVTs in learning classifiers from data, perhaps the most important is a preference for comprehensible and simple, yet accurate and robust classifiers (Pazzani et al., 1997) in many practical applications of data mining. The availability of AVT presents an opportunity to learn classification rules expressed in terms of abstract attribute values, leading to simpler, easier-to-comprehend rules in terms of hierarchically related values. Thus, the rule (*odor = pleasant*) → (*class = edible*) is likely to be preferred over [(*odor = a*) ∧ (*color = brown*)] ∨ [(*odor = l*) ∧ (*color = brown*)] ∨ [(*odor = s*) ∧ (*color = brown*)] → (*class = edible*) by a user familiar with the odor taxonomy shown in Figure 9.2.

Another reason for exploiting AVTs in learning classifiers from data arises from the necessity, in many application domains, for learning from small data sets where there is a greater chance of generating classifiers that over-fit the training data. A common approach used by statisticians when estimating from small samples involves shrinkage (Duda et al., 2000) or grouping attribute values (or more commonly class labels) into bins when too few instances match any specific attribute value or class label to estimate the relevant statistics with adequate confidence. Learning algorithms that exploit AVT can potentially perform shrinkage automatically, thereby yielding robust classifiers. In other words, exploiting information provided by an AVT can be an effective approach to performing regularization to minimize over-fitting (Zhang and Honavar, 2003).

Several algorithms for learning classifiers from AVTs and data as shown in Figure 9.2 have been proposed in the literature. These works show that AVTs can be exploited to improve the accuracy of classification, and in many instances reduce the complexity and increase the comprehensibility of the resulting classifiers (Dhar and Tuzhilin, 1993; Han and Fu, 1996; Hendler et al., 1996; Taylor et al., 1997; Zhang et al., 2002; Zhang and Honavar, 2003; Kang et al., 2004; Zhang and Honavar, 2004; Wu et al., 2005). Most of these algorithms exploit AVTs to represent the information needed for classification at different levels of abstraction.

One crucial problem of using taxonomy is that AVTs specified by human experts are unavailable in many domains. Even when a human-supplied AVT is available, it is interesting to explore whether alternative groupings of attribute values into an AVT might yield more accurate or more compact classifiers. Against this background, we explore the problem of automated construction of AVTs from data to see whether AVTs are useful for generating accurate and compact classifiers.

9.1.6 Descriptions of Experiments

For evaluation, we describe experiments on UCI data sets that compare the performances of AVT-NBL and the standard naive Bayes learner (NBL). The results show that the AVTs generated by AVT learner are competitive with human-generated AVTs (where such AVTs are available). AVT-NBL, using AVTs generated by AVT learner, achieved classification accuracies comparable to or better than those obtained by NBL; and the resulting classifiers were significantly more compact than those generated by NBL.

We extended our exploration to word taxonomy for unstructured data such as text and sequences and with similar arguments (Kang et al., 2005). Word taxonomies present the possibility of learning classification rules that are simpler and easier to understand when the terms in the rules are expressed as abstract values. With previous work (Kang et al., 2004; Zhang and Honavar, 2004), abstraction of similar concepts by means of attribute value taxonomy (AVT) proved useful in generating concise and accurate classifiers. Against this background, we introduced word taxonomy-guided naive Bayes learner for the multinomial event model (WTNBL-MN)—a word taxonomy-based generalization of the standard MBL algorithm for the multinomial model.

Word taxonomy is not available in many domains, creating a need for automated construction of word taxonomy. Hence, we describe a word taxonomy learner (WTL) that automatically generates word taxonomies from sequence data by clustering words based on their class conditional distribution. To evaluate word taxonomies with WTNBL-MN, we conducted experiments using two classification tasks: (1) assigning Reuters news wire articles to categories and (2) and classifying protein sequences via their localizations. We used WTL to generate word taxonomies from the training data. The generated word taxonomies were provided to WTNBL-MN to learn concise naive Bayes classifiers that used abstract words of WT.

Finally, we explored the effectiveness of propositionalized attribute taxonomy (PAT) applied to multivariate data (Kang and Sohn, 2009). To provide a motivating example of PAT, we proposed a *University* data set with *student* and *professor* attributes. Figure 9.3 shows human-made attribute value taxonomies. The *student* attribute has values including *freshman, sophomore, junior, senior, master,* and *phd.* The attributes of *professor* are *lecturer, assistant, associate,* and *professor.* There are many ways to abstract *student* attribute values. In Figure 9.3, we generated *undergrad* and *grad* values by abstraction. We can see that all the attribute values in *student* are partitioned as *undergrad* and *grad* attribute values.

We cannot generate new abstract values from *phd* and *lecturer* in this approach because *phd* is a value of the *student* attribute and *lecturer* is a value of the *professor* attribute. In other words, in a multivariate modeling and AVT approach, one data set comprises multiple attributes and each attribute has a numeric value or a set of nominal values. Most previous research focused on abstraction of values in an attribute but did not consider abstraction of values from different attributes.

The real world often reveals similarities between the values of different attributes, and thus the abstract values of the values from different attributes may be more useful than the abstract values of the values of one attribute. For example, when we want to group the people in the example by one criterion (whether he or she can professionally review an academic paper draft), we can treat *master* and *phd* with the values from the *professor* attribute as in the PAT shown in Figure 9.4

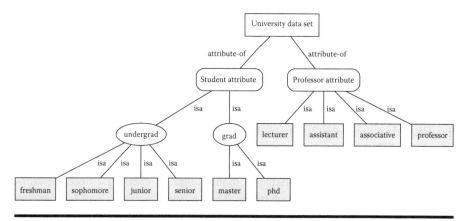

Figure 9.3 Human-made attribute value taxonomies of *University* data set.

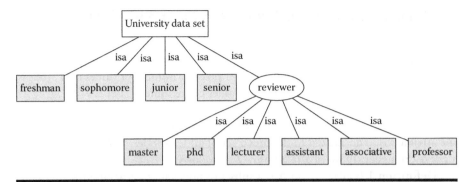

Figure 9.4 Human-made propositionalized attribute taxonomies of *University* data set. Note that original attributes are removed and a new *reviewer* attribute is added by abstraction.

made by human experts. Note that in the figure, the original attributes (*student* and *professor*) are removed, and a new *reviewer* attribute is added by abstraction.

As illustrated in the example, while the previous two approaches are only interested in abstraction of values within one attribute, it would be interesting to explore whether a set of values from different attributes can be grouped together to reflect a useful concept. To facilitate this grouping, an attribute must be propositionalized into a set of Boolean attributes, each of which corresponds to a value of the original attribute. The hierarchical abstraction of those propositionalized attributes will produce a PAT.

Because of these issues, we introduce PAT-NBL—a propositionalized attribute taxonomy-based generalization of the standard naive Bayes learning algorithm. PAT-NBL uses bottom-up search techniques over the PAT to find a useful abstraction for classification. This PAT is not available in most domains, so we used a PAT learner (propositionalized attribute taxonomy learner; (Kang and Sohn, 2009) that automatically propositionalizes attributes and generates taxonomies from the attributes by clustering based on their class conditional distributions.

To evaluate PATs with PAT-NBL, we will show and discuss experimental results with data sets from the UCI machine learning repository (Blake and Merz, 1998). We used PAT learner to generate PAT from the training set of UCI benchmark data and provided the generated PAT to PAT-NBL to learn naive Bayes classifiers incorporated with abstract values of PAT.

9.2 Learning Taxonomies from Data

We start with definitions of preliminary concepts necessary to describe the taxonomy-aware machine learning algorithms. We then precisely define the problem as learning classifiers from taxonomy and data.

9.2.1 Definitions of Attribute Value Taxonomy (AVT)

Let $A = \{A_1, A_2, ..., A_n\}$ be a set of nominal attributes. Let $V_i = \{v_i^1, v_i^2, ..., v_i^{m_i}\}$ be a finite domain of mutually exclusive values associated with attribute A_i where v_i^j is the jth attribute value of A_i and m_i is the number possible number of values of A_i, that is, $|V_i|$. We say that V_i is the set of primitive values of attribute A_i. Let $C = \{C1, C2, ..., C_k\}$ be a set of mutually disjoint class labels. A data set is $D \subseteq V_1 \times V_2 \times ... \times V_n \times C$. Let $T = \{T_1, T_2, ..., T_n\}$ denote a set of AVT such that T_i is an AVT associated with the attribute A_i, and *Leaves(T_i)* denotes a set of all leaf nodes in T_i. We then define a cut δ_i (Haussler, 1988) of a taxonomy T_i as follows:

Definition 1 (Cut)—A cut δ_i is a subset of nodes in T_i satisfying the following two properties: (1) for any leaf 1 $Î$ *Leaves(T_i)*, either 1 $Î\delta_i$ or 1 is a descendant of a node n $Î$ δ_i; (2) for any two nodes f, g $Î$ δ_1, f is neither a descendant nor an ancestor of g. For example, {*Bad, a, l, s, n*} is a cut through the AVT for *odor* shown in Figure 9.2. Note that a cut through T_i corresponds to a partition of the values in V_i. Let $\Delta = \{\delta_1, \delta_2, ... \delta_n\}$ be a set of cuts associated with AVTs in $T = \{T_1, T_2, ... T_n\}$. This definition of cut can be applied to any of the taxonomies discussed in this chapter including AVT, WT, and PAT.

Definition 2 (Refinement and Abstraction)—We say that a cut $\hat{\delta}_i$ is a refinement of a cut δ_i if $\hat{\delta}_i$ is obtained by replacing at least one node v $Î$ δ_i by its descendants. Conversely, δ_i is an abstraction of $\hat{\delta}_i$. Figure 9.5 illustrates a refinement process in taxonomy T. The cut $\gamma_2 = \{A, B, C, D\}$ in T_2 has been refined to $\delta = \{A, B_1, B_2, C, D\}$ by replacing B with its two children B_1, B_2, and $\delta_1 = \gamma_1$ and $\delta_3 = \gamma_3$. Therefore $\Delta = \{\delta_1, \delta_2, \delta_3\}$ is a refinement of $\Gamma = \{\gamma_1, \gamma_2, \gamma_3\}$ and the corresponding hypothesis $h(\Delta)$ is a refinement of $h(\Gamma)$. Note that this definition of cut can be applied to any of the taxonomies discussed in this chapter including AVT, WT, and PAT.

Definition 3 (Instance Space)—Any choice of Δ defines an input space I_Δ. If there are a node $Î\Delta$ and $Ï$ *Leaves(T)*, the induced input space I_Δ is an abstraction of the original input space I.

With a data set D, AVT T and corresponding valid cuts, we can extend our definition of instance space to include instance spaces induced from different levels of

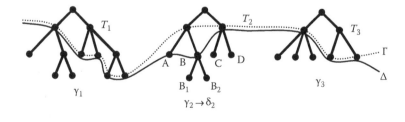

Figure 9.5 Cut refinement over AVT. The cut $\gamma_2 = \{A, B, C, D\}$ in T_2 has been refined to $\delta = \{A, B_1, B_2, C, D\}$ by replacing B with its two children B_1, B_2, and $\delta_1 = \gamma_1$ and $\delta_3 = \gamma_3$. Thus $\Delta = \{\delta_1, \delta_2, \delta_3\}$ is a refinement of $\Gamma = \{\gamma_1, \gamma_2, \gamma_3\}$.

abstraction of the original input space. Thus, taxonomy guided learning algorithms work on this induced input space.

9.2.2 Definition of Word Taxonomy (WT)

For word taxonomy over unstructured data such as text documents or sequences, we define abstraction based on the frequency of values associated with the same class label.

Let $\Sigma = \{w_1, w_2, ..., w_N\}$ be a dictionary of words, $C = \{c_1, c_2, ..., c_M\}$ a finite set of mutually disjoint class labels, and $f_{i,j}$ an integer frequency of word w_i in a sequence d_j. Sequence d_j is represented as an instance I_j, a frequency vector $< f_{i,j} >$ of w_i, and each sequence belongs to a class label in C. Finally, a data set D is represented as a collection of instances and their associated class labels $\{(I_j, c_j)\}$. Let T_Σ be a word taxonomy defined over the possible words of Σ. Let $Nodes(T_\Sigma)$ denote the set of all values in T_Σ and $Root(T_\Sigma)$ denote the root of T_Σ. We represent the set of leaves of T_Σ as $Leaves(T_\Sigma) \subseteq \Sigma$. The internal nodes of the tree correspond to *abstract values* of Σ.

Figure 9.6 illustrates a refinement process in word taxonomy T_Σ. The cut $\gamma = \{A, B\}$ is refined to $\hat{\gamma} = \{A_1, A_2, B\}$ by replacing A with A_1 and A_2. Thus, corresponding hypothesis $h_{\hat{\gamma}}$ is a refinement of h_γ. Note that there is only one WT for each data set and as many AVTs as the number of attributes in a multivariate data set.

9.2.3 Definition of Propositionalized Attribute Taxonomy (PAT)

First we define primitive attributes with their values. Then, we formally describe a class, instances, and a multivariate data set.

Let $A = \{A_1, A_2, ..., A_{|A|}\}$ be a set of nominal attributes. Let $V_{A_i} = \left\{ v_{A_i}^1, v_{A_i}^2, ..., v_{A_i}^{|V_{A_i}|} \right\}$ be a finite domain of mutually exclusive values associated with attribute A_i where $v_{A_i}^j$ is the jth attribute value of A_i and $|V_{A_i}|$ is the number of attribute values of A_i. Note that $v_{A_i}^j$ is used in the following definition of propositionalization. Let $C = \{C_1,$

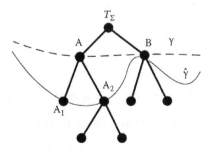

Figure 9.6   Cut refinement. The cut $\gamma = \{A, B\}$ is been refined to $\hat{\gamma} = \{A_1, A_2, B\}$ by replacing A with A_1 and A_2.

$C_2, ..., C_{|C|}\}$ be a set of mutually disjoint class labels. An instance I is a fixed tuple of attribute values such that $I \in V_{A_1} \times V_{A_2} \times ... \times V_{A_{|A|}}$. A data set D is a collection of instances and their associated class labels such that $D \in V_{A_1} \times V_{A_2} \times ... \times V_{A_{|A|}} \times \mathbb{C}$. We now explain propositionalization of the data set.

Definition 4 (Propositionalization)—Propositionalization is a function $f : V_{A_i} \to \tilde{\mathbb{A}}$ that, for each value $v_{A_i}^j \in V_{A_i}$ associated with $A_i \in A$, constructs a new Boolean attribute $\tilde{A}_l \in \tilde{\mathbb{A}}$. Propositionalized attribute value $\tilde{V}_{\tilde{A}_l}$ associated with $\tilde{A}_l$ is a Boolean value $\in \{True, False\}$, and a propositionalized data set $\tilde{D}$ is defined as $\tilde{D} \subseteq \tilde{V}_{\tilde{A}_1} \times \tilde{V}_{\tilde{A}_2} \times ... \times \tilde{V}_{\tilde{A}_{|\tilde{A}|}} \times \mathbb{C}$. An attribute $\tilde{A}_l$ of a propositionalized instance $\tilde{I}$ has a value *True* if and only if the original instance I has the corresponding attribute value $v_{A_i}^j$.

Let $\tilde{T}$ denote a PAT defined over the Boolean attributes $\in \tilde{\mathbb{A}}$ propositionalized from A. We represent the set of leaves of $\tilde{T}$ as *Leaves*$(\tilde{T}) \sqsubseteq \tilde{\mathbb{A}}$, and *abstract values* of $\tilde{\mathbb{A}}$ to internal nodes of the tree. We then define a cut (Haussler, 1988) γ through a taxonomy $\tilde{T}$ as follows.

A cut γ of $\tilde{T}$ induces a partition of propositionalized attributes $\tilde{\mathbb{A}}$. For example, in Figure 9.3, a cut {*undergrad, master, phd*} defines a partition over the values of a *student* attribute. Note that only one PAT applies to each data set, but many AVTs as the numbers of attributes in a multivariate data set.

Consider the *University* data set with *student* and *professor* attributes. The *student* attribute has values including *freshmen, sophomore, junior, senior, master* and *phd*. The *professor* attribute values are *lecturer, assistant, associate,* and *professor*. Let original instances in the data set be those in Table 9.1(a). After propositionalization, the resulting instances will be as in Table 9.1(b). Figure 9.7 illustrates an abstraction process in a taxonomy *T*. The cut s = {*undergrad, master, phd*} has been abstracted to r = {*undergrad, grad*} by replacing *master* and *phd* with *grad*.

Definition 5 (Propositionalized Instance Space)—Any choice of γ over $\tilde{T}$ defines a propositionalized instance space $\tilde{I}$ and if there is a note $\in \gamma$ and $\notin$ *Leaves* $(\tilde{T})$, the induced instance space $\tilde{I}$ is an abstraction of the instance space $\tilde{I}$, which is a propositionalization of the original input space I.

With a data set D, taxonomy $\tilde{T}$, and corresponding valid cuts, we can extend our definition of instance space to include those induced from different levels of abstraction of the propositionalized input space. Accordingly, a hypothesis h generated from an instance space $\tilde{I}$ is a refinement of h_γ associated with an instance space $\tilde{I}$. PAT-NBL and PAT learner work on this induced input space.

9.2.4 Algorithms of Learning Taxonomies from Data

9.2.4.1 Learning Attribute Value Taxonomies

We first describe AVT learner, an algorithm for automated construction of AVT from a data set of instances wherein each instance is described by an ordered tuple of N nominal attribute values and a class label. The problem of learning AVTs from

Table 9.1 Examples of Original (a) and Propositionalized (b) Instances of *University* **Data Set**

(a) Original instances	
Student	*Professor*
freshman	lecturer
sophomore	professor
freshman	associate
senior	assistant

(b) Propositionalized instances									
1	*2*	*3*	*4*	*Master*	*phd*	*lecturer*	*assistant*	*associate*	*professor*
T	F	F	F	F	F	T	F	F	F
F	T	F	F	F	F	F	F	F	T
T	F	F	F	F	F	F	F	T	F
F	F	F	T	F	F	F	T	F	F

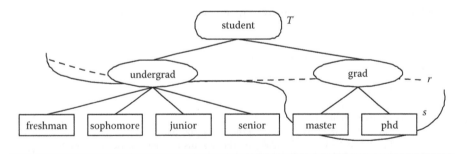

Figure 9.7 Cut abstraction. The cut *s* = *{undergrad, master, phd}* **has been abstracted to** *r* = *{undergrad, grad}* **by replacing** *master* **and** *phd* **with** *grad.*

data can be stated as follows. Given a data set $D \subseteq V_1 \times V_2 \times \dots \times V_n \times C$ and a measure of dissimilarity (or equivalent similarity) between any pair of values of an attribute, output a set of AVTs $T = \{T_1, T_2, \dots T_n\}$ such that each T_i (AVT associated with the attribute A_i) corresponds to a hierarchical grouping of values in V_i based on the specified similarity measure.

We use hierarchical agglomerative clustering (HAC) of the attribute values according to the distribution of classes that co-occur with them. Let $DM(P((x)\|P(y))$

denote a measure of pair-wise divergence between two probability distributions $P(x)$ and $P(y)$, where the random variables x and y take values from the same domain. We use the pair-wise divergence between the distributions of class labels associated with the corresponding attribute values to measure the dissimilarity between the attribute values. Thus, two values of an attribute are considered to be more similar to each other than any other pair of values if their class distributions are more similar to each other than the class distributions associated with any other pair of values for the same attribute.

The lower the divergence between the class distributions associated with two attributes, the greater is their similarity. The choice of this measure of dissimilarity between attribute values is motivated by the intended use of the AVT, namely the construction of accurate, compact, and robust classifiers. If two values of an attribute are indistinguishable from each other based on their class distributions, they provide statistically similar information for classification of instances.

The algorithm for learning AVT for a nominal attribute is shown in Figure 9.8. The basic idea behind AVT learner is to construct an AVT T_i for each attribute A_i by starting with the primitive values in V_i as the leaves of T_i and recursively adding nodes to T_i one at a time by merging two existing nodes. To aid this process, the algorithm maintains a cut d_i through the AVT T_i, updating the cut d_i as new nodes are added to T_i. At each step, the two attribute values to be grouped together to obtain an abstract attribute value to be added to T_i are selected from d_i, based on the divergence between the class distributions associated with the corresponding values. That is, a pair of attribute values in d_i are merged if they have more similar class distributions than any other pair of attribute values in d_i. This process terminates

---

begin

1. **Input:** data set D
2. For each attribute A_i:
3. For each attribute value v_i^j:
4. For each class label c_k: estimate probability $p(c_k | v_i^j)$
5. Let $P(C | v_i^j) = \{p(c_1 | v_i^j), \ldots, p(c_k | v_i^j)\}$ be class distribution associated with value.
6. Set $\delta_i \leftarrow V_i$; Initialize T_i with nodes in δ_i.
7. Iterate until $|\delta_i| = 1$:
8. In δ_i, find $(x, y) = argmin\{DM(P(C | v_i^x) \| P(C | v_i^y))\}$
9. Merge v_i^x and v_i^y $(x \neq y)$ to create new value v_i^{xy}.
10. Calculate probability distribution $P(C | v_i^{xy})$.
11. $\lambda_i \leftarrow \delta_i \cup \{v_i^{xy}\} \setminus \{v_i^x, v_i^y\}$.
12. Update T_i by adding nodes v_i^{xy} as a parent of v_i^x and v_i^y.
13. $\delta_i \leftarrow \lambda_i$.
14. **Output:** $T = \{T_1, T_2, \ldots, T_n\}$

end

Figure 9.8 Pseudocode of AVT learner.

when the cut d_i contains a single value that corresponds to the root of T_i. If $|V_i| = m_i$, the resulting T_i will have $(2m_i-1)$ nodes when the algorithm terminates.

In cases of continuous valued attributes, we define intervals based on observed values for the attribute in the data set. We then generate a hierarchical grouping of adjacent intervals, selecting at each step two adjacent intervals to merge using the pair-wise divergence measure. A cut through the resulting AVT corresponds to a discretization of the continuous valued attribute. A similar approach can be used to generate AVTs from ordinal attribute values.

9.2.4.2 Learning Word Taxonomies

The problem of learning a word taxonomy from sequence data can be stated as follows. Given a data set represented as a set of instances in which an instance is a frequency vector $<f_i, c>$ of a word $w_i Î S$, associated class label c, and a similarity measure among the words, output word taxonomy T_S corresponds to a hierarchical grouping of words in S based on the specified similarity measure. Since this problem is similar to the problem for learning AVT, we take a similar approach of applying AVT learner to word taxonomy learner (WTL).

9.2.4.3 Learning PAT

We use hierarchical agglomerative clustering (HAC) of Boolean attributes based on the distribution of class labels that co-occur with the attributes when they are "true." The pseudocode for PAT learner is shown in Figure 9.9. The basic idea is

```
begin
    1.  Input: propositionalized data set D̃
    2.  For each attribute Ã_i ∈Ã :
    3.  For each class c_k ∈ C:
    4.  Estimate probability distribution p(c_k|Ã_i)
    5.  Let P(C|Ã_i) = {p(c_1|Ã_i),...,p(c_k|Ã_i)} be class distribution associated with attribute Ã_i.
    6.  γ ← Ã
    7.  Initialize T̃ with nodes in γ.
    8.  Iterate until |γ| = 1:
    9.  Find (x, y) = argmin {DM (P (C|x) ||P(C|y))}, where x, y ∈ γ and x ≠ y
    10. Merge x and y to create a new value z.
    11. Calculate probability distribution P (C|z).
    12. γ̂ ← γ ∪ {z} \ {x, y}.
    13. Update T_ΣP by adding nodes z as parents of x and y.
    14. γ ← γ̂.
    15. Output: T_ΣP
end
```

Figure 9.9   Pseudocode of PAT learner.

to construct a taxonomy $\tilde{T}$ by starting with the primitive attributes in $\tilde{A}$ as the leaves of $\tilde{T}$ and recursively adding nodes to $\tilde{T}$ one at a time by merging two existing nodes.

Let $DM(P(x)\|Q(x))$ denote a measure of pair-wise divergence between two probability distributions P and Q of the random variable x. We use a pair-wise measure of divergence between the distributions of the class labels associated with the corresponding Boolean attributes as a measure of dissimilarity. The lower the divergence between the class distribution of two attributes, the greater is their similarity. The choice of this measure is motivated by the intended use of propositionalized attribute taxonomy for a PAT-aware algorithm to generate classifiers. If two attributes are indistinguishable with respect to their class distribution, they will provide statistically similar information for classification of instance.

The algorithm maintains a cut γ through the taxonomy $\tilde{T}$, updating the cut γ as new nodes are added to $\tilde{T}$. At each step, the two words to be grouped to yield an abstract word to be added to $\tilde{T}$ are selected from γ based on the divergence between the class distributions associated with the corresponding words. That is, a pair of words in γ is merged if they have more similar class distributions than any other pair of words in γ. This process terminates when the cut γ contains a single word that corresponds to the root of $\tilde{T}$. Overall, the algorithm iterates $\left(|\tilde{A}|-1\right)$ times of merging, and at each merging it adds one more abstract node to the taxonomy. Hence, the resulting $\tilde{T}$ will have $\left(2|\tilde{A}|-1\right)$ nodes when the algorithm terminates.

9.2.5 Pair-Wise Divergence Measures

Similiarities between two probability distributions can be measured by several methods. We tested 13 divergence measures for probability distributions P and Q, including J-divergence. Jensen–Shannon divergence, and arithmetic and geometric mean divergence.

J-divergence (Topsøe, 2000)—Also known as Jeffreys–Kullback–Liebler divergence, this method is a symmetric version of Kullback–Liebler (KL) divergence. J-divergence between two probability distributions P and Q is defined as:

$$J(P\|Q) = (K(P\|Q) + K(Q\|P)) = \sum (p_i - q_i)\log\left(\frac{pi}{qi}\right)$$

where Kullback–Liebler divergence, also known as relative information, directed divergence, relative entropy, and function of discrimination, is given by:

$$K(P\|Q) = \sum \left(p_i \log\left(\frac{p_i}{q_i}\right)\right)$$

Kullback–Liebler divergence is a natural measure for dissimilarity of distributions. It is nonnegative and reflexive; it is asymmetric and does not satisfy triangle inequality.

Jensen–Shannon divergence (Slonim et al., 2006)—This is a weighted information gain technique also called Jensen difference divergence, information radius, and Sibson–Burbea–Rao–Jensen–Shannon divergence:

$$I(P \| Q) = \frac{1}{2} \left[\sum p_i \log\left(\frac{2p_i}{p_i + q_i} \right) + \sum q_i \log\left(\frac{2q_i}{p_i + q_i} \right) \right]$$

Jensen–Shannon divergence is reflexive, symmetric, and bounded. Figure 9.10 shows an AVT of an *odor* attribute generated by AVT learner (with binary clustering).

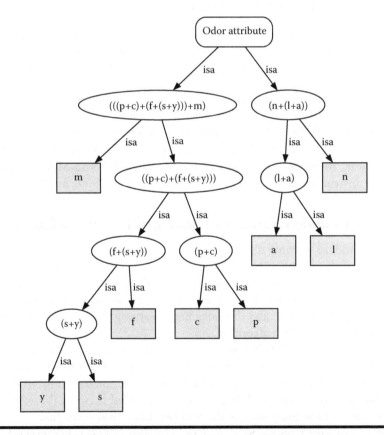

Figure 9.10 AVT of *odor* attribute of UCI's AGARICUS-LEPIOTA mushroom data set generated by AVT learner using Jensen–Shannon divergence (binary clustering).

Arithmetic and geometric (A&G) mean divergence (Taneja, 1995)—
Popularly known as backward Jensen–Shannon divergence, the formula is:

$$T(P \| Q) = \sum \left(\frac{p_i + q_i}{2} \right) \log \left(\frac{p_i + q_i}{2\sqrt{p_i q_i}} \right)$$

It is the KL divergence between the arithmetic and geometric means of two distributions. Since the results from different symmetric divergence measures do not reveal remarkable differences, we limit discussion to the Jensen–Shannon divergence measure.

9.3 Evaluation of Taxonomies

Our approach to evaluating AVTs generated by AVT learner arose because an AVT that captures relevant relationships among attribute values can generate simple and accurate classifiers from data, just as an appropriate choice of axioms in a mathematical domain can simplify proofs of theorems. Thus, the simplicity and predictive accuracy of the learned classifiers based on alternative choices of AVT can be used to evaluate the utility of a corresponding AVT in specific contexts. Similar arguments are applicable for WTL and PAT learner. For evaluation, it is necessary to discuss the learning algorithms that can exploit taxonomies. We explain AVT-NBL (Zhang and Honavar, 2004) for structured multivariate data, WTNBL-MN (Kang et al., 2005) for unstructured data, PAT-DTL (Kang and Sohn, 2009), and PAT-NBL.

9.3.1 AVT-Guided Variants of Standard Learning Algorithms

To make standard learning algorithm-aware taxonomies, we extend the standard learning algorithms in principled ways to exploit the information provided by AVT. AVT-DTL (Yamazaki et al., 1995; Zhang et al., 2002; Zhang and Honavar, 2003) and AVT-NBL (Zhang and Honavar, 2004) that extend the decision tree learning algorithm (Quinlan, 1993) and the naive Bayes learning algorithm (Langley et al., 1992) are examples of such algorithms.

The basic idea behind AVT-NBL is to start with the naive Bayes classifier based on the most abstract attribute values in AVTs and successively refine the classifier by a scoring function—a conditional minimum description length (CMDL) score suggested by Friedman et al. (1997) to capture trade-off between the accuracy of classification and the complexity of the resulting naive Bayes classifier.

The experiments reported by Zhang and Honavar (2004) using several benchmark data sets show that AVT-NBL is able to learn, via human-generated AVTs, substantially more accurate classifiers than those produced by naive Bayes learner (NBL) applied directly to the data sets and to data sets represented by a set of binary features that correspond to the nodes of the AVT (PROP-NBL). The classifiers generated by AVT-NBL are substantially more compact than those generated by NBL and PROP-NBL. These results hold across a wide range of missing attribute values in data sets. Hence, the performance of naive Bayes classifiers generated by AVT-NBL when supplied with AVTs generated by AVT learner provide useful measures of the effectiveness of AVT learner in discovering hierarchical groupings of attribute values that are useful in constructing compact and accurate classifiers from data.

9.3.2 WTNBL-MN Algorithm

If you understand the underlying idea of AVT-guided variants of standard learning algorithms, it is easy to understand the other taxonomy-aware algorithms because they are similar. The problem of learning classifiers from a word taxonomy and sequence data is a natural generalization of the problem of learning classifiers from sequence data. An original data set D is a collection of labeled instances $<I_i, C_j>$ where $I \hat{\in} I$. A classifier is a hypothesis in the form of function $h: I \rightarrow C$, whose domain is the instance space I and range is the set of class C. A hypothesis space H is a set of hypotheses that can be represented in some hypothesis language or by a parameterized family of functions. The task of learning classifiers from data set D is to induce a hypothesis $h \hat{\in} H$ that satisfies given criteria.

Learning classifiers from word taxonomy and data can be described by assuming a word taxonomy T_Σ over words Σ and a data set D. The aim is to induce a classifier $h_{\gamma^*}: I_{\gamma^*} \rightarrow C$ where γ^* is a cut that maximizes given criteria. Note that the resulting hypothesis space $H_{\hat{\gamma}}$ of a chosen cut $\hat{\gamma}$ is efficient in searching for both concise and accurate hypotheses. Word taxonomy-guided NBL has two major components: (1) estimation of parameters of naive Bayes classifiers based on a cut, and (b) a criterion for refining a cut.

9.3.3 Aggregation of Class Conditional Frequency Counts

We can estimate the relevant parameters of a naive Bayes classifier efficiently by aggregating class conditional frequency counts. For a particular node of a given cut, parameters of the node can be estimated by summing the class conditional frequency counts of its children (Zhang and Honavar, 2004).

Given word taxonomy T_Σ, we can define a tree of class conditional frequency counts T_f so that there is one-to-one correspondence between the nodes of word taxonomy T_Σ and the nodes of the corresponding T_f. The class conditional frequency counts associated with a nonleaf node of T_f are aggregations of the corresponding class conditional frequency counts associated with its children. Because a cut through word taxonomy corresponds to a partition of the set of words, the corresponding cut through T_f specifies a valid class conditional probability table for words. Therefore, to estimate each node of T_f, we simply estimate the class conditional frequency counts of primitive words in Σ that correspond to the leaves of T_f. Then we aggregate them recursively to calculate the class conditional frequency counts associated with their parent node.

9.3.3.1 Multinomial Model for Representing Text and Sequence

In a multinomial model, a sequence is represented as a vector of word occurrence frequencies $f_{i,j}$. The probability of an instance I_j given its class c_j is defined as follows:

$$P(d_j \mid c_j) = \left\{ \frac{\left(\sum_i^{|\Sigma|} f_{i,j} \right)!}{\prod_i^{|\Sigma|} (f_{i,j})!} \right\} \prod_i^{|\Sigma|} \{p_{i,j}^{f_{i,j}}\} \tag{9-1}$$

The term $\{(\sum_i^{|\Sigma|} f_{i,j})! / \prod_i^{|\Sigma|} (f_{i,j})!\}$ represents the number of possible combinations of words for the instance I_j. In Equation 9-1, p_{ij} is basically calculated as:

$$p_{i,j} = \frac{Count(c_j, w_i)}{Count(c_j)}$$

$Count(c_j, w_i)$ is the number of times word w_i appears in all the instances that have class labels c_j. $Count(c_j)$ is the total number of words in a particular class label c_j. With Laplacian smoothing, $p_{i,j}$ will be:

$$p_{i,j} = \frac{1 + Count(c_j, w_i)}{|\Sigma| + Count(c_j)}$$

Or, if we follow the Dirichlet prior, $p_{v_i, c}$ will be:

$$p_{v_i, c} = \frac{\bar{L} / |v| + Count(c, v_i)}{\bar{L} + Count(c)}$$

where $\bar{L}$ is an average length and $|v|$ is the number of values. If we consider the number of words in an instance (i.e., document length) (McCallum and Nigam, 1998) and assume that document length is independent of class for simplicity, we get:

$$P(v \mid c) = P(d) \left\{ \frac{d!}{\prod_i^{|v|} v_i!} \right\} \prod_i^{|v|} \{p_{v_i, c}^{v_i}\} \tag{9-2}$$

where $d = (\sum_i^{|v|} v_i)$ is the number of words in a particular instance (document length). In practice, document length may be class dependent:

$$P(v \mid c) = P(\mid d \mid \mid c) \left\{ \frac{d}{\prod\limits_i^{|v|} v_i!} \right\}^{|v|} \prod\limits_i \{ p_{v_i,c}^{v_i} \}$$

9.3.3.2 *Conditional Minimum Description Length of Naive Bayes Classifier*

We used a conditional minimum description length (CMDL; Friedman et al., 1997) score to grade the refinement of the naive Bayes classifier for the multinomial model.

Let v_j be a set of attribute values of jth instance $d_j \hat{\text{I}} D$, and $c_j \hat{\text{I}} C$ a class label associated with d_j. The conditional log likelihood of the hypothesis B given data D is:

$$CLL(B \mid D) = \mid D \mid \sum\limits^{|D|} \log\{P_B(c \mid v)\} = \mid D \mid \sum\limits^{|D|} \log \left\{ \frac{P_B(c)P_B(v \mid c)}{\sum\limits_{c_i}^{|C|} P_B(c_i)P_B(v \mid c_i)} \right\} \quad (9\text{-}3)$$

For a naive Bayes classifier, this score can be efficiently calculated (Zhang and Honavar, 2004):

$$CLL(B \mid D) = \mid D \mid \sum\limits^{|D|} \log \left\{ \frac{P_B(c)\Pi^{v_i \ominus}\{P_B(v_i \mid c)\}}{\sum\limits_{c_i}^{|C|} P_B(c_i)\Pi^{v_j \ominus}\{P_B(v_j \mid c_i)\}} \right\}$$

The corresponding CMDL score is defined as follows:

$$CMDL(B \mid D) = -CLL(B \mid D) + \left\{ \frac{\log \mid D \mid}{2} \right\} size(B)$$

where $size(B)$ is a size of the hypothesis B corresponding to the number of entries in the conditional probability tables (CPTs) of B. In the case of a naive Bayes classifier with a multivariate Bernoulli model, the equation is:

$$size(B) = \mid C \mid + \mid C \mid \sum\limits_{i=1}^{|v|} \mid v_i \mid \quad (9\text{-}4)$$

where $\mid C \mid$ is the number of class labels, $\mid v \mid$ is the number of attributes, and $\mid v_i \mid$ is the number of attribute values for an attribute v_i.

9.3.3.3 Conditional Minimum Description Length of Naive Bayes Classifier for Multinomial Model

Combining Equations 9-1 and 9-3, we can obtain the conditional log likelihood of the classifier B given data D under the naive Bayes multinomial model.

$$CLL(B \mid D) = |D| \sum_{j}^{|D|} \log \left\{ \frac{P(c_j) \left\{ \frac{\left(\sum_{i}^{|\Sigma|} f_{i,j} \right)!}{\prod_{i}^{|\Sigma|} (f_i, j)!} \right\} \prod_{i}^{|\Sigma|} \{ p_{i,j}^{f_{i,j}} \}}{\sum_{k}^{|C|} \left\{ P(c_k) \left\{ \frac{\left(\sum_{i}^{|\Sigma|} f_i, k \right)!}{\prod_{i}^{|\Sigma|} (f_i, k)!} \right\} \prod_{i}^{|\Sigma|} \{ p_{i,k}^{f_{i,k}} \} \right\}} \right\} \quad (9\text{-}5)$$

where $|D|$ is the number of instances, $c_j \hat{I} C$ is a class label for instance $d_j \hat{I} D$, $f_{i,j}$ is an integer frequency of word $w_i \hat{I} \Sigma$ in instance d_j, and $p_{i,j}$ is the estimated probability that word w_i occurred in the instances associated to class label j. The CMDL of a naive Bayes classifier for the multinomial model is defined as:

$$CMDL(B \mid D) = -CLL(B \mid D) + \left\{ \frac{\log |D|}{2} \right\} size(B)$$

where $size(B)$ is a size of the hypothesis B corresponding to the number of entries in conditional probability tables (CPTs) of B. Therefore, $size(B)$ is estimated as:

$$size(B) = |C| + |C||\Sigma| \quad (9\text{-}6)$$

where $|C|$ is the number of class labels and $|\Sigma|$ is the number of words.

9.3.3.4 Computation of CMDL Score

Because each word is assumed to be independent of others given the class, the search for the word taxonomy-guided naive Bayes classifier can be performed efficiently by optimizing the CMDL criteria for each word independently. Thus, the resulting hypothesis h intuitively trades off the complexity in terms of the number of parameters against the accuracy of classification. A hill-climbing search of the locally optimal cut can be achieved by top-down and bottom-up approaches. WTNBL-MN uses cut refinement for top-down search and cut abstraction for bottom-up search. The cut γ is initialized as child nodes of the root of the taxonomy T_S, and is refined for each node in the cut. The algorithm terminates when none of the candidate refinements of the classifier yields statistically significant improvements in CMDL scores. For binary clustered taxonomies, the algorithm stops after $|S| - 1$ iterations at the worst case. Figure 9.11 outlines WTNBL-MN with refinement.

```
begin
    1. Input: data set D and word taxonomy T_Σ
    2. Initialize cut γ to root of T_Σ
    3. Estimate probabilities that specify hypothesis h_γ
    4. Repeat until no change in cut γ
    5. γ̄ ← γ
    6. For each node v ∈ γ:
    7. Generate refinement γ^v of γ by replacing v with its children.
    8. Construct corresponding hypothesis h_{γ^v}.
    9. If CMDL(h_{γ^v}|D) < CMDL(h_γ̄|D), replace γ̄ with γ^v.
   10. If γ ≠ γ̄ , γ ← γ̄
   11. Output: h_γ
end
```

Figure 9.11   Pseudocode of WTNBL-MN.

9.3.4 *PAT-Guided Variants of Standard Learning Algorithm*

We explain two PAT-aware machine learning algorithms: PAT-guided decision tree learner (PAT-DTL) and PAT-guided naive Bayes learner (PAT-NBL). Basically, original data set D is a collection of labeled instances $< I, C >$ where I Î I. Let a classifier be a hypothesis in the form of function $h: I \rightarrow$ ç. A hypothesis space ì is a set of hypotheses that can be represented in a parameterized family of functions. The task of learning classifiers from the data set D is to induce a hypothesis h Î ì that satisfies criteria to maximize the performance.

The problem of learning classifiers from propositionalized attribute taxonomy and propositionalized data can be described as follows. Based on a propositionalized attribute taxonomy $\tilde{T}$ and a propositionalized data set $\tilde{D}$, the aim is induce a classifier $h_{γ^*}: \tilde{\mathbb{I}}_{γ^*} \rightarrow \mathbb{C}$ where $γ *$ is a cut that maximizes given criteria. Of interest is that the resulting hypothesis space $\mathbb{H}_{\hat{γ}}$ of a chosen cut $\hat{γ}$ is efficient in searching for both concise and accurate hypotheses.

9.3.4.1 *PAT-Guided Decision Tree Learner (PAT-DTL)*

The search for the locally optimal cut of PAT-DTL over the propositionalized attribute taxonomy is based on the accuracy of the decision trees generated from the training data as a model evaluation criterion. The accuracy for model selection is measured by a five-fold stratified cross-validation scheme to avoid over-fitting. The decision trees are constructed by a C4.5 decision tree learning algorithm (Quinlan, 1993). The algorithm terminates when no candidate refinements of the classifier yield statistically significant improvement in the model evaluation criterion.

Figure 9.12 outlines the PAT-DTL algorithm with abstraction. Because the algorithm uses abstraction, the cut $γ$ is initialized as leaves of propositionalized

---

begin

1. **Input**: propositionalized data set $\tilde{D}$ and propositionalized attribute taxonomy $\tilde{T}$
2. Initialize cut γ to leaves of $\tilde{T}$, *Leaves* $(\tilde{T})$
3. Estimate class conditional frequency counts and generate hypothesis h_γ
4. Repeat until no change in cut γ or $|\gamma| \leq 1$
5. $\bar{\gamma} \leftarrow \gamma$
6. $p_\gamma \leftarrow$ set of parents of all elements in γ
7. For each node $v \in p_\gamma$:
8. Generate abstraction γ^v of γ by substituting v for children $\in \gamma$ of v
9. Construct corresponding hypothesis h_{γ^v} using C4.5 algorithm.
10. If $CV5(h_{\gamma^v}) > CV5(h_{\bar{\gamma}})$ replace $\bar{\gamma}$ with γ^v.
11. If $\gamma \neq \bar{\gamma}$, $\gamma \leftarrow \bar{\gamma}$
12. **Output**: h_γ

end

Figure 9.12   Pseudocode of PAT-DTL.

---

begin

1. **Input**: propositionalized data set $\tilde{D}$ and propositionalized attribute taxonomy $\tilde{T}$
2. Initialize cut γ to the leaves of $\tilde{T}$, *Leaves* $(\tilde{T})$
3. Estimate class conditional frequency counts and generate hypothesis h_γ
4. Repeat until no change in cut γ or $|\gamma| \leq 1$
5. $\bar{\gamma} \leftarrow \gamma$
6. $p_\gamma \leftarrow$ set of parents of all elements in γ
7. For each node $v \in p_\gamma$:
8. Generate abstraction γ^v of γ by substituting v for children $\in \gamma$ of v
9. Construct corresponding hypothesis h_{γ^v}.
10. If $CMDL(h_{\gamma^v}|D) > CMDL(h_{\bar{\gamma}}|D)$, replace $\bar{\gamma}$ with γ^v.
11. If $\gamma \neq \bar{\gamma}$, $\gamma \leftarrow \bar{\gamma}$
12. **Output**: h_γ

end

Figure 9.13   Pseudocode of PAT-NBL.

attribute taxonomy *Leaves*$(\tilde{T})$, and abstracted for each parent of the nodes in the cut. For binary clustered taxonomy, the algorithm stops after $|\tilde{\mathbb{A}}|-1$ iterations at the worst case.

9.3.4.2 PAT-Guided Naive Bayes Learner (PAT-NBL)

We now explain the PAT-NBL algorithm. As noted above, taxonomy-aware algorithms share the common idea of performing regularization over a taxonomy. Figure 9.13 outlines the PAT-NBL algorithm with abstraction. The algorithm to compute CMDL scores is similar to the WTNBL-MN algorithm (Figure 9.11). We explained propositionalized instance spaces in PAT-DTL in detail in Section 9.3.3. To avoid duplication, we omit a detailed explanation of the PAT-NBL algorithm.

Propositionalized attribute taxonomy-guided naive Bayes learner (PAT-NBL) is a bottom-up multilevel PAT-guided hill-climbing search algorithm in a hypothesis space. PAT-NBL is composed of two major components: (1) computation of counts based on the given PAT, and (2) construction of a hypothesis based on the counts. Since we already explained these ideas in Section 9.3.2, we omit the explanation here.

9.4 Experiments Evaluating Taxonomies

9.4.1 Experiments for AVT

Figure 9.14 shows the experimental setup. The AVTs generated by AVT learner are evaluated by comparing the performance of naive Bayes classifiers produced by applying NBL and AVT-NBL to the original data set (see Figure 9.14). As benchmarks, we chose 37 data sets from the UCI data repository (Blake and Merz, 1998). Among the data sets chosen, AGARICUS-LEPIOTA and NURSERY had AVTs supplied by human experts. A botanist prepared the AVT for AGARICUS-LEPIOTA. The one for NURSERY data was based on our understanding of the domain.

In each experiment, we randomly divided each data set into three equal parts and used a third of the data for AVT construction using AVT learner. The remaining two thirds were used to generate and evaluate the classifier. Each set of AVTs generated by AVT learner was evaluated for error rate and the sizes of the resulting classifiers (as measured by the number of entries in CPTs). The error rate and size estimates were obtained using 10-fold cross-validation on the part of the two thirds set aside for evaluating the classifier. The results reported correspond to averages of the 10-fold cross-validation estimates obtained from the three choices of AVT construction and AVT evaluation. This process prevents information leakage between the data used for AVT construction and the data used for classifier construction and evaluation.

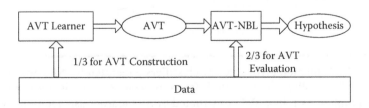

Figure 9.14   Evaluation setups of AVTs with AVT-NBL.

Ten-fold cross-validation experiments were performed to evaluate human expert-supplied AVTs on the AVT evaluation data sets used in the experiments for the AGARICUS-LEPIOTA and NURSERY data sets.

We also evaluated the robustness of the AVTs generated by AVT learner by using them to construct classifiers from data sets with varying percentages of missing attribute values. The data sets with different percentages of missing values were generated by uniformly sampling from instances and attributes to introduce the desired percentages of missing values.

Our results for NBL and AVT-NBL revealed the following:

1. AVTs generated by AVT learner are competitive with human-generated AVTs when used by AVT-NBL. The results shown in Figure 9.15 indicate that AVT learner is effective in constructing AVTs that are competitive with human expert-supplied AVTs for use in classification with respect to error rates and sizes of the resulting classifiers.

2. AVT learner can generate useful AVTs when no human-generated AVTs are available. No human-supplied AVTs were available for most of the data sets. Figure 9.16 shows the error rate estimates for naive Bayes classifiers generated by AVT-NBL using AVTs generated by AVT learner and classifiers generated by NBL applied to the DERMATOLOGY data set. The results suggest that AVT learner, using Jensen–Shannon divergence, can generate AVTs that, when used by AVT-NBL, produce classifiers that are more accurate than those generated by NBL. Additional experiments with other data sets

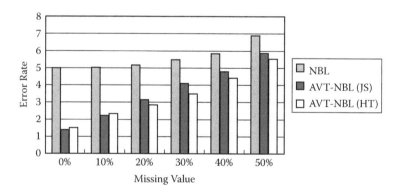

Figure 9.15 Estimated error rates of classifiers generated by NBL and AVT-NBL on AGARICUS-LEPIOTA data with different percentages of missing values. HT = human-supplied AVT. JS = AVT constructed by AVT learner using Jensen–Shannon divergence.

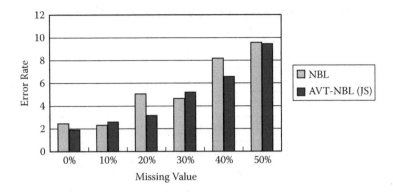

Figure 9.16 Error rate estimates of standard NBL compared with AVT-NBL on dermatology data. JS = AVT constructed by AVT learner using Jensen–Shannon divergence.

produced similar results. Table 9.2 shows classifier accuracies of the original UCI data sets for NBL and AVT-NBL using AVTs generated by AVT learner. A 10-fold cross-validation was used for evaluation and Jensen–Shannon divergence used for AVT generation. The user-specified number for discretization was 10. Thus, AVT learner can generate AVTs that are useful to construct compact and accurate classifiers from data.

3. AVTs generated by AVT learner, when used by AVT-NBL, yield substantially more compact naive Bayes classifiers than those produced by NBLs. Naive Bayes classifiers constructed by AVT-NBL generally had fewer parameters than those from NBL (see Figure 9.17). Table 9.3 shows classifier sizes measured by the number of parameters on selected UCI data sets for NBL and AVT-NBL using AVTs generated by AVT learner.

These results suggest that AVT learner is capable of grouping attribute values into AVTs so that the resulting AVTs, when used by AVT-NBL, result in compact yet accurate classifiers.

9.4.2 Experiments for Word Taxonomy

The results of experiments described in this section indicate that WTNBL-MN coupled with WTLs usually generates more concise and often more accurate classifiers than those of the naive Bayes classifiers for the multinomial model. We conducted experiments with two sequence classification tasks: text (word sequence) classification and protein (amino acid sequence) classification. In both cases, word taxonomies were generated using WTL and a classifier was constructed using WTNBL-MN on the resulting WT and sequence data.

Table 9.2   Accuracy of Classifiers Generated by NBL and AVT-NBL on UCI Data Sets*

Data	NBL	AVT-NBL
Anneal	86.30±2.25	**99.00±0.65**
Audiology	73.45±5.76	**76.99±5.49**
Auto	56.10±6.79	**86.83±4.63**
Balance-scale	90.40±2.31	**91.36±2.20**
Breast-cancer	71.68±5.22	**72.38±5.18**
Breast-w	95.99±1.45	**97.28±1.21**
Car	85.53±1.66	**86.17±1.63**
Colic	77.99±4.23	**83.42±3.80**
Credit-a	77.68±3.11	**86.52±2.55**
Credit-g	75.40±2.67	75.40±2.67
Dermatology	97.81±1.50	**98.09±1.40**
Diabetes	76.30±3.01	**77.99±2.93**
Glass	48.60±6.70	**80.84±5.27**
Heart-c	83.50±4.18	**87.13±3.77**
Heart-h	83.67±4.22	**86.39±3.92**
Heart-statlog	83.70±4.41	**86.67±4.05**
Hepatitis	84.52±5.70	**92.90±4.04**
Hypothyroid	95.28±0.68	**95.78±0.64**
Ionosphere	82.62±3.96	**94.59±2.37**
Iris	**96.00±3.14**	94.67±3.60
Kr-vs-kp	87.89±1.13	**87.92±1.13**
Labor	89.47±7.97	89.47±7.97
Letter	64.12±0.66	**70.54±0.63**
Lymph	83.11±6.04	**84.46±5.84**
Mushroom	95.83±0.43	**99.59±0.14**

Table 9.2 (Continued)   Accuracy of Classifiers Generated by NBL and AVT-NBL on UCI Data Sets*

Data	NBL	AVT-NBL
Nursery	90.32±0.51	90.32±0.51
Primary-tumor	**50.15±5.32**	47.79±5.32
Segment	80.22±1.62	**90.00±1.22**
Sick	92.68±0.83	**97.83±0.47**
Sonar	67.79±6.35	**99.52±0.94**
Soybean	92.97±1.92	**94.58±1.70**
Splice	95.36±0.73	**95.77±0.70**
Vehicle	44.90±3.35	**67.85±3.15**
Vote	90.11±2.80	90.11±2.80
Vowel	**63.74±2.99**	42.42±3.08
Waveform-5000	**80.00±1.11**	65.08±1.32
Zoo	93.07±4.95	**96.04±3.80**

* Error rates calculated by 10-fold cross validation with 95% confidence interval.

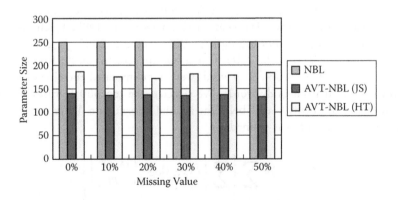

Figure 9.17   Size (number of parameters) of the standard NBL compared with AVT-NBL on AGARICUS-LEPIOTA data. HT = human-supplied AVT. JS = AVT constructed by AVT learner using Jensen–Shannon divergence.

Table 9.3 Parameter Sizes of Classifiers from Use of NBL and AVT-NBL on Selected UCI Data Sets

Data	NBL	AVT-NBL
Audiology	3720	**3600**
Breast-cancer	104	**62**
Car	88	**80**
Dermatology	906	**540**
Kr-vs-kp	150	**146**
Mushroom	252	**124**
Nursery	140	**125**
Primary-tumor	836	**814**
Soybean	1919	**1653**
Splice	864	**723**
Vote	66	66
Zoo	259	**238**

9.4.2.1 Text Classification

The Reuters 21578 Distribution 1.0 data set* consists of 12,902 news wire articles in 135 overlapping topic categories. We built binary classifiers for the 10 most populous categories of text classification (Dumais et al., 1998; Joachims, 1998; McCallum and Nigam, 1998; Sandler, 2005; Keerthi, 2005; Joachims, 2005; Gabrilovich and Markovitch, 2005; Carvalho and Cohen, 2005; Rooney et al., 2006; Zhang and Lee, 2006). Stop words were not eliminated and title words were not distinguished from body words. We selected the top 300 features based on mutual information with class labels. The mutual information $MI(x, c)$ between a feature x and a category c is defined as:

$$MI(x,c) = \sum^{x} \left\{ \sum^{c} \left\{ P(x,c) \log \frac{P(x,c)}{P(x)P(c)} \right\} \right\}$$

We followed the ModApté split (Apté et al., 1994) in which 9,603 stories are used to build classifiers and 3,299 stories test the accuracy of the resulting model. We reported the break-even points, the averages of precision and recall when the

---

* Publicly available at http://www.daviddlewis.com/resources/testcollections/reuters21578/

difference between the two was at a minimum. Precision and recall of text categorization are defined as:

$$\text{Precision} = \frac{|\text{detected documents in the category (true positives)}|}{|\text{documents in the category (true positives + false positives)}|}$$

$$\text{Recall} = \frac{|\text{detected documents in the category (true positives)}|}{|\text{detected documents (true positives + false positives)}|}$$

Table 9.4 shows the break-even point of precision and recall and the size of the classifier (from Equation 9-6) for the 10 most frequent categories. WTNBL-MN usually shows similar performance in terms of break-even performance, except in the case of the *corn* category, while the classifiers generated by WTNBL-MN were smaller than those generated by NBL. Figure 9.18 shows the precision–recall curve (Fawcett, 2003, 2006) for the *grain* category. WTNBL-MN generated a naive Bayes classifier that is more compact than (but performs comparable to) the classifier generated by NBL.

Table 9.4   Break-Even Points of Classifiers from Use of NBL-MN and WTNBL-MN on 10 Largest Categories of Reuters 21578 Data

	NBL-MN		WTNBL-MN		Number of Documents	
Data	*Break-even*	*Size*	*Break-even*	*Size*	*Train*	*Test*
Earn	**94.94**	602	94.57	**348**	2877	1087
Acq	89.43	602	89.43	**472**	1650	719
Money-fx	64.80	602	**65.36**	**346**	538	179
Grain	74.50	602	**77.85**	**198**	433	149
Crude	**79.89**	602	76.72	**182**	389	189
Trade	**59.83**	602	47.01	**208**	369	118
Interest	**61.07**	602	59.54	**366**	347	131
Ship	82.02	602	82.02	**348**	197	89
Wheat	**57.75**	602	53.52	**226**	212	71
Corn	**57.14**	602	21.43	**106**	182	56
Average (top 5)	80.71	602	**80.79**	**309.20**		
Average (top 10)	**72.14**	602	66.75	**280**		

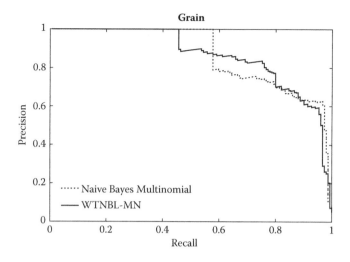

Figure 9.18 Precision–recall curves for *Grain* category.

WTNBL-MN did not show good performance for the *corn* category, possibly because conditional minimum description length trades off the accuracy of the model against its complexity, which may not necessarily optimize precision and recall for a particular class. As a consequence, WTNBL-MN may terminate refinement of the classifier prematurely for class labels with low support, i.e. when the data set is unbalanced.

9.4.2.2 Protein Sequences

We applied the WTNBL-MN algorithm to two protein data sets with a view to identifying their localizations (Reinhardt and Hubbard, 1998; Andorf et al., 2006).

The first data set contained 997 prokaryotic protein sequences derived from the SWISS-PROT data base (Bairoch and Apweiler, 2000). It included proteins from three subcellular locations: cytoplasmic (688 proteins), periplasmic (202 proteins), and extracellular (107 proteins).

The second data set contained 2,427 eukaryotic protein sequences derived from SWISS-PROT (Bairoch and Apweiler, 2000) and included proteins from four subcellular locations: nuclear (1,097 proteins), cytoplasmic (684 proteins), mitochondrial (321 proteins), and extracellular (325 proteins).

For these data sets,* we conducted 10-fold cross validation. To measure performance, the following measures (Yan et al., 2004) were applied and the results for the data sets are reported:

---

* These datasets are available to download at http://www.doe-mbi.ucla.edu/~astrid/astrid.html

$$\text{Correlation coefficient} = \frac{TP \times TN - FP \times FN}{\sqrt{(TP + FN)(TP + FP)(TN + FP)(TN + FN)}}$$

$$\text{Accuracy} = \frac{TP + TN}{TP + TN + FP + FN}$$

$$\text{Sensitivity}^+ = \frac{TP}{TP + FN}$$

$$\text{Specificity}^+ = \frac{TP}{TP + FP}$$

TP is the number of true positives, FP is the number of false positives, TN is the number of true negatives, and FN is the number of false negatives. Figure 9.19 shows the amino acid taxonomy constructed for the prokaryotic protein sequences. Table 9.5 shows the results for the two protein sequences. For both data sets, the classifiers generated by WTNBL were more concise and performed more accurately than the classifier generated by NBL based on the measures reported.

9.4.3 Experiments for PAT

9.4.3.1 Experimental Results from PAT-DTL

In this section, we explore certain performance issues of the proposed algorithms through various experimental settings: (1) performance of PAT-DTL compared with that of C4.5 decision tree learner to see whether taxonomies (as ontologies) can help the algorithm to improve the performance; (2) dissimilarity measures for comparing two probability distributions to see whether the algorithm assesses taxonomies from different disciplines; and (3) comprehensibility of the hypothesis to see whether humans can comprehend the generated hypothesis.

Comparison with C4.5 decision tree learner—We conducted experiments on 37 data sets from the UCI Machine Learning Repository (Blake and Merz, 1998). We tested four settings: (1) C4.5 (Quinlan, 1993) decision tree learner on the original attributes, (2) C4.5 decision tree learner on propositionalized attributes, (3) PAT-DTL with abstraction, and (4) PAT-DTL with refinement. Ten-fold cross-validation was used for evaluation. Taxonomies were generated using PAT learner and a decision tree was constructed using PAT-DTL on the resulting PAT and data.

The results of experiments indicate that none of the algorithms showed the highest accuracy over most data sets. Table 9.6 shows classifier accuracy and tree size on UCI data sets for C4.5 decision tree learner on the original attributes, C4.5 decision

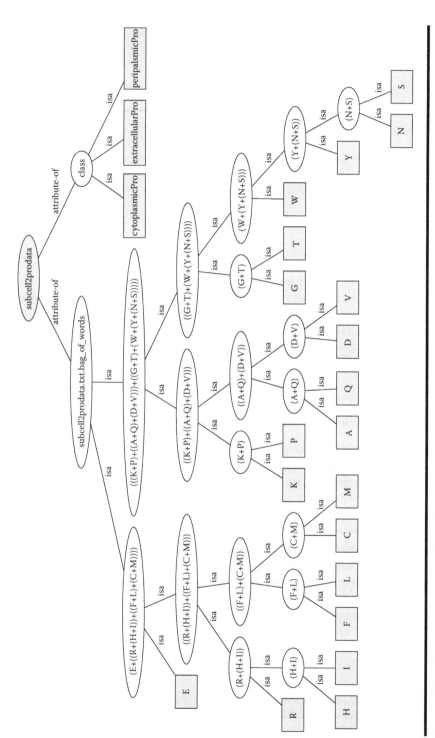

Figure 9.19 Taxonomy from prokaryotic protein localization sequences constructed by WTL.

Table 9.5 Localization Prediction Results of Use of NBL-MN and WTNBL-MN on Prokaryotic (a) and Eukaryotic (b) Protein Sequences

(a) Prokaryotic protein sequences					
NBL-MN	*Correlation Coefficient*	*Accuracy*	*Specificity*[+]	*Sensitivity*[+]	*Size*
Cytoplasmic	71.96±2.79	88.26±2.00	89.60±1.89	93.90±1.49	42
Extracellular	**70.57±2.83**	**93.58±1.52**	**65.93±2.94**	83.18±2.32	42
Periplasmic	51.31±3.10	81.85±2.39	53.85±3.09	72.77±2.76	42
WTNBL-MN	*Correlation Coefficient*	*Accuracy*	*Specificity+*	*Sensitivity+*	*Size*
Cytoplasmic	**72.43±2.77**	**88.47±1.98**	**89.63±1.89**	**94.19±1.45**	**20**
Extracellular	69.31±2.86	93.18±1.56	64.03±2.98	83.18±2.32	**20**
Periplasmic	**51.53±3.10**	81.85±2.39	53.82±3.09	**73.27±2.75**	**40**
(b) Eukaryotic protein sequences					
NBL-MN	*Correlation Coefficient*	*Accuracy*	*Specificity*[+]	*Sensitivity*[+]	*Size*
Nuclear	61.00±1.94	80.72±1.57	82.06±1.53	73.38±1.76	46
Extracellular	36.83±1.92	83.11±1.49	40.23±1.95	53.85±1.98	46
Mitochondrial	25.13±1.73	71.69±1.79	25.85±1.74	61.06±1.94	46
Cytoplasmic	44.05±1.98	71.41±1.80	49.55±1.99	81.29±1.55	46
WTNBL-MN	*Correlation Coefficient*	*Accuracy*	*Specificity*[+]	*Sensitivity*[+]	*Size*
Nuclear	60.82±1.94	80.63±1.57	81.70±1.54	73.66±1.75	24
Extracellular	38.21±1.93	84.01±1.46	42.30±1.97	53.23±1.99	36
Mitochondrial	25.48±1.73	72.35±1.78	26.29±1.75	60.44±1.95	34
Cytoplasmic	43.46±1.97	71.24±1.80	49.37±1.99	80.56±1.57	32

Error rates calculated by 10-fold cross validation with 95% confidence interval.

Note: '+' symbol after specificity and sensitivity means the criteria are measured for the positive class label.

Table 9.6 Accuracy and Tree Size of DTL (C4.5 Decision Tree Learner): Results for Original and Propositionalized Data and PAT-DTL with Abstraction and Refinement on UCI Data Sets

Data	DTL (Original)		DTL (Propositionalized)		PAT-DTL (Abstraction)		PAT-DTL (Refinement)	
	Accuracy	Size	Accuracy	Size	Accuracy	Size	Accuracy	Size
Anneal	98.78±0.72	49	99.33±0.53	27	99.11±0.61	27	90.31±1.93	11
Audiology	77.88±5.41	54	76.11±5.56	49	74.34±5.69	39	46.46±6.50	3
Autos	83.90±5.03	103	80.98±5.37	57	77.56±5.71	45	44.88±6.81	3
Balance-scale	69.60±3.61	13	69.60±3.61	13	73.28±3.47	11	73.92±3.44	11
Breast-cancer	75.52±4.98	6	72.03±5.20	17	70.28±5.3	43	3.43±5.12	7
Breast-w	94.99±1.62	26	95.71±1.50	25	96.14±1.43	21	96.85±1.29	5
Car	92.36±1.25	182	96.88±0.82	137	96.59±0.86	109	85.47±1.66	23
Colic	85.05±3.64	6	81.52±3.97	45	84.51±3.70	31	86.41±3.50	3
Credit-a	87.25±2.49	25	85.80±2.60	17	85.94±2.59	9	85.36±2.64	3
Credit-g	72.10±2.78	63	69.90±2.84	139	72.10±2.78	63	73.00±2.75	5
Dermatology	93.99±2.44	41	96.17±1.97	15	96.99±1.75	19	30.60±4.72	1
Diabetes	78.26±2.92	22	75.78±3.03	23	75.78±3.03	23	73.70±3.11	3
Glass	73.83±5.89	42	74.77±5.82	33	70.56±6.11	29	55.14±6.66	9
Heart-c	78.88±4.60	34	80.53±4.46	33	82.18±4.31	15	82.84±4.25	5

Heart-h	79.93±4.58	11	78.23±4.72	11	77.89±4.74	13	**82.65±4.33**	3
Heart-statlog	81.85±4.60	15	81.85±4.60	15	81.48±4.63	17	**82.22±4.56**	5
Hepatitis	82.58±5.97	10	81.94±6.06	19	**84.52±5.70**	7	83.23±5.88	7
Hypothyroid	**99.47±0.23**	48	99.44±0.24	25	99.36±0.25	23	97.00±0.54	7
Ionosphere	89.17±3.25	27	**92.88±2.69**	17	91.74±2.88	15	**92.88±2.69**	3
Iris	94.00±3.80	4	94.00±3.80	5	**94.67±3.60**	5	88.67±5.07	5
Kr-vs-kp	**99.44±0.26**	59	**99.44±0.26**	57	99.34±0.28	45	72.84±1.54	5
Labor	80.70±10.25	8	87.72±8.52	11	82.46±9.87	9	**89.47±7.97**	3
Letter	78.63±0.57	10520	**82.90±0.52**	3437	81.72±0.54	2937	68.30±0.64	2047
Lymph	**78.38±6.63**	30	77.03±6.78	23	74.32±7.04	23	77.03±6.78	7
Mushroom	**100.00±0.00**	30	**100.00±0.00**	17	99.98±0.03	15	98.52±0.26	3
Nursery	97.05±0.29	511	**99.40±0.13**	379	99.06±0.17	347	66.25±0.81	3
Primary-tumor	39.82±5.21	88	38.64±5.18	101	**44.54±5.29**	97	38.64±5.18	19
Segment	95.32±0.86	324	**95.37±0.86**	131	95.11±0.88	109	78.10±1.69	21
Sick	**97.85±0.46**	36	97.75±0.47	33	97.69±0.48	27	97.61±0.49	7
Sonar	79.81±5.46	31	79.81±5.46	31	**81.73±5.25**	21	76.44±5.77	3
Soybean	91.51±2.09	93	91.95±2.04	85	**93.85±1.80**	67	70.72±3.41	31

(Continued)

Table 9.6 (Continued) Accuracy and Tree Size of DTL (C4.5 Decision Tree Learner): Results for Original and Propositionalized Data and PAT-DTL with Abstraction and Refinement on UCI Data Sets

Data	DTL (Original)		DTL (Propositionalized)		PAT-DTL (Abstraction)		PAT-DTL (Refinement)	
	Accuracy	Size	Accuracy	Size	Accuracy	Size	Accuracy	Size
Splice	94.04±0.82	229	94.04±0.82	145	**94.17±0.81**	115	87.93±1.13	55
Vehicle	**71.99±3.03**	220	71.28±3.05	121	70.21±3.08	133	62.41±3.26	33
Vote	**96.32±1.77**	11	95.86±1.87	11	95.40±1.97	11	95.63±1.92	3
Vowel	**80.91±2.45**	424	**80.91±2.45**	239	76.87±2.63	229	46.46±3.11	135
Waveform-5000	**76.48±1.18**	595	76.44±1.18	857	75.04±1.20	683	68.76±1.28	37
Zoo	92.08±5.27	21	90.10±5.82	17	**93.07±4.95**	15	85.15±6.94	9
# of wins	**14**	2	10	0	8	0	9	35

Error rates estimated using 10-fold cross validation with 95% confidence interval.

tree learner on propositionalized attributes, and PAT-DTL that uses abstraction and refinement. Ten-fold cross-validation was used for evaluation.

In terms of accuracy, the decision trees generated by C4.5 performed better on average (21 of 37 data sets). With regard to tree size, PAT-DTL coupled with PAT learner usually generated more concise decision trees (35 of 37 data sets). However, PAT-DTL often produced comparably accurate classifiers to those of C4.5 decision tree inducer (17 of 37 data sets). PAT-DTL with refinement generally yielded the most concise trees, but for 9 of 37 data sets tested, it yielded decision trees that were also the most accurate. Figure 9.20 shows the decision trees generated by C4.5 on the original data and PAT-DTL with refinement. The tree with 5 nodes generated by PAT-DTL shows better accuracy than that with 34 nodes (six or seven times larger) generated by C4.5.

Execution time of PAT-DTL—PAT-DTL is a generalization of the C4.5 decision tree learning algorithm with regularization over taxonomies. At each refinement or abstraction step, PAT-DTL runs C4.5 multiple times to generate hypotheses and perform k-fold cross validation. Thus, the algorithm takes more time and space than the original C4.5 decision tree learning algorithm. However, the increase of complexity is linear with respect to the number of nodes in the taxonomy—equal to $(2|\tilde{A}|-1)$ where $|\tilde{A}|$ is the number of propositionalized attribute values. Table 9.7 shows the classifier evaluation values for executing efficiency on UCI data sets for C4.5 decision tree learner on the original attributes, C4.5 decision tree learner on propositionalized attributes, and PAT-DTL using abstraction and refinement.

Note that PAT-DTL with refinement requires less complexity than PAT-DTL with abstraction. It is because PAT-DTL with refinement starts from the cut at the top of the taxonomy which induces the the smallest instance space, and gradually expands the input space through refinements over taxonomies. But PAT-DTL with abstraction starts from the cut at the bottom of the taxonomy, inducing the largest instance space; it gradually shrinks the input space through abstractions over taxonomies. Also, DTL on the propositionalized data sets usually takes more time than DTL on the original data sets because propositionalization generates data sets with more attributes.

Taxonomies with Different Dissimilarity Measures—There are several ways to measure similarities of two probability distributions. One may wonder what the optimal measure for taxonomy construction to produce concise and accurate classifiers is. Thus, it is of interest to compare several dissimilarity measures from an experimental view.

We conducted experiments with three dissimilarity measures on selected data sets from the UCI Machine Learning Repository (Blake and Merz, 1998). Table 9.8 shows classifier accuracy and tree size of the PAT-DTL algorithm (refinement) coupled with Jeffreys–Kullback–Liebler (JKL), Jensen–Shannon (JS), and arithmetic and geometric mean (AGM) divergences on selected UCI data sets. The table indicates that none of the three divergence measures was always superior for taxonomy construction with concise and accurate classifiers.

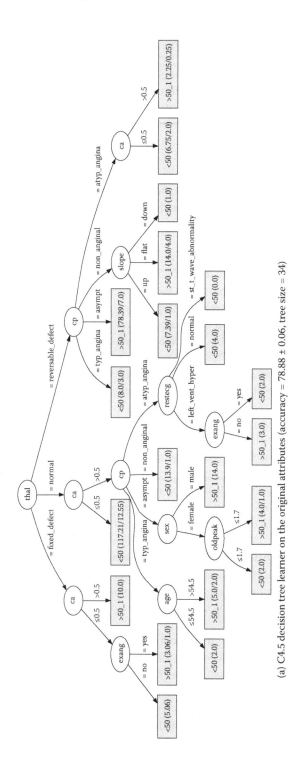

(a) C4.5 decision tree learner on the original attributes (accuracy = 78.88 ± 0.06, tree size = 34)

Figure 9.20(a) **Decision tree learned by C4.5 and PAT-DTL (with specialization) for Cleveland Clinic Foundation's Heart Disease (*heart-c*) data.**

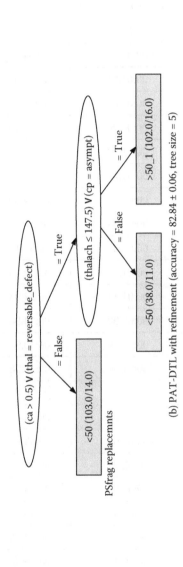

(b) PAT-DTL with refinement (accuracy = 82.84 ± 0.06, tree size = 5)

Figure 9.20(b) Decision tree learned by C4.5 and PAT-DTL (with specialization) for Cleveland Clinic Foundation's Heart Disease (*heart-c*) data.

Table 9.7 Running Times (Minutes:Seconds) of DTL (C4.5 Decision Tree Learner) for Original and Propositionalized Data and PAT-DTL with Abstraction and Refinement on UCI Data Sets

Data	DTL (Original)	DTL (Propositionalized)	PAT-DTL (Abstraction)	PAT-DTL (Refinement)
Anneal	00:01.69	00:02.91	22:55.76	03:07.08
Audiology	00:01.60	00:02.24	18:31.92	00:27.70
Autos	00:01.29	00:01.81	10:45.95	00:24.68
Balance-scale	00:00.95	00:00.85	00:06.30	00:04.86
Breast-cancer	00:01.06	00:06.90	04:27.15	00:40.29
Breast-w	00:01.20	00:01.13	01:23.71	00:13.82
Car	00:01.31	00:01.75	01:12.98	00:27.00
Colic	00:01.05	00:01.35	05:54.09	00:17.09
Credit-a	00:01.09	00:01.83	04:36.33	00:18.07
Credit-g	00:01.49	00:03.60	16:53.16	00:30.69
Dermatology	00:01.05	00:01.42	32:59.23	00:31.77
Diabetes	00:00.97	00:01.13	00:34.93	00:05.18
Glass	00:00.92	00:00.98	00:13.50	00:04.14
Heart-c	00:01.24	00:01.16	00:30.92	00:05.70
Heart-h	00:01.48	00:01.66	00:26.08	00:07.10
Heart-statlog	00:01.17	00:01.43	00:24.71	00:08.94
Hepatitis	00:01.05	00:01.04	00:43.84	00:06.34
Hypothyroid	00:03.26	00:05.63	33:05.69	08:54.18
Ionosphere	00:01.48	00:02.22	60:29.00	01:05.04
Iris	00:00.84	00:00.99	00:03.76	00:03.64
Kr-vs-kp	00:04.09	00:05.52	60:56.00	02:21.48
Labor	00:00.85	00:00.87	00:13.60	00:02.96
Letter	00:14.10	04:20.12	840:57.00	420:00.12
Lymph	00:00.80	00:00.86	00:49.24	00:03.65
Mushroom	00:02.84	00:22.05	563:58.00	11:07.54

Table 9.7 (Continued)   Running Times (Minutes:Seconds) of DTL (C4.5 Decision Tree Learner) for Original and Propositionalized Data and PAT-DTL with Abstraction and Refinement on UCI Data Sets

Data	DTL (Original)	DTL (Propositionalized)	PAT-DTL (Abstraction)	PAT-DTL (Refinement)
Nursery	00:05.09	00:12.90	21:03.24	00:47.45
Primary-tumor	00:01.54	00:01.76	01:18.51	00:09.23
Segment	00:01.91	00:13.05	04:38:55	02:55:53
Sick	00:04.58	00:07.67	43:01.48	02:53.22
Sonar	00:01.06	00:01.09	03:53.15	00:19.08
Soybean	00:01.70	00:02.48	10:16.57	04:15.50
Splice	00:01.50	00:05.77	803:08.00	22:07.00
Vehicle	00:00.77	00:01.12	09:38.08	01:27.03
Vote	00:00.65	00:00.47	00:17.29	00:03.47
Vowel	00:00.63	00:01.69	05:00.22	01:12.13
Waveform-5000	00:02.22	00:17.27	917:01.00	55:23.00
Zoo	00:00.46	00:00.42	00:04.47	00:02.63

Examination of the results of experiments shown in Table 9.8 indicates that all three divergence measures (JKL, JS, and AGM) yielded PATs that, when used by PAT-NBL, produced classifiers with similar accuracy. Of the 13 divergence measures we tested, Hellinger discrimination (Topsøe, 2000), symmetric diversion, and triangular discrimination (Topsøe, 2000) showed similar performances. Thus, PAT learner appears able to use a broad class of measures of similarity of attribute values based on class distributions associated with the respective values to generate PATs that are useful for constructing compact and accurate classifiers from data.

Comprehensibility of hypothesis—Figure 9.21 shows an example of PAT for the subset of attributes in the UCI repository's Balance Scale Weight and Distance Database (*balance scale*). The leaf nodes (gray boxes) correspond to the original attribute values of the *balance scale* data set and the dotted lines show the original attribute–value relationships. After propositionalization, each leaf node is treated as an attribute. The solid lines represent ISA relationships; therefore the nodes with solid lines represent a taxonomy. If we remove all the dotted lines and nodes inside the dotted box in the figure, we can see the taxonomy more clearly.

The *balance scale* data set has only four attributes, but most data sets have many more attributes and their taxonomies are too big to fit on one page. To aid

Table 9.8   Accuracy and Tree Size of PAT-DTL with Refinement Coupled with Divergences* on Selected UCI Data Sets

Data	PAT-DTL(JKL)		PAT-DTL(JS)		PAT-DTL(AGM)	
	Acccuracy	Size	Accuracy	Size	Accuracy	Size
Anneal	**92.43±1.73**	5	90.31±1.93	11	76.17±2.79	1
Audiology	**47.35±6.51**	7	46.46±6.50	3	46.46±6.50	3
Autos	**71.22±6.20**	13	44.88±6.81	3	45.37±6.82	9
Balance-scale	72.80±3.49	7	73.92±3.44	11	**74.40±3.42**	7
Breast-cancer	70.28±5.30	1	**73.43±5.12**	7	69.23±5.35	5
Breast-w	**97.14±1.24**	5	96.85±1.29	5	**97.14±1.24**	5
Car	81.13±1.84	7	85.47±1.66	23	**94.16±1.11**	61
Colic	85.22±3.63	3	**86.41±3.50**	3	**86.41±3.50**	3
Credit-a	85.22±2.65	3	**85.36±2.64**	3	84.93±2.67	5
Credit-g	73.50±2.74	7	73.00±2.75	5	**73.80±2.73**	15
Dermatology	**36.89±4.94**	5	30.60±4.72	1	30.60±4.72	1
Diabetes	**78.39±2.91**	5	73.70±3.11	3	73.70±3.11	3
Glass	**71.96±6.02**	19	55.14±6.66	9	63.08±6.47	13
Heart-c	**83.50±4.18**	5	82.84±4.25	5	**83.50±4.18**	5
Heart-h	**84.01±4.19**	5	82.65±4.33	3	82.99±4.29	3
Heart-statlog	80.00±4.77	5	82.22±4.56	5	**82.96±4.48**	5
Hepatitis	**83.23±5.88**	5	**83.23±5.88**	7	**83.23±5.88**	5
Hypothyroid	**99.13±0.30**	11	97.00±0.54	7	97.22±0.52	7
Ionosphere	**96.01±2.05**	3	92.88±2.69	3	92.31±2.79	3
Iris	94.00±3.80	5	88.67±5.07	5	**96.00±3.14**	5
Kr-vs-kp	66.05±1.64	3	72.84±1.54	5	**85.83±1.21**	5
Labor	87.72±8.52	3	**89.47±7.97**	3	85.96±9.02	5
Letter	55.91±0.56	527	68.30±0.64	2047	67.22±0.65	3261
Lymph	53.38±8.04	3	**77.03±6.78**	7	73.65±7.10	3
Mushroom	**99.70±0.12**	3	98.52±0.26	3	99.41±0.17	3

Table 9.8 (Continued)   Accuracy and Tree Size of PAT-DTL with Refinement Coupled with Divergences* on Selected UCI Data Sets

Data	PAT-DTL(JKL)		PAT-DTL(JS)		PAT-DTL(AGM)	
	Acccuracy	*Size*	*Accuracy*	*Size*	*Accuracy*	*Size*
Nursery	66.25±0.81	3	66.25±0.81	3	**70.97±0.78**	5
Primary-tumor	33.63±5.03	9	**38.64±5.18**	19	30.68±4.91	1
Segment	84.07±1.49	23	78.10±1.69	**21**	**87.10±1.37**	41
Sick	96.85±0.56	3	**97.61±0.49**	7	97.14±0.53	3
Sonar	75.48±5.85	3	**76.44±5.77**	3	**76.44±5.77**	13
Soybean	**87.41±2.49**	63	70.72±3.41	**31**	68.08±3.50	53
Splice	80.31±1.38	17	**87.93±1.13**	55	67.67±1.62	5
Vehicle	**68.79±3.12**	35	62.41±3.26	33	66.43±3.18	17
Vote	**95.63±1.92**	3	**95.63±1.92**	3	**95.63±1.92**	3
Vowel	**55.76±3.09**	133	46.46±3.11	135	49.90±3.11	185
Waveform-5000	**79.88±1.11**	63	68.76±1.28	37	71.38±1.25	39
Zoo	**92.08±5.27**	15	85.15±6.94	9	85.15±6.94	13
# of wins	19	20	11	24	14	21

* Error rates estimated using 10-fold cross validation with 95% confidence interval.
Jeffreys–Kullback–Liebler divergence = JKL. Jensen–Shannon divergence = JS. Arithmetic and Geometric Mean divergence = AGM.

understanding of the interpretation of the taxonomy and the generated decision tree, we show the Cleveland Clinic Foundation's Heart Disease (*heart-c*) data set from the UCI repository. We already showed the decision trees of the *heart-c* data set generated by C4.5 and PAT-DTL in Figure 9.20. Figure 9.22 shows the attribute–value relationships for the subset of attributes in *heart-c*. The data set has 13 attributes (*age, sex, cp, trestbps, chol, fbs, restecg, thalach, exang, oldpeak, slope, ca,* and *thal*). It is hard to show clearly the attribute–value relationships and the taxonomy for the original data set with 13 attributes on a page, so we choose 4 (*cp, thalach, ca,* and *thal*) from the 13 for presentation based on the results in Figure 9.20(b).

Figure 9.22(a) shows the original attribute-value relationship of the subsets of the *heart-c* data set. After propositionalization (Figure 9.22(b)), each attribute value will be considered as having 0 and 1 values. If the original attribute has a certain value, the propositionalized attribute will have a 1 value. Figure 9.23 shows the taxonomy generated from the propositionalized attributes of *heart-c* shown in Figure 9.22(b).

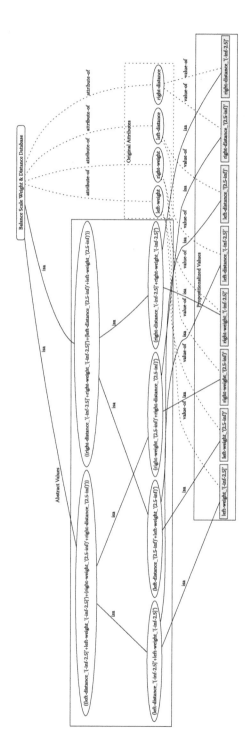

Figure 9.21 Propositionalized attribute taxonomy of Balance Scale Weight and Distance (*balance scale*) data. Dotted lines show original attribute–value relationship.

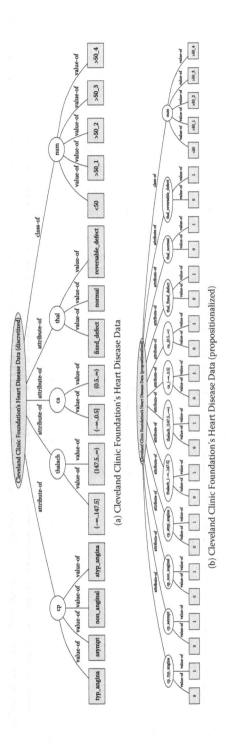

(a) Cleveland Clinic Foundation's Heart Disease Data

(b) Cleveland Clinic Foundation's Heart Disease Data (propositionalized)

Figure 9.22 **Attribute–value relationships for subset of attributes in Cleveland Clinic Foundation's Heart Disease (*heart-c*) data.**

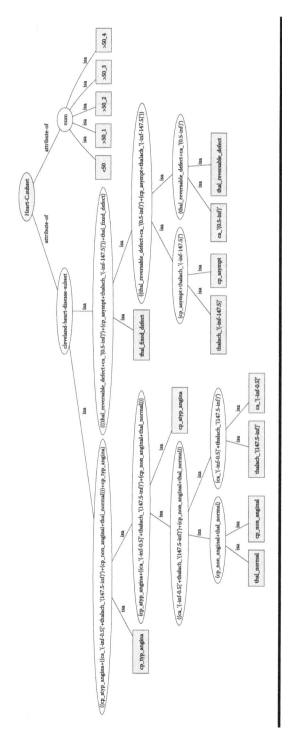

Figure 9.23 Propositionalized attribute taxonomy of Cleveland Clinic Foundation's Heart Disease (*heart-c*) data. Jensen–Shannon divergence measure was used to estimate dissimilarity.

The leaf nodes in Figure 9.23 are propositionalized attributes and each internal node represents merging of all of its descendant leaf nodes. The taxonomy is generated automatically by PAT learner and may not be easily readable for humans. However, in many applications, taxonomies specified by human experts are unavailable. Manual construction of taxonomies requires a great deal of domain expertise, and in case of large data sets with many attributes and many values for each attribute, manual generation of PATs is extremely tedious and not feasible in practice. Considering this drawback, PATs generated automatically by PAT learner are useful in constructing concise and accurate classifiers when used with PAT-DTL.

9.4.3.2 Experimental Results from PAT-NBL

Comparison with naive Bayes learner and model selection criteria—To assess how PAT-NBL algorithms evaluate taxonomies, we conducted experiments on data sets from the UCI Machine Learning Repository (Blake and Merz, 1998) with the following learning algorithm settings:

1. Naive Bayes learner
2. PAT-NBL algorithm with conditional log likelihood (CLL; Friedman et al., 1997) criterion
3. PAT-NBL algorithm with conditional minimum description length (CMDL) criterion
4. PAT-NBL algorithm with conditional Akaike information criterion (CAIC, a conditional version of Akaike information criterion; Akaike, 1973) represented as:

$$CAIC(B \mid D) = -CLL(B \mid D) + size(B)$$

To compare the performance of the algorithms, we adapted the *t*-test with 10-fold cross-validation. Table 9.9 shows classifier accuracy and tree sizes on UCI data sets for NBL on the original attributes, and PAT-NBL with CLL, CMDL, and CAIC. The results described in this section reflect that none of the algorithms showed the highest accuracy over all data sets. As to sizes of the generated classifiers (measures of compactness), PAT-NBL coupled with PAT learner (Kang and Sohn, 2009) usually generated more concise naive Bayes classifiers. The size of a naive Bayes classifier can be measured by Equation 9.4.

Figure 9.24 illustrates one of the generated propositionalized attribute taxonomies of the UCI Balance Scale Weight and Distance data set using PAT learner (Kang and Sohn, 2009). After the original data set (the relation is shown in Figure 9.24(a)) is propositionalized (Figure 9.24(b)), each propositionalized attribute is binary (true or false). Using the class-conditional distribution of each attribute when it is true, we can find a pair of attributes whose similarities are maximum (or whose divergences are minimum). Based on the divergence measure, we repeated hierarchical agglomerative clustering to generate the PAT shown in Figure 9.24(c).

Table 9.9 Accuracy and Parameter Size of NBL on Original Data Sets and PAT-NBL with CLL, CMDL, and CAIC on UCI Data Sets

Data	NBL (Original)		PAT-NBL (CLL)		PAT-NBL (CMDL)		PAT-NBL (CAIC)	
	Accuracy	Size	Accuracy	Size	Accuracy	Size	Accuracy	Size
Anneal	96.66±1.18	768	89.87±1.97	54	89.87±1.97	54	89.87±1.97	54
Autos	71.71±6.17	798	66.83±6.45	791	53.17±6.83	231	55.12±6.81	252
Balance-scale	70.72±3.57	27	75.20±3.39	24	75.20±3.39	24	75.20±3.39	24
Breast-cancer	71.68±5.22	104	73.08±5.14	102	72.73±5.16	66	72.73±5.16	66
Breast-w	97.00±1.27	60	97.28±1.21	58	97.28±1.21	58	97.28±1.21	58
Dermatology	97.81±1.50	906	98.09±1.40	900	98.36±1.30	564	98.09±1.40	582
Heart-statlog	83.33±4.45	46	84.07±4.36	44	84.07±4.36	44	84.07±4.36	44
Hepatitis	85.16±5.60	74	84.52±5.70	72	85.16±5.60	54	83.87±5.79	60
Hypothyroid	98.62±0.37	272	97.91±0.46	268	97.91±0.46	268	97.91±0.46	268
Ionosphere	90.60±3.05	292	89.46±3.21	290	92.31±2.79	110	92.02±2.83	112
Kr-vs-kp	87.89±1.13	150	85.01±1.24	148	77.72±1.44	96	81.88±1.34	100
Labor	91.23±7.34	72	92.98±6.63	70	89.47±7.97	48	89.47±7.97	48
Mushroom	95.83±0.43	252	94.25±0.51	250	96.66±0.39	156	94.76±0.48	182
Segment	91.52±1.14	1204	91.04±1.16	1197	88.83±1.28	651	88.83±1.28	658

Sonar	85.58±4.77	164	**86.06±4.71**	162	83.65±5.03	**70**	84.13±4.97	72
Splice	95.52±0.72	864	**95.64±0.71**	861	91.88±0.95	213	51.58±1.73	**21**
Vehicle	**62.65±3.26**	296	62.29±3.27	292	59.34±3.31	**188**	61.35±3.28	200
Vote	**90.11±2.80**	66	88.51±3.00	64	88.74±2.97	**52**	88.51±3.00	64
Waveform-5000	80.74±1.09	393	**81.24±1.08**	390	80.14±1.11	**159**	80.54±1.10	168
Zoo	93.07±4.95	259	**96.04±3.80**	252	**96.04±3.80**	**245**	**96.04±3.80**	252

Accuracy estimated using 10-fold cross validation with 95% confidence interval.

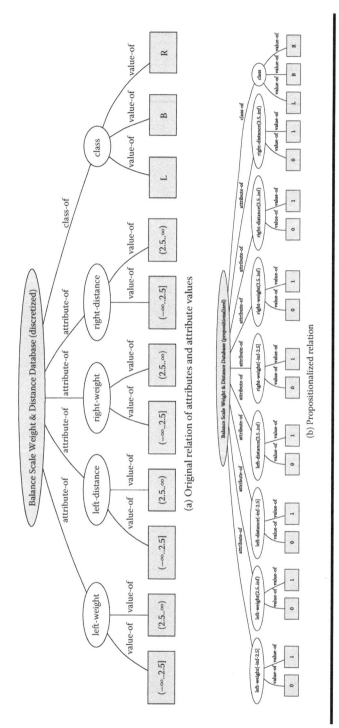

(a) Original relation of attributes and attribute values

(b) Propositionalized relation

Figure 9.24 UCI's Balance Scale Weight and Distance data set.

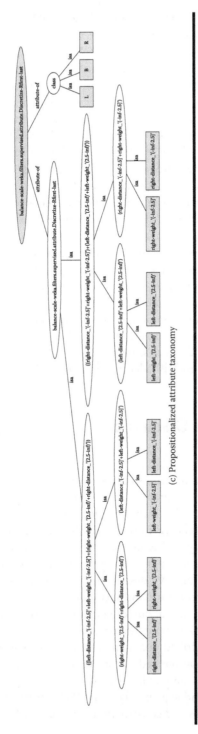

(c) Propositionalized attribute taxonomy

Figure 9.24 (Continued) UCI's Balance Scale Weight and Distance data set.

Comparison with data sets augmented with PAT—Zhang et al. (2006) presented attribute value taxonomy guided naive Bayes learner (AVT-NBL), an algorithm that exploits AVTs to generate naive Bayes classifiers that are more compact and often more accurate than classifiers that do not use AVTs. Zhang et al. included the comparison of their algorithm on original benchmark data sets with the standard naive Bayes learner on propositionalized data sets. To generate the propositionalized data sets, after taxonomy construction for each attribute in the original data, they appended abstract attributes of the constructed taxonomy (all nonleaf nodes in the taxonomy) to the original data as extra attributes. Unlike their propositionalization, we propositionalized original data first, then generated one large propositionalized attribute taxonomy. One of main weaknesses of using propositionalized data is that because of clear dependency relationships among the attributes of the propositionalized data, the performance of the learning algorithm degrades if it relies on an assumption that each attribute is independent of the other attributes like naive Bayes learners. Unlike standard naive Bayes classifiers on propositionalized data, PAT-NBL can also perform regularization over a taxonomy using model selection criteria to minimize over-fitting from learning.

Table 9.10 shows a comparison of PAT-NBL with CLL criteria and the standard naive Bayes learning algorithm on propositionalized data sets. None of the learning algorithms exhibited superior accuracy. However, PAT-NBL with CLL criteria generated more compact naive Bayes classifiers (shown in the size columns in Table 9.10) than those from the standard NBL algorithm on propositionalized data sets.

9.5 Summary and Discussion

9.5.1 Summary

We represented ontologies in various data structures (list, tree or directed acyclic graph, and directed/undirected graph). Graphs are very powerful data structures for expressing ontology for machine learning algorithms, but inferences using graphs for evaluation are widely believed to be intractable. Taxonomy is one of the most common forms of ontology and is useful for constructing compact, robust, and comprehensible classifiers, although human-designed taxonomies are unavailable in many application domains. We described data-driven evaluation of ontologies using machine learning algorithms and introduced cutting-edge taxonomy-aware algorithms for automated construction of taxonomies inductively from both structured (UCI repository data) and unstructured (text and biological sequence) data.

More precisely, we described taxonomy construction algorithms such as AVT learner, an algorithm for automated construction of attribute value taxonomies (AVTs) from data, word taxonomy learner (WTL) for automated construction of word taxonomy from text and sequence data, and PAT learner, an algorithm for propositionalization of attributes and construction of taxonomy from propositionalized

Table 9.10 Accuracy and Parameter Size of PAT-NBL with CLL on UCI Benchmark Data Sets and NBL on Propositionalized UCI Benchmark Data Sets

	PAT-NBL (CLL)		NBL (Propositionalized)	
Data	Accuracy	Size	Accuracy	Size
Anneal	**89.87±1.97**	**54**	89.31±2.02	2886
Autos	66.83±6.45	**791**	**78.54±5.62**	5187
Balance-scale	75.20±3.39	**24**	**88.48±2.50**	195
Breast-cancer	**73.08±5.14**	**102**	72.73±5.16	338
Breast-w	**97.28±1.21**	**58**	97.14±1.24	642
Dermatology	**98.09±1.40**	**900**	**98.09±1.40**	2790
Heart-statlog	**84.07±4.36**	**44**	83.70±4.41	482
Hepatitis	84.52±5.70	**72**	**90.97±4.51**	538
Hypothyroid	**97.91±0.46**	**268**	93.32±0.80	1276
Ionosphere	89.46±3.21	**290**	**91.74±2.88**	2318
Kr-vs-kp	85.01±1.24	**148**	**87.80±1.13**	306
Labor	**92.98±6.63**	**70**	89.47±7.97	546
Mushroom	94.25±0.51	**250**	**95.55±0.45**	682
Segment	**91.04±1.16**	**1197**	88.14±1.32	4193
Sonar	86.06±4.71	**162**	**99.04±1.33**	4322
Splice	95.64±0.71	**861**	**95.92±0.69**	2727
Vehicle	62.29±3.27	**292**	**67.02±3.17**	2596
Vote	88.51±3.00	**64**	**90.11±2.81**	130
Waveform-5000	**81.24±1.08**	**390**	63.62±1.33	4323
Zoo	**96.04±3.80**	**252**	94.06±4.61	567

Accuracy estimated using 10-fold cross validation with 95% confidence interval.

attributes. These taxonomy learning algorithms recursively group values based on a suitable measure of divergence between the class distributions associated with the values to construct taxonomies. They can generate hierarchical taxonomies of nominal, ordinal, and continuous valued attributes.

For evaluation of the generated taxonomies, we described taxonomy-aware machine learning algorithms such as AVT-NBL, a generalization of the naive Bayes learner for multivariate data using AVTs, WTNBL-MN, a generalization of the naive Bayes learner for the multinomial event model for learning classifiers from data using word taxonomy, PAT-NBL, a generalization of the naive Bayes learner to exploit propositionalized attribute taxonomy (PAT), and PAT-DTL, a generalization of the decision tree learner to exploit propositionalized attribute taxonomy (PAT). The experiments reported in this chapter show that:

- AVT learner, WTL, and PAT learner are effective for generating taxonomies that, when used by AVT-NBL, WTNBL-MN, PAT-DTL, and PAT-NBL, a principled extension of the standard algorithm for learning naive Bayes classifiers, result in classifiers that are substantially more compact (and often more accurate) than those obtained by the standard naive Bayes learner (that does not use taxonomies).
- The taxonomies generated by AVT learner, WTL, and PAT learner are competitive with human-supplied taxonomies (in the cases of benchmark data sets in which human-generated taxonomies were available) in terms of both error rate and sizes of the resulting classifiers.

9.5.2 K-ary Taxonomies

The taxonomies generated by taxonomy learners are all binary trees. Hence, for example, one might wonder whether *k*-ary AVTs yield better results when used with AVT-NBL. Figure 9.25 shows an AVT of the *odor* attribute generated by AVT learner (with quaternary clustering). Table 9.11 shows the accuracy of AVT-NBL when *k*-ary clustering is used by AVT learner. AVT-NBL generally works best when binary AVTs are used, because reducing internal nodes in AVT learner will eventually reduce the search space for possible cuts in AVT-NBL, generating a less compact classifier.

Considering that taxonomies are sufficiently complicated but tractable data structures for representing ontology, we have presented a systematic way of evaluating ontologies for machine learning tasks.

9.5.3 Related Work

Several groups explored the problem of learning classifiers from attribute value taxonomies (AVTs) or tree-structured attributes. Research has focused on the analysis of the correlation of the propositionalized attribute values (PATs) from different attributes in a data set in terms of inducing decision trees (Kang and Sohn, 2009).

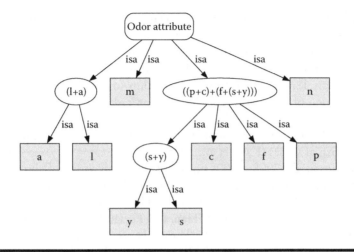

Figure 9.25 AVT of *odor* attribute of UCI's AGARICUS-LEPIOTA mushroom data set generated by AVT learner using Jensen–Shannon divergence (with quaternary clustering).

Table 9.11   Accuracy of Classifiers Generated by AVT-NBL Coupled with *k*-ary (2, 3, and 4) AVT Learner on Selected UCI Data Sets

Data	2-ary	3-ary	4-ary
Nursery	90.32±0.51	90.32±0.51	90.32±0.51
Audiology	**76.99±5.49**	76.55±5.52	**76.99±5.49**
Car	86.17±1.63	86.17±1.63	86.17±1.63
Dermatology	**98.09±1.40**	97.54±1.59	97.54±1.59
Mushroom	99.59±0.14	99.73±0.11	**99.75±0.11**
Soybean	**94.58±1.70**	94.44±1.72	94.44±1.72

Accuracy estimated using 10-fold cross validation with 95% confidence interval.

In their work, Kang and Sohn adopted decision tree with the accuracy measure of five-fold cross-validation as a stopping criterion. This chapter showed the exploration of naive Bayes classifiers, and we applied various criteria of probabilistic graphic models to measure the accuracy of hypotheses.

Zhang and Honavar (2003; 2004) developed decision tree learners and naive Bayes learners regularized over attribute value taxonomy. Zhang and Honavar (2004) presented attribute value taxonomy guided naive Bayes learner (AVT-NBL), an algorithm that exploits AVTs to generate naive Bayes classifiers that are more compact and often more accurate than classifiers that do not use AVTs. The algorithm potentially performs regularization to minimize over-fitting from learning with relatively small data sets. These works primarily focused on attribute value taxonomy for multivariate data sets. Kang et al. (2004) designed the attribute value taxonomy learner (AVT learner) algorithm to assist AVT-NBL with automatic generation of taxonomies for classification tasks. They extended those algorithms into word taxonomy-guided naive Bayes learner with multinomial model (WTNBL-MN) and word taxonomy learner (WTL) to deal with sequences represented as a bag of values (Kang et al., 2005).

des Jardins et al. (2008; 2000) suggested the combination of abstraction hierarchies and tree-structured conditional probability tables to learning structured Bayesian networks. Taylor et al. (1997) and Hendler et al. (1996) described the use of taxonomies in rule learning. Han and Fu (1996) proposed a method for exploiting hierarchically structured background knowledge for learning association rules. Flavian et al. (2005) designed TRIPPER, a modified version of RIPPER for exploiting taxonomies of propositionalized attributes.

Gibson et al. (1998) introduced STIRR, an iterative algorithm based on nonlinear dynamic systems for clustering categorical attributes. Ganti et al. (1999) designed CACTUS, an algorithm that uses intra-attribute summaries to cluster attribute values. Neither was aimed at creating and using taxonomies to improve performance of classification tasks.

Pereira et. al. (1993) described distributional clustering for grouping words based on class distributions associated with the words in a text classification. Yamazaki et al. (1995) described an algorithm for extracting hierarchical groupings from rules learned by FOCL (an inductive learning algorithm; Pazzani and Kibler, 1992) and reported improved performance on learning translation rules from examples in a natural language processing task. Slonim and Tishby (2006) described a technique (the agglomerative information bottleneck method) that extended the distributional clustering approach described by Pereira et al. (1993), using Jensen–Shannon divergence for measuring distances between document class distributions associated with words and applied it to a text classification task.

Baker and McCallum (1998) reported improved performance on text classification using a technique similar to distributional clustering and a distance measure that, upon closer examination, can be shown to be equivalent to Jensen–Shannon divergence (Slonim et al., 2005, 2006). Dimitropoulos et al. (2006) augmented an internet autonomous system (AS) taxonomy to the data set for ASe classification and successfully classified 95.3% of ASes with expected accuracy of 78.1%. Culotta et al. (2007) used edit distance with costs and feature-based ranking models to duplicate database records. These works focus mainly on clustering of words, but they did not apply the generated taxonomy for regularization to generate more concise classifiers.

9.5.4 Future Directions

We are considering several important directions for future research. First, the ontology learners described in this research are confined to taxonomic structures. However, it is interesting to consider a data structure that has more powerful expression but is still tractable by contemporary computer algorithms. Therefore, we plan to extend the learning algorithms discussed in this chapter to generate data structures that can express tangled hierarchies such as directed acyclic graphs (DAGs). Eventually, we are interested in a data structure that can describe ontologies as expressively as possible, but remain manageable by modest learning and reasoning algorithms.

Second, although we proposed various empirical results, most data sets we have studied are benchmark data sets used primarily by machine learning communities. Hence, we are interested in learning taxonomies from data for a broad range of real-world applications such as census data analysis, learning classifiers from relational data (Atramentov et al., 2003), protein function classification (Wang and Stolfo, 2003), and identification of protein–protein interfaces (Terribilini et al., 2006; Yan et al., 2003).

Third, all the algorithms proposed in this chapter focus on eliciting ISA relations to generate taxonomies. However, more types of relations exist among objects in ontological representations, part–whole relations, for example. Thus, it will be interesting to develop algorithms for learning hierarchical ontologies based on part–whole and other relations instead of ISA relations captured by a taxonomy.

Finally, we will investigate the feasibility for applying ontology-aware machine learning algorithms to other widely used machine learning algorithms including support vector machines (SVM) learning algorithms (Purdy et al., 2003) and others.

References

Akaike, H. 1973. Information theory and an extension of the maximum likelihood principle. In *Proceedings of Second International Symposium on Information Theory,* pp. 267–281.

Andorf, C., D. Dobbs, and V. Honavar. 2006. Learning classifiers for assigning protein sequences to subcellular localization families. In *Proceedings of Annual Meeting of International Society for Computational Biology,* Fortaleza, Brazil.

Apté, C., F. Damerau, and S. M. Weiss. 1994. Towards language-independent automated learning of text categorization models. In *Proceedings of 17th Annual International ACM SIGIR Conference on Research and Development in Information Retrieval,* Springer Verlag, New York, pp. 23–30.

Ashburner, M., C. Ball, J. Blake et al. 2000. Gene ontology: Tool for the unification of biology. *Nature Genetics 25*: 25–29.

Atramentov, A., H. Leiva, and V. Honavar. 2003. A multi-relational decision tree learning algorithm: Implementation and experiments. *Lecture Notes on Artificial Intelligence,* 2835: 38–56.

Bairoch, A. and R. Apweiler. 2000. The SWISS-PROT protein sequence database and its supplement. *Nucleic Acids Research, 28*: 45–48.

Baker, L. D. and A.K. McCallum. 1998. Distributional clustering of words for text classification. In *Proceedings of 21st Annual International ACM SIGIR Conference on Research and Development in Information Retrieval*, Springer Verlag, New York, pp. 96–103.

Berners-Lee, T., J. Hendler, and O. Lassila. May 2001. The semantic web. *Scientific American.*

Blake, C. and C. Merz. 1998. UCI repository of machine learning databases.

Brank, J., M. Grobelnik, and D. Mladeníc. 2005. Survey of ontology evaluation techniques. In *Proceedings of Eighth International Information Society Multiconference*, pp. 166–169.

Brewster, C., H. Alani, S. Dasmahapatra et al. 2004. Data-driven ontology evaluation. In *Proceedings of Fourth International Conference on Language Resources and Evaluation*, Lisbon.

Carvalho, V.R. and W.W. Cohen. 2005. On the collective classification of email speech acts. In *Proceedings of 28th Annual International ACM SIGIR Conference on Research and Development in Information Retrieval*, Springer Verlag, pp. 345–352.

Cimiano, P., S. Staab, and J. Tane. 2003. Automatic acquisition of taxonomies from text: Fca meets nlp. In *Proceedings of ECML/PKDD Workshop on Adaptive Text Extraction and Mining*, Cavtat-Dubrovnik, Croatia, pp. 10–17.

Culotta, A., M. Wick, R. Hall et al. 2007. Canonicalization of database records using adaptive similarity measures. In *Proceedings of 13th ACM SIGKDD International Conference on Knowledge Discovery and Data Mining*, San Jose, CA, pp. 201–209.

des Jardins, M., L. Getoor, and D. Koller. 2000. Using feature hierarchies in Bayesian network learning. In *Proceedings of Fourth International Symposium on Abstraction, Reformulation, and Approximation*, Springer Verlag, New York, pp. 260–270.

des Jardins, M., P. Rathod, and L. Getoor. 2008. Learning structured Bayesian networks: Combining abstraction hierarchies and tree-structured conditional probability tables. *Computational Intelligence, 24*: 1–22.

Dhar, V. and A. Tuzhilin. 1993. Abstract-driven pattern discovery in databases. *IEEE Transactions on Knowledge and Data Engineering, 5*: 926–938.

Dimitropoulos, X., D. Krioukov, G. Riley et al. 2006. Revealing the autonomous system taxonomy: The machine learning approach. In *Proceedings of Passive and Active Measurement Workshop.*

Duda, R.O., P.E. Hart, and D.G. Stork. 2000. *Pattern Classification*, 2nd ed., Wiley-Interscience, New York.

Dumais, S., J. Platt, D. Heckerman et al. 1998. Inductive learning algorithms and representations for text categorization. In *Proceedings of Seventh International Conference on Information and Knowledge Management*, pp. 148–155.

Fawcett, T. 2003. ROC graphs: Notes and practical considerations for researchers. Technical Report HPL-2003-4, Hewlett Packard Laboratories.

Fawcett, T. 2006. ROC graphs with instance-varying costs. *Pattern Recognition Letters, 27*: 882–891.

Friedman, N., D. Geiger, and M. Goldszmidt. 1997. Bayesian network classifiers. *Machine Learning 29*: 131–163.

Gabrilovich, E. and S. Markovitch. 2005. Feature generation for text categorization using world knowledge. In *Proceedings of Nineteenth International Joint Conference for Artificial Intelligence*, Edinburgh, pp. 1048–1053.

Gangemi, A., C. Catenacci, M. Ciaramita et al. 2006. Modelling ontology evaluation and validation. In *The Semantic Web: Research and Applications*, Vol. 4011, *Lecture Notes in Computer Science*, pp. 140–154.

Ganti, V., J. Gehrke, and R. Ramakrishnan. 1999. CACTUS: Clustering categorical data using summaries. In *Proceedings of Fifth ACM SIGKDD International Conference on Knowledge Discovery and Data Mining*, pp. 73–83.

Gibson, D., J. Kleinberg, and P. Raghavan. 1998. Clustering categorical data: An approach based on dynamical systems. *Very Large Data Bases, 8*: 222–236.

Grefenstette, G. 1994. *Explorations in Automatic Thesaurus Discovery.* Kluwer Academic, Norwell, MA.

Gulla, J.A. and V. Sugumaran. 2008. An interactive ontology learning workbench for non-experts. In *Proceedings of Second International Workshop on Ontologies and Information systems for the semantic web*, ACM Press, New York, pp. 9–16.

Han, J. and Y. Fu. 1996. Exploration of the power of attribute-oriented induction in data mining. In *Advances in Knowledge Discovery and Data Mining.* AIII/MIT Press, Cambridge, MA.

Haussler, D. 1988. Quantifying inductive bias: AI learning algorithms and Valiant's learning framework. *Artificial Intelligence, 36*: 177–221.

Hendler, J., K. Stoffel, and M. Taylor. 1996. Advances in high performance knowledge representation. Technical Report CS-TR-3672, University of Maryland Institute for Advanced Computer Studies.

Joachims, T. 1998. Text categorization with support vector machines: Learning with many relevant features. In *Proceedings of 10th European Conference on Machine Learning*, Chemnitz, Germany, pp. 137–142.

Joachims, T. 2005. A support vector method for multivariate performance measures. In *Proceedings of 22nd International Conference on Machine Learning*, Bonn, pp. 377–384.

Kang, D.K., A. Silvescu, J. Zhang et al. 2004. Generation of attribute value taxonomies from data for data-driven construction of accurate and compact classifiers. In *Proceedings of Fourth IEEE International Conference on Data Mining*, Brighton, UK, pp. 130–137.

Kang, D.K. and K. Sohn. 2009. Learning decision trees with taxonomy of propositionalized attributes. *Pattern Recognition, 42*: 84–92.

Kang, D.K., J. Zhang, A. Silvescu et al. 2005. Multinomial event model based abstraction for sequence and text classification. In *Abstraction, Reformulation and Approximation, 6th International Symposium*, Edinburgh, *Lecture Notes in Computer Science*, pp. 134–148.

Keerthi, S.S. 2005. Generalized LARS as an effective feature selection tool for text classification with SVMs. In *Proceedings of 22nd International Conference on Machine Learning*, Bonn, pp. 417–424.

Kohavi, R. and F. Provost. 2001. Applications of data mining to electronic commerce. *Data Mining and Knowledge Discovery, 5*:, 5–10.

Kohler, J., K. Munn, A. Ruegg et al. 2006. Quality control for terms and definitions in ontologies and taxonomies. *BMC Bioinformatics, 7*: 212–223.

Langley, P., W. Iba, and K. Thompson. 1992. Analysis of Bayesian classifiers. In *National Conference on Artificial Intelligence*, pp. 223–228.

Lozano-Tello, A. and A. Gómez-Pérez. 2004. Ontometric: A method to choose the appropriate ontology. *Journal of Database Management* 15.

Maedche, A. and S. Staab. 2002. Measuring similarity between ontologies. In *Proceedings of 13th International Conference on Knowledge Engineering and Knowledge Management, Ontologies and the Semantic Web*, London, pp. 251–263.

McCallum, A. and K. Nigam. 1998. A comparison of event models for naive Bayes text classification. In *Proceedings of AAAI Workshop on Learning for Text Categorization*.

Noy, N., R. Guha, and M. Musen. 2005. User ratings of ontologies: Who will rate the raters? In *Proceedings of AAAI Spring Symposium on Knowledge Collection from Volunteer Contributors*, Stanford, CA.

Pazzani, M. and D. Kibler. 1992. The role of prior knowledge in inductive learning. *Machine Learning, 9*: 54–97.

Pazzani, M.J., S. Mani, and W.R. Shankle. 1997. Beyond concise and colorful: Learning intelligible rules. In *Knowledge Discovery and Data Mining*, pp. 235–238.

Pereira, F., N. Tishby, and L. Lee. 1993. Distributional clustering of English words. In *Proceedings of 31st Annual Meeting of ACL*, pp. 183–190.

Porzel, R. and R. Malaka. 2004. A task-based approach for ontology evaluation. In *Proceedings of ECAI Workshop on Ontology Learning and Population*, Valencia, Spain.

Purdy, P.M., P.J. Moreno, P.P. Ho et al. 2003. A Kullback-Leibler divergence-based kernel for SVM classification in multimedia applications. In *Advances in Neural Information Processing Systems*, Vol. 16, MIT Press, Cambridge, MA.

Quinlan, J.R. 1993. *C4.5: Programs for Machine Learning*, Morgan Kaufmann, San Francisco.

Reinhardt, A. and T. Hubbard. 1998. Using neural networks for prediction of the subcellular location of proteins. *Nucleic Acids Research, 26*: 2230–2236.

Rooney, N., D. Patterson, M. Galushka et al. 2006. A scaleable document clustering approach for large document corpora. *Information Processing and Management, 42*: 1163–1175.

Sandler, M. 2005. On the use of linear programming for unsupervised text classification. In *Proceedings of 11th ACM SIGKDD International Conference on Knowledge Discovery in Data Mining*, Chicago, pp. 256–264.

Shadbolt, N., T. Berners-Lee, J. Hendler et al. 2006. The next wave of the web. In *Proceedings of 15th International Conference on World Wide Web*, Edinburgh.

Slonim, N., G.S. Atwal, G. Tkaik et al. 2005. Information-based clustering. In *Proceedings of National Academy of Sciences of United States of America*, Princeton University, Princeton, NJ.

Slonim, N., N. Friedman, and N. Tishby. 2006. Multivariate information bottleneck. *Neural Computation, 18*: 1739–1789.

Smith, B., J. Köhler, and A. Kumar. 2004. On the application of formal principles to life science data: A case study in the gene ontology. In *Proceedings of First International Workshop on Data Integration in the Life Sciences*, Leipzig, Vol. 2994, *Lecture Notes in Computer Science*, pp. 79–94.

Taneja, I. 1995. New developments in generalized information measures. *Advances in Imaging and Electron Physics, 91*: 37–135.

Taylor, M., K. Stoffel, and J. Hendler. 1997. Ontology-based induction of high level classification rules. In *SIGMOD Workshop on Research Issues in Data Mining and Knowledge Discovery*.

Taylor, M.G., K. Stoffel, and J. A. Hendler. 1997. Ontology-based induction of high level classification rules. In *DMKD*.

Terribilini, M., J.H. Lee, C. Yan et al. 2006. Prediction of RNA-binding sites in proteins based on amino acid sequence. *RNA, 12*: 1450–1462.

Topsøe, F. 2000. Some inequalities for information divergence and related measures of discrimination. *IEEE Transactions on Information Theory, 46*: 1602–1609.

Undercoffer, J.L., A. Joshi, and J. Pinkston. 2003. Modeling computer attacks: An ontology for intrusion detection. In *Proceedings of Sixth International Symposium on Recent Advances in Intrusion Detection*, Vol. 2516, *Lecture Notes in Computer Science*.

Vasile, F., A. Silvescu, D.K. Kang et al. 2005. TRIPPER: Rule learning using taxonomies. In *Proceedings of AAAI Workshop on Human Comprehensible Machine Learning,* Pittsburgh, PA.

Wang, K. and S. J. Stolfo. 2003. One class training for masquerade detection. In *ICDM Workshop on Data Mining for Computer Security,* Melbourne, FL.

Welty, C. and N. Guarino. 2001. Supporting ontological analysis of taxonomic relationships. *Data Knowledge Engineering, 39*: 51–74.

Wu, F., J. Zhang, and V. Honavar. 2005. Learning classifiers using hierarchically structured class taxonomies. In *Proceedings of Symposium on Abstraction, Reformulation, and Approximation,* Edinburgh, Vol. 3607, pp. 313–320.

Yamazaki, T., M.J. Pazzani, and C.J. Merz. 1995. Learning hierarchies from ambiguous natural language data. In *Proceedings of International Conference on Machine Learning,* pp. 575–583.

Yan, C., D. Dobbs, and V. Honavar. 2003. Identification of surface residues involved in protein–protein interaction: A support vector machine approach. In *Intelligent Systems Design and Applications,* Springer Verlag, Berlin, pp. 53–62.

Yan, C., D. Dobbs, and V. Honavar. 2004. A two-stage classifier for identification of protein–protein interface residues. In *Proceedings of 12th International Conference on Intelligent Systems for Molecular Biology/Third European Conference on Computational Biology,* pp. 371–378.

Zhang, D. and W. S. Lee. 2006. Extracting key substring-group features for text classification. In *Proceedings of 12th ACM SIGKDD International Conference on Knowledge Discovery and Data Mining,* New York, pp. 474–483.

Zhang, J. and V. Honavar. 2003. Learning decision tree classifiers from attribute value taxonomies and partially specified data. In *Proceedings of 20th International Conference on Machine Learning,* Washington, DC.

Zhang, J. and V. Honavar. 2004. AVT-NBL: An algorithm for learning compact and accurate naive Bayes classifiers from attribute value taxonomies and data. In *Proceedings of International Conference on Data Mining.*

Zhang, J., D.K. Kang, A. Silvescu et al. 2006. Learning accurate and concise naive Bayes classifiers from attribute value taxonomies and data. *Knowledge and Information Systems, 9*: 157–179.

Zhang, J., A. Silvescu, and V. Honavar. 2002. Ontology-driven induction of decision trees at multiple levels of abstraction. In *Proceedings of Symposium on Abstraction, Reformulation, and Approximation,* Vol. 2371, *Lecture Notes in Artificial Intelligence.*

Chapter 10

Automatic Evaluation of Search Ontologies in the Entertainment Domain Using Natural Language Processing

Michael Elhadad, David Gabay, and Yael Netzer

Ben-Gurion University, Beer Sheva, Israel

Contents

10.1 Introduction

Faceted search is a popular interaction method that allows users to navigate through complex unfamiliar data [1,2]. It has been widely used in recent e-commerce sites and spread by software providers such as Endeca. Faceted search supports the information need for exploratory search [3], corresponding to a shift in information retrieval from a focus on navigational queries and document ranking to higher level goals of content extraction, user goal recognition, and content aggregation [4].

When using a faceted search interface, a user first submits a general query, then navigates through several facet hierarchies that describe the result set. The navigation allows a user to interactively refine his query and discover further facets that may guide him through the document repository and help him discover relations he did not know when first issuing his query. Typically, faceted search applications show possible refinements to the current query together with a number of search results brought into focus by refinement. These counts provide helpful quantitative feedback to users and guidance when exploring the data.

The effectiveness of this interaction strategy relies heavily on the quality of the metadata associated with the documents: which attributes (facets) describe the documents and the hierarchy of values associated to each facet. In many applications such as e-commerce Web sites, information architects carefully prepare this metadata in the form of a search ontology [2,5,6]. Some researchers have also investigated automatic and semi-automatic methods to construct such search ontologies by mining information in document repositories and related resources [7–9].

When manually maintaining a search ontology or acquiring it automatically, a pressing need exists to evaluate its quality. In this chapter, we present a new method to evaluate search ontologies [10] that we tested specifically in the entertainment domain. A semantic search engine enables users to search for movie and song recommendations. The search engine relies on an explicit internal ontology of the domain that captures structured representations of objects (movies, actors, directors, etc.). The ontology is acquired and maintained semi-automatically from semi-structured resources (such as IMDb and Wikipedia). The ontology supports improved search experience at different stages: content indexing, query interpretation, and search result ranking and presentation (faceted search, aggregated search result presentation, search result summarization).

This chapter focuses on evaluating the quality of an ontology as it impacts the search process. As noted by [11], one can distinguish ontology evaluation methods at three levels: structural (measuring properties of ontology viewed as a formal graph), usability (access method—through API or search tools, versioned, annotated, or licensed) and functional (services the ontology delivers to applications). The method we present addresses functional evaluation; that is, we investigate how one can measure the adequacy of an ontology to support a semantic search engine.

As part of this functional evaluation, we distinguish two forms of information needs expressed by users: fact finding (user expects to retrieve a precise set of results or navigate to a specific movie) and exploratory search (user seeks recommendations for several movies according to nonspecific requirements). The ontology provides services to the application for both types of information needs, but this chapter concentrates on support for exploratory search.

The key idea of our method is that one can evaluate the functional adequacy of an ontology by investigating a corpus of textual documents anchored to the ontology. The documents are collected automatically and associated to ontology individuals. The documents do *not* correspond to the document repository covered by the search engine and are used only for ontology evaluation. Hypotheses about the ontology can then be transformed into classification tests on this test corpus.

We first review previous work in ontology evaluation and ontology-based information retrieval (ObIR). We then present our ontology evaluation method and a set of experiments illustrating the method to evaluate the functional adequacy of our ontology in the entertainment domain. The experiments validate the adequacy of the specific ontology acquired as part of our semantic engine for exploratory search and provide specific, concrete indications on how to improve the ontology.

10.2 Dimensions of Ontology Evaluation

Evaluation of ontologies is complicated because they vary in domains, sizes, purposes, languages, and more. Therefore, it is not possible to define a general ontology evaluation paradigm. In addition, evaluation depends on the way the ontology was constructed: (1) manually by scholars or domain experts or (2) as the product of an automatic or semi-automatic process. In most applications, ontology quality is best measured in terms of cost–profit effectiveness. Ontology evaluation can focus on one or more of the following dimensions:

- *Structural evaluation*: identifying structural properties of the ontology viewed as a graph-like artifact [12]
- *Usability*: assessing pragmatic aspects of the ontology, i.e., metadata and annotation [13]
- *Functionality*: measuring how well an ontology serves its purpose as part of a larger application

It is also useful to distinguish between extrinsic and intrinsic evaluation methods. Extrinsic evaluation of qualities requires external information such as expert opinion, a corpus representing the domain knowledge (data-driven evaluation), or a particular task that defines the context of the evaluation. Intrinsic evaluation reflects the quality of the ontology as a stand-alone body of knowledge. Naturally, intrinsic evaluation primarily reflects structural properties.

The method we propose is extrinsic. We assess the adequacy of an ontology to support exploratory search (in the form of faceted search) by constructing a set of textual documents derived from the ontology and testing hypotheses on this data set. The methodology is data-driven and automatically provides concrete feedback to the maintainer. The set of naturally occurring documents on which we perform the evaluation provides an approximation of expert opinion.

10.3 Search Ontologies

The usage of an ontology in our project was motivated by a wish to improve the search experience, i.e., we were interested in evaluating a search ontology as defined in the scope of ObIR. Semantic search involves techniques that go beyond the mere appearance of query words in possibly relevant documents and aims at capturing a deeper representation of the searched space and the knowledge embedded in it. Although searches are widely conducted on the Internet, user satisfaction studies indicate general dissatisfaction with irrelevant search results (low precision) or an excessive numbers of results.

Using an ontology can better support user expectations at the cost of restricting the scope of a search engine to a specific domain. We investigated the entertainment domain. For such limited scope search, semantic technology helps the engine find more relevant documents by using links among concepts (movies with the same actor and similar plot), cluster results along semantic attributes to improve navigation (faceted search) [14], and conceptual indexing (search for *spy* and get *james bond*) [8].

We refer to the elements of an ontology using specific terminology. An ontology describes *concepts* using a description language (e.g., OWL [15]). Concepts denote a *class of individuals* and are related to each other through *relations*. One of the most important relations is *specialization*, indicating, for example, that a *child* concept is a subset of a more general *parent* concept. When an ontology is populated, each concept is "filled" by specific individuals. For example, the *Movies* concept would be filled by thousands of individuals that denote each movie instance in the ontology. Each individual is described by its concepts (classes to which it belongs), a set of data properties (e.g., release date), and relations to which it belongs (e.g., a movie individual stands in relation to individuals of the actor class). The names of the individuals, classes, and relations determine the *terms* defined by the ontology. To define the evaluation of a search ontology, we refer first to distinct types of searches that represent different types of information needs [16,17]:

Fact finding—A precise set of results is requested. The number of retrieved documents is expected to be small (for instance, a specific movie in the entertainment domain) and may correspond to a return visit to a site or a short search session.

Exploration—A user's need is to obtain a general understanding of the search topic; high precision or recall is not required. For instance, the user explores a movie repository to find interesting movies according to his current mood or similarity with known movies [3].

According to this information needs distinction, Strasunskas and Tomassen [17] propose a set of evaluation measures for a search ontology:

■ Generic quality evaluation to check that the ontology is syntactically correct and is closely related to the domain.

■ Searching task fitness by applying a different measure for each search task. Fact-finding fitness for a cluster of concepts is a function of the number of individuals, properties, and data types of all concepts in the cluster. Exploratory search fitness is a function of the number and distribution of subclasses.

■ Search enhancement capability measures how useful the ontology is for query expansions that improve recall and precision. Recall enhancement capability is a function of the number of equivalent classes. Precision enhancement capability is a function of the number of concept properties.

Such metrics are useful to evaluate ontologies in the same sense that code complexity metrics are useful when developing software or readability indices when assessing the quality of text. They correspond to what we call intrinsic measures. These metrics capture the intuition that the search ontology properly supports the operation of a search engine but do not provide concrete feedback on the functional adequacy of the ontology to the domain.

To illustrate the limitations of such intrinsic measures, it is possible to design an ontology to obtain high scores on all metrics with no knowledge of the domain in a completely artificial manner by optimizing the distribution of ontology individuals across classes. To reuse the software development analogy, code complexity measures are useful to identify "bad codes" (functions that are too long, for example), but they do not help assess the correctness or robustness of the codes. Beyond such metrics, we wish to define functional quality criteria for search ontologies. Gulla et al. [8] define the following desirable properties in a search ontology:

- *Concept familiarity*: the terminology introduced by the ontology is strongly connected to user terms in search queries.
- *Document discrimination*: the concept granularity in the ontology is compatible with the granularity of users' queries. This granularity compatibility allows good grouping of search results according to the ontology concept hierarchy.
- *Query formulation*: the depth of the hierarchy in the ontology and the complexity and length of user queries should be compatible.
- *Domain volatility*: the ontology should be robust in the presence of frequent updates.

This classification of functional quality criteria is conceptually useful, but does not provide a methodology or concrete tools to evaluate a given ontology. This is the task addressed in this chapter, specifically for exploratory search. The evaluation method we introduce relies on the fact that given an ontology individual (in our domain, a movie), we can automatically retrieve large quantities of textual documents (movie reviews) associated to the individuals. On the basis of this automatically acquired textual corpus, we can perform automatic linguistic analysis that determines whether the ontology reflects the information we mine in the texts.

Note that we focus on evaluating the ontology and its adequacy to the domain as a search ontology. We do not simulate the search process or measure specifically how the ontology affects steps in search operation (such as indexing, query expansion, result set clustering). Accordingly, the evaluation we suggest, although informed by the task (we specifically evaluate a search ontology), is not a task-based evaluation (we do not evaluate the ontology on a search benchmark).

10.4 Experimental Setting: Ontology for Semantic Search in the Entertainment Domain and Test Corpus

We illustrate our ontology evaluation method in the context of the entertainment domain. We first describe the experimental setup. Our objective is to support exploratory search over a set of documents describing movies, actors, and related information in the domain. The ontology we evaluate is automatically acquired from semi-structured data sources (IMDb, Wikipedia, and other similar sources). Table 10.1 shows the size of the ontology we used. As is appropriate for a search ontology, the ontology is wide and shallow.

Table 10.1   Size of Movies Ontology

Classes	33
Class individuals	351,066
Relations	27
Movies	8,446
Persons	116,770

The first step of our ontology evaluation method was compiling from the domain a corpus of texts distinct from the documents used for acquisition of the ontology. We then used standard natural language processing (NLP) techniques to evaluate the ontology by testing various hypotheses on the collected corpus and report on three experiments:

- *Measuring coverage and term alignment*: we attempted to test the adequacy of the ontology with respect to concept familiarity (cf. Section 10.3). This coverage experiment is discussed in Section 10.5.
- *Measuring classification fitness on movie genres*: we attempted to test the potential of the ontology to properly organize movies into genres. Genre (comedy, drama, etc.) is a critical metadata attribute of movies. This classification experiment is described in Section 10.6.
- *Measuring topic identification fitness*: we assessed the capacity of the ontology to capture the notion of movie topics that describe what a movie is about; topics are distinct from genres. They are most often described by keywords. This topic experiment is described in Section 10.7.

Each experiment exploits a different NLP technique. For the coverage and term alignment experiment, we used fuzzy string matching techniques and named entity recognition (NER). For the classification experiment, we used text classification, and for the topic experiment, LDA topic modeling [18]. We used the same test corpus for all experiments and constructed it such that documents were aligned to ontology individuals. We constructed the corpus automatically by mining movie reviews from the Web. We collected professional, edited reviews taken from Robert Ebert's Web site,* additional professional and user reviews published on the Metacritic Web site,† and 13 similar Web sources. The key metadata collected for each document is a unique identifier indicating the movie to which the text is associated. The corpus we constructed contained 11,706 reviews (of 3,146 movies) and 8.7 million words (average of 749 words per review).

---

* http://rogerebert.suntimes.com
† http://www.metacritic.com

10.5 Evaluating Ontology Coverage of Query Terms

10.5.1 Objective

Consider a fact-finding search scenario. A user seeks precise results and knows what results should be attained. The main services expected from the search ontology to support this scenario are: (1) production of highly precise results and wide coverage for terms used in the queries; (2) providing entity recognition functionality to allow fuzzy string matching and identifying terminological variations; and (3) identifying anchors, i.e., minimal facts that identify a movie (for example, title, publication year, main actors, main keywords). For a populated ontology, we want to assure that the individuals in the ontology match the entities in the actual domain (the ontology describes the correct set of individuals). We also want to verify that the way the ontology individuals are retrieved corresponds to the terminology used in actual search queries (the ontology uses the correct terms to refer to individuals). Our experiment assesses these two dimensions by testing hypotheses on the test corpus.

10.5.2 Hypothesis

We wanted to test whether the terminology used in the ontology to refer to entities (movies, actors, directors) corresponded to the terminology used in queries. We had no access to a search query log or manually annotated data that would match terms in a query log to ontology individuals. Instead, we used our test corpus as a proxy; we considered that naturally occurring text about movies is similar (as far as references to movies and actors) to queries users would submit.

The task we addressed was unsupervised; the corpus was not annotated manually (an expensive operation). We wanted to assess the extent to which a named entity in text could be mapped to a term in the ontology. The hypothesis we formulated is that if an ontology has good term coverage, named entities found in text will be found in the ontology (high coverage) and mapping from a named entity found in text to an individual in the ontology will be accurate (no ambiguity).

10.5.3 Assessing Ontology Coverage

To assess the ontology coverage, we measured the overlaps between named entities that appeared in the corpus and the terms that appeared in the ontology. We first gathered a collection of potential named-entity labels in the corpus. In professional reviews, named entities are generally marked in the html source. User reviews are not edited nor formatted. For such reviews, we relied on the OpenCalais* named entity recognizer (NER) to tag named entities in the corpus. This system recognizes multiword expressions that refer to proper names of people, organizations,

---

* http://www.opencalais.com/

and products. We then extracted all person names from the textual corpus and searched the labels for each entity in the ontology.

Results show that 74% of the named-entities that appear in professional reviews also appear as terms in our ontology. For user reviews (nonedited), the figure is 50%.

The main reasons for mismatches lay in orthography variations (accents or transliteration differences), mentions of people not related to a movie in the reviews, and aliasing or spelling variations (mostly in user reviews). We conclude that the coverage of people entities in the ontology is satisfactory. However, whether a search for these entities will find them or will find the intended individuals in the ontology is not certain. This fuzziness is caused by term variation (as observed especially in user reviews) and term ambiguities.

10.5.4 Assessing Terminological Precision

To investigate terminological variation, we measured the ambiguity levels of named-entity labels. By ambiguity, we refer to the possibility that a single name refers to more than one ontology individual. Variation relates to the opposite case—one ontology individual can be described by various terms in text.

We measured the level of terminological variation for each ontology individual, i.e., given a single ontology individual (e.g., an actor), how many variations of the name are found in the corpus? Bilenko and Mooney [19] used a similar method in a different setting. To identify variations in the text, we used the StringMetrics similarity matching library.* We experimented with the Levenstein, Jaro-Winkler, and q-gram similarity measures. For example, using such similarity measures, we could match *Bill Jackson* (a name often used in blogs to informally refer to the actor) with *William Jackson* (the name under which the actor is described in the ontology). Such flexibility in aligning query terms with ontology terms increases search system recall but also risk of precision loss is introduced when two distinct individuals in the ontology can be named by the same term. For example, if an ontology contains an actor named *Bill Johnson* and another named *William Johnson,* a fuzzy string matching would confuse the two actors.

To measure the practical impacts of the name variability and ambiguity factors, we extracted information from the corpus of movie reviews we collected. We first developed a NER specialized to the Movies domain. (The OpenCalais NER we used above properly tags person names, but cannot distinguish actors and directors or identify movie names.) We manually tagged a corpus of 200 movie reviews from the Ebert corpus, to indicate the occurrences of movie names and actor names. We then applied the YAMCHA[†] package to train an automatic NER system on our corpus. YAMCHA uses a support vector machine (SVM) classifier to recognize named entities in text based on features describing each word. We used two

---

* http://www.dcs.shef.ac.uk/sam/stringmetrics.html
[†] http://chasen.org/~taku/software/yamcha/

different sets of features to train the system: (1) whether words started with capital letters (strong indications of a proper name) and (2) whether names occurred in a gazette (manually compiled list of proper names). We also used contextual features (properties of words around the words to be classified).

The main challenges a statistically trained NER system addresses are (1) identifying a sequence of several words as a single named expression (for example, *Bill Gates 3rd*) and (2) recognizing through generalization that words that do not appear in a predefined gazette of names are similar in their distribution to known names, so that terms not observed earlier as proper names are properly recognized as such. A NER system must also use contextual information to avoid tagging a word that does appear in the gazette but is not used as a proper name (for example, *Bill paid the bill*). Finally, a NER system must distinguish between proper names referring to actors and movies.

Table 10.2 summarizes the results of the trained NER system. The system on average is capable of properly identifying 92% of the movies named in the reviews and 94% of the persons.

Let us now consider a given text as a search query. If we apply our NER system to the text of the query, we will properly tag named movies or actors. The issue we now address is how successful we will be in aligning a named entity in the query with the corresponding individual in the ontology? For a version of the ontology including 117,556 individuals referring to persons, taking into account surnames only, we found that 83% of the names may refer to more than one instance of the ontology. We also found that over 18 name variations on average for each ontology instance actually occurred in the corpus.

10.5.5 Conclusion: Ontology Terminological Coverage

In conclusion, while the coverage of the ontology originally looked promising, we found that based on name variability and ambiguity, aligning a query with

Table 10.2 Performance of Named Entity Recognizer on Movies Domain

	Precision	Recall	F
Movie exact match	91.56	92.43	91.87
Movie boundary match	91.80	92.66	92.10
Person exact match	97.68	93.76	95.67
Person boundary match	97.84	93.92	95.83
Average accuracy	99.32		
Average boundary accuracy	99.34		

ontology individuals remained an acute challenge. In this experiment, we used the corpus of reviews as a representative set of search queries. Note that we do not claim that reviews are similar to actual search queries. We only claim that the way movies and actors are named in naturally occurring reviews is a good indication of how they will be named in search queries.

This exercise indicates how a textual corpus aligned with an ontology and mature language technology (named-entity recognition and flexible string similarity) allows us to measure a complex property of an ontology. This evaluation provides a score for the ontology and also indicates which specific named entities are used in the corpus, how often, which confusions can be expected when disambiguating query terms, and how to improve the terminology-related services provided by the ontology. The data set we collected can be used to specifically tune the specific method to be used to align named entities with ontology individuals. The next section demonstrates how the more complex task of measuring the clustering adequacy of an ontology can be assessed using text classification techniques.

10.6 Evaluation of Ontology Classification Fitness

10.6.1 Objective

Consider an exploratory search scenario. Precision and recall cannot be measured because the user does not know a priori what he expects. Different criteria have been proposed to assess the quality of an exploratory search system [21]. We do not attempt a full task-based (and expensive) evaluation. Instead, we identify quality criteria for exploratory search that enable specific ways through which an ontology can improve user experience. The services expected from the ontology are: (1) clustering individuals by similarity to address the need to present large result-sets; (2) presenting result sets using a faceted search GUI to provide efficient browsing and query refinement; and (3) identifying paths of exploration through which movies are identified (period, genre, actors, etc.) to structure a sequence of queries. Our task was to assess the adequacy of our ontology to provide the services listed above. Again, we adopted a corpus-based method. Our evaluation method translated tests on the ontology into tests on our aligned test corpus.

10.6.2 Hypothesis

The fitness of an ontology to support exploratory search is a function of the number of classes that organize the range of individuals. We take this definition a step forward: the structure of ontology classes is valid if it produces a balanced view of the world domain (represented by the documents) and if the explicit characteristics of the structure can be identified implicitly in the documents. The ontology induces a classification over its individuals. Each class (e.g., actor, genre) may be viewed as a dimension for classification of the texts that represent the domain. The ontology provides effective classification services if it meets two criteria:

- The ontology classification is useful if the induced classification is well balanced, enabling the user to explore the data set efficiently (for exploratory purposes).
- The ontology classification is adequate if the classification induced by the ontology is valid with respect to the domain represented by texts.

Accordingly, we formulate the following hypothesis. If the ontology indicates that some movies are "clustered" according to one of the dimensions, then documents associated to these movies should also be found to be associated by a text classification engine trained on the classification induced by the ontology.

10.6.3 Classification Experiment

The general procedure we performed to test this hypothesis is the following:

Step 1: Choose a dimension to test (we report here on genres).

Step 2: Induce a set of categories (subsets of movies). The subclasses of this dimension and the movies instantiated under each subclass define a clustering of the movies. For example, if we evaluate the genre dimension, we cluster movies according to their genre property. In our ontology, this produces about 30 subsets of movies (one for each genre value).

Step 3: Gather texts (from the reviews corpus, texts not used in the acquisition process of the ontology) related to these movies and form a collection ($Text_{ij}$, $movie_i$).

Step 4: Train a classifier on a subset ($Text_{ik} \ \grave{E} \ Text_{ij}$) of the texts ($Text_{ik}$, $movie_i$, $category_i$), where $category_i$ is the category induced by the ontology.

Step 5: Test the trained classifier on withheld data ($Text_{ij}$, $movie_i$) and compute accuracy, precision, and recall with respect to the category.

Several reasonable options can perform the text classification task in Step 4, with different methods of text representation and different classifiers. For text representation, we viewed texts as bags of words, i.e., unigrams, and represented each text as a Boolean vector in which each coordinate indicated the presence or absence of a string in the text. We tested several options of preprocessing on the texts and selecting features (strings taken into account when representing text) with and without stemming* and with and without filtering noise words. We selected features using mutual information (MI) or TF/IDF and different numbers of features (top 300 or 1,000).

---

* We used classical Porter Stemmer for the experiment.

For feature selection, in TF/IDF, we chose words with the highest values as features for the entire corpus. In MI, the features with the highest mutual information associated with the class were chosen (a different set of features used for every class). MI-based feature selection is inspired by [22]. The reference indicates that this method yields best results for text categorization by topic on a standard news corpus. We used two methods for classification: linear and quadratic support vector machines (SVMs) and multinomial naive Bayes (MNB) as implemented in the Weka toolkit [23].

10.6.4 Results

We applied the classification procedure to the classifications induced by the genre dimension. The classifiers were trained on the reviews corpus. We performed five-fold cross-validation on the corpus. The best text representation was established by testing the genre classifier on the task of classification of one class against all. For each possibility, we tested both SVM and naive Bayes as classifiers. Sixteen different experimental settings were tested:

- TF/IDF versus MI
- Vectors of 300 features versus vectors of 1,000 features
- Stemmed words versus raw words
- Filtered noise words versus unfiltered noise words

Classification by genre—A genre, according to IMDb.com, is defined as "simply a categorization of certain types of art based upon their style, form, or content. Most movies can easily be described with certain umbrella terms, such as westerns, dramas, or comedies." The tested ontology included 23 genre subclasses. We performed the classification process described above, and found that the best combination was MI, 300 features, no stemming, noise filtering, and naive Bayes classifier. Among the several ways to measure the performance of a binary classifier, a common measure in natural language processing is the *F*-measure is defined by:

$$\frac{2TP}{2TP + FP + FN}$$

where *TP* is the number of elements in the positive class that were correctly classified, *FP* is the number of elements in the negative class, falsely classified as positive, *TN* is the number of correctly classified negative elements, and *FN* the number of elements in the positive class classified as negative. *F*-measure takes values between 0 (always mistaken) and 1 (always correct) and combines in a single metric the desire to obtain high precision while maintaining high recall. For our task, we found the Matthews correlation coefficient (MCC) more suitable. MCC is calculated by:

$$\frac{TP \times TN - FP \times FN}{\sqrt{(TP + FN)(TP + \text{FP})(TN + FN)}}$$

The values of MCC range from –1 (always wrong) to 1 (always correct). The average *F*-Measure is 0.49, and the average MCC is 0.43 (results shown in Table 10.3). The average *F*-measure and MCC are reasonably high. For comparison, we tested a baseline classifier by creating 25 random classes of 1,000 movies. We performed the same classification procedure. The results showed average *F*-measures lower than 0.16 and extremely low accuracy.

This indicates that the corpus-anchored ontology evaluation does not capture random patterns of text classification. In other words, knowledge extracted from the ontology helped us classify text previously unseen in the domain covered by the ontology. This overall high performance on text classification validates our basic hypothesis that we can perform tests on the ontology by computing properties of the corresponding test corpus.

We are now interested in investigating how we can exploit the details of the quantitative analysis of the trained text classifiers to learn specific properties of the ontology. In a typical classification scenario, the classifier is the object of evaluation (typically, several classifiers are compared on the same data set), and hence the correlation between class size and *F*-measure is not an issue. We want to evaluate the classes, not the classifier. The advantage of MCC over *F*-measure arises because MCC, unlike *F*-measure, is not affected by positive class size. A random binary classifier that considers only the observed probability P of the positive class in the training set and not the content is expected to yield an *F*-score of P. Its MCC is expected to be 0. Another point in favor of MCC is that it is symmetrical and thus more suitable for classifying pairs of genres that exhibit no natural choice of the positive class.

The results indicate that some genres are very well defined (sport, family, documentary) and others cannot be recovered by analyzing the texts of the reviews (history, war, biography, adult, short).* While these figures provide a first assessment of the quality of each genre category, pair-wise classification provides finer grained tests of the level to which pairs of genres can be distinguished. In pair-wise classification, we first classify each pair of genres (e.g., drama versus history) and then calculate the average accuracy measure over all pairs. Pair-wise classification indicates genre pairs that are similar (with low accuracy measures). Table 10.4 shows a subset of the results revealing best and worst cases. We reported MCC and error rates for these tests. Pair-wise classification was accurate: the overall error rate was

---

* The music and musical genres are derived from IMDb genres and are apparently confusing.

Table 10.3 MCC, *F*-Measures, and Error Rates of One-versus-All Classification Engine Sorted by MCC

Genre	Percent Error	F-Measure	MCC
Sport	2.49	0.72	0.71
Family	5.59	0.63	0.60
Documentary	1.01	0.61	0.56
Adventure	11.88	0.63	0.56
Comedy	21.19	0.71	0.56
Thriller	20.06	0.68	0.54
Action	14.00	0.62	0.53
Science Fiction	7.94	0.55	0.52
Animation	5.68	0.54	0.52
Horror	8.88	0.54	0.51
Fantasy	7.47	0.53	0.50
Music	3.85	0.50	0.48
Drama	22.18	0.84	0.47
Western	2.35	0.43	0.46
Crime	16.96	0.49	0.39
Romance	23.17	0.46	0.31
Musical	1.73	0.27	0.29
Mystery	12.50	0.35	0.28
History	5.30	0.29	0.28
War	5.97	0.26	0.23
Biography	6.25	0.23	0.22
Adult	6.43	0.19	0.18
Short	20.91	0.24	0.18

Table 10.4 Pair-Wise Classification of Genres

Pair	Percent Error	MCC
Sport–Fantasy	4.76	0.89
Crime–Family	7.60	0.82
Biography–Science Fiction	9.96	0.78
Drama–Animation	1.49	0.77
Horror–Thriller	7.15	0.27
Drama–War	12.23	0.23
History–Biography	38.28	0.23
Drama–History	0.51	−0.002

below 12.4%, and did not exceed 38.2% for any pair of classes. Overlap between two categories is possible. For example, a movie can belong both to action and drama genres. We trained and tested only on movies that belonged to one genre of pairs tested.

10.6.5 Ontology Classification Fitness: Conclusions

Our method of translating tests of ontology properties into tests on an aligned textual corpus allowed us to quantitatively assess a complex property of the ontology: can it be used to cluster search results in a manner that would be recognized by experts in the domain? We translated this test of the ontology to a test on the aligned textual corpus. The results indicate that overall the ontology provided accurate classifications (average *F*-measure of 0.49 versus 0.16 for random clustering). Importantly, the method provided specific feedback on pairs of classes in the ontology. Using pair-wise classification, we can measure a priori high confusion between pairs of classes (e.g., drama versus history).

10.7 Evaluating Ontology Coverage of Query Topics

10.7.1 Objective and Hypothesis

In this section, we suggest a methodology to deal with an ontology that contains a vast number of classes that lack hierarchical (flat and wide) structures. From a search perspective, this situation is undesirable because it is most likely unbalanced. From an evaluation perspective, directly applying the classification-based evaluation discussed above on such flat and wide relations will not be effective because text classification is not effective on a large number of small categories.

We illustrate this issue with the case of keywords associated to movies. Keywords in IMDb and accordingly in our entertainment ontology are based on what Szomszor et al. [24] call free-for-all tagging. Users can add new keywords that are then moderated to prevent spamming. Overall, the ontology contains 10,529 unique keywords. The relation between keywords and films is many-to-many: many keywords per movie, too many or too few (as few as *one*) movies per keyword, and many keywords may be only weakly connected to movie content.

Take, for example, the keywords associated with the *Bonnie and Clyde* movie: bank robbery and celebrity criminal may be good search terms; but old woman, joke, face slap, and marriage intuitively do not characterize the plot. Bad search terms are too general or too specific. Overly specific terms may be useful in searching for a specific movie ("I'm looking for that movie with snakes and planes and forgot its name") but most likely would not aid an exploratory search.

Hence, for search purposes, we wish to cluster keywords into more manageable and useful exploratory dimensions. After we cluster them into a small number of topics, we can use the same classification-based evaluation method to test the quality of the clusters. In a more abstract manner, we relate to a specific property of the ontology (wide and shallow relations such as keywords) as the reflection of a hidden property in the domain (smaller set of unlabeled topics). While the concrete ontology relation does not directly help the search engine for exploratory purposes, the underlying hidden property may provide quantifiable benefits for exploratory search. Again, our method leads us to translate this hypothesis into practical tests on our aligned textual corpus.

10.7.2 Experiment

We applied a clustering method based on latent Dirichlet allocation (LDA) [18] to cluster the keywords in our application. LDA is a generative probabilistic model for collection of discrete data. Its main assumption is that a document (represented as a bag of words) is a mixture of topics, and each word is generated by a topic with some probability. The mixture proportion of topics for each document and the topic–to-word generation probabilities means that words are learned from a given corpus in an unsupervised process. Three parameters (K, α, and b) control the number of topics, the sparsity of the document-to-topic distribution, and the sparsity of the topic-to-word distribution, respectively.

LDA has been used successfully in many text mining applications. In our application, we adopted it to learn possible topics from a set of keywords. The topics learned by LDA are clusters of keywords. To this end, we considered the list of keywords linked to a film to form a document and performed LDA on all such documents. Examples of the keyword clusters we acquired are shown in Figures 10.1 and 10.2. We configured the LDA to construct 100 clusters to partition the more than 10,000 distinct keywords found in the ontology. On average, the obtained clusters contained 20 keywords.

> 10 flashback-sequence mother-son-relationship hotel father-son-relationship restaurant face-slap
> premarital-sex bar car-accident hospital funeral los-angeles-california friendship drunk-scene beach
> blockbuster profanity title-spoken-by-character narration cemetery
> 72 based-on-novel character-name-in-title independent-_lm number-in-title acronym-in-title lost-_lm
> hobo kilt scottish-accent entire-title-is-capitalized-acronym clock-watcher party-lifestyle team-owner
> essex-wife wags team-captain wives-and-girlfriends aids once-upon-a-time-in-the-title m-a-s-h
> 83 based-on-novel character-name-in-title independent-_lm circus carnival clown amusement-park
> criminal-justice number-in-title acrobat gypsy midget roller-coaster fortune-teller side-show hypnotism
> trapeze elephant carousel ferris-wheel

Figure 10.1 LDA sets with highest *F*-measures.

> 87 kids-and-family cartoon looney-tunes merrie-melodies australia bugs-bunny australian popeye
> porky-pig daffy-duck part-live-action chicken william-tell-overture woody-woodpecker sylvester pig
> screen-song breaking-the-fourth-wall duck anvil
> 86 boxing baseball sport soccer american-football football basketball coach boxer training olympics
> golf athlete college competition dandy stadium reverse-the-polarity-of-the-neutron-ow early-sound
> locker-room
> 36 native-american murder horse sheri_ cowboy revenge gold outlaw spaghetti-western saloon ranch
> actor-shares-first-name-with-character bank-robbery desert cattle bandit texas shootout stagecoach arizona

Figure 10.2 LDA sets with highest MCC-measures.

10.7.3 Results

To test the validity of the clusters obtained via LDA, we used the method described in Section 10.6. We applied the procedure to the classification induced by the keyword cluster dimension. The classifiers were trained on the review corpus. As a baseline, we applied a very simple keyword clustering method based on word similarity (two keywords attach to the same cluster if they include a common word or words within a small edit distance). With such a simple clustering heuristic, the average *F*-measure obtained on text classification was extremely low (average = 0.07). Results improved significantly with LDA clustering (average *F*-measure = 0.48; average MCC measure = 0.28; average error rate =0.26).

**Table 10.5   One-to-all
Classification of Keywords**

Class	F	MCC
10	0.74	0.27
72	0.71	0.25
83	0.70	0.21
24	0.66	0.19
90	0.66	0.38
71	0.66	0.39
45	0.66	0.21
36	0.65	0.43

Table 10.5 shows the results of the text classification for some classes. While the results are not very high (as expected for the extremely noisy data set), they are much better than the baseline (range of 0.65 to 0.75 versus 0.07). The MCC and *F*-measure values allowed us to filter unreliable keyword clusters and compare the potential of each keyword cluster to help explore the data set.

10.8 Conclusions and Future Work

We presented a concrete ontology evaluation method based on use of a corpus of textual documents aligned with ontology individuals. We demonstrated how to operate such an evaluation of an ontology in the entertainment domain used to improve a semantic search engine. We first constructed an ontology-aligned textual corpus by developing a Web crawler of movie reviews. On the basis of this data set, we demonstrated the method on three increasingly abstract tests. We assessed how the ontology captured important terminology in the domain, how it supported clustering search results along coarse relations such as genre, and how it supported clustering search results along abstract relations such as topic.

We measured the ontology coverage of query terms and found that our ontology had wide coverage but lacked support for ambiguity resolution and terminological variation handling. We used techniques of fuzzy string matching and statistically trained named-entity recognition to identify specific ontology terms to be disambiguated.

Our classification experiment measured the adequacy of the ontology to support exploratory search along coarse relations such as genre. We formulated hypotheses that capture the quality criteria of an exploratory search system and tested them on our ontology-aligned textual corpus. Specifically when testing the classification adequacy of our ontology along the genre dimension, we found that most of the genres in the ontology induced high-quality text classifiers, but some (such as sport and music) did not induce appropriate classifiers. We used techniques of statistically trained text classification in these experiments.

Finally, in a topic experiment, we investigated how the noisy data provided by a cloud of unedited keywords acquired automatically into the search ontology can still provide useful classification results to help exploratory searching. We used the topic modeling technique (LDA algorithm) to translate wide and shallow ontology relations (keywords) to a set of topic clusters, then applied the technigue to cluster search results.

Our tests indicated that the proposed method of translating tests on the ontology into tests on an aligned text corpus provided useful feedback to information architects that can be used to directly improve the quality of a search ontology.

Acknowledgments

This research is supported by Deutsche Telekom at the BGU T-Laboratories of Ben-Gurion University of the Negev.

References

1. Tunkelang, D. 2009. *Faceted Search.* Synthesis Lectures on Information Concepts, Retrieval, and Services. Morgan and Claypool.
2. Hearst, M.A. and Preston-Smalley, C.C. 2006. Faceted metadata for information architecture and search. (CHI course).
3. White, R.W. and Roth, R.A. 2009. *Exploratory Search: Beyond the Query–Response Paradigm.* Synthesis Lectures on Information Concepts, Retrieval, and Services. Morgan and Claypool.
4. Baeza-Yates, R., Ciaramita, M., Mika, P. et al. 2008. Towards semantic search. *Natural Language and Information Systems,* 4–11.
5. Hearst, M.A. 2008. UIs for faceted navigation: Recent advances and remaining open problems. In *Proceedings of Workshop on Computer Interaction and Information Retrieval,* HCIR.
6. Stefaner, M., Sebastian-Ferre, S.P.J.K., and Zhang, Y. 2009. User interface design. In *Dynamic Taxonomies and Faceted Search: Theory, Practice, and Experience,* Vol. 25, Information Retrieval Series, Springer, Berlin.
7. Stoica, E., Hearst, M.A., and Richardson, M. 2007. Automating creation of hierarchical faceted metadata structures. In Sidner, C.L. et al., Eds., HLT-NAACL, Association for Computational Linguistics, pp. 244–251.
8. Gulla, J.A., Borch, H., and Ingvaldsen, J. 2007. Ontology learning for search applications. In *Proceedings of 6th International Conference on Ontologies, Databases and Applications of Semantics.*

9. Mimno, D. and McCallum, A. 2007. Organizing the OCA: Learning faceted subjects from a library of digital books. In *Proceedings of Seventh ACM/IEEE-CS Joint Conference on Digital Libraries*, ACM Press, New York, pp. 376–385.

10. Burkhardt, F., Gulla, J.A., Liu, J. et al. 2008. Semi-automatic ontology engineering in business applications. In *Proceedings of Third International AST Workshop: Applications of Semantic Technologies*.

11. Gangemi, A., Catenacci, C., Ciaramita, M. et al. 2006. Modelling ontology evaluation and validation. In *Proceedings of ESWC*, Vol. 45011, *Lecture Notes in Computer Science*, pp. 140–154.

12. Alani, H. and Brewster, C. 2005. Ontology ranking based on the analysis of concept structures. In *Proceedings of Third International Conference on Knowledge Capture*, Banff, pp. 51–58.

13. Gomez-Perez, A. 2001. Evaluation of ontologies. *International Journal of Intelligent Systems*, 16: 391–409.

14. Hearst, M.A. 2009. *Search User Interfaces*. Cambridge University Press.

15. McGuinness, D.L. and van Harmelen, F. 2004. OWL web ontology language overview. Technical Report REC-owl-features-20040210, W3C.

16. Aula, A. 2003. Query formulation in web information search. In *Proceedings of IADIS International Conference on WWW/Internet*, pp. 403–410.

17. Strasunskas, D. and Tomassen, S. 2008. Empirical insights on a value of ontology quality in ontology-driven web search. In *On the Move to Meaningful Internet Systems: CoopIS, DOA, ODBASE, GADA, and IS*, Monterrey, Mexico.

18. Blei, D.M., Ng, A.Y., and Jordan, M. 2003. Latent Dirichlet allocation. *Journal of Machine Learning Research*, 3: 993–1022.

19. Bilenko, M. and Mooney, R.J. 2003. Adaptive duplicate detection using learnable string similarity measures. In *Proceedings of Ninth ACM SIGKDD International Conference on Knowledge Discovery and Data Mining*, ACM Press, New York, pp. 39–48.

20. Kudo, T. and Matsumoto, Y. 2003. Fast methods for kernel-based text analysis. In *Proceedings of 41st Annual Meeting of Association for Computational Linguistics*, Sapporo, Japan, pp. 24–31.

21. White, R.W., Muresan, G., and Marchionini, G., Eds. 2006. *ACM SIGIR Workshop on Evaluating Exploratory Search Systems*, Seattle.

22. Dumais, S., Platt, J., Heckerman, D. et al. 1998. Inductive learning algorithms and representations for text categorization. In *Proceedings of Seventh International Conference on Information and Knowledge Management*, Bethesda, MD, pp. 2–7.

23. Witten, I.H. and Frank, E. 2005. *Data Mining: Practical Machine Learning Tools and Techniques*, 2nd ed., Morgan Kaufmann, San Francisco.

24. Szomszor, M., Cattuto, C., Alani, H. et al. 2007. Folksonomies: The semantic web, and movie recommendation. In *Proceedings of Fourth European Semantic Web Conference: Bridging the Gap between Semantic Web and Web 2.0*, Innsbruck, Austria.

SEMANTIC APPLICATIONS

Chapter 11

Adding Semantics to Decision Tables: A New Approach to Data and Knowledge Engineering?

Yan Tang and Robert Meersman
VUB STARLab, Brussels, Belgium

Jan Vanthienen
Katholieke Universiteit Leuven, Leuven, Belgium

Contents

11.1 Introduction

Decision tables have been investigated for more than 50 years. Research interests range largely from programming to control systems, robotics, databases, and so forth. Modern ontology technologies provide promising solutions for decision support reasoning and collaborative decision support. This chapter proposes a new approach to data and knowledge engineering using a semantic decision table (SDT), defined as a semantically rich decision table supported by ontology engineering (OE). An SDT contains all the features of generic decision tables such as correctness, completeness, and syntactical consistency. Our research provides a means to capture and examine decision makers' concepts and a tool for refining their decision knowledge and facilitating knowledge sharing in a scalable manner.

Many researchers have attempted to extend decision tables for different purposes in various fields in the past two decades. This chapter addresses fundamental aspects of SDTs including comparisons with different types of extensions. To demonstrate the advantages, we will show an application that supports ontology-based data matching in the domains of e-learning and training. The motivation for and challenges of this chapter are to:

- Demonstrate the advantages of SDTs brought forward by modern Semantic Web (SW) and OE technologies
- Explore possible applications of SDTs and demonstrate their usefulness
- Illustrate how SDTs can assist ontology-based data matching processes

Section 11.2 covers background including definitions, OE issues, and two extensions to decision tables. The SDT concept is explained in Section 11.3. Section 11.4 details our recent results from applying SDTs to data management and knowledge engineering. In particular, we use SDTs to support ontology-based data matching—a kind of semantic matching. Section 11.5 is the discussion evaluating this particular SDT application. We also discuss and illustrate the trend of applying the principles of OE to traditional decision tables and decision support systems (DSS) in general. Section 11.6 is the chapter conclusion.

11.2 Background

11.2.1 Decision Tables

Decision tables have been widely used in various fields such as judicial support systems, control systems, algorithms, and data management. Interest in decision tables continues to increase, particularly in the domains of data and knowledge management (Barry 1998, Hewett and Leuchner 2002, Lima et al. 2008).

A decision table is defined as a tabular method of showing the relationships of a series of conditions and the resultant actions to be executed (CSA 1970). Wets et al. (1996) define a decision table as a tabular representation used to describe and analyze procedural decision situations, where the state of a number of conditions determines the execution of a set of actions.

A decision table contains three basic elements: the *conditions*, the *actions* (or *decisions*), and the *rules*. A decision *condition* is constructed with a *condition stub* (or *condition subject* in Wets et al. 1996) and a *condition entry* (or *condition state* per Wets et al.). A condition stub is declared a *statement* of a condition. A condition entry provides a *value* assigned to the condition stub.

Table 11.1 is an example of a decision table for deciding which Chinese medicines should be given to a patient based on his symptoms. *Blood deficiency, Qi deficiency,* and *Indigestion* are condition stubs. *Yes and No* are condition entries. *Donkey-hide gelatin, Angelica X,* and *Eel* are *action stubs*. Asterisks (*) and the

Table 11.1   Example of a Decision Table

	1	2	3	4	5	6	7	8
Condition								
Blood deficiency[1]	Yes	No	Yes	No	Yes	No	Yes	No
Qi deficiency[2]	Yes	Yes	No	No	Yes	Yes	No	No
Indigestion	Yes	Yes	Yes	Yes	No	No	No	No
Decision								
Donkey-hide gelatin					*	*	*	
Angelica X	*	*	*		*	*	*	
Eel	*	*			*	*		

[1] Clinical indication in Chinese medicine. Blood is described as deficient when it cannot fulfill its basic functions due to weakness. www.acupuncturecollege.org.uk/acupuncture/Chinese-medicine/Glossary/Glossary)

[2] Clinical indication in Chinese medicine. Deficient or exhausted Qi arising from prenatal or postnatal factors. www.liferising.com/know/q9.html)

absence of asterisks are action entries. *Indigestion–Yes* is a *condition. Angelica X–** is an action. Each decision column in a decision table is a decision rule defined as a combination of (a set of) conditions and (a set of) actions. For instance, decision column 3 in Table 11.1 represents a decision rule: "if a patient has the symptoms of blood deficiency and indigestion, the prescription is Angelica X."

A decision table presents many outstanding advantages for nontechnical business users (Pooch 1974, Kohavi and Sommerfield 1998, Vanthienen and Wets 1994). For example, a decision table is easily learned; is readable and understandable; and is concise and precise.

11.2.2 Ontology Engineering

The emergence of ontology-based applications such as the Semantic Web (SW, Berners-Lee 1999) marks the importance of ontologies. In the field of computer science, an ontology is defined as "an explicit *specification* of a *conceptualization*" (Gruber 1993). Conceptualization is further defined by Guarino (1995, 1998) as an *intended model* within which a set of logical *axioms* is designed to account for the *intended meaning* of a *vocabulary*.

Formal ontology is designed to aid knowledge sharing and interoperation among agents. A well designed ontology has the basic characteristics of conceptualization, consistency and coherence, sharability, representation independency, interoperability, and extensibility and evolution (Staab and Studer 2004). A common reason for using domain ontologies is to provide a basis for reusing, sharing, and integrating valuable domain knowledge among agents and/or applications. In particular, we use ontologies as bridges to connect the modules of a system or the components of different systems in a cluster. The granularity of a cluster can be repeatedly expanded and finally become a globalized SW. Modern OE combines the following research fields and existing technologies.

Ontology modeling and visualization approaches—Unified modeling language (UML, OMG 2003), object role modeling language (ORM, Halpin 2001), and entity-relationship language (ER, Chen 1976) are probably the most used ontology modeling languages. We use Tiny Lexon browser modeling language (T-Lex, Trog et al. 2006) and semantic decision modeling language (SDRule-L, Tang and Meersman 2007, 2009) at STARLab. The former is mainly based on ORM notations and the latter is a special extension to ORM for decision support.

Ontology representation languages—Resource description framework (schema) language [(RDF(s)]* and web ontology language (OWL)† are the most used. Rule markup initiative languages (RuleML, Boley 2001, Boley et al. 2004) and ontology reference and ideal language (Ω-RIDL, Verheyden et al. 2004) are for more specific usages.

---

* ttp://www.w3.org/TR/rdf-schema/
† http://www.w3.org/TR/owl-ref/

Ontology creation methodologies—On the OnToWorld wiki website,* a general survey of the ontology capturing methodologies is explored. Among them, Methontology (Férnandez et al. 1997), the Grüninger and Fox method (1995), the Uschold and King method (1995), and CommonKADS (Schreiber et al. 1999) are probably the most common ones. Recently, a new direction of pushing the community theory and social network technologies to ontology capturing methodologies has been discovered, e.g., Meaning evolution systems (de Moor et al. 2006) and negotiation pattern language (NPL, Paschke et al. 2006).

Ontology-based applications—Many available ontology based applications apply to different domains such as medical decision support (Lima et al. 2008) and marketing analysis (Mavridis et al. 2006). As discussed, the Semantic Web is a well known ontology-based application. Readers may also consider SDTs as a kind of ontology-based application.

We define SDTs as ontology-based, semantically rich decision tables. A detailed discussion appears in Section 11.3. The next subsection provides background about decision tables and ontology followed by illustrations of two extensions to decision tables.

11.2.3 Extensions to Decision Tables

This section explains approaches for extending decision tables in the field of data management and knowledge representation.

11.2.3.1 Second-Order Decision Tables

Second-order decision tables (SODTs, Hewett and Leuchner 2002) are defined as *database relations*, in which rows have sets of atomic values as components. The initial intent of using SODTs was to trim large decision tables yielded by data mining. Shorter tables are easier to understand and can be managed and applied more efficiently. Research on mining techniques and classifiers is beyond the scope of this chapter. The issue here is the meaning of the SODT.

First-order and second-order decision tables are commonly used. The difference between them arises from their condition and action entries. The condition and action entries of SODTs are *second-order tuples*. More specifically, each entry (condition or decision entry) of a first-order decision table corresponds to a single value; while each entry of an SODT is a value set. Table 11.2 is an example of an SODT that is equivalent to Table 11.1.

11.2.3.1.1 Fuzzy Decision Tables

Fuzzy decision tables (FDTs, Chen et al. 1995, Wets et al. 1996) deal with uncertainties. FDTs are introduced here because crisp decision tables "only appear to

---

* http://semanticweb.org/wiki/

Table 11.2   Example of an SODT

Condition							
Symptoms	BD, QD, IN	BD, QD	BD, IN	QD, IN	BD	QD	IN
Decision							
Donkey-hide gelatin		Yes			Yes	Yes	
Angelica X	Yes	Yes	Yes	Yes	Yes	Yes	
Eel	Yes	Yes		Yes		Yes	

BD = blood deficiency; QD = Q_i deficiency; IN = indigestion.

Table 11.3   Example of a Fuzzy Decision Table

Condition						
Headache		No			A little	
Sleep	Good	About average	Bad	Good	About average	Bad
Decision						
Possible blood deficiency					*	*
Possible Qi deficiency			*			*

produce an accurate or nonfuzzy decision output. The imprecision inherent in decision making is not noticed." An FDT includes fuzziness in the condition and/or action/decision segments. For example, in Table 11.3, the condition entries for *short, about average, long, a little* and the action stubs (*possible* blood deficiency and *possible* Qi deficiency) are described with fuzzy words. The condition and/or action configuration in an FDT is a value in [0, 1]. This approach brings fuzzy logic to decision tables.

11.3 Semantic Decision Tables

The semantic decision table (SDT) concept (Tang and Meersman 2007, Tang and Meersman 2008, Tang et al. 2008) is introduced to deal with certain problems in designing decision tables within a community (decision group):

1. Ambiguity in the information representation of the condition stubs and action stubs. For example, Angelica X in Table 11.1 is ambiguous because

Angelica can refer to many species such as Angelica atropurpurea and Angelica arguta.

2. Conceptual duplication that occurs between conditions, actions, and decision rules. For example, in Table 11.1, the indigestion symptom may be included among the symptoms of the Qi definition.

3. Uncertainty in the condition entries, e.g., possible blood deficiency in Table 11.3 contains a certain level of uncertainty.

4. Difficulties in managing large tables (also known as the structural scalability problem).

5. Specification of hidden or meta decision rules. A hidden decision rule in Table 11.1 might be, "Donkey-hide gelatin is not easily digested; therefore, the doctor should not prescribe it for a patient who has indigestion problems."

We use domain ontologies to store semantics from an SDT. With OE technologies, we can easily disambiguate the decision items, check the conceptual duplications in a decision table, and specify the uncertainties of the condition entries. Just as an ideal ontology is extensible and scalable, an SDT is easy and ready to be extended. While constructing SDTs, hidden and implicit (meta) decision rules are specified and stored. Since the SDTs are formal commitments based on agreement within a decision group, they are easily shared.

An SDT is modeled in a three-layer format: (1) decision binary fact types called SDT lexons; (2) a commitment layer containing constraints and axioms of the fact types; and (3) decision tasks or applications. The three-layer format was based on the principles of developing ontology-grounded methods and applications (DOGMA, Meersman 2001, Spyns et al. 2002) and has served as the main research topic at the VUB STARLab for 10 years.

An SDT lexon is a quintuple like (γ, *disease, has, is of, symptom*), in which γ is the context identifier and points to the documents in which *disease* and *symptom* are defined; *has* and *is of* represent two roles. A lexon is a fact type.

An SDT commitment corresponds to an explicit instance of an intentional interpretation for a decision task. Semantic decision rules (including ontological constraints cited in some OE papers) are stored at this level. We primarily consider uniqueness, mandatory nature, subset, equality, exclusion, subtype, occurrence, and frequency when using SDT for data management.

An SDT is the result of annotating a decision table with ontologies. During the annotation process, the decision makers must specify all the hidden rules, for example, one with a mandatory constraint stating that "EACH disease has AT LEAST ONE symptom." This rule is written in semantic decision rule language (SDRule-L, Tang and Meersman 2009) as an SDT commitment: P1 = [*disease, has, is of, symptom*]: UNIQ (P1).

With these "extra" rules, we can benefit from the reasoning advantages brought forward by OE.

Among the many other interesting use cases of SDTs, one is to embed an SDT in a process and separate decision rules from the process to improve system tractability

(Tang and Meersman 2007). An important feasibility provided by SDTs is visualizing the results and decision rules in the form of decision tables when the decisions are taken in every decision process. SDTs also increase flexibility at the system management level because the knowledge engineers can create different algorithms and decision rules based on their needs.

Another interesting use is applying SDTs to visualize decision tables at different levels that contain instance data at the lowest level and (meta) decision rules at higher levels (Tang et al. 2008). The idea is to illustrate the meta decision rules of a decision table.

11.3.1 SDTs for Supporting Ontology-Based Data Matching

In the EC Prolix project,* an ontology-based data matching framework was required to enhance a matching engine in the domains of human resource management and e-learning. Note that *ontology-based data matching* is not the same problem as *ontology matching*. The goal of the latter is to resolve semantic inconsistency while integrating more than *two* ontologies. The goal of the former (the scope of our work) is to find the similarities between two data sets, each of which corresponds to one part of the ontology. There is only one ontology in that problem.

By considering this ontology as a connected network, the issue of ontology-based data matching (ODM) can then be viewed as finding connections between two subnetworks (Korn et al. 1996, Venkateswaran et al. 2006) and the related work of finding and measuring such connections. Venkateswaran et al. (2006) focus on finding data objects or web pages belonging to the same (or similar) contexts. Korn et al. (1996) used a two-phase method to discover data based on feature distance. Barrett et al. (2008) illustrate an algorithm of finding the shortest path between two nodes in a labeled and weighted network.

Our work does not focus on how to draw a boundary between searching spaces like that of Venkateswaran et al. (2006). We calculate similarity scores between two subnetworks (or nodes) based on the shortest path between the subnetworks. We use SDTs to grant semantics to the labeled arcs and weights of the ontology graph to provide an extra layer of conceptual analysis to a network. In the next subsection, we illustrate an example of semantic matching in e-learning and human resource management.

11.3.2 Human Resource Management Use Case

A human resource management (HRM) department uses text descriptions of *company values* (such as *trustworthy, straightforward,* and *heart*) to evaluate its employees. The results are recorded on evaluation forms. The training department uses competency notations of skills and abilities to categorize utilization of learning courses and materials. Each department uses its own supporting tools and terms.

---

* http://www.prolixproject.org/

To achieve better collaboration between departments and enhance the interoperability of the applications across departments, we developed an HRM ontology with which we annotate the company values and learning components. Each company value or learning material corresponds to one subgraph in the same ontology.

Figure 11.1 illustrates the use case by considering an ontology as a graph and an annotation result set as a subgraph. The subgraph indicated by *straightforward & heart* is the union of the annotation sets of *straightforward* and *heart*. The *course ITIl1* subgraph is the annotation set of *ITIL1*. Note that in our problem settings, every item (company values and learning) is annotated with the domain ontology. If a knowledge engineer cannot find a proper defined concept, then he or she must define the new concept by executing the ontology creation methods listed earlier. We now illustrate our approach based on this use case.

11.3.3 SDTs and GRASIM for Semantic Matching

Our matching strategy consists of the following steps: (1) label the arcs on an ontology graph; (2) choose an algorithm for calculating the shortest paths; and (3) convert the values of the shortest paths into a similarity score. SDTs are used to propose weights to end users for labeling the arcs in step (1). The default weights are calculated based on the decision rules stored in the SDTs.

After an engineer generates default weights based on the SDTs, he can update the weights if he is not satisfied with them. We also use the semantics in these SDTs to restrict the boundaries of the weights modified by the engineers.

Table 11.4 shows an SDT with which our semantic matching engine automatically assigns weights on the ontology graph. Figure 11.2 shows an example for applying the decision rule specified by column 2 of Table 11.4. $l_1 = \langle \gamma, \, CV, \, describe,$ *is described by, Network engineer*$\rangle$, $l_2 = \langle \gamma, \, Network \, engineer, \, is \, a \, supertype \, of, \, engineer \rangle$, $l_1 \in L \sqsubseteq \Omega$, $l_2 \in \Omega$ and $l_2 \notin L$. According to the decision rule, the weight range is [0, 50]. The engine can choose three different ways (pessimistic, optimistic, and moderate) to assign the exact values as the weights.

If it takes the pessimistic action, the largest permitted values will be assigned (see Table 11.5). If it takes the optimistic action, the smallest permitted values will be assigned (see Table 11.6). The moderate action will lead to a set of averages from the two situations above. As noted, a user can update the weights if he is unsatisfied with them. Table 11.7 shows an SDT containing user-specified weights. Note that not all the conditions from Table 11.4 are used in Table 11.7. Users only need to specify the weights based on the conditions they consider necessary to specify.

After the weights are assigned, we may choose any shortest path algorithm to find the shortest path for one node from one annotation subgraph (suppose it is G_1) to another node in the other annotation subgraph (suppose it is G_2). It is executed in step (2). In step (3), we convert the shortest path values into a similarity score that must fall in the range of [0, 1].

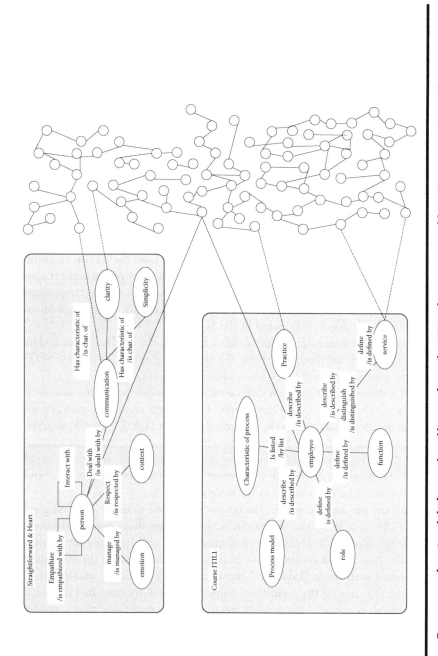

Figure 11.1 *Company values (straightforward and heart) from the HRM department and learning course (ITIL1) from training/e-learning department correspond to two sub-graphs of HRM ontology.*

Table 11.4 SDT for Deciding Default Weights of Arcs of Graph

Condition	1	2	3	n	...	n'
$int(r_1, r_2)$	is-a	{define, describe}	...	Has char. Of	...	N/A
$int(\bar{r}_1, \bar{r}_2)$	is-a	is-a	..	equal	...	N/A
$sub(t_1, t_1')$	Yes	Yes	...	Yes	...	No
$sup(t_1, t_1')$	Yes	No	...	No	...	No
$xor(t_1, t_1')$	Yes	No	...	Yes	...	No
Action						
Weight = 0				*		
0 <Weight <50		*				
Weight = 50					.	
50 <Weight ≤70						*
70 <Weight <100						
Weight = 100 (∞)	*					

Concept definitions of the condition stubs and action stubs

ID	Item	Explanation
CD1	t_1, t_2	Two terms in lexon $\langle \gamma, t_1, r_1, r_2, t_2 \rangle \in L$ where L is annotation set; each term t is a vertex in graph
CD2	r_1, r_2	Two roles in current lexon $\langle \gamma, t_1, r_1, r_2, t_2 \rangle; r_1/r_2 \rangle$; r_1/r_2 is marked on edge between t_1 and t_2
CD3	t_1', t_2'	Two terms in lexon $\langle \gamma, t_1', r_1', r_2', t_2' \rangle \in \Omega$ and $\langle \gamma, t_1', r_1', r_2', t_2' \rangle \notin L$ where Ω is complete ontology
CD4	$\langle \gamma, t_1', \bar{r}_1, \bar{r}_2, t_1' \rangle$	Lexon that links t_1 and t_1'. For all $l \in L$, t_1' is not a term in l. $\bar{r}_1$ and $\bar{r}_2$ are role pairs in this lexon.
CD5	$int(r_1, r_2)$	Possible interpretation of role pair
CD6	$sub(t_1, t_1')$	t_1 is subtype of t_1' ; t_1 is subclass of t_1' ; t_1 is child o t_1';...
CD8	$xor(t_1, t_1')$	Instance set of t_1 and instance set of t_1' do not overlap
CD7	$sup(t_1, t_1')$	t_1 is supertype of t_1' ; t_1 is superclass of t_1'; t_1 subsumes t_1';...

(Continued)

Table 11.4 (Continued)   SDT for Deciding Default Weights of Arcs of Graph

ID	Item	Explanation
CD9	Weight	Weight is integer and weight $\in [0,100]$
Value range of the condition entries		
ID	Condition Stub	Value Range
VR1	$int(r_1, r_2)$	is-a {define, describe}, has character Of, is character Of, N/A
VR2	$int(\bar{r}_1, \bar{r}_2)$	is-a, equal, N/A
VR3	$sub(t_1, t_1')$	Yes, No
VR4	$sup(t_1, t_1')$	Yes, No
VR5	$xor(t_1, t_1')$	Yes, No

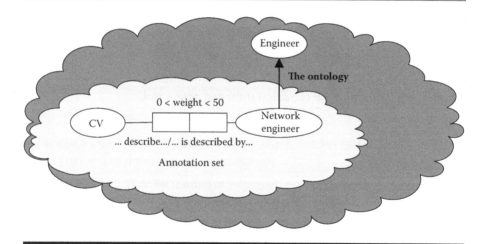

Figure 11.2   Example of application of decision rule specified in column 2 of Table 11.4.

Suppose G_1 has in total n_1 nodes and G_2 has n_2 nodes. The formula of calculating the similarity between G_1 and G_2 is designed as follows. It is called the graph-aided similarity (GRASIM) calculation:

$$S_1 = \lambda \times \frac{\sum_{i=1}^{n_1}\left(1 - \frac{sp(G_1 \cdot t_i, G_2 \cdot t_j)}{\bar{sp}(G_1 \cdot t_i, G_2 \cdot t_j)}\right)}{n_1} + (1+\lambda) \times \frac{\sum_{j=1}^{n_2}\left(1 - \frac{sp(G_2 \cdot t_i, G_1 \cdot t_j)}{\bar{sp}(G_2 \cdot t_i, G_1 \cdot t_j)}\right)}{n_2}$$

where $G_1 \cdot t_i$ indicates node t_i in subgraph G_1 ; $G_2 \cdot t_j$ indicates node t_j in subgraph G_2 and so forth. The function $sp(x, y)$ calculates the shortest path from the vertex x to y;

Table 11.5   SDT Containing Automatically Assigned (Pessimistic) Weights Based on Table 11.4

Condition	1	2	3	N	...	n"
$int(r_1, r_2)$	is-a	define, describe	...	Has char. Of	...	N/A
$int(\bar{r}_1, \bar{r}_2)$	is-a	is-a	..	Equal	...	N/A
$sub(t_1, t_1')$	Yes	Yes	...	Yes	...	No
$sup(t_1, t_1')$	Yes	No	...	No	...	No
$xor(t_1, t_1')$	Yes	No	...	Yes	...	No
Action						
Weight	100	49		0		70

Table 11.6   SDT Containing Automatically Assigned (Optimistic) Weights Based on Table 11.4

Condition	1	2	3	N	...	n"
$int(r_1, r_2)$	is-a	define, describe	...	Has char. Of	...	N/A
$int(\bar{r}_1, \bar{r}_2)$	is-a	is-a	..	Equal	...	N/A
$sub(t_1, t_1')$	Yes	Yes	...	Yes	...	No
$sup(t_1, t_1')$	Yes	No	...	No	...	No
$xor(t_1, t_1')$	Yes	No	...	Yes	...	No
Action						
Weight	100	1		0		51

the function $\overline{sp}(x, y)$ also calculates the shortest path from x to y. The difference between them represents the assigned weights on the arcs. The former takes user-defined particular weights (e.g., using Table 11.7), and the latter is calculated based on the pessimistic weights (Table 11.5). λ is a floating-point number within the range of [0, 1].

This section covers an application of SDT for semantic matching. The next section discusses the results of this application. We will also mention the trend of applying OE technologies to decision tables (in particular) and to decision support tools (in general).

11.4 Results

We chose Dijkstra's algorithm to calculate the shortest paths. The GRASIM similarity scores for the company values and the learning materials are shown in Figure 11.3 and

Table 11.7 SDT Containing User-Specified Wneights

Condition	1	2	3	4	...	n	...	m
$int(r_1, r_2)$	is-a	{define, describe}	Has char. Of	Is char. Of		Has char. Of	...	Is char. Of
$sub(t_1, t_1')$	Yes	Yes	Yes	Yes		No	...	No
Action								
Weight	100	25	50	100		35	...	25

Figure 11.4. The figures indicate which learning approaches are the most suitable for specific company values. For instance, the learning material titled *Cross-selling in Customer Service Call* is the most suitable answer for improving the *straightforward* company value. Their annotation sets are illustrated in Table 11.8 and Table 11.9, respectively.

We evaluated our matching strategy with the domain experts from the test bed in the Prolix project. First, the person who works both in HRM and the training department provided his view of the relevance levels (from 1 to 5) between the learning components and company values.

Relevance Level	Description
5	100% relevant
4	Very relevant
3	Relevant
2	Not very relevant
1	Not relevant

The *trustworthy* company value and the *technical organization of customer site* learning item yielded a relevance level 2—not very relevant. In the evaluation parameter set, we take into an account the range of GRASIM scores after running a complete test for the test case. The maximum score using GRASIM is 0.73 and the minimum is 0. We take 0.73/5 = 0.146 as the calibration for interpreting the relevance scores from end users. The relevance levels provided by the users are interpreted as shown in Table 11.10.

If a similarity score generated by GRASIM falls in the respected range (Table 11.10), this score is *completely satisfied*. If it does not fall in the value range, we must calculate the bias of the evaluation set: the minimum value of low boundary bias and high boundary bias. The pseudocode below shows the calculation:

```
IF (Similarity Score <Low Boundary)
  THEN Low Boundary Bias = Low Boundary - Similarity Score.
```

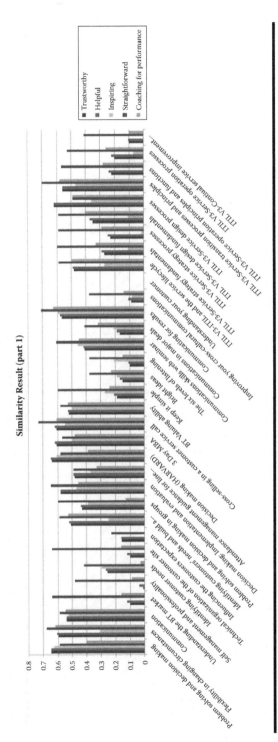

Figure 11.3 Similarity scores between listed learning materials and trustworthy, helpful, inspiring, straightforward, and coaching for performance company values. Scores are calculated with Dijkstra's algorithm using SDT and GRASIM.

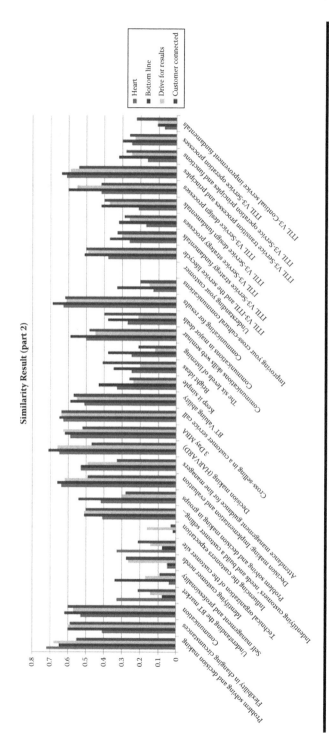

Figure 11.4 *Similarity scores between the listed learning materials and heart, bottom line, drive for results, and customer-connected company values. Scores are calculated with Dijkstra's algorithm using SDT and GRASIM.*

Table 11.8 Lexon Table: *Cross-Selling in Customer Service Call*

Head term	Role	Co-role	Tail term
Company	has characteristic of	is characteristic of	flexibility
Flexibility	is a	Is	key factor
key factor	is a	Is	factor
customer call centre	is part of	has part	company
CSA	is a	Is	person
Person	handle	is handled by	call
Person	help	is helped by	customer
Person	provide	is provided by	solution
Solution	has characteristic of	is characteristic of	efficiency
Solution	has characteristic of	is characteristic of	effectiveness
Person	cross-sell	is crossed-sold by	product
Person	prepare for	is prepared by	cross-selling call
Cross-selling call	is a	Is	call
...	...	...	...

Table 11.9 Lexon Table: *Straightforward*

Head term	Role	Co-role	Tail term
Person	has characteristics	is characteristics of	simplicity
Person	has characteristics	is characteristics of	clarity
Employee	has characteristics	is characteristics of	simplicity
Employee	has characteristics	is characteristics of	clarity
...	...	...	...

Table 11.10   Interpretation of Relevance Scores Provided by Users

Relevance Level	Low Boundary (>)	High Boundary (≤)
1	0	0.146
2	0.146	0.292
3	0.292	0.438
4	0.438	0.584
5	0.584	1

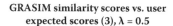

GRASIM similarity scores vs. user expected scores (3), λ = 0.5

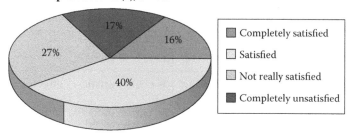

Figure 11.5   GRASIM evaluation results.

```
ELSE Low Boundary Bias = Similarity Score − Low Boundary
IF (Similarity Score <High Boundary)
 THEN High Boundary Bias = High Boundary-Similarity Score
ELESE High Boundary Bias = Similarity Score - High Boundary
```

For instance, if the similarity score for relevance level 4 is 0.45, the low boundary bias is 0.6 − 0.45 = 0.15 and the high boundary bias is 0.8 − 0.45 = 0.35. The bias is the smaller of 0.15 and 0.35: 0.15. We say a similarity score is *satisfied* if its bias is smaller than the calibration. A score is *not really satisfied* if its bias is smaller than twice the calibration; it falls in the neighbor similarity score ranges. If a similarity score does not match any of the above requirements, we say that it is *completely unsatisfied*.

The total numbers of completely satisfied, satisfied, not really satisfied, and completely unsatisfied scores are 32, 81, 55 and 33, respectively. Figure 11.5 shows the evaluation results.

Based on our observations, the factors that affect the satisfaction rate are as follows:

- Weights on the graph arcs stored in SDT. The ontology engineers must adjust the weights and thus need to know how to assign meaningful weights based on ontological commitments.
- The value of λ in GRASIM. Our ontology graph is directed. A lexon has forward and backward directions. The λ value is for balancing the results calculated from two directions. We observe that this value does not greatly affect the final similarity score if the weights on the arcs in two directions are well balanced. The value of λ significantly affects the score if the weights are not well balanced.
- Structure of the ontology. As GRASIM uses shortest path values to calculate similarity scores, the scores will more likely increase if more arcs (relations between concepts) are introduced.
- Two annotation sets. The annotation sets also affect the final similarity scores; they are two subgraphs in the ontology graph. When these two annotation sets almost fully overlap, the similarity score is very high. When they are completely disparate, the similarity score depends heavily on the shortest distance between the two graphs. If the shortest paths to all the nodes from these two subgraphs are small, the score is high. If they are large, the similarity score is low.
- Expertise level. Suppose we have expert A and expert B. Expert A is the domain expert who provides descriptions for the source materials used to create the ontology and annotation sets. Expert B is the evaluator who provides the expected similarity scores. The differences of the understandings of expert A and expert B of the competency objects will affect the evaluation results.

If all the above factors are well analyzed, a very good evaluation will result and GRASIM will work properly. How to adjust these factors in a continuously evolving evaluation environment presents an interesting future project.

11.5 Discussion

Knowledge engineers (including ontology engineers) are responsible for analyzing the raw materials provided by end users, helping them to formalize ontologies, and configuring the parameters in the matcher using SDTs. End users (including testers and evaluators) are considered nontechnical domain experts who are responsible for providing domain knowledge in documents. They also help test and evaluate matches.

Knowledge engineers annotate the learning materials and company values. In particular, they ask the company trainers (as end users) to provide textual description for learning component materials, and the HR manager to provide textual descriptions for company values. After the materials are annotated within the domain ontologies and the decision rules are properly presented in SDTs, tests are run; the results are illustrated in the next subsection.

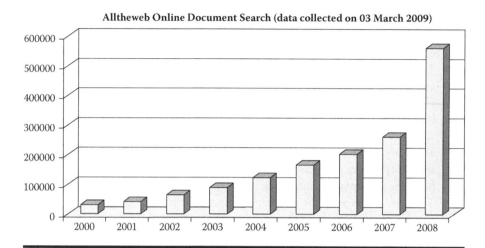

Figure 11.6 Number of online documents of decision tables along with semantics, 2000–2009.

11.5.1 Applying Ontology Engineering Technologies to Decision Tables

Many researchers have dealt with semantics using decision tables. Figure 11.6 shows the Alltheweb* statistics showing the numbers of online documents that contain discussions of both semantics and decision tables. In 2000, the number of online documents on semantics and decision tables was 30,000; it increased to 563,000 in 2008—more than 18 times the 2000 total. Apparently, decision tables and semantics continue to attract more research and public attention. We collected statistical data from Altavista[†] and Springer publications[‡] as well and made similar conclusions.

Statistical data is collected based on keywords. The technologies of supporting semantics in old publications are not the ones used for OE despite the notion of semantics that emerged earlier than the use of OE, to model semantics in computer science. Spoken language (ca. 700,000 BC) was one of the first key developments in semantics history. According to McComb (2004), spoken language, written language (ca. 20,000 BC), the Golden Age of ancient Greece (ca. 400 BC), the enlightenment (ca. 1700 AD), pragmatism (ca. 1870), linguistic advances (1930), and artificial intelligence (1960) are the milestones in the history of semantics.

---

* http://www.alltheweb.com/—this search engine is owned by Yahoo! Inc.
† Altavista is a Google-like Internet search engine. Users can use http://www.altavista.com/ to search online documents.
‡ Springer Verlag is an international publisher based in Heidelberg, Germany. It publishes scientific texts, academic reference books, conference proceedings, and peer-reviewed journals in many scientific fields, e.g., computer science, mathematics, and medicine.

Comparing two extensions of decision tables, the approach to SDTs uses OE technology to store semantics. Modern OE technologies can bring vigor to modeling semantics for decision tables. Generally, OE can endow decision support systems with easily interpretable formal semantics and promising future directions. Kasabov (2008) demonstrates the approach of combining data mining, machine learning modules, traditional statistical analysis, fuzzy rule reasoning, and ontology referencing for personalized biomedical decision support systems.

Mavridis et al. (2006) show a synergy of "fashionable" technologies for service-oriented architectures of market data filtering and gathering. Ontology and its engineering technologies establish the kernel of the semantic segment of this architecture. Basically, ontology provides a centralized knowledge block in distributed, time-evolving, and value-changing operational business environments.

Ceccaroni et al. (2002) use ontology to enhance existing wastewater decision support systems. Domain ontologies are used to integrate information among argument components to achieve better case-based and rule-based reasoning. Kashyap et al. (2006) illustrate how medical ontology can be used as classified references for clinical decision supporting systems.

These studies show the importance of and trend for combining OE and DSS. We can foresee that Semantic DSS* will tackle several challenges:

- Technological integration. Different decision support tools should communicate with each other seamlessly, without misunderstandings. Human effort related to implementation and integration of technologies should be minimized.
- Organizational integration. The interorganizational DSS† must comply with centralized resources—the ontologies—to achieve a desired level of organizational interoperability.
- Business rules and the Semantic Web. The SW approach reconnoiters a new way of combining the semantics and exploratory functionalities of the Internet. Business rules concerning activity monitoring, e-business, business process management, and other factors can be subject to reconnaissance using SW technologies.
- Smart objects for DSS. Smart objects such as smart phones, mobile devices, and intelligent pads will play important roles in Semantic DSS.
- Community-centralized DSS. Since the 1970s, the target users of DSS shifted slowly from single decision makers to decision groups. Decision groups tend to be more dynamic and virtual. This community aspect is an interesting challenge of Semantic DSS.
- Open world semantics for DSS. As claimed in de facto standards (CSA, 1970; Beitz et al. 1982), a decision table has the characteristics of completeness and correctness, as does a database-based DSS. If the semantic descriptions of SDT,

---

* SDT can be considered as a kind of Semantic DSS.
† DSS from different departments of a large company or DSS from different enterprises in a small and medium enterprise (SME) community

(or any other DSS) are taken from a distributed means (e.g., on the Web) under open world assumptions, we must again address the research issues surrounding "incomplete and incorrect" decision making and reasoning. This problem is similar to those arising from open world semantics for the SW, as examined by Fensel and van Harmelen (2007) and in the FP7 LarCK project.*

11.6 Conclusions and Future Work

Decision tables, as a means to support traditional machine learning or data mining algorithms, are often designed for or based on instance data. They are extracted from domain-specific knowledge that often mainly contains concrete *process* information of the domain. Decision makers normally take the background domain knowledge into account but it was not treated in our study as the kernel knowledge base and inferences for different applications that use decision tables.

SDTs are forged with domain ontologies. Thanks to modern technologies from OE, SDTs contain many semantically rich characteristics that a decision table does not have, such as self-organizing and self-layering of the tabular structures, and sharable and interoperable capabilities. SDTs can be easily embedded in ontology-based applications as ontological commitments.

This chapter discussed the notations of SDTs and one recent application in the field of semantic matching. Evaluation results for the SDT application were illustrated.

As a related aspect of SDTs, two extensions to tables were discussed. In order to draw attention to the trend of using OE in decision support systems, we collected data and made a thorough survey. We conclude that the DSS approach supported by OE is promising based on three points:

1. The statistics and related work of Semantic DSS shows that research interest in decision tables is growing, as is interest in using decision tables to deal with semantics or using semantics to deal with decision tables.
2. The importance of the link between semantics and decision tables has been always stressed. This chapter proposes SDTs as a new approach to decision tables combined with semantics. An SDT is generally considered a collection (or system) that contains decision table, semantics (domain ontologies), relevant support tools, algorithms, and methodologies. In a specific and narrow sense, an SDT is a (set of) decision table(s) annotated with domain ontology.
3. The related work of Semantic DSS shows that a trend in the field of semantics and decision tables is to use OE as the essence intelligence to capture, describe, store, and reason the decision semantics of decision tables. The same principles for an SDT can be applied to other decision support tools.

We illustrated the challenges of SDTs and Semantic DSS: technological integration, organizational integration, business rules and SW, smart objects for Semantic DSS,

---

* http://www.larkc.eu/

community-centralized DSS, and open world semantics for DSS. These challenges also represent our future work on SDTs.

References

Barrett, C., Bisset, K., Holzer, M. et al. 2008. Engineering label-constrained shortest-path algorithms. In *Proceedings of Fourth International AAIM Conference*, Shanghai, Lecture Notes in Computer Science Series.

Barry, G.B. 1998. Visualizing decision table classifiers. In *Proceedings of Information Visualization Conference*, Los Alamitos, CA, IEEE Computer Science Press, pp. 102–105.

Beitz, H. et al. 1982. *A Modern Appraisal of Decision Tables*. ACM Press, New York.

Berners-Lee, T. 1999. *Weaving the Web: Origins and Future of the World Wide Web*, Texere Publishing.

Boley, H. et al. December 17, 2004. Object-Oriented RuleML, *Version 0.9*. http://www. ruleml.org/indoo/indoo.html

Boley, H. 2001. Rule markup language: RDF-XML data model, XML schema hierarchy, and XSL transformations, Invited Talk, INAP, Tokyo.

Canadian Standards Association. 1970. *Z243.1-1970 for Decision Tables*.

Ceccaroni, L., Cortes, U., and Sanchez-Marre, M. 2002. OntoWEDSS: An ontology underpinned decision system for wastewater management. In *Proceedings of International Environmental Modelling and Software Society*, Lugano.

Chen, G., Vanthienen, J., and Wets, G. 1995. Using fuzzy decision tables to build valid intelligent systems. In *Proceedings of Sixth International Fuzzy Systems Association World Congress*, Sao Paulo.

Chen, P.P. 1976. The entity relationship model: Toward a unified view of data. *ACM Transactions on Database Systems*.

de Moor, A., De Leenheer, P., and Meersman, R. 2006. DOGMA-MESS: A meaning evolution support system for interorganizational ontology engineering. In *Proceedings of 14th International Conference on Conceptual Structures*, Aalborg, pp. 189–203.

Fensel, D., and van Harmelen, F. 2007. Unifying reasoning and search to web scale. *IEEE Internet Computing*, 11: 2.

Fernández, M., Gómez-Pérez, A., and Juristo, N. 1997. Methontology: From ontological art towards ontological engineering. In *Proceedings of AAAI Spring Symposium Series on Ontological Engineering*, Stanford, CA, pp. 33–40.

Goedertier, S. and Vanthienen, J. 2005. Rule-based business process modeling and execution. In *Proceedings of IEEE EDOC Workshop on Vocabularies, Ontologies, and Rules for the Enterprise*, Enschede, Netherlands.

Gruber, T.R. 1993. Toward principles for the design of ontologies used for knowledge sharing. In *Formal Ontology in Conceptual Analysis and Knowledge Representation*, Amsterdam, Kluwer.

Grüninger, M. and Fox, M. 1995. Methodology for design and evaluation of ontologies, In *Proceedings of IJCAI Workshop on Basic Ontological Issues in Knowledge Sharing*.

Guarino, N. 1998. Formal ontology and information system. In *Proceedings of FOIS*, Trento, Italy, pp. 3–15.

Guarino, N. 1995. Formal ontology, conceptual analysis and knowledge representation. *International Journal of Human–Computer Studies*, 43: 625–640.

Halpin, T.A. 2001. *Information Modeling and Relational Databases: From Conceptual Analysis to Logical Design*, San Francisco, Morgan Kaufman.

Hewett, R. and Leuchner, J.H. 2002. The power of second-order decision tables. In *Proceedings of Second SIAM International Conference on Data Mining*, Arlington, VA,

Kasabov, N. 2008. Data mining, modeling and knowledge discovery methods for personalised biomedical decision support systems. In *Proceedings of Fourth International Conference on Biomedical Engineering*, Kuala Lumpur, pp. 25–28.

Kashyap, V., Morales, A., and Hongsermeier, T. 2006. On implementing clinical decision support. In *Proceedings of AMIA Annual Symposium*, pp, 414–418.

Kohavi, R. and Sommerfield, D. 1998. Targeting business users with decision table classifier. In *Proceedings of Fourth International Conference on Knowledge Discovery and Data Mining*, New York, AAAI Press, pp. 249–253.

Korn, F., Sidiropoulos, N., Faloutsos, C. et al. 1996. Fast nearest neighbor search in medical databases. In *Proceedings of International Conference on Very Large Databases*, pp. 215–226.

Lima, E., Mues, C., and Baesens, B. 2008. Domain knowledge integration in data mining using decision tables: Case studies in churn prediction. *Journal of Operational Research Society*.

Mavridis, A., Koumpis, A., and Athanasiadis, I.N. 2006. Towards an intelligent decision support architecture in extended enterprises. In *Proceedings of Sixth International Conference on Recent Advances in Soft Computing*, Canterbury, U.K.

McComb, D. 2004. *Semantics in Business Systems: The Savvy Manager's Guide*, San Francisco, Morgan Kaufmann.

Meersman, R. 2001. Ontologies and databases: More than a fleeting resemblance. In *Proceedings of OES/SEO Workshop*, Rome.

Moreno-Garcia, A.M., Verhelle, M., and Vanthienen J. 2000. Decision tables: An overview of the existing literature. *Proceedings of Fifth International Conference on Artificial Intelligence and Emerging Technologies in Accounting, Finance, and Tax*, Huelva, Spain, Servicio de Publicaciones Universidad de Huelva.

Object Management Group. March 2003. Unified Modeling Language, Version 1.3, Chapter 6: Object Constraint Language Specification, Needham, MA. http://www.omg.org/spec/UML/1.3/

Paschke, A., Kiss, C., and Al-Hunaty, S. 2006. Negotiation pattern language: A design pattern language for decentralized (agent) coordination and negotiation protocols. In *E-Negotiation: An Introduction*, ICFAI University Press.

Pooch, U.W. 1974. Translation of decision tables. *ACM Computing Surveys*, 6: 125–151.

Schreiber, G., Akkermans, H., Anjewierden, A. et al. 1999. *Knowledge Engineering and Management: The CommonKADS Methodology*. Cambridge, MA, MIT Press.

Spyns, P., Meersman, R., and Jarrar, M. 2002. Data modeling versus ontology engineering. *SIGMOD Record*, 31: 12–17.

Staab, S. and Studer, R. 2004. *Handbook on Ontologies*, International Handbooks on Information Systems Series, Heidelberg, Springer Verlag.

Tang, Y. and Meersman, R. 2008. Toward building semantic decision tables with domain ontologies. In *Challenges in Information Technology Management*, World Scientific.

Tang, Y. and Meersman, R. 2007. On constructing semantic decision tables. In *Proceedings of 18th International Conference on Database and Expert Systems Applications*, Regensburg, Germany, Lecture Notes in Computer Science Series, pp. 34–44.

Tang, Y. and Meersman, R. 2007. Organizing meaning evolution supporting systems using semantic decision tables, In *Proceedings of 15th International Conference on Cooperative Information Systems*, Vilamoura, Portugal, Lecture Notes in Computer Science Series 4803, pp. 272–284.

Tang, Y., Meersman, R., and Vanthienen, J. 2008. Semantic decision tables: Self-Organizing and reorganizable decision tables. In *Proceedings of 19th International Conference on Database and Expert Systems Applications,* Turin, Italy, Lecture Notes in Computer Science Series.

Tang, Y., Spyns, P., and Meersman, R. 2007. Toward semantically grounded decision rules using ORM+. In *Proceedings of International Symposium on Rule Interchange and Applications,* Orlando, FL, Lecture Notes in Computer Science Series, pp. 78–91.

Tang, Y. and Meersman, R. 2009. SD rule markup language: Toward modeling and interchanging ontological commitments for semantic decision making. In *Handbook of Research on Emerging Rule-Based Languages and Technologies: Open Solutions and Approaches,* IGI Publishing.

Tang, Y. *Semantic Decision Tables: A New, Promising and Innovative Way of Reorganizing Your Decision Making Tool.*

Trog, D., Vereecken, J., Christiaens, S. et al. 2006. T-Lex: A role-based ontology engineering tool. In *Proceedings of On the Move to Meaningful Internet Systems,* Lecture Notes in Computer Science Series 4278, pp. 1191–1200.

Uschold, M. and King, M. 1995. Towards a methodology for building ontologies. In *Proceedings of IJCAI Workshop on Basic Ontological Issues in Knowledge Sharing.*

Venkateswaran, J., Kahveci1, T., and Camoglu, O. 2006. Finding data broadness via generalized nearest neighbors. In *Proceedings of Conference on Advances in Database Technology,* Lecture Notes in Computer Science Series 3896.

Vanthienen, J. and Wets, G. 1994. From decision tables to expert system shells. *Data and Knowledge Engineering* 13: 265–282.

Verheyden, P., De Bo, J., and Meersman, R. 2004. Semantically unlocking database content through ontology-based mediation. In *SWDB,* Lecture Notes in Computer Science Series 3372, pp. 109–126.

Wets, G., Witlox, F., Timmermans, H. et al. 1996. A fuzzy decision table approach for business site selection. In *Proceedings of Fifth IEEE International Conference on Fuzzy Systems,* Vol. 3, New Orleans, pp. 160-5–1610.

Chapter 12

Semantic Sentiment Analyses Based on Reputations of Web Information Sources

Donato Barbagallo, Cinzia Cappiello, Chiara Francalanci, and Maristella Matera

Politecnico di Milano, Milan, Italy

Contents

12.1 Introduction

Web 2.0 technologies enable active roles for users, who can create and share their contents very easily. This mass of information includes opinions about a variety of key interest topics (e.g., products, brands, services, and other subjects of interest) and represents a new and invaluable source of marketing information. However, the size of this information base and its pace of change make manual market monitoring almost impossible. Public and private organizations that aim to understand and analyze this unsolicited feedback need intelligent platforms that can support users in detecting and monitoring key topics. Hence, a trend is emerging toward automated market intelligence and the crafting of tools that allow reputation monitoring in a mechanized fashion. We present one such approach to define self-service environments that support the creation of dashboards, providing a personalized view of the Web information space through the integration of trustworthy services for information access and analysis.

To understand the idea, let us consider a usage scenario in the health, wellness, and cultural tourism domain—a tourism segment that is gaining momentum. Suppose that a tourist office wants to enhance its services by providing advice about the best restaurants in a given city. The employees of the office will have to search the Web for both institutional commentaries and user feedback on restaurants. For this purpose, they would greatly benefit from a set of functionalities that would search for the right information sources, evaluate relevant content, and finally integrate resulting suggestions into a unified view of the Web. Satisfying these needs raises a number of issues. First, Web sources should be selected to complement standard tourist information with Web 2.0 information from online communities. Since the quantity of information is vast, the platform should rely on the most dependable, active, and possibly authoritative sources. Second, the platform should offer a way to visually integrate information from multiple sources and allow users to bookmark the most reliable sources on specific subjects. Third, the platform should provide services to evaluate the overall sentiments of users on those subjects, thus integrating Web information into aggregate assessments of restaurants along the numerous decision dimensions that impact users' opinions.

This scenario highlights two fundamental requirements: (1) selection of dependable services that can fulfill specific information needs and quality requirements and (2) provision of tools to compose on demand the functionalities the users need. To our knowledge, little research has focused on satisfying both requirements exhaustively. While existing commercial tools provide aggregate sentiment analyses, their results (1) are mostly independent of the decision models of users and (2) do not account for the data quality issues related to the integration of sentiment analyses based on multisource and multidimensional information. Finally, they are generic and have limited semantic abilities to interpret natural language in a given domain.

Our approach proposes a comprehensive solution, in which mashup functionalities are exploited to help people create personalized Web access environments. Data quality analyses are adopted to help them select relevant and authoritative information sources that are then wrapped as data services supplying the information required to analyze the reputations of subjects of interest. Data quality techniques are also exploited to support the integration of sentiment analyses based on multisource and multidimensional information. The results of sentiment analyses are made available as *services* that can be mashed up, possibly with further services from the Web that complement the analysis. Users are thus enabled to create personalized environments through which they can analytically investigate the sentiment trends of their subjects of interest.

Section 12.2 illustrates the state of the art that clarifies the novel issues addressed by our research. Section 12.3 discusses the data quality dimensions relevant for sentiment analysis. Section 12.4 briefly presents the reference technology architecture, while Section 12.5 reports preliminary empirical results. The final sections present conclusions and outline our future work.

12.2 State of the Art

The approach proposed in this chapter is based on the reputation-based selection of relevant and reliable Web information sources. Previous work concentrated on trust of Web resources (Artz and Gil 2009), making a distinction between *content trust* and *entity* (source) *trust*. Other research contributions identify Web trustworthiness with popularity (as in the PageRank algorithm, Brin and Page 1998). Other algorithms are based on *hub and authority* mechanisms in the field of social network analysis (SNA, Kleinberg 1999). Recent works intended to evaluate authors' trustworthiness levels as in the SNA approach (Skopik et al. 2009).

The selection of sources providing dependable information has been loosely based on the definition of methods for assessing data quality (DQ). In the DQ field, the concept of reputation is the result of assessing several properties of information sources including *correctness, completeness, timeliness, dependability,* and *consistency* (Batini et al. 2009). The data quality literature provides a consolidated body of research on the quality dimensions of information, their qualitative and quantitative assessment, and their improvement (Atzeni et al. 2001, Gackowski 2006). However, trust-related quality dimensions, particularly reputation, are still open issues (Gackowski 2006).

In our approach, reputation is considered an information source, which represents an a priori assessment of the reputation of the information source based on its authority in its field and its ability to offer relevant answers to user queries based on historical data on the source collected by our platform. This approach is original in that it defines reputation as a context- and time-dependent characteristic of information sources, and leverages the ability of the platform to track a source's reputation over time. In previous research, we developed and tested a reputation monitor now integrated into our platform (Ardagna et al. 2005, 2006). In this proposal, we use source reputation as the basis for the assessment of the reliability and relevance of its content for sentiment analyses. We previously developed a semantic sentiment analyzer as part of a project funded by the City of Milan to implement a city brand decision model (Barbagallo et al. 2010a).

Sentiment analysis provides indicators that summarize the opinions contained in Web sources on a specific matter. Companies now find the Web an important resource for checking customers' appreciation for their products and services and even to investigate their brands' reputations—clearly online reviews can have negative impacts on sales (Hu et al. 2008) and Weblog mentions are highly correlated with sales (Liu et al. 2007).

In the literature, some approaches to sentiment analysis are based on document classification (Greene and Resnik 2009). Typically, these approaches provide a preliminary feature extraction using word frequencies (Liu et al. 2007), information gain, and genetic algorithms (Abbasi et al. 2008) based on lexicons such as WordNet (Godbole et al. 2007), and hidden Markov models (HMM, Mei et al. 2007). When the domain of interest is narrow and the language is specific, it is possible to use a corpus-based approach (O'Hare et al. 2009). These analyses can be integrated with social network analysis (SNA) to improve the assessment of information sources (Gloor et al. 2009, Glance et al. 2005). These approaches do not support access to the results of sentiment analyses. To overcome this limitation, we intend to integrate sentiment analyses with mashup technologies (Yu et al. 2008) to allow self-service composition of services embedding the results of sentiment analyses. Thanks to mashup technologies (Yu et al. 2008), an end user can self-construct a personalized analysis environment based on a combination of access and analysis services.

To ease the task of developing mashups, a variety of tools (Yahoo!, Ennals and Garofalakis 2007; Intel, and IBM, Yu et al. 2007) have recently emerged. Their main goal is to facilitate the mashing of components via simple, graphical or textual user interfaces, sets of predefined components, and abstractions from technicalities. While they all propose mechanisms to solve composition issues, none provides the users with support to create their own components to be added to the spectrum of predefined components. They also do not provide any support for selecting dependable services. Our approach capitalizes on an already functioning mashup engine (Mixup, Yu et al. 2007) and we extend it to achieve the easy creation of mashup components on top of sentiment analysis services and dependable Web resources.

The componentization of sentiment and Web services requires mechanisms for the construction of the presentation layer that take into account both service and user profiles. Further extensions support users in selecting dependable services based on the estimated quality of the underlying data sources. This selection is based on the availability of a quality model for mashup components that allows us to quantify the measure of each single component and the quality of the final mashup (Cappiello et al. 2009). Estimating quality based on such a model guides users to select quality components and mashup components to convey the necessary information.

12.3 Quality Dimensions for Sentiment Analysis

Our proposed technique for sentiment analysis performs an evaluation of the average opinion on a subject of interest measured on a qualitative five-point scale ranging from very negative to very positive. The input data to the sentiment analysis consists of a set of *snippets*, i.e., fragments of text providing comments on the subject of interest. Sentiment is evaluated first on individual snippets and then aggregated.

Most commercial tools providing sentiment analysis aggregate the evaluation of sentiment on individual snippets by calculating the mean value of a sentiment over the entire set of snippets or over a subset of snippets published on the Web within a specific time frame. Snippets that comment on the same subject of interest are usually stored in the same set even if they came from multiple heterogeneous Web sources. The mean value of a sentiment across a set of snippets is usually complemented by the total count of snippets retrieved to give users an indication of the level of interest on the subject. Schawbel (2008) provides a survey of existing tools that clearly indicates that the volume of talk on a subject and the average evaluation of sentiment on large data sets retrieved from a broad range of sources represent a common approach. We believe the approach raises a number of information quality issues that could lead decision makers to wrong interpretations and decisions. These issues relate mainly to (1) the selection of Web information sources and (2) the characterization, interpretation, and evaluation of the content of the sources. We now discuss how these two issues can be resolved using information quality assessment techniques.

12.3.1 Information Source Reputation

Common experiences of users searching the Web reveal how the identification of relevant information on a specific issue through Web browsing requires several iterations. Interesting sources may surface only after a relatively long search processes. In the work of Jiang et al. (2008), empirical evidence reveals quite a large probability (about 63%) that a relevant document will be found within a 1 to 120 rank range and that in more than 65% of cases, not even the top 300 ranked documents are expected to satisfy the user request.

Our approach tries to overcome this problem by proposing the adoption of typical data quality dimensions to assess the reputations of information sources. This in turn allows us to ensure a high degree of quality of retrieved information. Our operationalization of reputation draws from the data quality literature. In particular, we start from the classification of reputation dimensions provided by Batini et al. (2009) in which *accuracy*, *completeness*, and *time* represent the fundamental data quality dimensions in most contexts. *Interpretability, authority*, and *dependability* are suggested as additional dimensions to consider, especially when assessing the reputations of semistructured and nonstructured sources of information. We have identified four aspects that should be evaluated to assess the reputations of blogs and forums (two important forms of Web resources providing large numbers of users' opinions):

■ *Traffic: overall volume of information produced and exchanged in a specific time frame*
■ *Breadth of contributions: overall range of issues on which a source can provide information*
■ *Relevance: degree of specialization of a source in a specific domain (e.g., tourism)*
■ *Liveliness: responsiveness to new issues or events*

Table 12.1 summarizes the reputation metrics identified for the variables above (table columns) along the different data quality dimensions (table rows). As a general observation, our choice of metrics was driven by feasibility considerations. In particular, we defined only quantitative and measurable metrics. The data source on which metrics are computed is reported in parentheses. "Crawling" means manual inspection or automated crawling depending on the site. Some metrics are also derived from data published by Alexa (www.alexa.com), a well known service publishing traffic metrics for a number of Internet sites. It is worth noting that not all data quality dimensions apply to all variables (not applicable = N/A in Table 12.1).

As shown in Barbagallo et al. (2010b), after performing an experiment with over 100 queries submitted to Google through a principal component analysis, the original set of metrics was reduced to a group of three indicators *traffic, participation*, and *time* (Table 12.2). The table also shows the relation found through linear regression between each new dimension and Google search ranking. The relation between *traffic* and Google rank is significant and positive, meaning that *traffic* is a good predictor of Google positioning. The interaction of *participation* and Google rank is supported and the coefficient has a negative sign. Finally, *time* and Google rank are negatively related and the relation is significant: the better the results from such an indicator, the worse the results of a Google search.

These analyses confirm that the PageRank algorithm relates directly to traffic and inbound links, merely privileging the number of accesses rather than the actual interest of the users and the quality of such interactions. Indeed, the inverse relations between Google rank and *time* and *participation* indicate that highly participated websites may not be rewarded and may even be penalized in a Google search. To understand this result, consider the practical example of companies' institutional websites. These sites are often equipped with a forum or a blog monitored regularly by moderators or editorial units to avoid spam or attacks to the company

Table 12.1 Reputation Metrics

	Traffic	Breadth of Contribution	Relevance	Liveliness
Accuracy	N/A	Average number of comments to selected posts (crawling)	Centrality, i.e., number of covered topics (crawling)	N/A
Completeness	N/A	Number of open discussions (crawling)	Number of open discussions compared to largest Web blog/forum (crawling)	Number of comments per user (crawling)
Time	Traffic rank (www.alexa.com)	Age of source (crawling)	N/A	Average number of new discussions daily (www.alexa.com)
Interpretability	N/A	Average number of distinct tags per post (crawling)	N/A	N/A
Authority	Daily visitors (www.alexa.com); daily page views (www.alexa.com); average time spent on site (www.alexa.com)	N/A	Number of inbound links (www.alexa.com); number of feed subscriptions (Feedburner tool)	Number of daily page views per daily visitor (www.alexa.com)
Dependability	N/A	Number of comments per discussion (crawling)	Bounce rate (www.alexa.com)	Average number of comments for discussion per day (crawling)

N/A = not applicable.

Table 12.2 Componentization of Data Quality Metrics

Variable	Component	Relation with Google
Traffic rank	Traffic	Positive
Daily visitors		
Daily page views		
Number of inbound links		
Number of open discussions compared to largest Web blog/forum		
Average number of new discussions per day	Participation	Negative
Number of comments per discussion		
Average number of comments to post provided within 24 hours for discussion per day		
Bounce rate	Time	Negative
Average time spent on site		

reputation. It is easy to observe that such websites are always well positioned, usually at the top of the list, and are also the most visited because they represent a gate to a company and its products and services. Nevertheless, institutional websites are not always the most interesting or truthful sources of information, because negative comments can be removed by moderators. In such cases, independent forums or blogs may be more reliable information sources for reviews, but usually they are not highly ranked by Google unless they have high traffic rates. As explained in Section 12.4, our approach tries to cover these issues via continuous monitoring of our reputation index and the creation of a database of relevant sources and related historical reputation data.

12.3.2 Information Source Characterization

Web information sources are heterogeneous; the same comment on a subject of interest may carry a different type of information, depending on the source where it is published. For example, a *tweet* (snippet from Twitter) represents an instant comment (with a very short life expectancy) that expresses an opinion of one individual. A tweet stating that "Milan is sunny" does not have the same meaning as a snippet from a weather forecasting site. Similarly, a weather forecast predicting that Milan will be sunny for the next few hours has a different meaning from a magazine comment providing general weather information for potential tourists. In this respect, Web information sources can be classified as:

1. Objective institutional sources (magazines or governmental tourism agencies)
2. Objective noninstitutional sources (hotel sites or sales agencies)
3. Subjective sources (such as Twitter)

Both objective and subjective sources can be further classified. For example, Twitter provides instant isolated comments. TripAdvisor provides a chain of question-and-answer comments with much longer time horizons that, from a Web perspective, are considered "historical." Both Twitter and TripAdvisor are vertical, i.e., specializing in the tourism domain, while Wikipedia is general (nondomain-specific). However, Wikipedia provides reference information that is useful in the tourism domain and should not be ignored.

Clearly, providing an average estimate of sentiment by gathering snippets from a variety of heterogeneous sources can be misleading. The magnitude of resulting interpretation errors may be significant. To demonstrate the impact of these quality issues on decision makers, let us consider *weather in Milan* as the subject of interest and assume that the content sentiment analysis module aggregates information from (1) an electronic tourist guide providing objective institutional information, (2) Expedia providing objective noninstitutional information, and (3) Twitter providing subjective information. Assume that the guide states that "Milan in winter is usually foggy," while Expedia shows a three-day rainy forecast, and Twitter provides 100 instant tweets stating that Milan is sunny. *Foggy* and *rainy* indicate negative sentiments and *sunny* is positive. The result of an average sentiment evaluation will be positive because the volume of snippets from Twitter clearly outnumbers the negative snippets from objective sources. This positive result is at variance with the still predominant image of Milan as a foggy city (Wordtravels 2010). Although the climate changes have almost eliminated fog in Milan, its objective institutional image remains foggy and evidence indicates the general perception is that Milan is a foggy city (Wordtravels 2010). This suggests that the institutional image of Milan provides a much more dependable indication of the general perception of Milan than the indication provided by a large number of instant subjective comments.

The example shows how the error of a flat average calculation of sentiment can be significant, to the point of ranking sentiment as very positive when in fact it is negative. The dependability and practical application of undifferentiated sentiment analysis tools are thus highly questionable. Quality issues become even more critical when considering content. For example, a snippet from a subjective source stating that "I am very bored today in Milan" represents an *autobiographic comment* with a negative sentiment that should not be attributed to the city. Conversely, a snippet such as "I believe that Milan is a boring city," although subjective, expresses an *opinion* that should be accounted for when assessing the city as a destination for tourists. Making a distinction between different types of snippets requires the ability to perform semantic interpretations of natural language within a specific domain.

Content may also be semantically biased, depending on the personal objectives of contributors. Psychological studies indicate that an individual tends to share positive feelings more easily than negative feelings. This general personal attitude is consistent with the results of Bruno and Radice (2009), indicating that most comments posted on social networks (around 80%) are positive. Negative comments remain largely unexpressed on subjective Web sources. Consider a decision maker who is comparing Milan to Madrid and assume that a sentiment analysis tool retrieves 10 very positive comments on Milan and 100 positive comments on Madrid of which 10 are very positive. An average assessment of sentiment will show that Milan is better than Madrid, since the 80 positive comments on Madrid decrease the average value of sentiment. However, people who do not comment on Milan may have negative feelings they are not inclined to share. Again, quality issues can be sufficiently critical to invalidate the results of sentiment analyses. Table 12.3 summarizes these data quality issues and translates them into design requirements for sentiment analysis tools. The two orthogonal sets of reputation metrics and source characterization outlined in Sections 12.3.1 and 12.3.2 can also be used to rank information services. Table 14.4 shows results for each combination of data quality and characterization metric.

12.4 Reference Technology Architecture

From a technical view, one novel aspect of our approach is the provision of an integrated environment through which users can query market monitoring services and also combine them with other external open services providing utility functions. In the context of market monitoring, Web users take actions to access and retrieve Web resources to find information about a key topic and possibly make some kind of choice or decision. We envision a platform that will enable users to compose and analyze several heterogeneous sources and resources to obtain an integrated view of what is available on the Web. As illustrated in the previous sections, the reliability and the relevance of the considered Web resources represent driving factors of the proposed platform. Further advantages come from the ability of a user to self-define a dashboard on which different services (data services, reputation-based filters, sentiment analysis services, and generic services providing analysis functionality) can be mashed up.

As shown in Figure 12.1, the organization of the platform architecture reflects the two previous aspects centered on two main blocks: one block collects the modules for sentiment and reputation analysis and another is devoted to the definition of the user dashboard. The modules for sentiment and reputation analysis are in charge of evaluating the quality of selected Web sources and, based on the

Table 12.3   Data Quality Issues in Sentiment Analysis

Quality Issue Related to Selection and Characterization of Web Information Sources	*Quality Issue Related to Interpretation and Evaluation of Web Information Source Content*
Characterization of institutional versus noninstitutional sources	Identification of labels describing subject of interest in a specific domain
Characterization of objective versus subjective sources	Identification of items characterizing labels
Characterization of general versus vertical sources	Content volatility
Characterization of person-to-person versus community sources	Content credibility
Characterization of instant versus historical sources	Content currency
Assessment of relevance of sources on subject of interest	Evaluation of subjective sentiment biases
Assessment of source general reputation	Characterization of autobiographic comments versus opinions
Assessment of impact of source on opinion making	Characterization of objective comments versus opinions
Assessment of source sentiment biases	Semantic interpretation of natural language in specific domain

Table 12.4   Orthogonal Representation of Characterization and Data Quality Dimensions

	Objective Institutional Source	*Objective Noninstitutional Source*	*Subjective Source*
Traffic	Travel.state.gov	About.com	Twitter
Time	Fco.gov.uk	TravelmagazineUSA	TripAdvisor
Participation	FastLane	Expedia	LonelyPlanet

results, to assess the sentiment about key entities. The second block capitalizes on the availability of services exposing the results of the data and sentiment analyses, and allows users to construct self-service environments in which they can combine interesting and trustworthy services that can support their decisions. The next sections provide details about the design of these two architectural components.

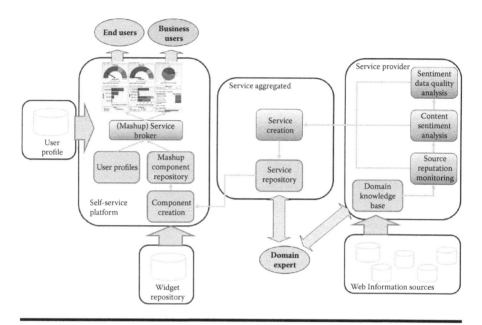

Figure 12.1   Reference technology architecture.

12.4.1 Reputation and Sentiment Analysis

The platform is designed to provide information about specific topics selected by users. On the basis of user requirements, a domain expert selects the most suitable Web sources. Sources are further analyzed by the Source Reputation Monitoring module that evaluates sources and assigns measures based on the criteria cited in Section 12.3. The assessments are updated continuously. The Source Reputation Monitoring module verifies and updates the quality levels of the data sources. This external analysis is combined with internal analysis of the retrieved information.

The Content Sentiment Analysis module assesses the sentiment on the key topic based on information from different sources. A Sentiment Data Quality Analysis module continuously monitors the quality of the data extracted by the Content Sentiment Analysis module. In practice, the role of this module is to consider and evaluate the heterogeneity of Web information sources that may affect the interpretation of the published content, in accordance with the quality dimensions outlined in Section 12.3.

All the search and assessment functionalities provided by the various modules must be transformed in services. The Service Creation module handles this transformation and creates the service metadata needed in a self-service environment to let users create their personal information access environments. The Service Creation module populates the Service Repository that stores a catalogue of data and other services, providing a binding with a dependable data source through a description of the data structure or generic Web services and enabling the retrieval of relevant information or providing additional analysis features. The latter are directly added to the Service Repository by the domain expert.

12.4.2 Self-Service Environment

The self-service environment is based on the availability of a mashup environment (Yu et al. 2007) through which a user can select some relevant components from the Mashup Component Repository and combine them to generate a new value. This environment allows users to combine services and data to create their own dashboards. With respect to the functionality provided by a full mashup engine, the self-service environment will constrain what users can do by providing a "sandbox" that filters ready-to-use services on the basis of their nature (e.g., data services, filters, generic utilities, etc.) and their mutual compatibility (syntactic and semantic). This will ease the composition task and also increase the degree of control over the quality of mashups created.

Nevertheless, users will not be limited in the types of applications they can build because the method addresses the great diversity of user needs. This is in line with the current trend in empowering users with tools to construct so-called situational applications (Jhingran 2006), i.e., applications created for a single purpose and user to solve an immediate business problem. In this case, especially in an enterprise context, complex solutions developed by an IT department would be too costly and perhaps not adequate for the specific decision process. Empowering users to self-define their applications can alleviate this problem.

To combine the services for sentiment analysis into a mashup, those extracted by the Service Repository must be componentized by the Component Creation module. In the componentization process, each service must be associated with a descriptor highlighting the properties useful for combination and choreography purposes, as required by the adopted mashup engine (Yu et al. 2007). When the services are not provided with a proper user interface, as occurs for pure data services, componentization requires the generation of a presentation layer. This process implies the identification of visualization "widgets" that best match the operations and the exchanged data, as indicated by the service descriptors (e.g., in the WSDL interfaces of SOAP Web services). The user can also take part in the construction of the presentation layer, for example, by selecting the most preferred visualization objects.

To compose a dashboard, a user selects both sentiment services as generated by the Service Aggregator module and generic external services, properly wrapped and described for mashup and stored in the Mashup Component Repository. The self-service environment supports the user in service selection: the Mashup Service Broker module is in charge of ranking the services in the Mashup Component Repository based on their ability to match the users' goals and profile. The technical quality of the mashup components is also taken into account (Cappiello et al. 2009). The component descriptors include annotations about quality dimensions, and the Mashup Service Broker takes the annotations into account to guide users in selecting components that maximize the quality of the final composition (Ardagna et al. 2005).

Note that users may also become providers of resources because their dashboards have the potential to be shared with other users. This in turn implies a sharing of the motivations and semantics behind the construction of the integrated view and the consequent choices and decisions. More specifically, a mashup-based dashboard provides feedback about the users' sentiments on the reputations of Web resources. If users share their own dashboards, they then share their behavior in the decision and selection process and behavior can then be analyzed to fine tune the assessment of the service's reputation (in other words, its acceptability). Addressing these user needs and fostering the social behavior of users in a business community can offer new opportunities to service providers and aggregators. By leveraging these opportunities, they can satisfy their own information requirements by gaining access to new sources of business intelligence information.

12.5 Implementation and Experimental Results

The architecture reported in Figure 12.1 is currently in a prototype form. Our implementation efforts to date have focused on the Sentiment Analysis and Sentiment Data Quality Analysis modules and will be discussed in more detail in the following section. Concerning the self-service environment, we adopted the Mixup mashup engine (Yu et al. 2007) and extended its design environment with a broker for generating recommendations about quality mashup components (Cappiello et al. 2009). Future steps will focus on constructing an editor able to ease the componentization of sentiment services by expert users (system administrators) and by the end users who want to construct self-service environments.

12.5.1 Content Sentiment Analysis Module

The Content Sentiment Analysis module integrates *WordNet* (Fellbaum 1998) with *Freeling* (Atserias et al. 2006) and *SentiWordNet* (Esuli and Sebastiani 2006a). The current version of the tool, named *SentiEngine*, has the following characteristics:

- *It focuses on English.*
- *It evaluates the sentiments of selected sources (namely Twitter, TripAdvisor, and LonelyPlanet) on a single label (i.e., it accepts single-label queries).*
- *It extracts from Web sources the snippets, including the target label, and does not consider the context of those sentences (i.e., the text in which they are embedded).*

■ *It selects the correct meanings of words within their synsets (sets of synonyms inside WordNet) based on the concept of domain. In particular, the experimentation to date focused on the tourism domain.*

The content sentiment analysis module is based on a heuristic approach to improve results that can be achieved simply by joining the workflows of the modules. Figure 12.2 shows the workflow executed by our tool from the input text to the final sentiment evaluation. White blocks identify application modules and grey blocks identify filters used to interpret from each module. As shown in the figure, the following filtering activities are executed:

Stopword removal—This activity is intended to eliminate from snippets the words that do not contribute to the evaluation of sentiment (stopwords, Silva and Ribeiro 2003) and include articles, pronouns, prepositions, conjunctions, and so on.

Synset selection—This step refines the results of sentiment evaluation based on the part-of-speech (POS) tagger. WordNet and SentiWordNet associate several synsets with lemmas, each one with an associated polarity (Esuli and Sebastiani 2006b). To reduce the noise from multiple synsets, this step eliminates all the synsets that do not correspond to the syntactic type provided by the POS tagger.

Domain disambiguation—A further filtering activity is performed via WordNetDomains. The importance of domain analysis in word sense

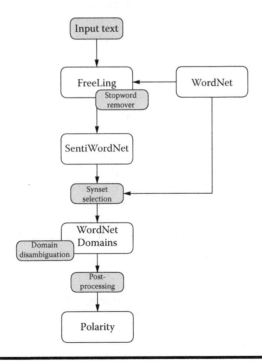

Figure 12.2   Sentiment evaluation process.

disambiguation is discussed by Magnini et al. (2002). Our engine disambiguates by selecting among remaining synsets based on their domains. Empirical experiments have proven that a well articulated sentence can be referred to multiple domains. WordNetDomains attributes each word to several domains. Our filter counts the number of words per domain, represented by at least one word in a sentence, and then eliminates the domains with scores below a given threshold (the value has been empirically set to 0.2).

Pattern correction rules—This filter applies a set of well known syntactic rules that refine the evaluation of sentiment:

1. *Adverb–adjective pattern* modifies the polarity of an adjective when matched with an adverb that emphasizes or deemphasizes the adjective sentiment. For example, *very nice* is more positive than *nice* while *a bit ugly* is less negative than *ugly*. Formally, the rule is expressed as:

```
IF (Pol⁺_adj < Pol⁻_adj) THEN invert (Pol⁺_adv, Pol⁻_adv);
ELSE DO nothing;
END IF,
```

where Pol^+_{adj} represents the positive sentiment component of the adjective, Pol^-_{adj} represents the negative sentiment component of the adjective, Pol^+_{adv} represents the positive sentiment component of the adverb, and Pol^-_{adv} represents the negative sentiment component of the adverb.

2. *Adverb–adverb pattern:* is similar to the previous one, but is applied when two adverbs such as *very badly* or *very nicely* reinforce each other. Formally, the rule can be expressed as:

```
IF (Pol⁺_adv2 < Pol⁻_adv2) THEN invert (Pol⁺_adv1, Pol⁻_adv1);
ELSE DO nothing;
END IF,
```

where Pol^+_{adv1} and Pol^+_{adv2} represent respectively, the positive sentiment component of the first and the second adverbs, while Pol^-_{adv1} and Pol^-_{adv2} represent the negative sentiment component of the first and second adverbs.

3. *Adverb–adverb–adverb/adjective pattern* can be considered an extension of rules 1 and 2 above. It is needed to deal with three-word patterns such as *very very ugly*. It applies the previous two rules repeatedly in groups of two, according to the following algorithm:

```
FOR (i = 3; i = 0; i--)
IF (word[i] is adverb AND word[i-1] is adverb) THEN
apply rule_2;
ELSE IF (word[i] is adjective AND word[i-1] is adverb)
THEN apply rule 1;
END IF
END FOR
```

4. *Not pattern* in which the *not* adverb involves specific interpretations to adjust the evaluation of the sentiment. For example, *not beautiful* is negative, i.e., the *not* adverb inverts the polarity of the *beautiful* adjective. *Not a bad city* is slightly negative (it does not mean that the city is *nice*) and does not need the adjective polarity inversion. For this reason, we adopted a rule to invert the polarities of all the words following a *not* lemma in a sentence until a stopword is found. Tests performed on a benchmark of sentences noted significant improvements of precision and recall when the *not* adverb is handled by this rule instead of rules 1 or 2 above. Precision increased from 32 to 56%, and recall from 28 to 51%.

Post-processing—this last filter is necessary to evaluate the sentiment of a sentence based on the evaluation of sentiment of individual words. We calculate the overall sentiment of a sentence as the mean value of sentiment of all nonzero sentiment words in the sentence. This last filter also excludes all the words that lack polarity. The polarity of the sentence is calculated as shown below and the formula is used for positive and negative polarities. The result is normalized to a five-point discrete scale.

$$Pol_+ = \frac{\sum_{k=1}^{n} Pol_+(k)}{n}$$

12.6 Empirical Results

As described above, a value of sentiment is attributed to individual snippets based on the following steps. A snippet is logically analyzed and different words are assigned polarities in the -1 to $+1$ range; -1 is very negative and $+1$ is very positive. Words with 0 polarity are eliminated because they are irrelevant to the sentiment computation. Sentiment is calculated as the summation of the sentiment of remaining words and normalized on a five-point scale. The semantic text interpretation embedded in the tool does not allow selection of subsets of words with non-null polarities that are referred to the subject of interest (label). This represents a limitation and involves interpretation errors. For example, "Madrid is more rainy than Milan" will be attributed identical negative polarities for both Madrid and Milan as subjects of interest. Current work is addressing this issue.

Figure 12.3 reports the results of a comparison of food quality in Madrid and Milan and makes a distinction between positive and negative comments. The labels considered were *food, dinner, lunch, meal, breakfast, restaurant, pub, eat*. A total of 250 snippets from Twitter were analyzed for each city. The graph reports an aggregate evaluation of sentiment obtained as a simple average of the sentiment

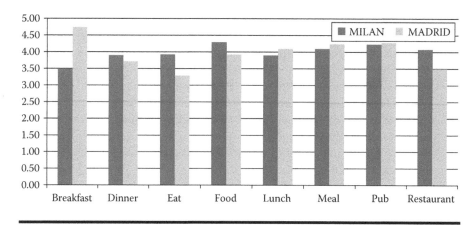

Figure 12.3   A comparison between the food in Madrid and Milan.

assessed for each label. Sentiment is rated on a 1 to 5 scale (1 = very negative, 5 = very positive). We obtained medium quality accuracy with a precision of 66% and a recall of 64% on a five-level based evaluation. Such values noticeably improve with a three-level evaluation, achieving a precision of 95% and a recall of 92%. Precision and recall assessments were based on a manual evaluation of the tool's results on the sample input.

Previous literature considered approaches similar to the one presented in this work. In particular, Agrawal and Siddiqui (2009) obtained an average precision of 85%, while Denecke (2008) found an accuracy level between 51 and 62% for English, and between 58 and 66% for German.

We further tested the validity of our platform by comparing the results of the analysis performed by our tool with analyses made with publicly available commercial tools. We created several Twitter accounts and published 52 tweets containing reserved and invented words to ensure that we could find all our tweets through a single search and that our tweets would not have been followed and commented by other users. The tweets constituted a benchmark that we used to evaluate the improvements in our engine performance during its development. They included many tricky sentences that can serve as difficult tests for our tool and for all the commercial ones. We then performed an automatic sentiment analysis of the 52 tweets, retrieved through our reserved words. Finally, we manually evaluated the result of each sentence sentiment produced by each tool.

Table 12.5 reports the results. As shown, some commercial tools were unable to find all the tweets we entered and our tool showed the best performance in terms of precision and recall. Our SentiEngine was able to find all the 52 tweets and to obtain the highest number of hits, i.e., number of times the tool correctly estimated positive, negative, and neutral sentences. Finally, SentiEngine showed the best tradeoff of precision and recall.

Table 12.5   Tool Performance Comparison

Tool	Found Tweets	Hits	Precision	Recall
Twitter sentiment	33	18	55%	35%
Twitrratr	52	8	53%	15%
Social mention	47	11	41%	21%
Tweetfeel	2	2	100%	4%
SentiEngine	52	33	69%	63%

12.7 Concluding Remarks

This chapter discussed a new approach to sentiment analysis. Its most novel aspect is its ability to evaluate a source's reputation and sentiment analyses along classical data quality dimensions. The classification of information sources and the assessment of the quality of their information improve the reliability of reputation and sentiment assessments, and provide users with a tool to select dependable sources for the analyses they need to perform. Users can thus perform more focused searches and devise more reliable interpretations.

Another novelty of our approach is the possibility for a user to construct a personal analysis environment through the lightweight combination of services (data services, analysis and reputation services, or generic services) based on mashups. Traditional dashboards are characterized by rigid structures; indicators present some aggregate data with no possibilities of personalizing an analysis (for example, through source selection) or integrating other services that may be useful to improve the analysis. Our approach tries to go beyond this limitation and enables users to quickly and easily create personalized views of analyses of selected information sources.

The ease and flexibility that characterize the construction of the analysis environment are in line with the current trend of creating *situational applications,* i.e., applications that serve a well defined purpose and are developed for a limited time horizon (Jhingran 2006). In our platform, mashups can be easily composed (by visually combining icons that represent the available services), and therefore users can create their own applications without the aid of expert developers. This modus operandi increases productivity. Many information composition tasks are not adequately supported by long-lived enterprise applications due, for example, to very specific needs and/or preferences that characterize the activities, or to immediate unexpected business problems. The ability to create a personalized application "on the fly" alleviates this problem.

Our current efforts are devoted to refining the algorithm for sentiment assessment, for example, by introducing term clustering to improve the analysis. We are also developing the visual environment to support user's ability to: (1) personalize the reputation filter and sentiment analysis services by means of suitable presentation layers and (2) guide the mashup of such services by means of quality-aware recommendations.

References

Abbasi, A., Chen, H., and A. Salem. 2008. Sentiment analysis in multiple languages: Feature selection for opinion classification in Web forums. *ACM Trans. Inf. Syst. 26*: 1–34.

Agrawal, S. and Siddiqui, T.J. 2009. Using syntactic and contextual information for sentiment polarity analysis. In *Proceedings of Second International Conference on Interaction Science: Information Technology, Culture, and Human,* Seoul, ACM Press, pp. 620–623.

Ardagna, D., Cappiello, C., Comuzzi, M. et al. 2005. A broker for selecting and provisioning high quality syndicated data. In *Proceedings of the International Conference on Information Quality.*

Ardagna, D., Cappiello, C., Francalanci, C. et al. 2006. Brokering multisource data with quality constraints. In *Proceedings of OTM Conferences,* pp. 807–817.

Artz, D. and Y. Gil. 2007. A survey of trust in computer science and the Semantic Web. *J. Web Sem. 5*: 58–71.

Atserias, J., Casas, B., Comelles, E. et al. 2006. Freeling 1.3: Syntactic and semantic services in an open-source NLP library. In *Proceedings of Fifth Conference on Language Resources and Evaluation.*

Atzeni, P., Merialdo, P., and G. Sindoni. 2001. Web site evaluation: Methodology and case study. In *Proceedings of DASWIS International Workshop on Data Semantics in Web Information Systems,* Yokohama.

Barbagallo, D., Cappiello, C., Francalanci, C. et al. 2010a. A reputation-based DSS: The INTEREST approach. In *Proceedings of 17th International Conference on Information Technology and Travel & Tourism.*

Barbagallo, D., Cappiello, C., Francalanci, C. et al. 2010b. Reputation-based selection of Web information sources. In *Proceedings of 12th Conference on Enterprise Information Systems.*

Batini, C., Cappiello, C., Francalanci, C. et al. 2009. Methodologies for data quality assessment and improvement. *ACM Comp. Surveys 41*: 1–52.

Brin, S., and L. Page. 1998. The anatomy of a large-scale hypertextual Web search engine. *Computer Networks 30*: 107–117.

Bruno, S. and L. Radice. 2009. Analisi della reputazione in Ambienti web 2.0: Una Metodologia orientata alla Data quality per la sentiment Analysis (Reputation analysis in Web 2.0. A data quality-oriented methodology for the sentiment analysis). Master's thesis, Politecnico di Milano.

Cappiello, C., Daniel, F., and M. Matera. 2009. A quality model for mashup components. In *Proceedings of ICWE,* pp. 236–250.

Denecke, K. 2008. Using SentiWordNet for multilingual sentiment analysis. In *Proceedings of IEEE 24th International Conference on Data Engineering Workshop,* pp. 507–512.

Ennals, R. and M.N. Garofalakis. 2007. MashMaker: Mashups for the masses. In *Proceedings of SIGMOD,* pp. 1116–1118.

Esuli, A. and F. Sebastiani. 2006a. SentiWordNet: A publicly available lexical resource for opinion mining. In *Proceedings of Fifth Conference on Language Resources and Evaluation.*

Esuli, A. and F. Sebastiani. 2006b. Determining term subjectivity and term orientation for opinion mining. In *Proceedings of 11th Conference of European Chapter of Association for Computational Linguistics.*

Fellbaum, C. 1998. *WordNet: An Electronic Lexical Database.* MIT Press, Cambridge, MA.

Gackowski, Z. 2006. Redefining information quality: The operations management approach. In *Proceedings of 11th International Conference on Information Quality,* pp. 399–419.

Glance, N., Hurst, M., Nigam, K. et al. 2005. Deriving marketing intelligence from online discussion. In *Proceedings of 11th ACM SIGKDD International Conference on Knowledge Discovery in Data Mining,* pp. 419–428.

Gloor, P.A., Krauss, J., Nann, S. et al. 2009. Web Science 2.0: Identifying trends through semantic social network analysis. In *Proceedings of International Conference on Computational Science and Engineering,* Vol. 04, pp. 215–222.

Godbole, N., Srinivasaiah, M. and S. Skiena. 2007. Large-scale sentiment analysis for news and blogs. In *Proceedings of First International Conference on Weblogs and Social Media,* pp. 219–222.

Greene, S. and Resnik, P. 2009. More than words: Syntactic packaging and implicit sentiment. In *Proceedings of Human Language Technologies: Annual Conference of North American Chapter of Association For Computational* Linguistics, pp. 503–511.

Hu, N., Liu, L., and J.J. Zhang. 2008. Do online reviews affect product sales? Role of reviewer characteristics and temporal effects. *Inf. Technol. Mgt. 9*: 201–214.

IBM. Mashup Center. http://www-01.ibm.com/software/info/mashup-center/

Intel. MashMaker. http://mashmaker.intel.com/web/

Jhingran, A. 2006. Enterprise information mashups: Integrating information, simply. In *Proceedings of VLDB,* pp. 3–4.

Jiang, S., Zilles, S., and R. Holte. 2008. Empirical analysis of rank distribution of relevant documents in Web search. In *Proceedings of International Conference on Web Intelligence and Intelligent Agent Technology,* pp. 208–213.

Kleinberg, J.M. 1999. Hubs, authorities, and communities. *ACM Comp. Survey 31*: 5.

Liu, Y., Huang, X., An, A. et al. 2007. ARSA: A sentiment-aware model for predicting sales performance using blogs. In *Proceedings of 30th Annual International ACM SIGIR Conference on Research and Development in Information Retrieval,* pp. 607–614.

Magnini, B., Pezzulo, G., and A. Gliozzo. 2002. The role of domain information in word sense disambiguation. *Nat. Language Eng. 8*: 359–373.

Mei, Q., Ling, X., Wondra, M. et al. 2007. Topic sentiment mixture: Modelling facets and opinions in weblogs. In *Proceedings of 16th International Conference on World Wide Web,* pp. 171–180.

O'Hare, N., Davy, M., Bermingham et al. 2009. Topic-dependent sentiment analysis of financial blogs. In *Proceedings of First International CIKM Workshop on Topic-Sentiment Analysis for Mass Opinion,* pp. 9–16.

Schawbel, D. 2008. Top 10 reputation tracking tools worth paying for. Mashable: the social media guide. http://mashable.com/2008/12/29/brand-reputation-monitoring-tools/

Silva, C. and B. Ribeiro. 2003. The importance of stop word removal on recall values in text categorization. In *Proceedings of International Joint Conference on Neural Networks,* pp. 1661–1666.

Skopik, F., Truong, H. L. and S. Dustdar. 2009. Trust and reputation mining in professional virtual communities. In *Proceedings of ICWE,* pp. 76–90.

Wordtravels. 2010. *Milan Travel Guide.* http://www.wordtravels.com/Cities/Italy/Milan

Yahoo!. Yahoo! Pipes. http://pipes.yahoo.com/pipes/

Yu, J., Benatallah, B., Saint-Paul, R. et al. 2007. A framework for rapid integration of presentation components. In *Proceedings of WWW,* pp. 923–932.

Yu, J., Benatallah, B., Casati, F. et al. 2007. Understanding mashup development. *IEEE Internet Comp. 12*: 44–52.

Chapter 13

Semantics and Search

Jon Atle Gulla

Norwegian University of Science and Technology, Trondheim, Norway

Jin Liu

T-Systems, Bonn, Germany

Felix Burkhardt, Jianshen Zhou, and Christian Weiss

Deutsche Telekom Laboratories, Bonn, Germany

Per Myrseth, Veronika Haderlein, and Olga Cerrato

Det Norske Veritas, Oslo, Norway

Contents

13.1 Introduction

Web search applications today are crucial for the efficient management and exploitation of information on the Internet. People use searches to find web sites of companies or services and check on items from tonight's movies to recommendations on books and products. A study by Kumar and Tomkins (2009) revealed that 9.0% of all page views on the Internet are visits to various search sites, including multimedia searches and searches of databases; 8.9% are direct referrals from searches; and another 3.5% are indirect referrals, resulting in a total of 21.4% of overall page views that are based on search.

Searching now supports a wide range of activities on the Internet. Whereas early use of web search engines concentrated on finding static data on a restricted range of topics, current information on the Internet is constantly changing and is useful for almost any activity or interest. A survey conducted by Careerbuilder. com in 2006 found that one in four employers used web searches to screen potential employees, and more than half the managers interviewed decided against hiring individuals after investigating their online activities. As shown in Figure 13.1, people now use search applications to retrieve information about very specific objects like persons, products, events, and places. This is not surprising because the Internet is now used actively and dynamically to publish information relevant to what is going on around us. The Internet responds faster to events than traditional news channels, allows a wider range of opinions and perspectives to be published, encourages communication and discussion, and offers almost infinite amounts of information.

At the same time, enterprises also observe the increasing importance of good search facilities for managing their internal activities and resources. To handle the

Category	Percent Queries
Organization	33.94
Notable person	13.08
Specific product	11.35
Media title	10.10
General product	8.56
Business category or service	7.69
Places	4.9
Ordinary person	4.42
Event	2.31
Health	1.35
Games	1.15
Real estate	1.15

Figure 13.1 Search categories on Internet. (*Source;* Kumar, R. and A. Tomkins, *IEEE Data Engineering Bulletin,* 32: 3–11, 2009.)

complexity of their businesses and take full advantage of their own competence, they need appropriate tools for documenting and retrieving business-critical information. This is a particular concern in evolving domains in which organizations change constantly and must relate to new market needs, procedures, technology, and staffing.

The sheer amount of information is one of the most challenging aspects of Internet and enterprise search applications, but other aspects also hamper the effectiveness of current search technology. The reliance of standard search applications on simple keywords is satisfactory for users who know exactly which words would appear in the documents they request. However, most users will not know in detail the wording of all documents, and the flexibility of natural languages makes it difficult to guess how words and phrases are used to describe phenomena. If terminologies change over time, a suitable keyword today may fail to identify relevant documents from the past. *Semantic search applications* address this language problem of current search technology. They offer mechanisms for dealing with document content rather than keywords and try to capture the variety and instability of terms used in documents and queries.

This chapter surveys prominent approaches to semantic search. After explaining the principles of semantic search in Sections 13.2 and 13.3, we discuss semantic indexing techniques in Section 13.4. Most research on semantic search relates to query processing and interpretation—the topic of Section 13.5. Section 13.6 is devoted to the use of semantics on the search result page, and Section 13.7 presents techniques for semantic navigation of result sets. The temporal or evolutionary dimension of search is discussed in Section 13.8, followed by conclusions in Section 13.9.

13.2 Semantic Representations

Words in natural language may be analyzed along syntactic and semantic lines. From a *syntactic* perspective, we note that words must be spelled and inflected according to certain morphological rules and combine into phrases or sentences following grammatical principles. In the syntactic realm we can decide whether the text is well formed with respect to morphological or grammatical rules, but not whether it is meaningful to the reader. *Semantics* refers to the meanings of words and compositions of words into phrases, sentences, and larger pieces of text. Every word is assumed to carry semantic content that combines with other words into meaningful messages to readers. We say that a word—or term—in the syntactic realm refers to some concept in the realm that constitutes the meaning of the term.

Figure 13.2 shows how the correspondence between syntactic terms and semantic concepts is modeled in *WordNet*, a semantic lexicon from Princeton University (Miller, 1995). A term may be used to refer to several concepts and a concept may form the meanings of several terms. The term *car* has five different meanings in WordNet, of which two are shown in the figure. The term may refer to a four-wheeled (specialized) motor vehicle and a generalization of more specialized cars like ambulances and station wagons. However, it may also refer to railroad cars that may be further specialized into luggage cars, cabin cars, and other types. A *car* may also be referred to by terms like *rail car* and *railway car*. Concepts in the semantic realm are semantically related by means of relations like *has_parts* and *is_member_of*. Semantic search applications go beyond traditional search engines by allowing users to search for documents on the basis of content rather than keyword matching. With traditional search applications based on the vector space model, query terms are matched—as they are—against inverted indices of terms appearing in the documents of the collection. The degree of match between the search terms and the document terms decides whether a particular document is deemed relevant to the query. This is often referred to as *syntactic search* because no attempt is made to analyze the structures of the terms or their semantic contents. With *morpho-syntactic search*, stemmers or lemmatizers are used to normalize query and/or index terms so that any inflection of a search term will match any inflection of the same lexical word in the index. This means

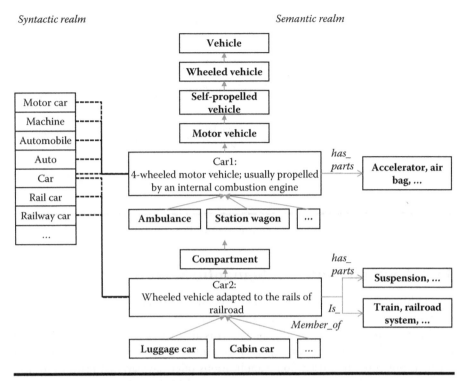

Syntactic realm

Semantic realm

Figure 13.2 Correspondence between terms and WordNet semantics.

that the *cars* search term will match the *car* index term; *written* will match the *write* index term, etc. Many current commercial search applications offer some form of morpho-syntactic search, often in combination with spell checking of query terms.

The next step up from traditional syntactic search is using dictionaries, thesauri, or ontologies to be match search terms against synonyms, instances, or other related terms in an index. A search for *cars* would return documents citing only *automobiles* because the dictionary informs the search application that cars and automobiles are synonyms. Since ontologies depict the semantic structures of a domain, we are now in a position to relate search terms to index terms based on semantic content and to reason about document content. Ultimately, this semantic approach has the capacity to help search engines match search terms against information that is not explicitly stated in the documents but can be inferred from them via the ontology. This is shown on the right side of Figure 13.3, in which the system realizes that cars are related to vehicles that run by means of engines. This type of human-like interpretation and reasoning is one of the main objectives of the Semantic Web initiative, although we still face fundamental and unsolved challenges in extracting semantic content from text and reasoning.

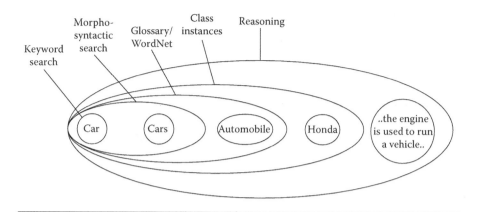

Figure 13.3 **Which documents are relevant to the *car* query?**

13.3 Layered Model of Semantic Search

The architecture of a search application is composed of components for indexing, querying, searching and ranking, result presentation, and result navigation. In a traditional search application, the query terms are matched against an index of all terms in the documents. A result page with ranked links to all the retrieved documents is presented to a user. Some applications offer navigational features to help a user specify a new and more precise query or drill down into the result set. All these stages operate on terms that are, by definition, meaningless to the application itself.

We can imagine a similar search process at a semantic layer (see Figure 13.4). Documents are indexed by means of semantic structures; queries include references to concepts, instances, and their relationships; retrieved documents are described by semantic content; and navigational links address semantic classification or refinement of result sets. However, in a real semantic search application, only some of the search stages operate at this semantic level and the others follow a traditional syntactic approach. We classify a search application as semantic if at least one of the stages of the search process establishes a correspondence between the syntactic and semantic realms. This correspondence is facilitated by an underlying ontology or other mechanism that exposes semantic aspects of text.

Common to all semantic applications is an explicit or implicit understanding of how ontological concepts or instances are referred to in the real world. Ontologies may be linked to terms in documents and queries in four basic ways:

■ *Syntactic correspondence: Concept names are assumed to be identical with the terms used to refer to them. For example, the* movie *concept is assumed to be cited by the same term in the real world as well.*

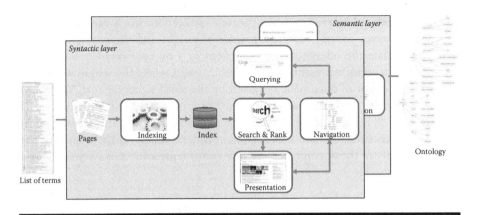

Figure 13.4   Search process and representations.

- *Morpho-syntactic correspondence: Concept names are assumed to be identical to the lemmas of the terms used to refer to them. A concept like* movie *will then be referred to by* movie, movies, movie's, *etc.*
- *Synonym correspondence: Concept names are linked to a set of synonyms that may all be used to refer to the concept. For a concept like* movie, *a synonym set may contain* movie, film, *and* motion picture.
- *Relative correspondence: This method involves relative relatedness among concepts and terms. A relative score, usually between 0 and 1, indicates to what extent a specific term is used to refer to a specific concept. A similar score reveals the likelihood that a concept is materialized by a particular term in the text. For example,* bank *refers to the concept of river banks with a score of 0.2 and to financial banks with a score of 0.6.*

We now discuss the various approaches or techniques of semantic searching. Extending existing frameworks (Hildebrand et al., 2007; Mäkelä, 2005; Mangold, 2007), we classify semantic search applications with respect to their approach to index matching, query processing, result presentation, and navigation. Many search applications use several semantic strategies; for reasons of simplicity we discuss them in isolation. We will also cover aspects of temporal search because these applications require a semantics not readily available from current ontologies.

13.4 Index Matching Approaches

Most semantic search applications make use of standard indexing mechanisms from the vector space model. Thy utilize both content- and link-related relevance calculations.

Content-related relevance—Most search applications use a variant of the tf-idf (*term frequency–inverse document frequency*) weight and the cosine similarity score to calculate the relevance of a document to a query. Every document and query is given a vector representation, $(w_{1j}, w_{2j}, \ldots, w_{kj})$, where the weight w_{ij} of each term i in the vector of document j is given by the tf-idf score: $w_{ij} = tf_{ij}{}^* idf_i = (fij/max\ fj){}^* log(N/n)$. tf_{ij} is the frequency of term i in j, max f_j is the max frequency of any term in j, N is the number of documents in the collection, and n is the number of documents that contain i. A document is deemed relevant to a query if the cosine similarity of the document and query vector representations (views) is above a certain threshold:

$$similarity(Q, D) = cos(\theta) = \frac{Q * D}{\|Q\| * \|D\|}$$

where Q and D are vector representations of the query and the document, and $\|Q\|$ and $\|D\|$ are the lengths of the vectors.

Link-related relevance—Web search applications also make use of link-related information using techniques similar to Google's Page rank algorithm (Page et al., 1997) or the Hypertext Induced Topic Selection (HITS) of Kleinberg (1999). PageRank is a probability distribution that models the likelihood that a person randomly clicking on links will arrive at a particular page. The idea is that links from other high-quality pages to a particular page count as a vote of confidence in that page and indicate the particular page is more important than other pages with fewer good links. The Page rank of a web page is given by:

$$PR(u) = \sum_{v \in B_u} \frac{PR(v)}{L(v)}$$

where $PR(u)$ is the page rank of page u, B_u is the set of all pages linking to u, and $L(v)$ is the number of links from v to other pages. When ranking documents with respect to a query, we boost documents with high Page rank scores, assuming that they have higher general quality than low score documents.

In addition, semantic search may involve graph traversals, semantic structure matching, or reasoning with implicit information. All these approaches assume that semantic aspects of documents can be extracted and used to set up semantically structured indices instead of or in addition to traditional indices. To what extent Page rank and cosine similarity can be applied to semantic indices remains unclear, although attempts have been made to define new ranking schemes like ReConRank to extend Page rank into the semantic realm (Hogan et al., 2006).

13.4.1 Named Entity Matching

Named entity recognition has been used to recognize occurrences of entity references in documents either by looking up carefully crafted entity dictionaries or by matching document text against regular expressions for types of entities. A regular expression can, for example, indicate that a word starting with a capital letter and followed by an *Ltd.* abbreviation is the name of a company. The range of entity types (person names, locations, dates) recognized is usually restricted and the types yield a minimal semantic characterization of entities. If an entity like *George W. Bush* is recognized at the beginning of a document, short forms of that entity (*George Bush* or simply *Bush*) may also be recognized.

The recognized entity references may go to a semantic index or be normalized for a traditional inverted index. Normalization means that all variants of an entity (like George W. Bush, President Bush, George Bush, and Bush) are combined and we calculate a total frequency for the entity rather than for each separate entity reference. Since the entities are typed, this algorithm can support entity searches based on type indications. For example, a query such as Q = LOCATION Deutsche Telekom may list and rank all entities of type location that are prominent in documents citing Deutsche Telekom. Presumably, the ranking should show cities and countries in which Deutsche Telekom is located or does business. Special named entity indices can be found in several search applications (Amaral et al., 2004; Duke et al., 2007; Kiryakov et al., 2004).

13.4.2 Graph Traversal

If a semantic index is set up and a query is mapped onto conceptual classes, the user's query may correspond to nodes in a graph-structured index. Finding relevant information means traversing a graph on the basis of the user's selected nodes, certain constraints, and some general search strategies. One traversal strategy may, for example, specify how the graph is traversed to find interesting instances of a particular class.

Graph-structured indices are used most often when the documents already have some inherent uniform structure, e.g., a particular XML format. It is not obvious that these structures are semantically sound or meaningful and they may not make much sense to a user. The approach tends to be more useful in professional settings in which the documents and index structures are understood and respected. The semantics are given by conventions in the community and may not be explicitly defined with ontology languages.

Graph-traversing strategies have been used in a number of search systems for XML documents: XSearch from Cohen et al. (2003) and XRANK from Guo et al. (2003). Recent systems like Tabulator (Berners-Lee et al., 2006) and Swoogle (Li et al., 2004) use similar strategies for RDF documents. The SSARK system of Anyanwu et al. (2005) uses a configurable ranking algorithm for ranking the associations between entities in the result set.

13.4.3 Conceptual Matching

The conceptual matching approach requires that both documents and queries be specified at a conceptual (semantic) level using similar conceptual structures. During retrieval, a document is deemed relevant to a query if its conceptual content subsumes the conceptual content of the query. Since there are no vector calculations of similarity scores, how relevant documents are to be ranked in the result set is not obvious.

If a document has semantic annotations that can be used to construct semantic indices, the search process is a matching of semantic query structures against semantic document structures. Separate concept indices are used in several search engines (Bonino et al., 2003; Celino et al., 2006; Davies et al., 2004; Finin et al., 2005; Heflin and Hendler, 2000; Lei et al., 2006). As shown in Figure 13.5 from Heflin and Hendler (2000), the SHOE search application asks the user to select an ontology before posting a query. Available categories from the ontology are presented to the user, and the user selects the relevant ones and specifies the details (properties) of the query. The categories and properties are all reflected in the document index. This strategy is in many ways similar to query reformulation strategies

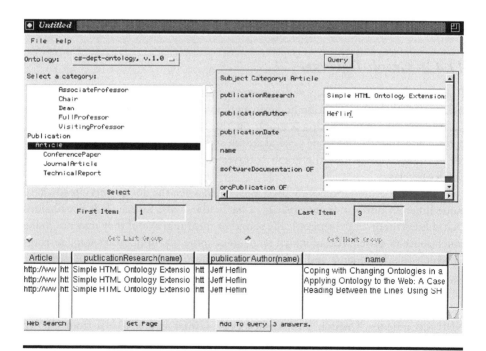

Figure 13.5 SHOE search interface. (*Source:* **Heflin, J. and J. Hendler. In** *Artificial Intelligence for Web Search: Papers from AAAI Workshop,* **2000, AAAI Press. pp. 35–40.)**

and navigation strategies, although the semantic structures are hard-coded into the index structure.

An extension to this approach is to allow the search application to use broader (more general) terms or narrower (more specialized) terms to extract a more suitable result set when the original search terms do not yield satisfactory answers. If, for example, a user query does not produce hits, the system may automatically expand the search with broader terms to retrieve documents that are at least somewhat related to the query. This matching strategy is adopted by SKOS, DOSE (Bonino et al., 2004) and Squiggle (Celino et al., 2006), among others.

13.4.4 Reasoning

Calculation of document relevance may also be computed based on information implicit in the documents. Given a query for B, a document with content A, and an ontology with axiom A $\rightarrow$ B (A implies B) or A $\leftrightarrow$ B (A is equivalent to B), the matching component may conclude that the document is relevant even though it does not explicitly answer the query. Common types of reasoning support include RDFS subsumption based on a user-selected RDF class, OWL identity classes, and various types of specialization and generalization reasoning. This technology is somewhat immature and does not scale well for a full-fledged search solution; experiments with this approach continue (Duke et al., 2007; Finin et al., 2005).

13.5 Querying Approaches

Standard querying interfaces include features that are also used in semantic search. These include syntactic operators like + and –, spell checking (e.g., with the Levenshtein algorithm), and phrasing of terms to be treated as phrases or colocations. In addition, semantics has been used in query disambiguation, controlled semantic querying, query reformulation, and query constraints.

13.5.1 Query Disambiguation

The purpose of query disambiguation is to identify the sense of ambiguous query terms. Ambiguities may stem from multiple word meanings (lexical ambiguity) or from multiple interpretations of complex expressions (structural ambiguity). In the first case, we often refer to the terms as homonyms because they share the same spelling with semantically different terms. Disambiguation is often used as part of more extensive semantic search strategies that involve lexical or ontological resources (Amaral et al., 2004; Burton-Jones et al., 2003; Guarino et al., 1999).

One approach is to use WordNet (Miller, 1995) synsets of isolated ambiguous terms to identify possible interpretations of a query. Take for example the term bank, which has ten WordNet senses (synsets) including "a financial institution"

1	Sloping land, especially a slope beside a body of water
2	Depository financial institution, banking concern, banking company (financial institution that accepts deposits and channels money into lending activities)
3	Long ridge or pile
4	Arrangement of similar objects in a row or in tiers
5	Supply or stock held in reserve for future use (especially emergencies)
6	Funds held by gambling houses or dealers in gambling games
7	Slope at a turn of a road or track; the outside is higher than the inside to reduce effects of centrifugal force (also cant, camber)
8	Container (usually with a slot in the top) for keeping money at home (also savings bank, coin bank, money box)
9	Building in which banking business is transacted (also bank)
10	Flight maneuver; aircraft tips laterally about its longitudinal axis, usually while turning

Figure 13.6 Different senses (synsets) of *bank* term in WordNet.

and "some sloping land beside water" (Figure 13.6). If the system presents possible senses of a term, the user may choose the correct one, and the system can use the additional terms of the chosen synset to direct the search toward this interpretation. If the user selects bank as a financial institution, the system may also include terms like banking concern and banking company in the query to ensure that the chosen interpretation is reflected in the documents retrieved.

When a query consists of several terms, we can use the structure of the ontology or lexicon to determine the most reasonable senses of the terms. Every term in WordNet is part of a hierarchy that links all terms of a particular part of speech together. By following these hierarchical links, we can establish a path between any two senses. The length of that path is often taken as an indication of how close these senses are semantically. In the WordNet lexicon, credit union and financial institution are considered very close, since credit union is only one link away from financial institution (credit union is a direct hyponym of financial institution). The semantic distance between the two concepts is set to 1. Let us now assume a query of N ambiguous terms, $Q = T_1, ..., T_N = \{S_{1,1}, ..., S_{K,1}\}, ..., \{S_{1,N}, ..., S_{M,N}\}$, of which $S_{i,j}$ is sense i of term j in the query. One approach to query disambiguation would be to assume that each term T_i can be replaced by exactly one sense S_{ki} and together form an unambiguous query, $Q' = S_{i,1}, ... S_{j,N}$, that minimizes the total semantic distance between any two terms in the query. Budanitsky and Hirst (2006) evaluated a number of techniques for calculating WordNet-based measures of semantic relatedness for this purpose.

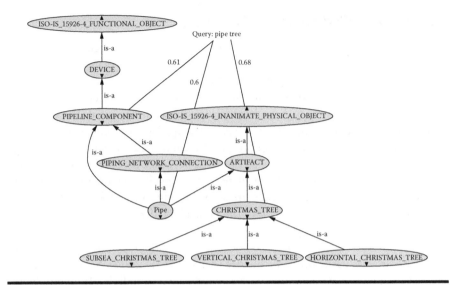

Figure 13.7 The *pipe* term matches several concepts in the ontology.

Similar strategies have been developed for calculating semantic relatedness between concepts in large ontologies as well. Figure 13.7 shows how the ISO 15926 petroleum ontology is used to disambiguate the query Q = *pipe tree* in Solskinnsbakk and Gulla (2008). Based on spelling similarities, the *pipe* term may refer to either the *pipe* concepts (similarity 0.6) or the *pipeline_component* concept (similarity 0.61), whereas *tree* matches only the *christmas tree* concept. The system selects *pipe* as the most likely interpretation due to the much closer semantic relationship of *christmas_tree* and *pipe* than between *christmas_tree* and *pipeline_component*. As seen from the figure, *pipe* and *christmas_tree* are only two edges away from each other in the ontology.

Sometimes a query includes abstract or general terms that may not make much sense as search terms but may be specialized into terms that are common in documents. Instead of presenting a very general result set, the system may ask directly which specialization the user is interested in. For example, when a user posts a *pipe tree* query in Figure 13.7, the system may suggest that *tree* may be specialized into subsea trees, vertical trees, and horizontal trees. The strategy serves as an alternative to providing specialization links on the result page or in combination with controlled concept vocabularies in queries.

Query disambiguation is a well understood method. Some systems use it inter-actively and ask a user to identify the correct sense before the search process is completed. Other systems search for all interpretations of the query and allow the user to drill down to the correct interpretation on the result page. However, since semantic search is normally restricted to a certain domain, the problem of hom-onyms is less critical than in unrestricted search spaces.

13.5.2 Controlled Semantic Querying

The earliest semantic search systems often let a user browse through a whole ontology and choose the concepts that best represented his information needs, then constructed a semantic query from the chosen concepts. This ensured that the query had a clearly defined semantic interpretation and the user could include concepts that she would not have been able to find on her own. The approach required either semantic indices or a separate mapping from concepts to terms. The GetData query language is an example of a controlled formal query language (Guha et al., 2003). This strategy is cumbersome when ontologies are huge and a user must inspect a large portion of results to specify her query. Many users are also uncomfortable because they are allowed only to use predefined concepts rather than their own terminologies. The controlled semantic query approach is thus rarely used in today's systems.

Later systems with controlled vocabularies adopted sentence template approaches to help users formulate queries (Amaral et al., 2004). Some systems use sentence templates in combination with semantic auto-completion from ontologies (Bernstein et al., 2006) and others use auto-completion in combination with free query input (Hyvönen et al., 2006).

13.5.3 Semantic Query Reformulation

Semantic query reformulation tries to add more flexibility than is possible with simple controlled vocabulary queries. The idea is to translate the original query into concepts that are then used for searching a semantically structured index. The process of recognizing concepts in query terms includes standard linguistic techniques like stemming and lemmatization, phrasing, and anti-phrasing. A substrategy is the use of auto-completion techniques, i.e., suggesting complete concept names as the user enters search terms. This strategy is often used in conjunction with navigation techniques. After identifying some concepts in the query, the system may present the relevant subparts of the ontology and let the user refine his original query with more specialized concepts.

Fang et al. (2005) present a search application that maps natural language queries onto ontology concepts, adds missing information from the ontology, and constructs a new query consisting of RDF tuples of concepts. Imagine a query Q = what do pandas in Tibet eat? Using the OWL ontology in Figure 13.8, the application builds a query RDF pattern that captures the relevant terms of the query: {<EAT, ?p, ?c> <TYPE, ?p, PANDA> <liveIn, ?p, TIBET>}. After binding the variable ?p to PANDA, the application finds ?c to be BAMBOO from the ontology and constructs an RDF tuple as the new semantic query: {<EAT, PANDAS in TIBET, BAMBOO>}.

It uses a semantic index consisting of a concept–document matrix. The weight of a particular concept c for a document d is given by the formula $R(d,c) = \sum_{i=1}^{Nd} r(t_i,c)$ where N_d is the number of terms in d, and $r(t_i,c)$ is the relevance between c and term

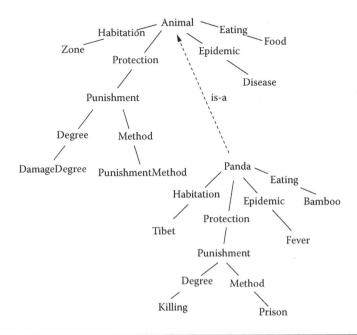

Figure 13.8 OWL ontology. (Source: Fang, W.D. et al. In *Proceedings of International Conference on Machine Learning and Cybernetics*, 2005.)

i in d. To calculate $r(t_i,c)$, the system compares the spellings of terms with the labels of concepts as follows:

$$r(t_i,c) = \begin{cases} 1.0 \ \textit{if } t_i = c \\ 0.7 \ \textit{if } t_i \ \textit{is a subclass of } c \\ 0.4 \ \textit{if } t_i \ \textit{has same superclass as } c \\ 0.2 \ \textit{if } t_i \ \textit{is a superclass of } c \textit{ or a subclass of a superclass of } c \\ 0 \ \textit{otherwise} \end{cases}$$

After the method constructs a query vector of concepts from the RDF tuple query, it can compute the relevance of documents with respect to the query following the standard cosine similarity measure.

In a similar approach, Lei et al. (2006) identified entities in queries and constructed formal queries in the Sesame SeRQL query language. Tran et al. (2007) constructed reformulated queries in description logic, and Zhou et al. (2007) constructed SPARQL queries from natural language queries. Calvanese et al. (2004) used some semantic rules to modify a query to work on a grid of search indices. A challenge with semantic queries is that they require semantic indices that suffer from severe performance issues linked to both the indexing of documents and the matching of queries with the index.

13.5.4 Syntactic Query Reformulation

With syntactic query reformulation, we map a syntactic query onto semantic concepts, interpret the query semantically, and map the result back to a syntactic query of weighted terms (Solskinnsbakk and Gulla, 2008). Unlike semantic query reformulation, this approach uses a standard inverted index based on term–document matrices and requires that ontologies be trained on a representative set of documents in the document collection. For every concept in the ontology, we allocate a set of relevant documents from this set and generate a concept signature for concept i, $C_i = (t_{i1}, \ldots, t_{in})$, as shown in Figure 13.9. The resulting concept signature for SCOPE PLANNING: C_{SP} = (scope planning:0.0097, project scope:0.0047, product:0.0043, project work:0.0008, project:0.0001), tells us that the scope planning term is the most relevant reference to the concept, but terms like project scope and product may also be used to describe aspects of the concept. This signature is a vector of weighted nouns and noun phrases characteristic of the concepts as described in the documents.

Technically, the weights are calculated using tf-idf scores of stemmed terms in the documents. From the query vector Q = (tqi, ..., tqn), we compute the cosine similarity with all concepts C_i of the ontology and build a new query vector, Q' = (c1, ..., cK), that includes all concepts C_i that had similarity scores above threshold α. Q' is the semantic interpretation of Q and has already dealt with possible ambiguities of the query. Due to the similarity calculations, the top ranked concepts are semantically close to the whole set of terms of Q and not only to individual terms. A syntactic query Q" is finally generated by adding the concept signatures of all concepts included in Q':

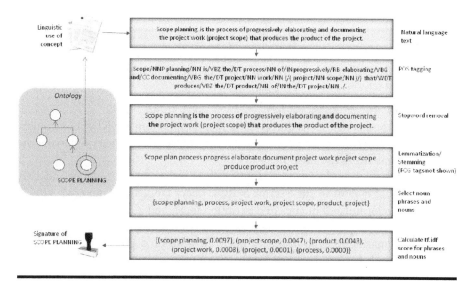

Figure 13.9 Generating the signature of SCOPE_PLANNING concept.

$$Q''' = C_i + \ldots + C_K = (t_{Qi}, \ldots, t_{Qn}).$$

Figure 13.10 demonstrates the approach with a small example. From the concept signatures, we know that the bank term is related to the FINANCIAL_BANK concept with a weight of 0.5 and to RIVER_BANK with a weight of 0.2. Since this query contains no other query terms, the term will be mapped onto FINANCIAL_BANK due to the higher weight. After the term is disambiguated in this manner and mapped onto suitable concepts, the concepts are mapped back to query terms to form a new expanded syntactic query. In the figure, the semantic query $Q' =$ (FINANCIAL_BANK) is mapped to the weighted query $Q'' =$ (bank:0.5 "banking company":0.9 "credit union":0.6).

In this way, we managed to both disambiguate the query and add other semantically related terms for better recall. The approach has the advantage of being used on top of a standard search engine that supports weighted search terms. Since it tends to add in more terms though, it tends to be better for recall than precision. Formica et al. (2008) have a similar approach, SenSim, that depends on a reference ontology with an ISA hierarchy weighted on the basis of a probability distribution. Burton-Jones et al. (2003) use hypernyms from WordNet and the DAML ontology library to expand queries. Similar strategies are used by Pinheiro et al. (2004), Revuri et al. (2006) and Rocha et al. (2004). The Inquirus2 metasearch engine expands queries with the users' information need category (Glover et al., 2001).

13.5.5 Complex Constraint Queries

Some semantic systems allow users to formulate precise semantic queries using complex semantic operators and references to ontology concepts and instances. In the SemSearch system, for example, a user may specify to which RDFS or OWL class a result should belong (Lei et al., 2006). Another example is GRQL, which allows users to build graph pattern queries by navigating the ontology graphically (Athanasis et al., 2004).

Formal constraint queries may accurately represent user information needs, though they are complex and time-consuming to formulate. Even when graphical

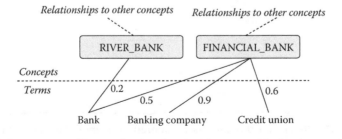

Figure 13.10   Correspondence between concepts and terms.

formalisms are used, special training is needed for users to compose such queries. Furthermore, modeling the user's information needs so accurately only makes sense if the exact content of all documents can be extracted and modeled correspondingly at indexing time.

13.6 Results

In addition to ranked lists of documents, semantic search applications may display metadata of recognized concepts in queries and result sets or provide conceptual summaries of documents or whole result sets.

13.6.1 Metadata

Many semantic search systems divide the result page into two sections: one for the standard list of ranked documents and the other for a structured list of metadata. This requires interpretation of a query as referring to a particular entity or topic that is structurally described in the ontology. The metadata section can also be used to refine the query by changing the attributes of one or more of the metadata presented.

Squirrel is an experimental search engine that uses metadata with drill-down facilities as an integral part of the result page (Duke et al., 2007). As seen from Figure 13.11, every document is displayed with relevant metadata, and important

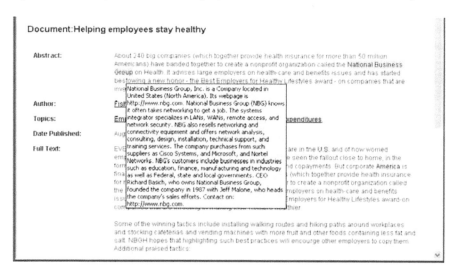

Figure 13.11   Retrieved documents presented with metadata and annotations. (*Source:* Duke, A., T. Glover, and J. Davies. In *Proceedings of Fourth European Semantic Web Conference,* Innsbruck, *2007, pp. 341–355.*)

terms of the documents are annotated with explanatory text. A related strategy in which user-centered facets are used to cluster result documents is implemented in Suominen et al. (2007).

13.6.2 Conceptual Summarization

Conceptual summarization techniques are applied to extract ontological concepts, instances, and relationships characteristic to the documents and present them as structured semantic summaries. The summaries may cover a search as a whole or each individual document in the result set. For most systems, this means presenting a list of conceptual keywords or tags. This is a text mining technique that can be done on-the-fly on the result page. However, a list of three or four keywords does not necessarily give a satisfactory summary to a domain nonexpert.

SenseBot is an example of a commercial search engine that generates tag cloud summaries of the document result set. The top part of Figure 13.12 tells us that

Figure 13.12   Result page from SenseBot (www.sensebot.net).

Eiffel Tower and Paris are the top two concepts describing the documents retrieved for query eiffel tower.

If no semantics are used, the summaries typically consist of the terms ranked on the basis of statistical scores like tf-idf. More advanced semantic approaches maintain ontologies in which each concept is given a vector representation, like the scope-planning concept signature in Figure 13.8 or the centroid representation used in the Rocchio text classification technique. Conceptual summarization is the process of categorizing text with respect to the concepts in the ontology using standard categorization techniques like Rocchio, k nearest neighbor, and naive Bayes (Manning et al., 2008). With the Rocchio approach, we build a centroid vector for each concept of the ontology. This centroid, A_C, is the vector average or center of mass of documents that were manually determined earlier to describe the concept:

$$A_c = \frac{1}{|D_C|} \sum_{d \in D_C} V(d)$$

where D_C is the set of documents describing concept C, and $V(d)$ is the normalized vector representation of document d in D_C. A document or document set is represented by a vector R. The conceptual summary of the document (set) is given by the ranked list of concepts C_i that has a cosine similarity with R above a certain threshold α:

$$\text{similarity}(R, A_{C_i}) = \cos(\theta) > \alpha$$

In Figure 13.12, the document set retrieved for the Eiffel Tower query shows the highest cosine similarity with the Eiffel Tower, Paris, city, construction, and restaurant ontology concepts.

13.7 Navigation

Several search applications add navigational features to result pages for easy selection of the most interesting parts of a result set.

13.7.1 Hierarchical Refinement

A search application may suggest generalizing or specializing a query by providing concept names that are hierarchically related to the concepts identified in the query. The strategy is basically similar to automatic query specialization except that the user is left to choose. The functionality is supported by several systems (Duke et al.,

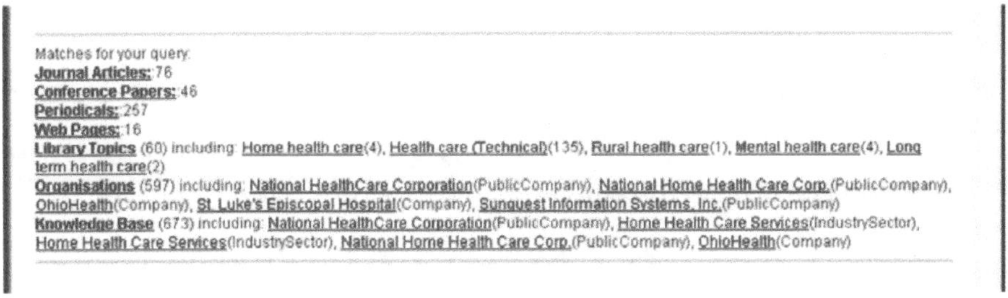

Matches for your query:
Journal Articles: 76
Conference Papers: 46
Periodicals: 257
Web Pages: 16
Library Topics (60) including: Home health care(4), Health care (Technical)(135), Rural health care(1), Mental health care(4), Long term health care(2)
Organisations (597) including: National HealthCare Corporation(PublicCompany), National Home Health Care Corp.(PublicCompany), OhioHealth(Company), St. Luke's Episcopal Hospital(Company), Sunquest Information Systems, Inc.(PublicCompany)
Knowledge Base (673) including: National HealthCare Corporation(PublicCompany), Home Health Care Services(IndustrySector), Home Health Care Services(IndustrySector), National Home Health Care Corp.(PublicCompany), OhioHealth(Company)

Figure 13.13   Links for drilling into search result set in Squirrel.

2007; García et al., 2003; Moench et al., 2003), and they usually use standardized taxonomies to provide drill-down functionality on the result page. The hierarchical links shown in Figure 13.13 for Squirrel are semantic categories used to classify the documents at index time.

13.7.2 Faceted Search

In faceted search applications, we use multiple classification schemes to describe a range of document dimensions. The method provides a more fine-grained description than those offered by taxonomies, although the same dimensions can also be modeled within extensive ontologies. Normally, the relevant facets are derived from an analysis of the document text, so that aggregated views of these facets are available when the documents are retrieved and presented as the result set to a query.

Figure 13.14 illustrates some of the facets used to describe document result sets in Endeca's topic search. The initial result set is listed at right and the user is encouraged to drill into the result set using the facets listed at left. Choosing for example, *futures trading* in *organization* and the Beverly Hills location, the system will display only documents that satisfy the query and deal with futures trading and Beverly Hills. Ben-Yitzhak et al. (2008) present an extended faceted search application in which business intelligence features are added to the standard drill-down functions of faceted search. Another system from Hyvönen et al. (2003) builds facets from ontology concepts and combines them with recommendation functionality.

13.7.3 Ontology Rules and Navigators

In the SmartSearch project of Deutsche Telekom Laboratories (Burkhardt et al, 2008), a technique similar to faceted search is used to interpret and refine posted search queries. Within a limited domain, so-called navigators offer drill-down functionality based on ontological category classification. Figure 13.15 shows the results from posting a *new bruce willis* query. In the standard ranked list of documents

Figure 13.14 Faceted search with Endeca (www.endeca.com).

Figure 13.15 Navigational search with SmartSearch.

under *pages*, several recent movies starring Bruce Willis are listed in the *movie* navigator on the left side. An internal rule system uses a movie ontology to match *bruce willis* to an instance of the *actor* concept and *new* to movies that are less than 5 years old. If a user clicks on the *Live Free or Die Hard* link under *movies*, the output displayed in Figure 13.16 appears. The result page now consists of documents referring to this particular movie, while the navigators extend to movies that are similar (based on a tf-idf ranking)—actors who appear in the movie and companies connected to it. Again, this technique is based on a navigational rule that connects

Figure 13.16   Navigational search with SmartSearch.

instances of movies to similar movies, actors, and companies. With the help of navigators, the user is assisted in exploratory search (the user may have only a vague idea of his needs and the target documents are not known).

The navigational rules state which information from the ontology should be used to interpret queries, retrieve relevant information from the ontology, and construct drill-down semantic navigators. For example, the system retrieves *The Untouchables* movie to respond to a *james bond mafia movies* query because the ontology determines that this movie deals with the mafia and includes Sean Connery, an actor who played James Bond. In a search for *Brangelina movies*, the system presents the *Mr. and Mrs. Smith* movie because the main characters are played by Brad Pitt and Angelina Jolie and the ontology defines *Brangelina* as this group of two actors. To date, these rules have been manually crafted and are domain-specific—sufficient for the concrete task of creating a flexible and intelligent movie search interface. Whether it will be possible to partially automate the generation of such rules for this and other domains remains to be seen.

13.8 Temporal Aspects of Search

Normally, search applications assume that documents are time-independent and express content that is meaningful and valid over time. Users do not normally worry about dates of documents. In some cases, though, dates may severely affect document retrieval and ranking; for example, a user is seeking only published information or information from particular time periods, or a user may post queries that make use of terms that are not used at the time of publication, even though the document content is relevant to the query.

One observation with ranking based on cosine similarity and PageRank is that older documents tend to receive higher scores than newer ones. Since older documents are more likely to be known to a large community, often more links lead to them, giving them a higher PageRank and thereby higher relevance score than recently published documents. For developing domains like scientific disciplines in which new information tends to be more reliable and relevant than old information, this effect of PageRank may be unfortunate. Yu et al. (2004) present a timed page rank score TPR that boosts documents that have been recently published:

$$TPR(A) = Aging(A) * PR^T(A)$$

$$PR^T(A) = (1 - d) + d * \left(\frac{w_1 * PR^T(p_1)}{C(p_1)} + \cdots + \frac{w_n * PR^T(p_n)}{C(p_n)} \right)$$

where $PR^T(A)$ is the time-weighted PageRank score of paper A, $PR^T(p_i)$ is the time-weighted PageRank score of paper p_i that links to paper A, $C(p_i)$ is the number of outbound links of paper p_i, and d is a dampening factor set to 0.85. A time weight, w_i, has a value that reduces exponentially with citation age. Aging(A) is an aging factor for paper A set to 1 for brand new papers, and which declines linearly with time down to 0.5. Initial experiments with papers about particle physics suggest that the new score better reflects the relevance of new papers and better captures the likelihood that later papers include citations to them.

More generally, a user may want to retrieve documents from particular time periods. Systems like GEIN support this by storing temporal data as part of the metadata of documents (see Figure 13.17). Every document or catalog item in GEIN is associated with a number of valid time periods, a number of semantic categories, a number of geographical locations, and a specific item class (Tochtermann et al., 1997). When searching for information sources, a user may add a temporal restriction to the query that specifies the relevant period, e.g., all documents about emission levels in Munich from 1990 to 1995. Grandi et al. (2005) developed a similar approach, but included a more fine-grained temporal system with attributes for validity time, efficacy time, transaction time, and publication time.

If a document date is not known, it may be feasible to estimate it using temporal mining or information extraction. Statistical techniques for estimating dates of documents were suggested by Kanhabua and Nørvåg (2009) and deJong et al. (2005). These methods rely on extensive training data and are suitable for documents that contain no direct or indirect time indications. Sometimes temporal phrases in

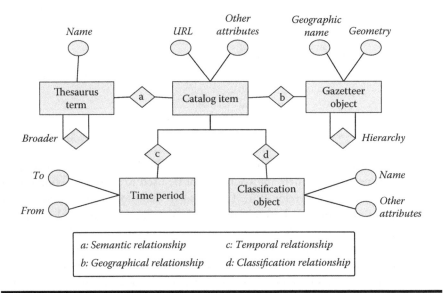

Figure 13.17 **Valid time periods associated with documents (catalog items) in GEIN.**

documents can be extracted and interpreted with appropriate information extraction techniques. Kalczynski and Chou (2005) define a t-zoidal fuzzy time representation that can model both direct time stamps such as 1990 and temporal content of phrases (last month, several days ago). By adding the fuzzy time representations of every time reference extracted from a document, the system can compute a tf-idf-like score for every calendar date relevant to the document. A query is assumed to contain an exact date and the system will calculate date similarities between the query and all documents following a standard cosine similarity. Unlike temporal mining, the fuzzy approach allows every document to be relevant to different time periods with different weights. If no proper time indication is cited in the text, however, the approach will fail and temporal mining will be the only option.

The examples above assume that the terminology relevant to queries does not change over time. The same query terms would be used for retrieving information about the same topic at different time points, independently of any terminological changes in the domain. Obviously, this is a simplification that is not satisfactory for searches of evolving or unstable domains. For example, using *Berlin* as a search term to look for information about the capital of Germany in the 1970s would not work because Bonn was the capital of West Germany until reunification in 1990.

With the ontologies at hand, we can model the validity of terminology over time. In Eder and Koncilia's approach (2004), every concept is modeled in OWL and, when necessary, associated with a start date and/or end date. The OWL specification below shows how they model the fact that class DegreeCourseSchema is a valid concept from 1 January 1990:

```
<owl:Class rdf:ID="DegreeCourseSchema">
     <rdfs:subClassOf>
          <owl:Restriction>
               <owl:onProperty rdf:resource="#vtStart"/>
               <owl:hasValue rdf:datatype="&xsd;date">
               1990-01-01
               </owl:hasValue>
          </owl:Restriction>
          . . .
```

Since OWL does not allow such time stamps to be added to relations (data properties or object properties), their approach cannot be used to model evolving ontologies in general. Van Atteveldt et al. (2008) solve this problem by modeling all properties as time-stamped classes, leading to an ontology that is problematic for reasoning and structural clarity. A more conventional approach would be to model the time-stamped structure as a separate metamodel or temporal ontology structure from which snapshot ontologies for particular time periods may be extracted.

A concept is normally understood with reference to a *term*, an *intension*, and an *extension*. The term, also known as a *symbol* or *signifier*, is a word used in the real world to refer to the concept. The intension, often called *reference* or *signified*, is the meaning or sense of the concept, and the extension or *referent* is the set of real-world objects to which the concept applies. Whereas the intension of *car* is our understanding of the concept, the extension is the set of all imaginable and unimaginable cars. Generally, terminological changes fall into three distinct categories (see Figure 13.18).

Change of term—A particular term is gradually replaced by another term that has the same basic meaning. We consider them synonyms, even though they tend to be used in slightly different periods. Although we prefer the *car* term to *automobiles*, the *automobiles* term was used originally for this concept. In an

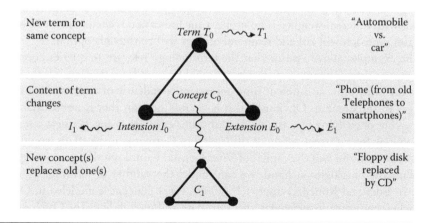

Figure 13.18   Terminological changes over time.

ontology, these variants are modeled as time-stamped synonyms or term variants of classes.

Change of term content—A concept may change semantically, even though the term referring to the concept stays the same. Both its intension and extension may be affected by this change, which is often the result of new technology or of deeper insight into the matter. The *phone* term has been used for more than 100 years but our understanding of phones and their relationships to other concepts have changed significantly. Ontologically, OWL properties and subclass structures must be modeled as time-dependent.

Change of concept—The most fundamental change appears when some concepts go out of fashion and other related ones gradually take their places. There need not be a 1:1 correspondence between the concepts, and they usually differ somewhat in terms, intensions, and extensions. An example is the replacement of floppy disks by CDs for the common purpose of storing computer data. In the ontology, floppy disks and CDs have separate structures, but the structures will show certain functional commonalities.

For a semantic search application, it is not sufficient to know whether certain concepts are relevant at a particular time. The need is to know how concepts evolve and relate to new concepts over time, allowing us to translate the original search terms into terms more useful for the desired period. Conceptually, searches in evolving domains involve three basic steps:

1. *Query disambiguation with respect to user's intended time frame $[t0', t0'']$. This step makes use of a snapshot of the ontology and is similar to semantic disambiguation discussed above.*
2. *Time-dependent query mapping. The original query is translated into a set of time-dependent queries that for each time period is the best semantic replication of the original query.*
3. *Semantic search within time periods. Each time period can be compared to a separate language in a multilingual search application. The time-dependent queries can be dealt with using the semantic approaches above and snapshot ontologies for the indicated time periods.*

The critical part of the search process is the temporal mapping of queries. Given a query Q_0 for time period $[t_0', t_0'']$, the system needs to propose a set of new queries, $Q_1[t_1', t_1''] \dots, Q_n[t_n', t_n'']$, in which the aggregate of these time periods corresponds to the original time period $[t_0', t_0'']$, and each Q_i is the query semantically most similar to Q_0 for the period indicated. Q_0 contains terms referring to concepts at the user's reference time. In Q_i, concepts C_0 in Q_0 that are not relevant in $[t_i', t_i'']$ are replaced with semantically close and time-relevant concept(s) C_i. This includes access to C_i's properties and structures for semantic query processing. In case only the reference T_0 is irrelevant and the underlying concept is valid, T_0 is replaced with time-relevant T_i as a reference to C_0 in the query.

Translating a query Q_0 to time-relevant queries $Q_1, \ldots Q_n$ requires that all ontology elements be time stamped, and relevant semantic links between time periods, be established for related concepts and terms. This calls for new approaches to ontology evolution and management that enable us to produce snapshot ontologies for particular points of time and represent the semantic relationships between these ontologies. Due to the complexities of such approaches, evolving ontologies have so far not been exploited in semantic search applications.

13.9 Conclusions

Semantic search applications are based on the same general search architecture found in popular web search engines like Google and Yahoo! Some research prototypes employ only semantic components; most systems adopt semantic approaches only for parts of their architectures and combine them with a standard syntactic search machinery. Certain systems use semantic indices instead of traditional inverted files, these include: systems that define semantic query languages or map standard queries to semantic representations, systems that present results in terms of semantic structures and summaries, and systems that offer semantic navigation of result sets. Often the semantic part is realized as a semantic layer on top of a conventional search engine core.

To be classified as a semantic search application, a system must provide an explicit semantic representation of categories, words, or texts. Early semantic applications often defined their own formal languages for this purpose. Current research emphasizes the use of standard semantic ontology languages like RDF(S) and OWL. Although ontologies have proven useful in semantic search applications, we also see their limitations for temporal searches or searches in terminologically unstable domains. To date, we have no standardized approach to modeling terminological changes in ontologies, and this complicates their use in domains with evolving terminologies.

In recent years, we witnessed a number of new commercial search applications that claim to offer semantic search functionality. These include Hakia, SenseBot, Powerset, DeepDyve, Cognition, and Kosmix, among others. While their approaches vary, they tend to rely on statistical NLP and limited use of semantic lexical resources. Few attempts have been made to define domain knowledge or ontologies, and we have omitted these systems from our analysis of semantic search applications.

A particular case that was not analyzed in this chapter is the Swoogle semantic search engine that retrieves and even reasons about formal semantic representations. Swoogle, however, is not a general purpose search application and is restricted to retrieving ontologies or files with embedded RDF content on the Internet. Since Swoogle cannot deal with documents that are not defined semantically in the first place, it does not help us organize and manage the vast amounts of information already available on the Internet or in enterprises. Semantic document structures are also assumed by the OWLIR system in Shah et al. (2002).

In spite of all these commercial systems, we see few real semantic search applications in the marketplace. The scalability problems of ontology-driven applications may partly explain the current lack of commercial systems. The most successful applications are built on top of standard search engines to take advantage of well tested and scalable search architectures. However, certain other concerns must be addressed in more detail for semantic search applications to become more widely used. As semantic search applications rest on semantic domain representations like ontologies and taxonomies, it is often difficult and/or expensive to employ the applications in new domains. Ontology engineering is tedious and costly, and very few freely available ontologies can be plugged into general semantic search applications. Also, the usability of many semantic search applications has not been given enough attention, and many applications require users to have intimate knowledge of various formal representation languages. When these issues have been appropriately resolved, we may see more search applications that truly allow computers to store, retrieve, and understand information the way humans would.

References

Amaral, C. et al. Design and implementation of a semantic search engine for Portuguese. In *Proceedings of Fourth International Conference on Language Resources and Evaluation,* Lisbon, 2004, pp. 247–250.

Anyanwu, K., A. Maduko, and A. Sheth. SemRank: Ranking complex relationship search results on the semantic web. In *Proceedings of 14th International Conference on World Wide Web,* Chiba, Japan, 2005, ACM Press, pp. 117–127.

Athanasis, N., V. Christophides, and D. Kotzinos. Generating on-the-fly queries for the semantic web: ICS-FORTH graphical RQL interface (GRQL). In *Proceedings of Third International Semantic Web Conference,* Hiroshima, 2004, pp. 486–501.

Ben-Yitzhak, O., N. Golbandi, N. Har'El, et al. Beyond basic faceted search. In *Proceedings of International Conference on Web Search and Web Data Mining,* Palo Alto, CA, 2008, pp. 33–44.

Berners-Lee, T. et al. Tabulator: Exploring and analyzing linked data on the Semantic Web. In *Proceedings of Third International Semantic Web User Interaction Workshop,* Athens, GA, 2006.

Bernstein, A. et al., Ginseng: A guided input natural language search engine for querying ontologies. In *Proceedings of JENA User Conference,* Bristol, UK, 2006.

Bonino, D., F. Corno, and L. Farinetti. DOSE: A distributed open semantic elaboration platform. In *Proceedings of 15th IEEE International Conference on Tools with Artificial Intelligence,* Sacramento, CA, 2003.

Bonino, D. et al. Ontology-driven semantic search. *WSEAS Transactions on Information Science and Applications, 1*: 1597–1605, 2004.

Budanitsky, A. and G. Hirst. Evaluating WordNet-based measures of lexical semantic relatedness. *Computational Linguistics, 32*: 13–47, 2006.

Burkhardt, F., J.A. Gulla, J. Liu, et al. Semi automatic ontology engineering in business applications. In *Proceedings of Workshop on Applications of Semantic Technologies,* 2008.

Burton-Jones, A. et al. A heuristic-based methodology for semantic augmentation of user queries on the Web. In *Proceedings of 22nd International Conference on Conceptual Modeling,* Chicago, 2003, pp. 476–489.

Calvanese, D. et al. What to ask a peer: Ontology-based query reformulation. In *Proceedings of Ninth International Conference on Principles of Knowledge Representation and Reasoning,* Whistler, BC, 2004, AAAI Press, pp. 469–478.

Celino, I. et al. Squiggle: A semantic search engine for indexing and retrieval of multimedia content. In *Proceedings of First International Workshop on Semantic-Enhanced Multimedia Presentation Systems,* Athens, 2006, pp. 20–34.

Cohen, S. et al. XSEarch: A semantic search engine for XML. In *Proceedings of 29th International Conference on Very Large Data Bases,* Berlin, 2003, pp. 45–56.

Davies, J., R. Weeks, and U. Krohn. QuizRDF: Search technology for the Semantic Web. In *Proceedings of 37th International Conference on System Sciences,* Hawaii, IEEE Computer Society, 2004.

Duke, A., T. Glover, and J. Davies. Squirrel: An advanced semantic search and browse facility. In *Proceedings of Fourth European Semantic Web Conference,* Innsbruck, 2007, pp. 341–355.

Eder, J. and C. Koncilia. Modelling changes in ontologies. *On the Move to Meaningful Internet Systems Workshops,* Lecture Notes in Computer Science Series 3292, 2004, pp. 662–673.

Fang, W.D. et al. Toward a semantic search engine based on ontologies. In *Proceedings of International Conference on Machine Learning and Cybernetics,* 2005.

Finin, T. et al. Information retrieval and the Semantic Web. In *Proceedings of 38th Annual International Conference on System Sciences,* Hawaii, 2005, IEEE Computer Society.

Formica, A., M. Missikoff, E. Pourabbas, et al. Weighted ontology for semantic search. *OTM Conferences, 2:* 1289–1303, 2008.

García, E. and M.Á. Sicilia. Designing ontology-based interactive information retrieval interfaces. In *Proceedings of Workshop on Human Computer Interface for Semantic Web and Web Applications,* Lecture Notes in Computer Science 2889, 2003, pp 152–165.

Glover, E.J. et al. Web search your way. *Communications of ACM, 44:* 97–102, 2001.

Grandi, F., F. Mandreoli, R. Martoglia, et al. Enhanced access to e-government services: temporal and semantics-aware retrieval of norms. In *Semantic Web Applications and Perspectives: Proceedings of Second Italian Semantic Web Workshop,* University of Trento, Trento, Italy, December 2005.

Guarino, N., C. Masolo, and G. Vetere. OntoSeek: Content-based access to the Web. *IEEE Intelligent Systems, 14:* 70–80, 1999.

Guha, R., R. McCool, and E. Miller. Semantic search. In *Proceedings of Twelfth International Conference on World Wide Web,* Budapest, 2003.

Guo, L., F. Shao, C. Botev, et al. XRANK: Ranked keyword search over XML documents. *SIGMOD,* 2003.

Heflin, J. and J. Hendler. Searching the web with SHOE. In *Artificial Intelligence for Web Search: Papers from AAAI Workshop,* 2000, AAAI Press. pp. 35–40.

Hildebrand, M., J. von Ossenbruggen, and L. Hardman. An analysis of search-based user interaction on the Semantic Web. *INS-E0706,* 2007.

Hogan, A., A. Harth, and S. Decker, ReConRank: A scalable ranking method for semantic web data with context. In *Proceedings of Second Workshop on Scalable Semantic Web Knowledge-Based Systems,* 2006.

Hyvönen, E. and E. Mäkelä. Semantic autocompletion. In *Proceedings of First Asia Semantic Web Conference*, Beijing, 2006.

Hyvönen, E., S. Saarela, and K. Viljanen. Ontogator: Combining view- and ontology-based search with semantic browsing. In *Proceedings of XML Finland: Open Standards, XML, and the Public Sector*, Kuopio, Finland, 2003.

deJong, F., H. Rode, and D. Hiemstra. Temporal language models for the disclosure of historical text. In *Proceedings of AHC*, 2005.

Kalczynski, P.J. and A. Chou. Temporal document retrieval model for business news archives. *Information Processing and Management*. 41: 635–650. 2005.

Kanhabua, N. and K. Nørvåg. Using temporal language models for document dating. *ECML/PKDD, 2*: 738–741, 2009.

Kiryakov, A. et al. Semantic annotation, indexing, and retrieval. *Journal of Web Semantics, 2*: 49–79, 2004.

Kleinberg, J.M. Authoritative sources in a hyperlinked environment. *Journal of ACM, 48*: 604–632, 1999.

Kumar, R. and A. Tomkins. A characterization of online search behavior. *IEEE Data Engineering Bulletin, 32*: 3–11, 2009.

Lei, Y., V. Uren, and E. Motta. SemSearch: Search engine for the semantic web. In *Proceedings of 15th International Conference on Knowledge Engineering and Knowledge Management*, Poedbrady, Czech Republic, 2006.

Li, D. et al. Swoogle: A search and metadata engine for the semantic web. In *Proceedings of 13th ACM International Conference on Information and Knowledge Management*. Washington, 2004, pp. 652–659.

Mäkelä, E. Survey of semantic search research. In *Proceedings of Seminar on Knowledge Management on Semantic Web*, University of Helsinki, 2005.

Mangold, C. A survey and classification of semantic search approaches. *International Journal of Metadata, Semantics and Ontology, 2*, 2007.

Manning, C.D., P. Raghavan, and H. Schütze. *Introduction to Information Retrieval*, Cambridge University Press. 2008.

Miller, G.A. WordNet: A lexical database for English. *Communications of ACM, 38*: 39–41, 1995.

Moench, E. et al. SemanticMiner: Ontology-based knowledge retrieval. *Journal of Universal Computer Science, 9*: 682–696, 2003.

Page, L., S. Brin, R. Motowani, et al. PageRank citation ranking: Bringing order to the web. Stanford Digital Library working paper 0072, 1997.

Pinheiro, W.A. and A.M.d.C. Moura. An ontology based-approach for semantic search in portals. In *Proceedings of 15th International Workshop on Database and Expert Systems Applications*, IEEE Computer Society, 2004.

Revuri, S., S.R. Upadhyaya, and P.S. Kumar. Using domain ontologies for efficient information retrieval. In *Proceedings of 13th International Conference on Management of Data*, Delhi, 2006, pp. 170–173.

Rocha, C., D. Schwabe, and M.P.d. Aragão. A hybrid approach for searching the semantic web. In *Proceedings of Thirteenth International Conference on World Wide Web*, New York, 2004, pp. 374–383.

Shah, U. et al. Information retrieval on the semantic web. In *Proceedings of 11th International Conference on Information and Knowledge Management*, 2002, ACM Press, pp. 461–468.

Solskinnsbakk, G., and J.A. Gulla: Ontological profiles in enterprise search. In *Proceedings of 16th International Conference on Knowledge Engineering and Knowledge Management*, Acitrezza, Italy, 2008.

Stojanovic, N. On analysing query ambiguity for query refinement: The librarian agent approach. In *Proceedings 22nd International Conference on Conceptual Modeling*, Chicago, 2003, pp. 490–505.

Suominen, O., K. Viljanen, and E. Hyvönen. User-centric faceted search for semantic portals. In *Proceedings of European Semantic Web Conference*, Innsbruck, 2007.

Tochtermann, K., W.F. Riekert, G. Wiest, et al. Using semantic, geographical, and temporal relationships to enhance search and retrieval in digital catalogs. In *Proceedings of First European Conference on Research and Advanced Technology for Digital Libraries*, Pisa, September 1997.

Tran, D.T. et al. Ontology-based Interpretation of keywords for semantic search. In *Proceedings of Sixth International Semantic Web Conference and Second Asian Semantic Web Conference*, Busan, Korea, 2007, pp. 523–536.

Van Atteveldt, W., N. Ruigrok, S. Schlobach, et al. Searching the news using a rich ontology with time-bound roles to search through annotated newspaper archives. In *Proceedings of 58th Annual Conference of International Communication Association*, Montreal, 2008.

Yu, P.S., X. Li, and B. Liu. On the temporal dimension of search. In *Proceedings of 13th International World Wide Web Conference on Alternate Track Papers and Posters*, New York, 2004, pp. 448–449.

Zhou, Q. et al. SPARK: Adapting keyword query to semantic search In *Proceedings of Sixth International Semantic Web Conference and Second Asian Semantic Web Conference*, Busan, Korea, 2007, pp. 687–700.

Chapter 14

Toward Semantics-Based Service Composition in Transport Logistics

Joerg Leukel and Stefan Kirn

Universität Hohenheim, Stuttgart, Germany

Contents

14.1 Introduction

Logistics is a domain concerned with controlling and executing the flow of goods, services, and associated information from sources to destinations, e.g., from manufacturing site to point of sale. It can be characterized by multiple firms providing resources and services or delivering complex services to meet customer requirements. The need for coordination across firms is obvious, since few single firms deliver an entire product or service without contractors because they face division of labor for basic logistics services, increasing customer requirements that lead to greater specialization, and supply chain management (SCM).

The task of a *logistics system* is to transform goods with regard to location, time, and quantity. These transformations materialize into the concept of logistics service—a logical set of transformations. Logistics services are offered by firms such as shippers, packers, warehouses, and firms that provide more complex services. In this sense, a logistics system provides capabilities to deliver services to customers but does not define a priori the ways to implement the services.

The *problem* with logistics systems is finding the best solution for a given set of customer requirements. We will define this problem as a subclass of service composition, thus combining and linking services. The result is a composite logistics service. Composition has two dimensions: hierarchy (*part-of* relationships between services) and sequence (logical order of services). In prior research, we studied the mapping of logistics services to models, methods, and technologies of Web Service research (Karaenke and Kirn 2009) in particular, by employing languages for describing service level agreements (SLAs) formally defining obligations and guarantees in a service relationship.

We address the composition problem from the *perspective of interoperability*; hence, we aim to make the semantics of all relevant parts of logistics systems explicit, machine-readable, and exchangeable. Such a semantic description is based on the annotation principle, as adopted in Semantic Web services (Martin et al., 2007) by which service providers maintain their local descriptions while annotating them according to a shared conceptualization (ontology). We think that this approach is feasible in specific environments, such as regional logistics networks of shippers. We limit the scope to transport logistics and thus transport services.

Current representations of such services are not semantic. They can be found in intra-organizational information systems such as ERP and inter-organizational information systems such as logistics marketplaces and SCM. We enrich these representations by using description logic (DL) that allows for reasoning about customer requirements and answering more expressive queries during service discovery and composition. These are key features, because customer requirements are often expressed in an abstract form—searching for transportation of hazardous goods without specifying vehicle types and load-securing measures.

The objectives of this chapter are to (1) develop a semantic model for transport services and (2) apply the model to a use case scenario to demonstrate its feasibility and usefulness. The next section defines the basic assumptions relevant to the domain and problem. After that, we present our semantic model, followed by a section on preliminary validation and discussion. We also review related work and finally draw conclusions and outline avenues of future research.

14.2 Basic Assumptions

This section defines the basic terms and formalisms for logistics systems, transport services, and composite transport services.

14.2.1 Logistics System

Definition 1: A logistics system consists of nodes participating in transforming goods with regard to location, time, and quantity. The inter-relations between nodes are constituted by the possible flow of goods (e.g., modes of transportation). Nodes represent the storage of goods at locations such as warehouses. A logistics system model is represented by a directed graph $LS = (N, F)$, where N is the set of all nodes and F is the set of all possible flows of goods with $F \subseteq N \times N \times TM \times TU$. Each f is a four-tuple, $f = (n_j, n_k, tm, tu)$, with flow from n_j to n_k using a transportation means $tm \in TM$ (e.g., truck) and transport unit $tu \in TU$ (e.g., container). The following integrity constraints must hold:

Let $\bullet n = \{m | (m,n) \in F\}$, hence the set of input nodes of n; then at least one $n \in N$ exists with $|\bullet n| = 0$. Thus, at least one node has no incoming flows, i.e., representing origin of goods.

Let $n \bullet = \{m | (n,m) \in F\}$, hence the set of output nodes of n; then at least one $n \in N$ exists with $|n \bullet| = 0$. Thus, a least one node has no outgoing flows, i.e., representing final destination of goods.

For all $n \in N$: $|n \bullet| + |\bullet n| \geq 1$. Thus, the graph LS is (weakly) connected.

14.2.2 Transport Service

Definition 2: A transport service is a possible service flow from a logistics service provider to a logistics service consumer. The set of all such services forms a transport service flow model, which is a directed graph $SF = (A, S, M)$. A is the set of all actors. S is the set of all possible elementary service flows. Each $s \in S$ is a tuple

$s = (a_j, a_k)$, with service flow from a_j to a_k. M is a relation that maps each s to one or more f in LS. Thus each service flow s relates to $|M(s)|$ flows of goods in L. The following integrity constraints must hold:

Let $\bullet a = \{b|(b,a) \in S\}$, then at least one $a \in A$ exists with $|\bullet a| = 0$, i.e., actor that is not a logistics service requester.

Let $a\bullet = \{b|(a,b) \in S\}$, then at least one $a \in A$ exists with $|a\bullet| = 0$, i.e., actor that is not a logistics service provider.

SF is (weakly) connected.

For any s, if $|M(s)| \geq 2$, then $t = |M(s)|$, and there must exist a walk w_s in LS with $w_s (n_i, m_1, ..., m_t, n_j)$ and $n_i, n_j \in N$.

14.2.3 Composite Transport Service

Definition 3: A composite transport service is a composition of two or more transport services in SF. It is defined as a four-tuple $cs = (a_j, a_k, CE, WF)$. The composite service is offered by actor $a_j \in A$ to actor $a_k \in A$. CE denotes the composition elements. WF denotes the workflow, i.e., logical sequence of all $ce \in CE$. The following integrity constraints must hold:

Let CS be the set of all composite services. A composite service cs may contain elementary and other composite services, i.e., $\forall cs_i: CE \subseteq S^* \cup CS\backslash cs_i$. WF describes a directed tree (A', S') with $A' \subseteq A, S' \subseteq S$.

Figure 14.1 illustrates the inter-relationships of these formalisms: LS represents a two-stage logistics system with transportation of goods from three sources via a

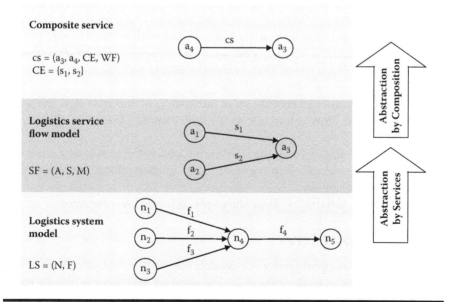

Figure 14.1 Examples of logistics system, service flow, and composite service.

hub (n_4) to the final destination (n_5). There are two service providers: a_1 offering transportation from sources to the hub and a_2 offering transportation to the destination site; these services are consumed by a_3. In addition, the actor a_4 is a so-called third party logistics provider (3PL) offering a composite service combining both services, and therefore covers all transportation relationships in *LS*.

14.3 Semantic Model for Service Composition

This section develops the semantic model for transport services. It augments the logistics system and service flow model with additional formal semantics of each element and discusses classifications and constraints of each element. A semantic description may be grounded on respective domain ontologies, but viable ontologies for logistics do not provide explicit, formal, and machine-readable representation (Leukel and Kirn 2008). Therefore, we provide a core conceptualization of the domain based on logistics systems and SCM theory (Storey et al. 2006). We define the semantics using the SHOIN description logic due to its expressiveness (Baader et al. 2007); SHOIN is also the underlying logic of the OWL DL Web ontology language (W3C 2004).

14.3.1 Semantics of Logistics System

14.3.2 Semantics of Nodes (N)

The informal meaning is that each node represents a physical location where goods can be stored for a limited time. The nodes can be classified by several methods.

Geographical–political classification—One can adopt ISO 3166 defining standard codes for all country names (ISO 2010). However, this classification is flat, with disjunction of all classes as the only semantics. Thus, we define a functional role *(N, Country):locatedIn* with $T \sqsubseteq 1locatedIn$ and add assertions for all ISO countries by respective individual, e.g., *{CAN}:Country* for Canada, *{FRA}:Country* for France, etc., with *{CAN}* $\sqsubseteq$ *{FRA}*, etc. The decision to choose individuals over subconcepts is made because each country exists only once (e.g., there is no instance of a *Sweden* concept). We could also incorporate additional information about countries into the ontology by adding roles and making assertions about those individuals.

Geographical–logistics classification—The United Nations Code for Trade and Transport Locations (UN/LOCODE) is a classification specifically designed for the domain (UNECE 2010). It (1) adds a second level to ISO 3166 consisting of about 42,000 locations, (2) defines the logistics functions of each location (port, rail terminal, road terminal, airport, postal exchange office, intermodal transfer, border crossing), and (3) gives the respective geographical coordinates.

With regard to (1), we add a *Location* ⊑ *Country* subconcept, enumerate its members, e.g., *{MRN}:Location*, and then link each location to one country, thus by a functional role *(Location,Country):belongsTo,* then *({MRN},{CAN}):belongsTo* as an example. With regard to (2), functions are expressed by a role *(Location,Function): hasFunction*. Membership in *Function* is restricted by *Function* ⊑ *{Port}*⊔*{RailTe rmin}*...⊔*{BorderCrossing}*, and all locations are related to at least one function, e.g., *({MRN},{Port}:hasFunction*. With regard to (3), a functional role *(Location,C oordinate):hasCoordinate* with $T ⊑ 1hasCoordinate$ is needed, which is then used to give the coordinate of each location, e.g., *({MRN},{4535N07337}):hasCoordina te*. UN/LOCODE's locations and logistics functions are modeled as individuals, because they exist only once and an instantiation of respective concepts would be redundant.

   Other classifications—Locations may also be classified according to other criteria such as physical infrastructure (e.g., type of warehouse), more precise geographical details (e.g., firm-specific organization of sites and warehouses), types of goods that can be stored, or quantities (e.g., maximum inbound volume per time period). If two or more locations represent an aggregated location, an enumerated subconcept covering aggregation is defined; e.g., *Scandinavia* ⊑ *Location* ⊓ *({DNK}* ⊔ *{NOR}* ⊔*{SWE}* ⊔*{FIN})*.

14.3.2.1 Semantics of Flows (F)

A flow arises from forwarding goods from source to destination; hence each $f ∈ F$ asserts two functional roles: *(F,N):hasSource* with *({f},{n_j}):hasSource* and *(F,N):hasDestination* with *({f},{n_k}):hasDestination*. More precisely, a flow contains a number of transport units. For the former, we define a functional role *(F,Capacity):hasCapacity*. The latter is already part of the four-tuple *f*, but must be further specified (see 14.2.2.1.4 below).

14.3.2.2 Semantics of Transportation Means

The transportation means constitute the vehicles or infrastructures used for transportation; hence the functional role *(F,TM):usesMean*. A very basic classification is the UN/CEFACT Recommendation 19 (Code for Modes of Transport) (UN/ CEFACT 2010) that defines eight modes. We adopt it by defining a functional role *(TM,Mode):hasMode* and listing all individuals by *Mode* ⊑ *{Rail}*⊔...⊔*{Road}*. The decision for individuals is made because each mode exists only once, e.g., a mode cannot be instantiated.

14.3.2.3 Semantics of Transport Units (TUs)

A transport unit is an item to be transported; hence role *(F,TU):transports*. This item has its own structure forming a hierarchy of load units, e.g., pallet → case →

bottle → sparkling water. Thus, we extend *TU* by the *Object* ⊑ *TU* subconcept and a transitive role *(Object,Object):containsObject*, e.g., *({MyEuroPalette},{MyCoveringB ox}):containsObject* with {MyEuroPalette}:Object and *{MyCoveringBox}:Object*. For classifying such objects, we consider two approaches: (1) defining categories of load units; (2) defining categories of goods.

The former is subject of the UN/CEFACT Recommendation 21 (Codes for Passengers, Types of Cargo, Packages and Packaging Materials) (UN/CEFACT 2010); we adopt it by making *Object* a subconcept of load unit (*Object* ⊑ *LoadUnit*) and adding further subconcepts, e.g., DM ⊑ *LoadUnit* (for crate, bulk, plastic), MC ⊑ *LoadUnit* (for crate, milk), etc., with DM ⊑ MC, etc. The decision to use subconcepts arises from the need to capture individuals, e.g., pallets belonging to the same pallet concept but identified to define returns of used pallets.

The latter is subject of categorization standards for goods (UNSPSC 2010; eCl@ss 2010). Basically, such standards build a classification hierarchy and to an extent enrich the categories with properties describing instances. This area attracted semantic web researchers early, and led to RDF Schema and OWL-based representations (also known as product ontology), respectively (Klein 2002; Hepp 2006). Such ontologies can be easily incorporated into our semantic model by making *Object* a subconcept of the *Product* root concept of the product ontology, e.g., *Object* ⊑ *Eclass*.

14.3.2.4 Semantic Integrity of TM and TU

Due to physical restrictions, not all modes can transport all units. For example, aircraft cannot transport standard containers used for road and rail transportation. Such restrictions can be defined by semantic integrity constraints over concepts and roles. Since the elements of *TM* are individuals (not concepts), we first collect the relevant individuals in new subconcepts of *TM*, and then state the restriction by universal or existential quantifiers; the role *usesMean* must be inverted, i.e., *usedBy* ⊑ *usesMean⁻* which becomes inverse-functional. There are two cases:

1. Inclusion of transport units: a transport mode *tma* must use only the explicitly stated units given as subconcepts $TU_1,...,TU_n$ of *LoadUnit* (or *Product*). We define therefore *TMA* ⊑ *{tma}*, *TUA* ⊑ TU_1 ⊔ ... ⊔ TU_n, and *TMA* ⊑ *TM* ⊓ ∀*usedBy*.(F ⊓ ∀*transport*.*TUA*).
2. Exclusion of transport units: a transport mode *tmb* may use any, but not the explicitly stated transport units. We define therefore *TMB* ⊑ *{tmb}*, *TUB* ⊑ TU_1 ⊔ ... ⊔ TU_n, and *TMB* ⊑ *TM*⊓∀*usedBy*.(F⊓∀*transport*. *TUB*).

Figure 14.2 gives an overview of the semantic model (without constraints).

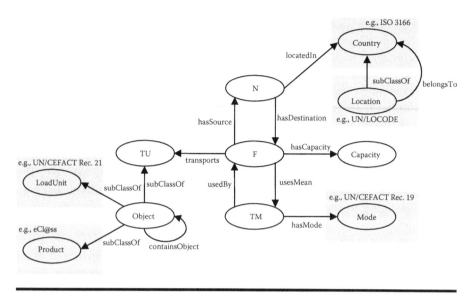

Figure 14.2   Semantic network for logistics system.

14.3.3 *Semantics of Transport Service*

14.3.3.1 *Semantics of Service Flows (S)*

A service flow results from a transport service between a provider a_j and consumer a_k; hence each $s{\in}S$ asserts two functional roles: *(A, S):provides* with *({a_j},{s}):provides* and *(S,A):consumedBy* with *({s},{a_k}):consumedBy*. The service flow can be described by additional nonfunctional properties outside the scope of our current model.

14.3.3.2 *Semantics of Actors*

The informal meaning is the role that an organizational unit (firm, department, person) fulfills in a logistics system; such a role should not be confused with the role construct of DL. Roles for the logistics domain can be retrieved from domain categorizations that often define a multilevel hierarchy of actors, e.g., the North American Industry Classification System (NAICS) (US Census Bureau 2010). If such a categorization is used, it can be adopted by placing a role between A and the root concept *ActorRole*, e.g., *(A,NAICS):isActorOf.*

14.3.3.3 *Semantic Integrity of M*

A mapping from transport services to flows is allowed if the service fulfills the physical restrictions for implementing the flow. For instance, a flow of railway containers by railroad requires an actor of rail transports; other actors are not allowed. We extend the definition of actor concepts by restrictions that must hold for any individual of the concept. First, we assemble the relevant individuals of *TM* and *TU* in new subconcepts, and then state the restriction by universal quantifiers. There are several cases:

1. Inclusion of transport units and transport means, i.e., an actor a_1 implements only flows with the explicitly given transport units $(tu_1,...,tu_n)$ and transportation means $(tm_1,...,tm_m)$. We define therefore *Actor1* $\sqsubseteq$ $\{a_1\}$, *TUA* $\sqsubseteq$ $\{tu_1\}\sqcup...\sqcup\{tu_n\}$, *TMA* $\sqsubseteq$ $\{tm_1\}\sqcup...\sqcup\{tm_m\}$, and *Actor1* $\sqsubseteq$ *A*$\sqcap\forall$*provides.(S*$\sqcap\forall$*implements.(F*$\sqcap\forall$*transports.TUA*$\sqcap\forall$*usesMean.TMA))*.
2. Exclusion of transport units and transport means, i.e., by negating the role fillers of *transports* and *usesMean* in 1 above.
3. Combinations of 1 and 2, and also adding constraints on the roles *hasCapacity*, *hasSource*, and *hasDestination*. Note that defining semantic integrity constraints of *TU* and *TM* can help reduce the number of constraints over *M*.

14.3.3.4 Semantics of Composite Transport Services (CS)

A composite service contains multiple elementary services, thus we add the role *(CS,S):containsService*. Expressing semantic constraints on the workflow *WF* over all concepts and roles of the model is possible by applying constructs of a semantic workflow definition language such as BPEL4SWS (Karastoyanova et al. 2008). These constraints are beyond the scope of the current model. Figure 14.3 gives an overview of the second part of the semantic model that links to *F* (without constraints).

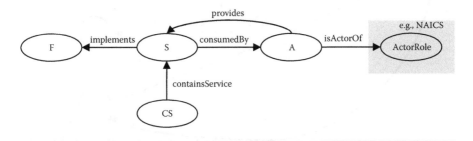

Figure 14.3   Semantic networks for transport service and composite transport service.

14.4 Preliminary Validation

In this section, we provide a preliminary validation of the proposed model. We describe the experimental design, report the results, and discuss the implications.

14.4.1 Validation Scenario

The purpose of the experiment is to demonstrate the feasibility and usefulness of the model. With regard to discovering and composing services fulfilling customer requirements, we consider the setup shown in Figure 14.4 that describes a logistics system for distributing incoming freight (via an airport) to final customers by road transportation. This scenario is the subject of a cooperative research project known as InterLogGrid (Intermodal Logistics and IT Services). The problem is finding the best set of transportation services for a (large) volume of freight for various customers. For most such situations, service contracts are not settled by long-term agreements and provide only short-term allocation of transport resources. We consider three logistics service providers: Provider 1 can serve only pallet transportation, Provider 2 can serve only container transportation, Provider 3 can serve only Customer 2 and Customer 4 (see Table 14.1).

14.4.2 Semantic Modeling

We instantiate and extend the proposed model to the scenario. Next, we transform given requirements (Table 14.2) known for the logistics scenario into axioms and facts (Table 14.3).

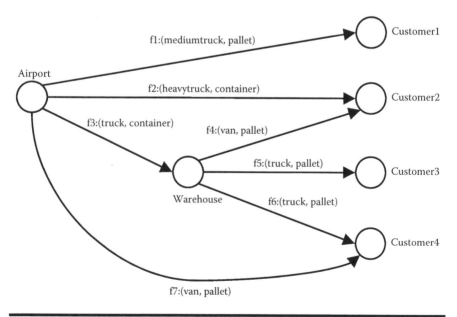

Figure 14.4 Overview of logistics system of scenario.

Table 14.1   Transportation Services by Service Providers

Service Provider	Service Flow	Service Consumer	Flow of Goods
SP1	s1	Customer 1	f1
	s2	Customer 2	f4
	s3	Customer 3	f5
	s4	Customer 4	f6
	s5	Customer 4	f7
SP2	s6	Customer 2	f2
	s7	Warehouse	f3
SP3	s8	Customer 2	f2
	s9	Customer 2	f4
	s10	Customer 4	f6
	s11	Customer 4	f7

Table 14.2   Requirements

ID	Requirement
R1	TM: all transportation means belong to road mode of UN Recommendation 19
R2	TM and TU: vans transport only pallets
R3	TM and TU: heavy trucks may not transport aquatic plants; eCl@ss code ACE892004
R4	N and TU: Customer 4 cannot handle containers
R5	M: Provider 2 handles only containers via two types of trucks
R6	S: due to a conflict of interest, Provider 2 is not allowed to serve Customer 4
R7	CS: because of provider policy, services by Provider 2 cannot be part of a composite service

Table 14.3   Additional Axioms and Facts for Requirements

ID	Additional Axioms and Facts
R1	{truck}:TM; {mediumtruck}:TM; {heavytruck}:TM; {van}:TM ({truck},{Road}):hasMode; ({mediumtruck},{Road}):hasMode; ({heavytruck},{Road}):hasMode; ({van},{Road}):hasMode
R2	TMVan⊑{van}; TUVan⊑OE TMVan⊑TM⊓∀usedBy. (F⊓∀transports.TUVan)
R3	TMHeavyTruck⊑{heavytruck}; TUNoHeavyTruck⊑ACE892004 ACE892004⊑Product TMHeavyTruck⊑TM⊓∀usedBy. (F⊓∀transports. ¬TUNoHeavyTruck)
R4	Customer4⊑{Customer4}; isSource⊑hasSource– Customer4⊑N⊓∀isSource.(F⊓∀transports. CN)
R5	SP2⊑{SP2}; TMSP2⊑{heavytruck}⊔{truck} SP2⊑A⊓∀provides.(S⊓∀implements. (F⊓∀usedMean.TMSP2⊓∀transports.CN)
R6	SP2⊑{SP2}; Customer4⊑{Customer4} SP2⊑A⊓∀provides.(S⊓∀consumedBy. ¬Customer4)
R7	providedBy⊓provides– CS⊑∀containsService. (S⊓∀providedBy. ¬SP2)

14.5 Discussion

The validation scenario shows that the proposed model can be used for describing both the setup and additional requirements. We have in total transformed seven exemplary types of requirements into DL axioms and facts. Evidence indicates that the proposed model provides a core set of constructs. These constructs were extended, i.e., we defined additional semantic integrity constraints that must hold. In principle, such constraints may affect most possible combinations of constructs (e.g., warehouses allowing only specific types of products, customers requiring special types of trucks because of loading and unloading restrictions at their sites, etc.). This wide range of constraints is due to the complexity of logistics services that require physical resources and diverse operational strategies. Further extending the coverage of the model would necessarily increase its size and complexity. For the sake of clarity and due to limited space, we have limited its scope.

The model has two implications for parties interested in automated service composition. First, it provides a formal conceptualization of the domain that may be used to represent actual logistics services in service-oriented computing (SOC), and hence to specify Web services representing physical services. This approach extends the scope of SOC to noncomputational services—another key characteristic of service science. The experience from our previous research (Karaenke and Kirn 2009) indicated that logistics problems can be solved by representation by means of SOC. Second, the model unfolds parts of the true complexity of service discovery and composition in a relevant real-world domain; it thus can serve to advance service composition algorithms. The present work did not study such algorithms.

14.6 Related Work

Semantics-based approaches in logistics are rather specialized subjects. For instance, SchemaWeb (http://www.schemaweb.info) and DAML Ontology Library (http://www.daml.org/ontologies) repositories return only one entry each for logistics and both are even no logistics, but production respectively product ontologies.

When widening the scope, one can identify a topic as part of other ontologies. Very often, these ontologies concern a particular domain or function within logistics so we will provide an overview. The work of Wendt et al. (2002) describes how to derive common logistics concepts for scheduling from merging two domain-specific ontologies, but the planned ontology has not been published. Pawlasczyk et al. (2004) describe the role of logistics ontologies in mass customization and consider the enterprise ontology (Uschold et al. 1998) as a starting point without giving a specification. Haugen and McCarthy (2000) propose to extend the REA ontology beyond internal accounting to supporting logistics and e-commerce. Gailly and Poels (2005) provide a method for defining this ontology using UML and OWL. Fayez et al. (2005) propose an OWL representation of the supply chain operation reference model (SCOR) for supply chain simulation but do not provide details on their implementation.

Ye et al. (2008) propose an ontology-based architecture for addressing the problem of semantic integration and use custom ontologies for supply chain management based on OWL DL. The ontology engineering process was not made explicit. Brock et al. (2005) argue against the use of logistics ontologies because of the "rigid and inflexible" nature of ontologies that would contradict characteristics of logistics. In particular, they claim that it is unrealistic to believe in formulating an "all-inclusive canon that would stand the test of time." They relate this proposition to information systems in general, and propose to define somewhat lightweight abstractions such as multiperspective taxonomies for the logistics domain.

Other relevant fields are web services research and service-oriented computing (SOC). A first stream is adopting the service paradigm for logistics management software to provide the functionality of logistics and SCM software by an integrated set of (web) services (Cheng et al. 2009). The second is adopting the service paradigm to represent logistics systems—or their parts—by (web) services. In this sense, the electronic representations become subjects of web service coordination and its specific body of knowledge. The work presented belongs to the latter stream. To the best of our knowledge, the problem of specifying and searching for logistics services and their composition has not been addressed by focused research. Conversely, a wealth of research covers web services, in particular Semantic Web services, related to service composition that may be incorporated into logistics service composition (Kona et al. 2008; Fujii and Suda 2006). By employing DL to conceptualize a domain, the proposed model can be regarded as a first step toward filling this research gap.

14.7 Conclusions

This chapter proposed a semantic model for transport services and demonstrated its usefulness in a scenario of distribution logistics. We defined the problem of finding the best solution for a given set of customer requirements as a subclass of service composition, thus combining and linking (logistics) services. A key prerequisite for determining compositions is a rich conceptualization that allows specification of relevant constraints that must be fulfilled. Such a conceptualization is missing in the current body of knowledge. We therefore studied the problem from the perspective of interoperability. We employed the SHOIN description logic. Preliminary validation indicated that the proposed model provides a core set of constructs and thus can be used for specifying semantic constraints sufficiently.

The proposed model has several limitations. First, validation was restricted to a small and artificial scenario, although it was derived from a cooperative research project involving logistics service providers. This validation method is not sufficient to actually prove validity and effectiveness. Second, the model is a basic component required for service composition, but does not specify composition algorithms or semantic search queries. Third, the model has not yet been integrated with the technology stack of SOC, e.g., SLA models, semantic service descriptions, and semantic workflow models.

Therefore, current and future work comprises (1) mapping the semantic model to service models of semantic web services, in particular OWL-S; (2) selecting and adopting service composition algorithms; and (3) developing a tool for semi-automated logistics service discovery and composition.

Acknowledgement

The work presented in this paper was funded by the German Federal Ministry of Education and Research as part of the InterLogGrid project (BMBF 01lG09010E).

References

Baader, F., Horrocks, I., and U. Sattler. 2007. Description logic. In *Handbook of Knowledge Representation*, Amsterdam: Elsevier, pp. 135–179.

Brock, D.L., Schuster, E.W., Allen, S.J. et al. 2005. Introduction to semantic modeling for logistical systems. *Journal of Business Logistics 26*: 97–117.

Cheng, J.C.P., Law, K.H., Jones, A. et al. 2009. Service oriented and orchestration framework for supply chain integration. In *International Design Engineering Technology Conference and Computers and Information Engineering Conference*.

eCl@ss. 2010. *International Standard for the Classification and Description of Products and Services.* http://www.eclass-online.org.

Fayez, F., Rabelo, L., and M. Mollaghasemi. 2005. Ontologies for supply chain simulation modeling. In *2005 Winter Simulation Conference*.

Fujii, K. and T. Suda. 2006. Semantics-based dynamic web service composition. *International Journal of Cooperative Information Systems 15*: 293–324.

Gailly, F. and G. Poels. 2005. Development of a formal REA-ontology representation. In *Open INTEROP Workshop on Enterprise Modeling and Ontologies for Interoperability (EMOI)*, CEUR Workshop Proceedings 160.

Haugen, R. and W.E. McCarthy. 2000. REA: A semantic model for Internet supply chain collaboration. In *OOPSALA Business Objects and Component Design and Implementation Workshop VI: Enterprise Application Integration*.

Hepp, M. 2006. *eClassOWL 5.1. Products and Services Ontology for e-Business. User's Guide.* http://www.heppnetz.de/eclassowl.

ISO. 2010. *ISO 3166: Country Codes.* http://www.iso.org/iso/country_codes.

Karaenke, P., Micsik, A. and S. Kirn. 2009. Adaptive SLA Management along value chains for service individualization. In *International Symposium on Service Science*, pp. 217–228.

Karastoyanova, D., van Lessen, T., Leymann, F. et al. 2008. *WS-BPEL Extension for Semantic Web Services (BPEL4SWS).* ftp://ftp.informatik.uni-stuttgart.de/pub/library/ncstrl.ustuttgart_fi/TR-2008-03/TR-2008-03.pdf.

Klein, M. 2002. *DAML+OIL and RDF Schema representation of UNSPSC.* http://www.cs.vu.nl/~mcaklein/unspsc.

Kona, S., Bansal, A., Blake, M.B. et al. 2008. Generalized semantics-based service composition. In *IEEE International Conference on Web Services*, pp. 219–227.

Leukel, J. and S. Kirn. 2008. A supply chain management approach to logistics ontologies in information systems. In *11th International Conference on Business Information Systems*, LNBIP Series, Vol. 7.

Martin, D., Burstein, M., McDermott, D. et al. 2007. Bringing semantics to web services with OWL-S. *World Wide Web Journal 10*: 243–277.

Pawlaszcyk, D., Dietrich, A.J., Timm, I.J. et al. 2004. Ontologies supporting cooperation in mass customization: a pragmatic approach. *International Conference on Mass Customization and Personalization: Theory and Practice in Central Europe*.

Storey, J., Emberson, C., Godsell, J. et al. 2006. Supply chain management: Theory, practice and future challenges. *International Journal of Operations and Production Management 26*: 754–774.

Supply-Chain Council. 2006. *Supply Chain Operations Reference Model (SCOR®), Version 8.0.* http://www.supply-chain.org.

UNECE. 2010. *United Nations Code for Trade and Transport Locations.* http://www.unece.org/cefact/locode/.

UN/CEFACT. 2010. *List of Trade Facilitation Recommendations*. http://www.unece.org/cefact/recommendations/rec_index.htm.

UNSPSC. 2010. *United Nations Standard Products and Services Code*. http://www.unspsc.org.

U.S. Census Bureau. 2010. *North American Industry Classification System (NAICS)*. http://www.census.gov/cgi-bin/sssd/naics/naicsrch?chart=2007.

Uschold, M., King, M., Moralee, S. et al. 1998. Enterprise ontology. *Knowledge Engineering Review 13*: 31–89.

W3C. 2004. OWL Web ontology language. http://www.w3.org/TR/owl-guide/.

Wendt, O., Stockheim, T., Grolik, S. et al. 2002. Distributed ontology management prospects and pitfalls on our way to a web of ontologies. In *Dagstuhl Workshop*, Event 02212, DFG-SPP 1083.

Ye, Y., Yang, D., Jiang, Z. et al. 2008. An ontology-based architecture for implementing semantic integration of supply chain management. *International Journal of Computer Integrated Manufacturing 21*: 1–18.

Chapter 15

Ontology-Driven Business Process Intelligence

Jon Espen Ingvaldsen

Norwegian University of Science and Technology, Trondheim, Norway

Contents

15.1 Introduction

Many companies have adopted enterprise resource planning (ERP) systems that support their business processes. ERP systems have rich functionality for supporting the operational sides of companies. Although leading vendors of ERP systems have incorporated analytical modules and data warehousing into their platforms, it is not easy to validate the quality of supported business processes. According to Casati and Shan (2002), a key problem for process analysis technologies is the difficulty of gaining business insights. The extracted reports are presented at a very low level of abstraction and do not support any kind of business level analysis. Another issue is the lack of explorative capabilities in existing analysis environments. Traditional business intelligence and data warehousing solutions tend to rely on predefined and mostly template-driven reports designed by data warehousing professionals. Report readers cannot easily modify them (Evelson and Brown 2008; Watson et al. 2001). The ability to perform explorative data analysis is bounded by the functionality of a report and the data it is defined to gather.

ERP and other process-aware information systems log events related to actual business process executions. Proper analysis of event logs can provide valuable and important knowledge, and help organizations improve the quality of their services. Business process intelligence (BPI) is a process-centric approach that can answer many questions related to the quality and nature of business process executions. BPI relates to "a set of integrated tools that supports business and IT users in managing process execution quality" (Grigori et al. 2004) and refers to applications of various measurement and analysis techniques. Process mining, statistical analysis, and data mining are all techniques that can be applied as parts of BPI solutions and projects. Process mining allows discovery of real business flow models from event log structures. Statistical analysis enables investigations of quantitative process measures and performance indicators, while data mining can be used to reveal hidden and underlying patterns related to historic business process executions.

The main challenges related to BPI include harmonization of data from multiple sources and turning detailed and system-technical event log structures into meaningful process information. Ontologies can be applied in BPI to provide a shared understanding and accurate representation of domain concepts. Event logs enriched with ontological annotations and significant context information structures also have potential for utilizing search technologies.

In this chapter, we will present an iterative process analysis approach based on search technology and ontologies and implemented in the Enterprise Visualization Suite (EVS) BPI system. This approach utilizes ontologies for harmonization, analysis, and presentation of business process aspects. Throughout the chapter we will focus on the importance of ontologies in the process analysis approach and demonstrate how ontologies and searches are fundamental for structuring process mining models and analysis perspectives, and providing an explorative analysis environment. We will use an event log from a call center at a banking company (Wells Bank) as example data to describe the approach and functionality in EVS. These data stem from a call center system in a real bank, but data and ontology structures were modified to keep the original organization and its employees anonymous.

In Section 15.2, we describe the call center process at Wells Bank and the event log used for examples throughout this chapter. Section 15.3 describes the construction of EVS and its modules. The analysis approach (EVS BPI Cycle) is described in Section 15.4. We will describe each analysis phase with examples and results from Wells Bank. Section 15.5 presents related work. A discussion on how to use BPI results and the importance of ontologies are covered in Section 15.6, followed by conclusions in Section 15.7.

15.2 Example Data: Wells Bank

The event log we use gathers information from events executed by an automated voice recognition unit (VRU) and human operators. An incoming call is first handled by the VRU that routes the call further to a human operator via automated steps carried out by a VRU server. The employees at this call center have different skills and serve different functions. For example, not all employees have competence to serve English speaking customers or assist the stock trading group. The event log is stored in Semantically Annotated Mining eXtensible Markup Language (SA-MXML) and annotated with concepts from two external ontologies. One ontology describes aggregation between concepts related to the activities found in the event log, while the other describes the organizational hierarchy from employees, to groups, to higher organizational units.

MXML is the event log format used by the open source process mining framework ProM. SA-MXML is an extended version of MXML that incorporates ontological concept annotations on event log elements. The ontology structures in SA-MXML are provided in external Web Service Modeling Language (WSML) files. WSML is a formal language that provides a framework of different language variants to describe semantic web services. It is a frame-based language with an intuitive human readable syntax and XML, RDF exchange syntaxes, and a mapping to Web Ontology Language (OWL; Lausen et al. 2005).

The event log used for examples in this chapter describes operations carried out in the first week of January 2009. A fraction of this event log is shown below. We can see how the workflow model elements and originator elements are annotated with ontological concepts.

```
<ProcessInstance id="33139" description="Handle Customer Call">
<Data>
          <Attribute name="Process_ID">33139</Attribute>
     </Data>
     <AuditTrailEntry>
          <Data>
               <Attribute name="VRU Output">NC</
Attribute>                    </Data>
<WorkflowModelElement modelReference=
"file://CallCentreTasks.wsml#VRU">VRU
</WorkflowModelElement>
          <EventType>start</EventType>
          <Timestamp>2009-01-01T11:23:55.000+11:00</
Timestamp>
          <Originator modelReference=
"file://CallCentreOriginator.wsml#VRU_Server">VRU_Server
</Originator>
     </AuditTrailEntry>
     <AuditTrailEntry>
          <Data>
               <Attribute name="VRU Output">NC</Attribute>
          </Data>
          <WorkflowModelElement modelReference=
"file://CallCentreTasks.wsml#VRU">VRU
</WorkflowModelElement>
          <EventType>complete</EventType>
          <Timestamp>2009-01-01T11:24:04.000+11:00</
Timestamp>
          <Originator modelReference=
"file://CallCentreOriginator.wsml#VRU_Server">VRU_Server
</Originator>
     </AuditTrailEntry>
     <AuditTrailEntry>
          <Data>
               <Attribute name="VRU Output">NC</Attribute>
          </Data>
          <WorkflowModelElement modelReference=
"file://CallCentreTasks.wsml#New_Customer">New_Customer
</WorkflowModelElement>
          <EventType>start</EventType>
          <Timestamp>2009-01-01T11:24:05.000+11:00</
Timestamp>
          <Originator modelReference=
"file://CallCentreOriginator.wsml#Michael">Michael
</Originator>
          </AuditTrailEntry>
          <AuditTrialEntry> …
```

Every tag in our event log is a semantically defined class in an underlying ontology (Van Dongen and Van der Aalst 2005; Aalst 2008), and the log data form instances of these classes. The *process instance* elements are the core building blocks in MXML for describing sequences of related events. The name of an event in MXML is audit trail entry. Such elements gather information about the activity carried out (*work flow model element*), event type, time stamp showing when the event occurred, and user (*originator*) executing the event. The data tag is used to add information about the event context.

The fraction from the MXML file shows one instance of the process *Handle Customer Call* and its first three events. The events describe the start and completion of the automated steps in the process and the start of a new customer registration. As we can see, the first two events are executed by the VRU server, and the VRU completion finishes 9 seconds after the VRU starts. The third event is executed by an employee named Michael. He picks up the phone 1 second after the VRU operation finishes and he starts serving the customer. The service is a registration of a new customer.

Both the *WorkflowModelElement* and the *Originator* are annotated with a concept in an external ontology. In our example, the *VRU WorkflowModelElement* is annotated with the ontological concept *VRU* found in the *CallCentreTasks.wsml* file. The *New Customer WorkflowModelElement* and all originators are annotated similarly. To each *AuditTrailEntry* in this example, an attribute is added under a data tag to provide additional information about the output from the VRU. Based on automated phone interactions with customers, the VRU decides the service to which the customer should be forwarded. The *VRU Output* attribute contains the value of this routing decision (*NC* = new customer, *ST* = stock trading, *RS* = regular service, and *SE* = service in English). When MXML is parsed in EVS, such data attributes are also treated as categorical and ontological information. Based on the MXML file and the two ontology files, the process mining algorithms can extract knowledge about the process flows and relate these flows to different ontological concepts and aggregation levels.

EVS is designed to handle the full complexity of real ERP systems like SAP. In the database of SAP, resource and document changes are logged only as they are completed (not scheduled or started). Therefore, EVS considers events as atomic without any state information. In MXML, an event has a type and can proceed through different stages such as schedule, start, and complete. EVS does not distinguish between different types of events and considers each event as a single-staged and completed happening with one execution time stamp. As a result, an event with multiple stages in MXML is converted into multiple events in EVS with one event for each stage.

Using event logs with only single-stage events produces some implications for the potential of some process mining algorithms. Multistage events are core building blocks for process mining algorithms that try to identify and describe parallelism in business flow (Wen et al. 2004). Even without multiple stages in the event logs, we can still discover the nature of real business flows and extract meaningful and valuable process models enriched with statistics and contextual information.

15.3 Architecture

EVS is a process mining framework developed by Businesscape AS. An overview of the architecture is shown in Figure 15.1. The backbone of the EVS architecture and its search functionality is a graph database integrated with an Apache Lucene search engine. The graph database consists of serialized trace networks and the search engine enables fast retrieval of the traces based on textual queries. Adapters for importing event data are developed for MXML (and SA-MXML), Excel, and SAP database tables. The first version of the SAP adapter is described in Ingvaldsen and Gulla (2007).

The trace networks in the graph database are structured according to a defined upper ontology. Figure 15.2 shows this upper ontology and three related application ontologies. The upper ontology aims at defining generic and universally valid concepts that integrate the application ontologies in a BPI context. As in ontology languages like OWL, every instance and defined class is a member of the thing class. A trace is a sequence of events ordered by the execution time stamp. In addition to containing time stamp information, events refer to defined business processes (optional) and a set of static context entity instances involved in their executions.

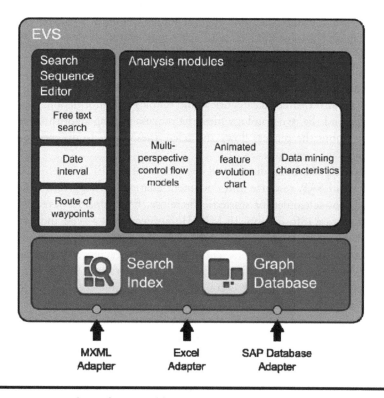

Figure 15.1   Overview of EVS architecture.

a)

b)

Figure 15.2 **(a) Figure notation. (b) Upper ontology and three related application ontologies.**

Context entities describe a set of property values (i.e., value of a purchase order, expected delivery date of ordered goods) and refer to other context entities by use of associations or part-of relationships (i.e., a purchase order can be associated with a vendor, and a user can be part of a group). Business processes, context entities, and events can be classified as nodes in drill-down hierarchies.

The application ontologies define concepts specific to the settings of actual BPI projects. In Figure 15.2, we can see that four application ontologies are attached to the upper ontology. These ontologies are (1) an event class ontology that describes the breakdown structures of defined services, (2) an organizational hierarchy, and

(3) a small ontology describing VRU outputs. Note that Figure 15.2 shows only the class level of the upper ontology and the application ontologies.

The instance levels of the ontologies appear in Figure 15.3. In (a), the part-of relationships between instances in the organizational hierarchy are described. Wells Bank consists of two departments that further consist of groups and employees and/or servers. Figure 15.3(b) shows how the data attributes from MXML are interpreted as ontological information where the XML attribute name is used to construct an ontological class, while the attribute values are considered instances of this class. In our example, we have a data attribute named VRU Output. This attribute name is used to construct a unique ontological class. The four output values for this data attribute are considered as instances of this class. Figure 15.3(c) shows a trace that was constructed based on our MXML example. It contains three events that are instances of three event classes (VRU Start, VRU Complete, and New Customer Start) and refer to three context entity instances (VRU Server, NC, and Michael). The trace neighbors have further relations into the application ontologies and eventually the upper ontology.

All the ontologies and trace structures are merged together in the graph database of EVS. We will refer to this merged ontology structure as the ontology throughout this chapter. The traces are indexed and made searchable for users. Textual names and descriptions in their neighborhood networks are gathered to form a searchable index row for each trace. For our trace 33139, phrases from the related ontologies like VRU Start, Michael, Team 4, IT Department, CRM, etc. are included to create an indexed and searchable description.

Ingvaldsen and Gulla (2008) describe indexing of traces in an earlier prototype version of EVS. This prototype used Lucene both for indexing of searchable terms and for object serialization. In the current version of EVS, the responsibility for serialization of object structures is handled by the graph database, while the search engine and its index are responsible for making the object structures searchable.

Both databases and search engines are concerned with similar functions to store, access, and manage information. In contrast to databases, a search engine is more loosely organized, with no schema that define data attributes. The Lucene API uses field names to assign text segments to different attributes of the indexed items, but does not restrict the type of text that can be stored in a field (Konchady 2008).

In addition to the graph database and search index, we have a user interface for querying traces and three different modules for analyzing different aspects of the dataset and highlighted trace clusters.

15.4 Process Analysis Approach

In EVS, the user can either explore the data through custom search queries or by browsing the data through the ontological drill-down hierarchy. These hierarchies traverse drill-down relationships in the ontologies. As shown in Figure 15.4, both subclass-of

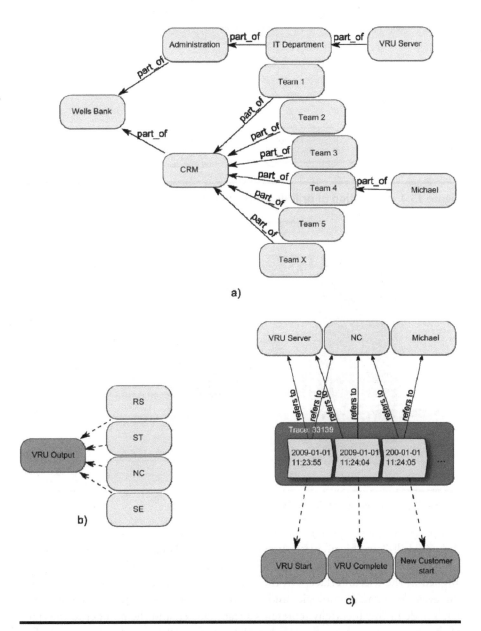

Figure 15.3 (a) Instance level in organizational hierarchy (only a subset of employees is shown). (b) Instances related to VRU output ontology. (c) Example of trace and its relations to context entity instances and event class definitions.

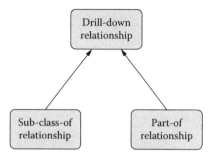

Figure 15.4   Definition of drill-down relationships.

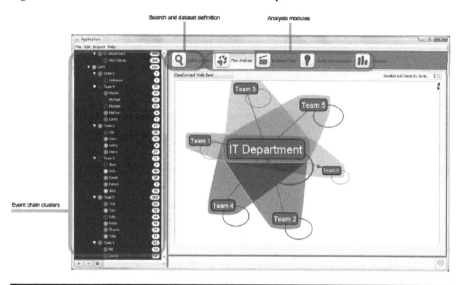

Figure 15.5   Screenshot from EVS.

and part-of relationships are considered drill-down relationships. By exploring data through drill-down hierarchies, a user can increase and decrease the level of detail.

The screenshot in Figure 15.5 shows how search and ontological browsing are aligned in the user interface. On the left side of the screenshot, we can recognize the event log-related ontologies and structures from Figure 15.2 and Figure 15.3. Each node in this hierarchy represents a trace cluster, and the number to the right of the cluster name shows the number of traces the respective clusters contain. For the node New Customer start, the population size is 57. This means that there are 57 traces with the event class New Customer start in their contexts.

On the right side of the screenshot, we show the main panel where the user can define datasets and investigate them through several analysis modules. In Figure 15.5, the flow analysis module is currently selected and displayed. The approach for analyzing process data in EVS appears in Figure 15.6. The approach

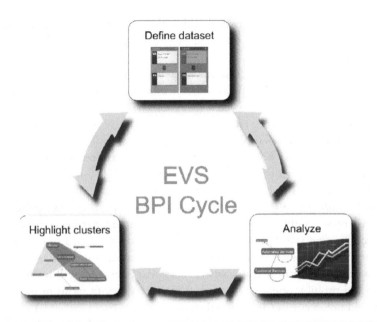

Figure 15.6 Analysis approach.

starts with defining a dataset that sets restrictions on which traces should be included in the analysis. After the dataset is defined, the user can select search-based or ontology-based trace clusters that should be highlighted throughout the analysis and interactively explore the data. Throughout the analysis, the user can always step back and reformulate search queries or highlight different trace clusters.

15.4.1 Defining Datasets

A user can define a dataset by chaining a set of queries that are run against the search index to retrieve relevant traces. In EVS, three query types are available: free text search, date interval, and route of waypoints. By operating on defined subsets of the data, a user can narrow the investigations to regions of interest; for example, to review the processes only within a certain department or processes that involve a specific set of vendors or event classes.

15.4.1.1 Free Text Search

Free text search is a very flexible way of retrieving a custom set of traces. The user specifies a set of terms that should occur in the context of relevant process instances. The free text search queries can also utilize the Apache Lucene search syntax and term modifiers to form more sophisticated queries. The term modifiers relevant for retrieving traces include:

- Wild card search: Both single (?) and multiple (*) wild card searches are supported. To retrieve traces executed by either *Daniel* or *David*, we can use a wildcard search like Da*.

- Fuzzy search: This search is useful when we are not sure about the spelling of a term. Lucene supports fuzzy search based on the Levenshtein distance or edit distance algorithm. To do a fuzzy search, we use the tilde (~) symbol at the end of a single word term. If we form a search such as Garry~ we would get hits on both *Gary* and *Gerry*.

- Boolean operators: Boolean operators allow terms and phrases to be combined through logic operators. Lucene supports AND (+), OR, NOT, and the minus sign (–) as Boolean operators. To search for traces that contains either *Stock Trading* or *Arthur*, we can use the Stock Trading OR Arthur query. Similarly we could use the AND operator to search for traces containing both *Stock Trading* and *Arthur*. The required operator (+) is used to retrieve traces that must contain certain terms or phrases. A search query like +Customer can be used to retrieve traces where "customer" must occur. The NOT operator and prohibit operator (–) work similarly to specify terms or phrases that should not occur in the retrieved traces.

- Grouping: Parentheses are used to group clauses and form subqueries. To search for either *Arthur* or *Stock Trading* and *VRU*, we can use the query (Arthur OR Stock Trading) AND VRU.

By combining the term modifiers we get very expressive and sophisticated search queries that can be used to retrieve a customized and specific subset of traces. Apache Lucene Query Syntax, 2010 contains a more extensive description of available term modifiers.

15.4.1.2 Date Interval

Date interval queries are used to impose restrictions on the time frame within which relevant traces must be contained. These queries select out traces that have a first event occurrence after or equal to the start limit of the time frame and a last event occurrence before or equal to the end limit of the time frame. Figure 15.7 shows an example of a defined time frame with a start and end time stamp. The horizontally stretched boxes represent traces, and their horizontal positions and widths represent their start time stamps and durations. For instance, trace 1 has a longer duration between its first and last event than trace 2. Traces 1, 3, and 4 started before trace 2. Traces 2, 3, and 5 are considered relevant for this date interval query, while partially overlapping and nonoverlapping traces are considered irrelevant.

Route-of-waypoint queries are alternatives to free text search; the user forms a search query based on predefined terms from the ontology. These queries are very useful for enforcing restrictions on which ontological elements through which the traces in our dataset must pass. Figure 15.8 shows a screenshot from a route-of-waypoints

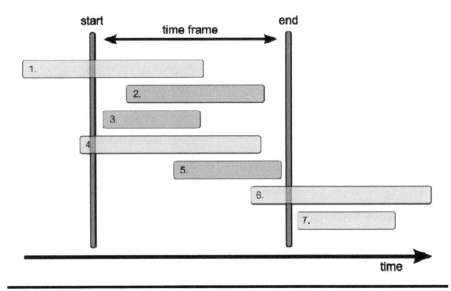

Figure 15.7   Examples of traces considered relevant for time frame.

query definition. The user has specified that relevant traces must pass through the event classes *VRU start* and VRU *complete*. As we also can see, a route of waypoints can involve any element from the ontology and the query may also be specified to involve teams, users, and VRU outputs. The user can select any combination of ontology elements that relevant traces must pass through to be considered relevant.

15.4.1.3 Search Sequences

When we search for traces in practice, it is commonly necessary to combine query elements. For instance, is it typically useful to define a date interval together with a free text search or route-of-waypoints. EVS provides functionality for combining search elements through search sequences. A search sequence acts as a conjunction element in the overall dataset definition, and can also be selected as highlighted clusters in the analysis phase. The user can form multiple search sequences and compare two or more result sets against each other.

Figure 15.9 shows two search sequences. Both queries contain three search query elements, where the first is a date interval query, the second is a route-of-waypoints, and the third is a free text search. The two first query elements are the same for both search sequences, and to show that the two first query elements in *Search B* (right search sequence) are references to the query element definitions in *Search A* they are visualized as partly transparent. Their original query element is marked when the user puts the mouse pointer over the referring query elements. The use of references instead of duplications is chosen to simplify maintenance and modification of queries. If the user in our example wants to modify the dates in the date interval queries of both

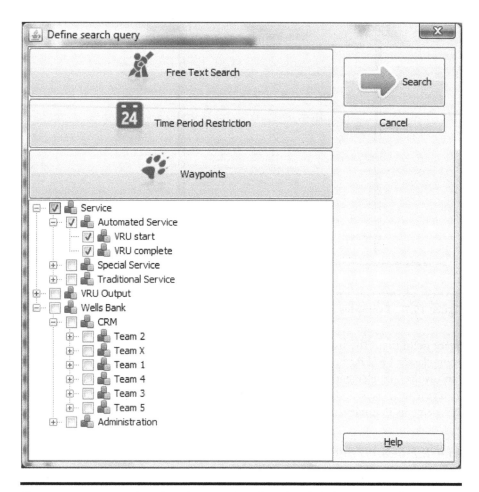

Figure 15.8 Screenshot showing user interface for defining routes-of-waypoints queries.

Search A and Search B, he or she can change all by one modification in Search A. When the user forms the search sequences, he or she can select whether to define and include a new query element in the sequence or refer to existing query elements.

The first query element ensures that we extract data from a defined time period. This period is January 1 to January 7 of 2009. The second query element states that all traces must involve VRU complete, VRU start, and automated service. The third query elements in the two search sequences demonstrate free text search and the use of term modifiers. This dataset definition with two search sequences implies that traces must either be relevant for *Search A* or *Search B* to be included in the analysis dataset.

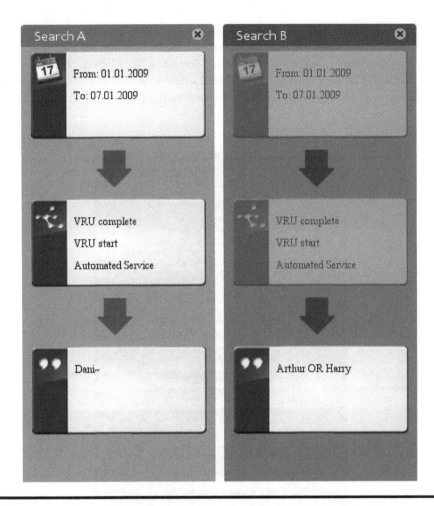

Figure 15.9 **Examples of two search sequences, each containing three query elements.**

15.4.2 Group Highlighting

Group highlighting is used to structure and visually mark subsets of datasets throughout an analysis. Both ontologically defined elements and search sequences represent trace clusters that can be highlighted. Search- and ontology-based clusters can be seen as alternatives to automated trace clustering approaches (a comparison of the two approaches is described further in Section 15.5). EVS does not currently provide functionality for automatic trace clustering, but it is designed to align search- and ontology-based trace clusters with outputs from automated clustering algorithms.

Figure 15.10 shows a screenshot from the set of trace clusters the user can highlight. As we can see, two search sequences (*Search A* and *Search B*) and ontological elements (*Service, Traditional Service, VRU Output, Team X,* etc.) are available for highlighting. The colored circle icon left of the cluster name shows the color that will represent and visualize the cluster in further analysis.

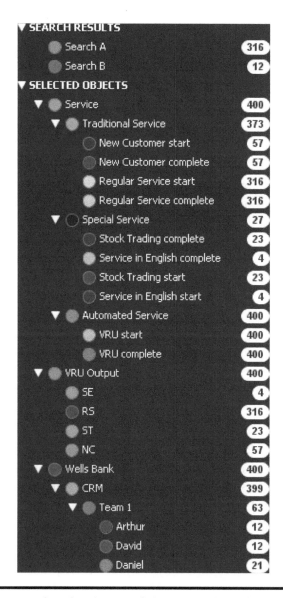

Figure 15.10   Screenshot showing set of clusters available for highlighting.

15.4.3 Analysis Modules

EVS consists of three analysis modules that focus on visualizing and describing different aspects of the traces. These modules are multiperspective control flow models, evolution charts, and cluster characteristics.

15.4.3.1 Multiperspective Control Flow Models

Good business process models are missing in many organizations. Models are typically absent, incorrect, or outdated. If process models exist in an explicit form, their quality typically leaves much to be desired. Process models created for documentation and communication purposes tend to present a "Power Point" reality that may not be followed in day-to-day operations. According to Aalst (2009), process models should not be static; they should allow for interactivity and various context-dependent views.

Although event logs alone accurately reflect process executions, they are still useless for many analysis purposes because they lack the abstraction level required from (business) analysts for understanding business operations. Conversely, abstract flow models on a higher business level do not reflect all the details necessary to reveal all improvement potentials. To provide both conceptual and actual information in the same analysis environment, we must relate the different perspectives to each other (Casati and Shan 2002). Semantically annotated event logs allow extraction from process models at multiple abstraction levels.

The multiperspective control flow model module in EVS creates a visual graph of control flow relationships among elements from the ontology. The order between events in a trace and the ontological elements they involve forms a basis for constructing control flow models on multiple aggregated levels. In the user interface of this analysis module, the user selects an ontological root class and an appropriate drill-down level. A flow model is then constructed based on ontological elements found at the specified level below the root class. This creates an interactive environment in which the user can easily change process perspective and drill down to detailed levels.

Figures 15.11 and 15.12 show the control flow between subclasses of the *Service* and *Wells Bank* ontological classes. These root classes and a specified drill-down level below form the perspective of the extracted control flow models. The sizes of the boxes in the model represent the number of times an element is involved. Similarly, the widths of the edges represent the number of times a source element is directly followed by a target element in the current dataset. Sized boxes and edge widths together visualize the load distribution throughout the model flow (*load* is the number of times a process step or flow relationship occurs in the dataset).

Note that Figures 15.11 and 15.12 show only the control flows for two ontological class hierarchies. If the *VRU output* class had drill-down relations to other classes in the application ontologies, we could show control flow for this perspective also. In principle, any ontological class can set the modeling perspective. If more

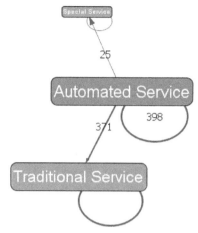

a) Root class: Service, drilldown level: 1

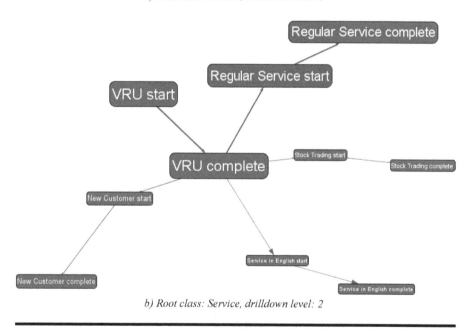

b) Root class: Service, drilldown level: 2

Figure 15.11 **(a) Models showing control flow between elements at different classification levels below the ontological *Service* class. (b) Service control flow at one and two classification levels below *Service* class.**

ontological elements were involved in the event executions and available in the event log, we would have an even larger portfolio of potential process perspectives.

Figure 15.11(a) shows an aggregated level of business flow between services. The processes at the call center start with an automated service (VRU operation), followed by a traditional or specialized service. The sizes of the boxes and widths of

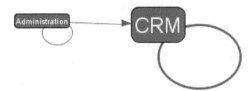

a) Root class: Wells Bank, drilldown level: 1

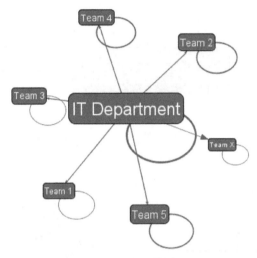

b) Root class: Wells Bank, drilldown level: 2

Figure 15.12 **(a) Model showing control flow between elements at different classification levels below the ontological *Wells Bank* class. (b) and (c) Organizational control flow after digging one, two, and three aggregation levels down.**

the edges indicate that automated and traditional services are more often executed than specialized services. In this model screenshot, the user has the mouse over the *Automated Service* box and the load on incoming, outgoing, and cyclic flows is shown as frequency labels on the edges. *Automated Service* is directly followed 371 times by *Traditional Service*, 25 times by *Special Service*, and 398 times by itself. In Figure 15.11(b) we step down a level in the ontological hierarchy to get a more detailed picture of the same service perspective.

Figure 15.12 changes the focus to depict the flow between ontological elements at the level just below the Wells Bank class in the organization hierarchy. The flow in such organizational models is typically interpreted and described as a handover of work. Note that the main flow starts at the administration department, followed by operations in the CRM department.

By stepping one level down in the organizational hierarchy, the flow moves from the IT department to different CRM teams. This extracted model reveals no

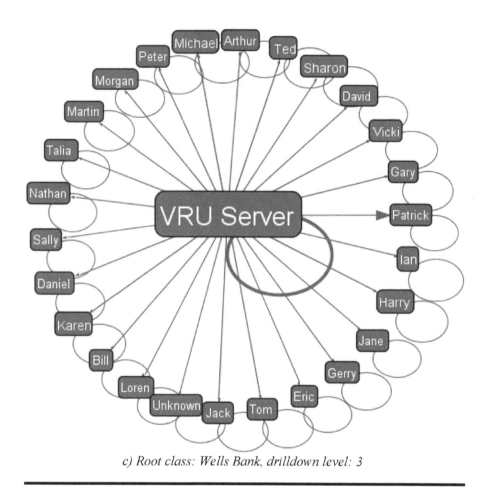

c) Root class: Wells Bank, drilldown level: 3

Figure 15.12   (Continued) a) Model showing control flow between elements at different classification levels below the ontological *Wells Bank* class. (b) and (c) Organizational control flow after digging one, two, and three aggregation levels down.

interactions (in the context of logged business processes) between the teams. In Figure 12(c), we see the same phenomenon at the lowest level (servers and employees) in the organizational hierarchy. The cause lies in the nature of the call center processes. The process is considered finished when a customer service operator ends a phone conversation, and in our sample data no customer was forwarded from one operator to another during a phone call.

The multiperspective control flow models use background coloring on process paths to highlight selected trace clusters. In Figure 15.13, four different VRU outputs are selected as highlighted trace clusters, and we can see how they are involved through the service and organizational perspectives of the

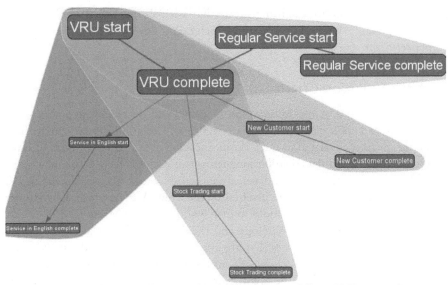

a) Root class: Service, drilldown level: 2, highlight the four different VRU output values

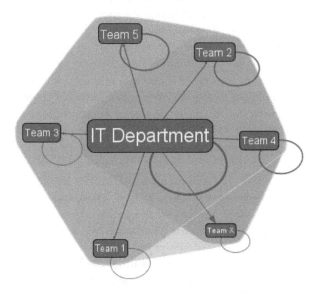

b) Root class: Wells Bank, drilldown level: 2, highlight the four different VRU output values

Figure 15.13   Highlighted trace clusters. Four VRU output values are selected as highlighted trace clusters. (a) Highlighted clusters on flow between services. (b) Same highlighted clusters on flow between organizational units.

processes. This group highlighting shows that VRU outputs consistently decide which manual services will follow and which teams cover different areas of customer service.

15.4.3.2 Evolution Charts

The presence of time stamp information in events and traces makes it possible to animate the evolution of property values over time. Evolution charts animate how numerical properties related to trace clusters develop over a period of time. A standard scatter plot shows data distributions across two dimensions (X-axis and Y-axis). Evolution charts, on the other hand, reveal data across five dimensions (X-axis, Y-axis, color, size, and time). They were inspired by the TrendAnalyzer from GapMinder and use such animated visualizations to map world data (GapMinder 2010).

Based on concepts in the ontology and their internal flow relationships, EVS constructs a large set of features that are available for statistics and data mining. Duration measures are one such set of features that can be valuable for describing trace cluster characteristics. The event log typically describes traces with different profiles. Traces cover different business areas; some overlap partly or completely with each other, while others are separated. As a result, we must specify start and end points when we describe duration values. When the event log is read into the search index, the system remembers all possible starting points and end points for successive event executions. These combinations are used to construct and present a set of possible duration features. An example of a duration feature is the time elapsed from *VRU complete* to *Regular Service start*. Another set of features counts the number of occurrences for each ontological concept. Two examples are the number of times *Martin* or *VRU complete* was involved in the traces.

Each trace cluster is visualized as a bubble whose radius is a function of cluster size (number of traces contained in cluster). The vertical and horizontal positions of the trace cluster bubble depend on numerical features selected by the user, who can also specify the animation speed, aggregation period, and number of animation steps between the first and last event in the visualized dataset.

Evolution charts make it possible to perform high level analyses such as identifying long-term trends, and targeted analyses for gauging the impacts of a specific change. An example of a high level analysis is investigating how business processes measures (like durations and loads) develop relative to each other and over time in different organizational units. Targeted analysis, on the other hand, may investigate how these organizational units develop before and after a large marketing campaign.

Figure 15.14 shows two screenshots from an animation sequence in an evolution chart. We selected organizational teams as the highlighted clusters. Each cluster is represented as a colored bubble. The discovered model in Figure 15.11 revealed that *Regular Service* is the most commonly requested service. In the chart, we set the duration between *Regular Service start* and *Regular Service complete* to indicate time spent servicing a customer as a horizontal feature, and duration between

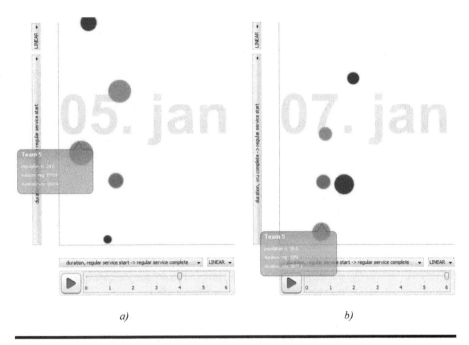

a)   *b)*

Figure 15.14   Two screenshots of evolution chart module. (a) Snapshot of animation on January 5. (b) Snapshot of same data on January 7.

VRU complete and *Regular Service start* to show response time before the phone is answered by an operator as a vertical feature. We specified the animation to break the time period into seven key frames (one per day), and calculate average values based on the period between current animation time and 1 day back.

The two animation snapshots show how the horizontal and vertical feature values change over time and move the bubble locations. The cluster diameters (defined by the cluster sizes) have changed slightly over this period. On January 5, *Team 5* had a service time for regular services of 67 seconds, a response time of 29 seconds, and processed a total of 24 customer calls. On January 7, their service time almost doubled to 126 seconds and response time dropped below 4 seconds; they processed a total of 16 customer calls. We can see how Team 5 scored relative to the other teams. As the animation screenshots show, a lot of volatility appears when we extract and visualize customer service measures on a daily basis. With an event log containing data for longer time periods, the same analysis would be able to show longer trends and pinpoint teams that are typically slow to answer the phone and start servicing customers.

15.4.3.3 Data Mining Characteristics

The data mining module has the potential of discovering unknown and valuable patterns that characterize the highlighted trace clusters. Like evolution charts, data mining modules select feature candidates from the ontological concepts and their internal flow relationships. One feature different from evolution charts is that a data mining module operates on both numerical and categorical features. One set of common categorical features is based on ontological elements in the traces. In EVS, such features are considered Boolean if they have a true (1) or false (0) value.

Figure 15.15 shows how potential features are presented. A user can navigate through this hierarchy and select those feature candidates that should be included in

Figure 15.15   Screenshot showing hierarchy of potential data mining features.

the data mining algorithms. In the figure, the user selected all duration features and all service concepts as potential features to describe traces carried out by *Team 1*.

The ability to manually select a set of feature candidates gives a user control over the solution space and the types of descriptions the data mining operation can produce. This is useful to prevent the data mining algorithm from constructing rules that are obvious, redundant, or of little knowledge value.

After a user finishes feature selection, a dataset is created. Figure 15.16 shows a fraction with the first six traces of a bigger dataset. Each column represents a feature and the feature name is written vertically in the column headers. The traces are represented as rows with a set of feature values. This dataset shows examples of duration features and values. Column 2 represents a feature named *duration, vru complete → new customer start* that describes the time elapsed between the first occurrence of *VRU complete* and the first following occurrence of *New Customer start*. Only the first

'duration, vru start -> vru complete'	'duration, vru complete -> new customer start'	'duration, vru complete -> new customer complete'	'duration, service in english start -> service in english complete'	'duration, vru start -> stock trading complete'		'team 2'	loren	'it department'	michael	Eric	david	administration	sally	sharon	class
13000	1000	25000	?	?		1	0	1	0	0	0	1	0	0	0
6000	?	?	?	?	...	1	0	1	0	0	0	1	0	0	0
13000	?	?	?	?		0	0	1	0	0	0	1	0	0	0
5000	?	?	?	?		0	0	1	0	0	1	1	0	0	0
5000	?	?	?	183000		0	0	1	0	0	0	1	0	0	1
5000	?	?	?	?		1	0	1	0	0	0	1	0	0	0

Figure 15.16   Fraction of dataset.

trace involves these two activities and has such a value (1,000 ms). Question marks in the dataset represent unknown or missing values. The dataset also shows examples of categorical features created from relations to ontological elements. *Team 2* is one ontological class related to the first two as well as the last trace in our dataset.

The last column in the dataset is the classification feature. This feature has a 1 (true) value if the respective trace is a member of the highlighted trace cluster to be characterized. We want to classify all traces that involve service operators in *Team 1*. The classification feature has a 1 (true) value if *Team 1* is involved and a 0 (false) value if it is not. Based on such datasets, the system can run data mining algorithms to find rules that describe outcomes of the classification feature.

In EVS, the J48 algorithm from the WEKA Machine Learning Library (Hall et al. 2009) is used on the dataset to extract a descriptive decision tree model. J48 is an open source version of the C4.5 algorithm developed by J. Ross Quinlan (1993). The decision tree is a classic way to represent information from a machine learning algorithm and offers a fast and powerful way to express structures in data. One of the most useful characteristics of decision trees is their comprehensibility. Rules in a decision tree are represented in a tree structure with a feature test at each node. If these tests are well chosen, a surprisingly small tree is sufficient to accurately classify test objects. A test object enters the tree at the root node, and a test is applied at each node to determine which child node the test object will encounter next. Various algorithms identify, structure, and select a set of test nodes, but the goal is the same: choose the test that best discriminates among the target classes (Berry and Linoff 1997). To classify an unknown instance, it is routed down the tree according to the values of the features tested in successive nodes. When a leaf is reached, the instance is classified according to the class assigned to the leaf (Witten and Frank 2005).

The following is an extracted decision tree model that describes traces involving *Team 1*. All duration features and organizational units at all aggregation levels were selected as descriptive feature candidates. The numbers in parentheses at the end of each leaf node indicate the number of classified and misclassified examples in this leaf node.

```
stock trading complete = true
| duration, vru start -> stock trading start <= 11000: false
(3.0/1.0)
| duration, vru start -> stock trading start > 11000: true
(11.0/1.0)
stock trading complete = false: false (186.0/24.0)
Number of Leaves :   3
Size of the tree :   5
Correctly Classified Instances 343 85.75 %
Incorrectly Classified Instances 57 14.25 %
```

This decision tree model says that if *stock trading complete* is involved in the trace and the duration from the start of the VRU operation until the customer is serviced is equal to or below 11 seconds, *Team 1* is most likely not involved. This rule is supported by three of four correctly classified instances. The decision tree continues stating that if *stock trading complete* is involved and the duration value exceeds 11 seconds, *Team 1* is most likely involved. The last rule says that if *stock trading complete* is not involved, *Team 1* is not involved. The decision rule model is constructed on a training set and evaluated against a test set. By default, EVS constructs both the training and test datasets by randomly selecting 50% of the entries from the total dataset. This decision tree model classifies about 85% of the traces correctly. In summary, it tells us that Team 1 almost exclusively handles the stock trading service and their customers tend to spend at least 11 seconds from the time they call until they are serviced by human operators.

15.5 Related Work

15.5.1 Semantics

In our work, we used external ontologies to form searchable contexts around traces to create hierarchical breakdown structures for analyzing them. Within the process mining research community, significant work has also been done to use ontologically annotated event logs for reasoning (Alves de Medeiros et al. 2007; Celino et al. 2007). The Semantic LTL Checker is a ProM plug-in that allows semantic verification of properties in SA-MXML logs based on linear temporal logic (LTL) (Alves de Medeiros et al. 2008). This tool would enable our Wells Bank example company to verify whether specific teams operate certain services.

15.5.2 "Spaghettiness"

Existing process mining techniques perform well on structured processes, but have problems representing and visualizing less structured ones (Van der Aalst and Günther 2007). When we apply process mining on event logs with many distinct activities, the results are often complex spaghetti-like model structures that are difficult to understand. Process mining algorithms such as heuristic mining have been created to extract the main flow of business processes and handle real-life noise and exceptions (Weijters et al. 2006).

Trace clustering is an approach in process mining that applies data clustering techniques to event logs to extract homogeneous subsets. Data clustering techniques such as sequence clustering (Ferreira 2009; Veiga and Ferreira 2009) and self-organizing maps (SOMs) (Song et al. 2009; Mans et al. 2009) have successfully been applied in process mining projects to identify natural clusters that group traces with similar characteristics. By splitting the event logs into clusters, process mining can be applied on each subset where much of the overall complexity and detail are reduced or even eliminated.

In our work, we show how clusters of traces can be defined by combining index-ing of traces, search queries, and ontological structures. Similarly to trace cluster-ing, ontology-based clusters or custom search queries create homogeneous subsets of traces that potentially hide overall model complexity and detail. The advantage is that trace clustering does not rely on any ontological structure related to the event logs. Also, the clustering algorithms can be optimized to find the set of clusters that show minimal overlap and maximum internal flow dependencies. However, since the clusters are identified automatically, how to label them and understand why certain clusters are grouped is not always obvious. Letting a user define the clus-ters manually though search queries or utilize ontological structures to construct them produces clusters with recognizable labels and meanings. Clusters based on ontological structures also have meaningful relationships to other ontology-based clusters. This enables a user to understand how separate models fit together and relate to each other.

Semantically annotated event logs also have the ability to transform the com-plexity of detailed models to more abstract and conceptual levels that describe gen-eral characteristics. The Ontology Abstraction Filter is another plug-in to ProM that utilizes semantic annotations in event logs. As in the multiperspective control flow module of EVS, a user can set a specific abstraction level to be used in visual-ization of discovered flow models (Funk et al. 2009).

Another work dealing with the spaghetti-like complexity of discovered pro-cess mining models is the Fuzzy Miner (Günther and Aalst 2007), a plug-in to ProM that addresses the mining of unstructured processes by using a mixture of abstraction and clustering. It attempts to hide visual noise automatically and group model elements that are likely to have low information values for a user. The user controls the level of model detail by setting a threshold value on a slider.

15.5.3 Rule Extraction

Decision mining, also referred to as decision point analysis, aims to detect data dependencies that affect the routing of a trace. In our MXML example data, VRU output is a variable that decides the routing from the automated VRU operation to the appropriate service operator. For example, the *NC* VRU output value would forward a customer to an operator handling new customers. With decision mining, a system potentially finds a decision point after completion of the VRU operation, and the routing from that point is based on four different VRU output values.

Decision Miner is a plug-in to ProM that uses decision trees to classify alterna-tive paths from a decision point. The output form is a business process model in which the outputs from the decision points are annotated with discovered decision rules (Rozinat and Aalst 2006). Decision Miner solves its classification problem in a manner similar to the data mining module of EVS. The difference is that EVS discovers characteristics of a manually selected cluster of traces, and Decision

Miner discovers characteristics for alternative paths in the process flows. Both use decision tree algorithms to model the data.

Casati and Shan (2002) describe a BPI system known as the HPPM Intelligent Process Data Warehouse (PDW) that makes extensive use of taxonomies to structure the analysis environment. As with EVS, nodes in distinct taxonomies can be used to define groups of traces. As an alternative to search sequences, PDW provides behavior templates to construct groups of interesting traces. An example of a behavior template is *Instances of process P that take more than N days to complete*, where *P* and *N* are variable values that must be provided by the user. PDW provides statistical functionality for calculating correlation values between selected groups. These correlation values are interpreted as indicators of cause effects.

15.6 Discussion

Search technology, and especially web and enterprise searching, has shown its applicability and power in allowing access to unstructured contents like web pages, documents, blog and wiki entries, and emails. Merging of structured, unstructured, and semi-structured data in search indices has enabled entirely new applications at the intersection of business intelligence and search. Enterprise search vendors like FAST (a Microsoft subsidiary) have begun to incorporate analytical functions like data visualization and reporting into their products (Evelson and Brown 2008; Owens, 2008). Business process intelligence solutions should take advantage of this convergence, giving users accessible insight and decision support.

In this chapter we have shown how BPI, along with search and ontologically structured event context information, can describe quality aspects of business processes and pinpoint improvement potentials. It is important to note that the information provided by this system is only one of several information sources behind effective change decisions. In the evolution charts in Section 15.3, we measured the time between completion of the voice machine (VRU) task until a human operator answered the phone, and the time used to service customers. These measures were extracted and visualized for all the teams at Wells Bank. The charts revealed that the values deviated significantly from day to day and from team to team. In many cases, it may be reasonable to cut process durations and minimize variances and flavors of process execution behavior to improve efficiency. However, in some business processes, typically those related to customer service, variances and case-dependent use of time and resources are beneficial.

If our teams at Wells Bank strived to keep service conversations as short as possible, the service quality from customers' viewpoint would most likely decrease. One consequence could be the need for customers to call multiple times to have their requests handled. If we now chart the service traces, we would see that the measures appear improved because service times dropped. However, as the number of traces increased, the overall efficiency and amount of time and resources spent on servicing the customers worsened. In summary, the outputs of BPI tools do not replace human business knowledge and other information sources, but BPI is a very valuable complement.

Workshops, on-the-job observations, and interviews are traditional techniques applied to gather good pictures of business processes. One of the biggest advantages of BPI tools over traditional techniques is their ability to describe processes that span both human and computer-assisted services. Many companies see the need to replace human operations with automated services carried out by computer agents to meet efficiency goals. In our Wells Bank case, the first step of customer service is handled by a voice machine. To gather knowledge about automated operations and how they merge into longer business process chains, traditional techniques are no longer adequate. We now need BPI tools like process mining that can trace event logs and reveal real business flows. For process mining algorithms, whether an operation is executed by a human operator or computer agent makes no difference.

Throughout this chapter we have seen how ontologies are fundamental for constructing searchable traces and trace clusters, enable drill-down capabilities, and extract process knowledge. For many BPI projects, custom application ontologies are unavailable. With little context information related to the executed events, the ability of BPI to provide information about business process qualities becomes significantly reduced. As complements to custom application ontologies, it is also possible to utilize common ontologies. Significant research work has focused on construction of enterprise ontologies. The main purpose of an enterprise ontology is to promote a common understanding among people across different enterprises and advance communications between people and applications and between different applications (Uschold et al. 1998; Dietz 2006). Pedrinaci et al. (2009) describe a set of common ontologies that specifically target business process analysis, extraction of metrics, and process mining. The upper ontology presented in this chapter targets integration and interpretation of event log structures. It is designed to be consistent with other enterprise ontologies, and at the same time be as minimal as possible so that it can apply to most process mining project settings. Although common ontologies do not provide custom details about a company's competitive uniqueness, they may be stand alone or applied with custom application ontologies as a middle layer below the upper ontology, thus giving BPI techniques valuable annotations and structure.

15.7 Conclusions

This chapter explained how search sequences and ontology structures provide entrance points for browsing and analyzing traces of events. As an alternative to automated clustering, search and ontology elements can be used to define trace clusters with meaningful names and interrelations. In the EVS BPI framework, trace clusters can be visually highlighted throughout an analysis, enabling analysts to investigate and compare specific data subsets. The involvement of ontologies enables BPI tools to understand more of the contexts around executed events. Statistical analysis and data mining algorithms get a richer set of features to model underlying data relationships, and process mining algorithms become capable of extracting multiperspective models that may be drilled down to show different perspectives and levels of detail.

For our example company, Wells Bank, these capabilities revealed process flows between organizational units and services at all defined aggregation levels. Bank users can form and analyze specific trace cluster-based relations to ontological concepts or search expressions. For example, they can cluster and highlight all traces that involve the same service team, and further investigate flows, trends, performances, and characteristics for each team via different analysis modules.

Knowledge about a company's business processes comes from many sources and in different formats including human knowledge, text documents, graphic models, source codes of legacy systems, and configurations of ERP systems (Van der Aalst 2009). Event logs provide valuable information that accurately and objectively describe flows and performance measures for executed business processes. However, to gather other quality aspects of business processes, like customer opinions and product reviews, we must process and use unstructured data sources (blogs, forums, web pages). The use of search technologies in BPI solutions can merge structured, unstructured, and semi-structured data and open it for entirely new applications that can align information fragments and visualize more complete process pictures.

Acknowledgments

We would like to thank George Varvaressos, Principal Consultant, Business Process Mining, for providing us with the basis for the event log we used throughout this chapter.

References

Alves de Medeiros, A.K., W.M.P. van der Aalst, and C. Pedrinaci. 2008. Semantic process mining tools: core building blocks. In *16th European Conference on Information Systems*, Galway.

Alves de Medeiros, A.K., C. Pedrinaci, W.M.P. van der Aalst, et al. 2007. An outlook on semantic business process mining and monitoring. *OTM 2007 Workshops*, Lecture Notes in Computer Science Series 4806, pp. 1244–1255.

Apache Lucene Query Syntax, http://lucene.apache.org/java/2_3_2/queryparsersyntax.html (accessed January 12, 2010).

Berry, M. and G. Linoff. 1997. *Data Mining Techniques for Marketing, Sales and Customer Support*. Wiley Interscience, New York.

Casati, F. and M. Shan. 2002. Semantic analysis of business process executions. In *8th International Conference on Extending Database Technology,* Springer, pp. 287–296.

Celino, I., A.K. Alves de Medeiros, G. Zeissler, et al. 2007. Semantic business process analysis. In *Proceedings of Workshop on Semantic Business Process and Product Lifecycle Management, Third European Semantic Web Conference,* CEUR Workshop Proceedings 251, pp. 44–47.

Dietz, J.L.G. 2006. *Enterprise Ontology: Theory and Methodology.* Springer.

Evelson, B. and M. Brown. 2008. Search + BI = Unified Information Access. Forrester Research.

Ferreira, D.R. 2009. Applied sequence clustering techniques for process mining. In *Handbook of Research on Business Process Modeling.* Information Science Reference Series, IGI Global, pp. 492–513.

Funk, M., A. Rozinat, A.K. Alves de Medeiros, et al. 2009. Improving product usage monitoring and analysis with semantic concepts. In *UNISCON,* Springer, pp. 190–201.

GapMinder, http://www.gapminder.org/ (accessed January 12, 2010).

Grigori, D., F. Casati, M. Castellanos, et al. 2004. Business process intelligence. *Computers in Industry 53*: 321–343.

Günther, C.W. and W.M.P. van der Aalst. 2007. Fuzzy mining: adaptive process simplification based on multi-perspective metrics. *International Conference on Business Process Management, Springer,* pp. 328–343.

Hall, M., E. Frank, G. Holmes, et al. 2009. The WEKA data mining software: an update. *SIGKDD Explorer 11*: 10–18.

Ingvaldsen, J.E. and J.A. Gulla. 2007. Preprocessing support for large scale process mining of SAP transactions. In *Business Process Management Workshops,* Springer, pp. 30–41.

Ingvaldsen, J.E. and J.A. Gulla. 2008. EVS process miner: Incorporating ideas from search ETL into process mining. In *Proceedings of 10th International Conference on Enterprise Information Systems,* pp. 340–347.

Konchady, M. 2008. *Building Search Applications: Lucene, LingPipe, and Gate.* Mustru Publishing.

Lausen, H., J. de Bruijn, A. Polleres, et al. 2005. *WSML: a language framework for semantic web services. Proceedings of W3C Workshop on Rule Languages for Interoperability.*

Mans, R.S., M.H. Schonenberg, M. Song, W.M.P. van der Aalst, and P.J.M. Bakker. 2009. *Biomedical Engineering Systems and Technologies, Communications in Computer and Information Science,* Volume 25. ISBN 978-3-540-92218-6. Springer Berlin Heidelberg, p. 425.

Owens, L. 2008. *The Forrester Wave: Enterprise Search Q2 2008.* Forrester Research, Inc.

Pedrinaci, C., I. Markovic, F. Hasibether, et al. 2009. Strategy-driven business process analysis. *12th International Conference on Business Information Systems,* Springer, pp. 169–180.

Quinlan, J.R. 1993. *C4.5: Programs for Machine Learning.* Morgan Kaufmann, San Francisco.

Rozinat, A. and W.M.P. van der Aalst. 2006. Decision mining in business processes. *BETA Working Paper Series, WP 164,* Eindhoven University of Technology.

Song, M., C.W. Günther, and W.M.P. van der Aalst. 2009. Trace clustering in process mining. *Business Process Management Workshops,* Springer, pp. 109–120.

Uschold, M., K. Martin, M. Stuart, et al. 1998. Enterprise ontology. *Knowledge Engineering Review* 13.

Van der Aalst, W.M.P and C.W. Günther. 2007. Finding structure in unstructured processes: The case for process mining. In *17th International Conference on Applications of Concurrency to System Design,* IEEE Computer Society Press, pp. 3–12.

Van der Aalst, W.M.P. 2008. Decision support based on process mining. In *Handbook on Decision Support Systems, Part 1, Basic Themes*, International Handbooks on Information Systems Series, Springer, Heidelberg, pp. 637–657.

Van der Aalst, W.M.P. 2009. Using process mining to generate accurate and interactive business process maps. *Business Information Systems Workshops,* Springer, pp. 1–14.

Van Dongen, B. F. and W. M. P. van der Aalst. 2005. A meta model for process mining data. In *Conference on Advanced Information Systems Engineering*, Porto, Portugal, Vol. 161.

Veiga, G.M. and D.R. Ferreira. 2009. Understanding spaghetti models with sequence clustering for ProM. business process intelligence. *BPI Workshop Proceedings.*

Watson, H., D. Annino, B. Wixom, et al. 2001. Current practices in data warehousing. *Information Systems Management 18*: 47–55.

Weijters, A., W.M.P. van der Aalst, and A.K. Alves de Medeiros. 2006. Process mining with the heuristics miner algorithm. Beta Working Paper WP166.

Wen, L., J. Wang, W.M.P. van der Aalst, et al. 2004. A novel approach for process mining based on event types. BETA Working Paper WP 118.

Witten, I.H. and E. Frank. 2005. *Data Mining: Practical Machine Learning Tools and Techniques*, 2nd ed., Morgan Kaufmann.

Chapter 16

Semantics for Energy Efficiency in Smart Home Environments

Slobodanka Tomic and Anna Fensel
Forschungszentrum Telekommunikation Wien GmbH, Vienna, Austria

Michael Schwanzer
University of Applied Sciences, Vienna, Austria

Mirna Kojic Veljovic and Milan Stefanovic
E-Smart Systems DOO, Beograd, Serbia

Contents

16.1 Introduction

Climate change due to rising CO_2 emissions is one of the biggest environmental challenges of the 21st century. Achieving 20% savings in energy consumption by 2020 through energy efficiency is one of the key measures to keep CO_2 emissions under control (EC ICT 2008). Intelligent, in particular, semantically enabled, solutions for home or building automation and management (building automation systems or BASs) can offer significant contributions to energy conservation. Potential savings that may be achieved through smart control of heating, ventilation, air conditioning, lighting, and other systems are estimated at 35% (EC ICT 2008). In addition, BASs provide advanced security and safety through alarms, leakage detection, fire detection and suppression, prevention of unlawful intrusions, and pollution reduction.

The global market for such systems has a significant size and potential, with an estimated average annual growth rate of 5%. Recent market research (Frost and Sullivan 2009) finds that the European building management and control system products market earned revenues of $1.62 billion in 2004 and estimates revenues to reach $1.84 billion in 2011 (Green Intelligent Buildings 2006). The European market is dominated by control box manufacturers and system integrators. Current BASs, however, offer limited intelligence commonly based on principles of on–off switching with scheduled or simple logic-based activation of attached peripherals.

To fully exploit the capabilities of building automation systems for the purposes of advanced energy management, they must be integrated with novel smart metering solutions or advanced metering infrastructure (AMIs; ESMIG 2009), also referred to as demand side management (DLMS 2009). Advanced metering is a new approach toward real-time energy consumption monitoring and supply optimization. AMI systems connect advanced meters deployed at the customer premises with the information and control system at the grid operator's side. The purpose of smart metering is to provide both energy suppliers and end customers with detailed information about temporal energy use and demands at different levels of aggregation, such as consumption per apartment, per building, per residential area, etc. This information can facilitate demand prediction and supply planning and optimization, and serve as a basis for adaptive energy pricing and advanced applications of semantic techniques to bring energy-related information to the users. DLMS implementation today is the basis for advanced systems for meter readings such as MESMET (2008) and OSP (2008).

A study of the impact of energy usage information on user behavior by Darby (2006) shows that a simple technology-enabled feedback to customers based on timely presentation of meter measurements can produce energy savings of about 3 to 15%. It is becoming increasingly important to understand how presentation of utility-related data, real-time consumption measurements, and tariffs influence user behavior, and also how such data can be used automatically by a home automation system that acts on behalf of a user.

16.1.1 Problem Statement

At present, environment control and energy management in standard home environments is rarely supported by advanced means. Most home systems accommodate simple building automation systems, for example, to regulate temperatures. Up-to-date information about the deregulated energy market, such as energy tariffs or available energy types, can be acquired via Internet access. Depending on the country (Smart Metering Project Map 2009), a typical home may already be equipped with a smart meter that may include a handy display and a service that offers access to a secured Web page to review energy consumption–time diagrams. Reviewing the diagrams enhances potential for energy saving that otherwise depends on customers' awareness of good practices like switching lights off, changing temperature levels at nights, and understanding tariffs.

To take this burden from the residents, more advanced home automation system may be deployed to intelligently control lights, heating, and ventilation according to the specific situation and tariffs, but it typically requires programming and a user who acts as an administrator. When appropriately programmed, these systems reduce energy cost, but the administrator must be aware of changes in tariffs and user requirements so that the system can be reprogrammed accordingly. Obviously, the performance of these system depends on proper administration—often criticized as too daunting a task for a typical homeowner. Significant improvement can be achieved only by using technology that can both connect the parts of the system that exchange information directly and also interact with a user in an intuitive and user-friendly way. Semantic technology and service-oriented design are the key pillars of such improvements.

In particular, the SESAME project (2009) uses ontology-based modeling and service-oriented design to integrate building automation and advanced metering in a truly flexible system controlled by user-generated policies. It is important to notice that such "semantic gluing" is not trivial; it requires understanding of many domain-specific issues—in this case, within the automation and energy domains.

The approach has not yet been explored broadly, partially because of proprietary developments in metering and data processing automation and the complexities of ontology management. Unlike today's competing products that offer manual, scheduled, or simple logic-based activation and setting of peripherals such as lights, heating, air conditioning, and access controls, SESAME is designed to operate on a common semantically described framework of multimodal factors including preferences and policies of users, operational factors of peripheral devices, sensors, and actuators, and external information characterizing the availability and cost of energy.

16.1.2 Chapter Organization

Section 16.2 defines the overall goals of the SESAME project and describes three representative innovative scenarios. Section 16.3 reviews the state of the art in related areas and positions our approach within the landscape of related activities. The architecture and technical details of the semantically-enabled SESAME system are described in Section 16.4. Section 16.5 provides a discussion and outlook.

16.2 SESAME Vision, Goals, and Illustrative Scenarios

16.2.1 Vision and Goals

SESAME's overall societal and technological vision and goals can be summarized easily. The system will help end customers to save energy and optimize their energy costs, while they control and maintain their living conditions. The goal is oriented to a potentially broad customer market. By integrating smart metering and building automation systems, users will have the means to monitor and control their environments and energy consumption in a holistic way, based on their own semantically specified policies. Such policies will regulate operations in physical spaces by turning off stand-by devices, switching to alternative energy generation sources, and controlling privacy and security settings.

Integrated functions will enable energy suppliers to facilitate energy savings for users and build diversified service portfolios and pricing schemes. These services will support direct integration of end customer metering information (now under exclusive control of AMI operators) and other energy-related information, such as tariffs, within the policy-based reasoning system of each end customer. This will enable consumers to better understand their energy consumption patterns and help them select the most efficient energy service portfolios and pricing schemes. As a means for advanced planning of resources, SESAME will provide suppliers with energy optimization services to facilitate global optimization. These services will allow customers to delegate optimization of their environments to an external entity via provisioning access to their devices and policies.

16.2.2 Scenarios for Energy Efficiency in Smart Home Environments

SESAME's innovative scenarios for energy efficiency address semantically different layers in the interactions of elements of the smart metering system and the home automation system. We will describe three representative scenarios: (1) operation of energy efficiency equipment, (2) definition and processing of user policies, and (3) sharing such policies socially on the semantic Internet.

16.2.2.1 Scenario 1: Intelligent Equipment for Controlling Peak Power Loads

Motivation: Decreasing peak load in a user's home or in a provider's substation region. A higher-than-predicted peak load may be a problem for both customers and utilities. The end customer may be required to pay higher energy prices for energy use during a "red" consumption period. A utility may encounter problems if the load on a substation region is higher than the predicted load because of an imbalance in the electrical grid.

Every device uses its maximum peak load when switched on. This load in a smart home is measured and stored in a central control element or universal control box (UCB). We further assume that major consumer appliances in the home are attached to small metering devices such as intelligent plugs that measure current power and can communicate with the UCB. After the switches turn on, for example, an air conditioning system, the UCB processes the request, taking into account the power needed to switch on the device, the current power load in the home, and the policies defined by the user and utility. The UCB reasons about whether to allow this request, act on potential warning information on the display, or simply queue the request with other requests.

Similarly, considering a broader region of several households, the power load can be managed by a smart concentrator colocated with a control meter at a transformer substation. All UCBs in the region communicate with the smart concentrator. For major consumers, they forward switch-on requests to the smart concentrator. Based on the power needed to switch on the major consumer's device, current power loads in the region, and policy defined by the utility, the smart UCB manages the load balance of its substation region. For example, when outside temperature exceeds 30°C, consumers probably want to turn on air conditioning. A smart concentrator will "serialize" these switching actions to keep the general peak load as low as possible.

16.2.2.2 Scenario 2: Demand–Response Policies in Interactions with Energy Market

Motivation: For utilities, the motivation is to provide demand response programs. For consumers, the motivation is active participation in the energy market. Suppliers want to reduce supply process risks.

As a result of implementing advanced metering infrastructure with smart meters owned and controlled by utilities and deployed at residences and sophisticated home automation systems and UCBs owned and controlled by consumers, a utility system can provide advanced demand–response programs involving energy suppliers, energy distributors, and energy consumers.

The suppliers control deliveries and prices of energy and sell their goods and services to new customers. Their basic interest is to supply the exact amounts of energy that customers will use, and deliver the required amounts to the grid. If they deliver more energy, the distributors will redeem it at unfavorable prices. If consumers use more energy than expected, a distributor increases its charges. Distributors deliver energy from suppliers to customers and charge for distribution, metering, and billing and settlement services.

Consider an imaginary customer named Mary who selected three different suppliers (Green Grid, Smart Supply, and OnDemand) and developed specific energy consumption policies based on their offerings:

- Switch on the electric boiler and simultaneously switch off the gas boiler when price for 1 kwh is 50% lower than price for 1 liter.
- Choose Green Grid if consumption is less than 3 kw.
- Choose the cheapest supplier if consumption exceeds 3 kw.
- Alert me if consumption is larger than 5 kw and switch off a predefined set of devices if consumption remains so for 15 minutes.
- Decrease consumption to desired level when you receive demand from a distributor.

Mary published all her energy consumer policies to her energy suppliers. The suppliers continuously monitor consumption of their customers and check their energy consumer policies, monitor market conditions, manage their energy tariffs, and decide whether to buy additional energy and at what price. The most interesting policies for suppliers specify exact preferred times or intervals of an automation activity such as: "Raise temperature 5° degrees at 17:00," or "Switch on dishwasher between 19:00 and 24:00." Conversely, distributors continuously monitor grid state. If the expected synchronization is lost, it instantly sends alerts to consumers and suppliers. Depending on the availability of energy resources and the state of the grid, restrictive actions such as switching off devices with highest consumptions using UCBs can be performed.

16.2.2.3 Scenario 3: Social Network Energy Policy Sharing

Motivation: Decrease energy consumption by exchanging semantic policies over the Internet.

At present, most users are aware of some simple best-practice rules that may help save energy in a household. The most familiar rule is turning all lights off when leaving.

With the SESAME system, rules that save money or bring other advantages to the home environment are translated into semantic policies. Based on the system interoperability that ontology-based design will facilitate, these policies may be published and shared and make saving energy easy and fun. For example, in an online game designed and set up in an existing social network site, people team up and compete with other teams to reach energy efficiency goals. "Using 20% less energy than last week" may be one of those goals. Members of a team may try to reduce their energy consumption by implementing promising semantic policies. The outcome of using selected policies may be directly posted by a team member's home automation system on the team page, allowing successful policies to be shared and implemented within a group. After a goal is reached, the winning team's policies are published so that everyone can benefit from what was learned. Such games are fun because playing with friends may save money on a utility bill. Furthermore, end users become energy aware and "fight for a good cause" within their social network.

These three scenarios show that integration of a smart home system with a smart metering (demand management) system—the vision and aim of the SESAME project—will have to address various interactions among the relevant stakeholders to create an intelligent environment integrating home and grid requirements and constraints.

Existing research on pervasive intelligent environments in general and smart home systems in particular offers valuable input on how semantic technology deals with flexible integration of heterogeneous devices, services, and user requirements and supports automated reasoning. In the novel scenario that we address, the new requirements of integration arise from attempts to make decisions based on contexts in the home environment and the broader context of energy demand control. The next section reviews approaches derived from smart home research and provides guidance for developing more complex energy-responsive systems.

16.3 Overview of Existing Semantically Enabled Modeling Approaches for Smart Homes

In recent years, advances in several research areas exerted significant impacts on the modeling and implementation of pervasive environments and smart homes. These topics include the design of context-aware middleware characterized by adaptability and flexibility, service-oriented functional modeling, agent technology for modeling and realization of interactions in environments with high uncertainty, and ontology-based modeling for context awareness and automated, policy-based decision making.

A smart home is a heterogeneous dynamic system that must be open for easy integration of interactions with many devices and services [centrally controlled lights, heating, ventilation and air conditioning (HVAC) systems, automated window blinds, lawn watering equipment, swimming pool systems, photovoltaic systems, other renewable energy devices, multimedia, comfort, and supervision services] to a variety of users. Integrated devices are highly heterogeneous and their configurations and maintenance often require special effort. However, particularly in home care applications, users are often nontechnical; devices and services must seamlessly cooperate to support users' needs by acting on their behalf (Henricksen et al. 2002). To operate in highly dynamic environments, the devices, services, and agents must be context-aware, where *context* is the information characterizing a specific transient situation (Dey and Abowd 2000).

Research has identified two essential requirements for building context-aware systems: a suitable context model and middleware level support. The middleware is the best place to deal with the context acquisition from physical sensors, databases, and agents; context interpretation and timely dissemination; and orchestration of more complex context-aware services. A very prominent middleware (software) platform used in smart home research focused on dynamically extensible embedded design is OSGI (2005; Bonino et al. 2008; Rodondo et al. 2008). Other technologies such as WSMX mashups, Yahoo pipes, Apple app. SDT, and Google Android are expected to play increasingly important roles in interactions with users.

The existing approaches to context model design may be classified as application-oriented, model-oriented, and ontology-oriented (Gu et al. 2004). Application-oriented approaches represent context relevant only for specific applications (Dey et al. 2001; Kindberg and Barton 2001). Therefore they lack formality and expressiveness and do not support knowledge sharing across different systems. The model-oriented approaches are commonly based on a formal context model such as the entity–relationship (ER) model of Harter at al. (2002) and the object–role model (ORM) of Henricksen et al. (2003) and are easily managed with relational databases. The model-oriented approaches lack knowledge sharing and context reasoning. The ontology-oriented approaches focus on context ontology and explore the benefits of automated context reasoning based on Semantic Web technologies.

Ontology-based knowledge modeling has received significant attention as a central concept of the Semantic Web (Berners-Lee and Fischetti 1999; Noy et al. 2001). Ontology is the shared understanding of some domains—a specification of a conceptualization—often conceived as a set of entities, relations, functions, axioms, and instances (Gruber 1993). Ontology-oriented approaches to smart home modeling address issues critical for realizing efficient, user-friendly, and cost-effective solutions. The benefits of the ontology-based modeling are knowledge sharing, logic inference at a high level, conceptual context at a low level, raw context, and existing domain knowledge reuse. Ontology languages such as RDF and OWL support the specification of concepts, relationships, and associated classification and reasoning mechanisms for data. OWL is presently the preferred language for defining ontologies, mainly because of its better expressiveness as compared to other ontology languages such as RDFS (Brickley and Guha 2003), its ability to support semantic interoperability and context knowledge sharing, and its automated reasoning.

Therefore, the ontology-based model has been established as a technology of choice for context-aware and smart home applications (Gu et al. 2004). Integrated within the service-oriented architecture (SOA), an ontology facilitates intelligent service discovery and composition (Tsai 2005; Papazoglou and Georgakapoulos 2003). The concepts of SOA support dynamic discovery of available functions and their invocation in a loosely coupled manner. Several SOA approaches that focus on specialization for automation-related architectures are known. Examples include Universal Plug and Play (UPnP, 2009), Devices Profile for Web Services (DPWS, 2009), OPC Foundation (OPC, 2009), and others. Another important open-source initiative is Service-Oriented Architecture for Devices (SOA4D, 2009), which is intended to foster an ecosystem for the development of service-oriented software components (SOAP messaging, WS-* protocols, service orchestration) adapted to the specific constraints of embedded devices.

Several context modeling approaches identify the need to differentiate between general context information (focused on users, tasks, and higher layer situations) and specific context information focusing on devices to support these tasks. This is an important direction that must be addressed when energy-specific ontology extensions are required.

A model proposed by Gu et al. (2004) and integrated within the Service-Oriented Context-Aware Middleware (SOCAM) is based on a common upper ontology for general context information and a set of low-level ontologies applying to different subdomains. OWL (Web Ontology Language; Smith et al. 2003) is used to create a semantic context representation describing the basic concepts of person, location, computational entity and activity, and properties and relationships among these concepts. The upper ontology captures general context knowledge; the domain-specific ontologies define the details of general concepts and their properties in each subdomain. The low-level ontology can be dynamically plugged into and unplugged from the upper ontology when the environment is changed.

Based on the means by which the context is obtained, the distinction between the direct and indirect contexts is made. Direct context is acquired from content provider services implemented by internal sensors or an external information server, and may be sensed or defined by a user. To model the quality of the sensed context, four quality parameters are defined: accuracy, resolution, certainty, and freshness. By automated reasoning based on first-order logic predicates, the deduced context can be inferred from sensed, aggregated, and defined contexts, taking also into account the quality of the context. Different services acquiring the sensed context from sensors or external information sources feed into the context knowledge database.

The proposed model can contain different contexts and their inter-relationships and captures the quality of sensed contexts. Context reasoning is the central component of the SOCAM architecture, and different context reasoning engines may be combined to establish confidence in inferred contexts before the applications act on them. The inference rules are used by the reasoning engine producing inferred higher level contexts. Similarly, Wang et al. (2004) define an extensible CONtext ONtology (CONON) for modeling context in pervasive computing environments. Location, user, activity (e.g., cooking, showering, sleeping), and computational entity are the most fundamental contexts for capturing the information about an executing situation. A set of upper-level entities in the upper ontology can be extended easily with specific ontology sets that define the details of general concepts and their features in each subdomain.

While energy-aware user behaviors may seem concentrated within their homes, this concept may need more flexibility. A user may prefer to save energy in any intelligent environment in which he or she roams. One interesting ontology-based modeling approach that provides direction for further work on this issue is a result of the European Union's ATRACO project (Goumopoulos and Kameas 2008). It designs a model of ambient ecologies (AEs) as conglomerates of devices and services that interact with each other, with the environment, and with people inhabiting the environment. The users are characterized along with their goals for comfort, mobility, or activity. N "activity sphere" is introduced to describe all the devices that temporarily surround a user in terms of the related domain model and the task-based applications they perform. The proposed system is based on the service-oriented architecture organization of the API, interfacing with the hardware modules and communication protocols, ontologies and ontology management modules, decision making mechanisms, planning modules, negotiation and learning mechanisms, intelligent agents, trust policies and privacy enforcement mechanisms, and composable interaction components.

The aim is to execute higher level tasks over inherently heterogeneous devices and services. Therefore, the focus is on establishing independence between a task description and its concrete realization via ontology modeling and ontology alignment mechanisms. Intelligent agents are used to implement transient component interactions for adaptive task planning, task realization, and enhanced human–machine interactions supporting user activity in changing contexts. ATRACO proposes an ontology-based approach to system adaptation within the activity sphere, where interfaces between the constituent environment ontologies and higher-level aim description are recalculated on demand based on availability of constituent passive entities (devices and services). The sphere also includes active entities: task and interaction agents, ontology manager, and sphere manager. Operation is based on aim ontology, local ontologies, and sphere ontology formed by aligning, merging, and mapping of local ontologies. The sphere components cooperate to realize user tasks and operate the devices and services according to a dynamically created sphere ontology.

Flexibility in creating complex services based on available devices and preferences in using them is one important requirement in integrating smart homes and demand management systems based on smart metering information. The ontology-based design proposed by Xu et al. (2009) addresses a service model in which requested applications cannot be fulfilled by a single device. The service model consists of a set of devices working together as specified in an application template (service composition) description. The smart home ontology is composed of a device ontology describing concepts related to devices; an environment ontology describing the natural environment and user profiles; a policy and preference ontology describing basic system constraints and preference rules covering device uses and functions; and as a core of the knowledge base, a function ontology describing the atomic or composed service functions.

The ontology is the blueprint of the knowledge base that interacts with the smart home active functions; the household data manager implements the registry for devices, the service manager, and the plan deployment component. A function request made by a user during run when a running device may be unavailable may require a new device added to the system or an unused device removed. The system executes a function plan based on previous requested functions. The plan is constantly adjusted when new function is requested or a device becomes unavailable. A function plan is generated based on device ontology, function ontology, and information about available devices, and thus involves knowledge query, plan construction, and plan deployment.

A knowledge query may result in several function plans; preferences are used to rank these plans and deploy the best one. During plan deployment, mapping from the high-layer function into specific protocols and interactions of devices is performed. Adding and removing devices will update the device registry. Ontology maintenance is a critical task in such a dynamic system. Adding items to ontologies may be required to represent new device or function concepts. Deleting items may be needed to keep the running ontology small.

Ontology management is a well researched topic addressed in many projects. EU FP6 includes Project Semantics Utilised for Process Management within and between Enterprises (SUPER, 2009), Project Data, Information, and Process Integration with Semantic Web Services (DIP, 2007), Semantically Enabled Knowledge Technologies (SEKT, 2006), and Project KnowledgeWeb

(KnowledgeWeb, 2007). One EU FP7 project is Reasoning on the Web with Rules and Semantics (REWERSE, 2009). Energy efficiency ontology design has been addressed by two other EU FP7 projects: Intelligent Self-Describing Technical and Environmental Networks (S-TEN, 2008) and SmartHouse/SmartGrid (SHSG, 2009).

One important aspect of ontology-based modeling is support for reasoning, in particular creation and management of user-specified policies. The SESAME project addresses issues of policy *pervasiveness, legislation, economy and governance,* and *reasoning.* In the area of policy pervasiveness, SESAME will extend the overall state of the art to smart metering environments. General studies of semantic policies already exist and support the policy-aware web approach and deployment of generic policy engine prototypes (Kagal and Berners-Lee 2005; Kolovski et al. 2005; Zhdanova et al., 2009). As to legislation, economy, and governance aspects of policy design, machine-readable policies will improve human–machine interactions in complex transactions and increase transparency and accountability.

Policies may control privacy protection and handling of transaction generated data. They can also specify a user's preferred product and service bundle, including accounting for energy consumption and billing from various providers in a competitive energy market. At present, reasoning with policies is normally achieved with general purpose reasoning engines in a generic manner using tools such as EULER (2009) or PYCHINKO (2009) reasoners, such as tools along with well established JENA (2009) and PROTÉGÉ (2009) to create and process ontologies.

Policy-based smart home systems assist users to modify behaviors of systems. A typical policy defines event conditions and actions (ECAs) as contexts (Dey et al. 2001). Raw sensor data are not used directly; they are interpreted or aggregated to produce high-level contexts. The way policies are integrated in a system determines the ease with which the system infers and can be changed.

One interesting ontology-based modeling approach that integrates service-oriented architecture and can provide services adapted to the needs of its inhabitants is proposed in Ricquebourg et al. (2007). The system takes into account the ambient context of its inhabitants and provides context-aware services. A four-layer architecture that manages data acquisition and context information is defined: it includes a perception layer that obtains information through sensors; a context layer that provides a semantic view of the perceived data; an inference layer that computes the contextual data; and an action layer that triggers actions decided by the inference layer. Within this architecture, the context model is based on ontology designed in OWL. The inference layer is based on SWRL. The ontology is filled with contextual data through the ontology service. SWRL allows reasoning from ontology through two types of inference rules, transforming low-level contextual data into high-level contextual concepts.

The back-chain rules model constraints in the ontology are directly injected into the OWL file; the forward-chain rules define the actions to be triggered on a specific context. The proposed architecture is characterized by a loose coupling of components achieved by using an event-driven bus. The sensors and inference engine publish events relevant for actions of actuators. For example, in a scenario where a user moves and a system automatically switches on the nearest lights, a rule that binds the location of an inhabitant with the location of a lamp is used; the sensors detect motion and the software driver publishes an event, specifying parameters including topic, time stamp, sensor identification, and measurement value. All services subscribing to this topic receive this event.

The ontology service subscribes to events of all sensors and uses their data to fill in the ontology at the appropriate place. For this purpose, the ontology is queried and the value of the respective individual sensor changed. Because individual entities are linked within the ontology, the context can propagate through back-chain rules. As a result of an ontology update with real sensor data, the follow-up actions are inferred based on forward-chain rules, and the events specifying actions are distributed to the services controlling actuators subscribed to such events. The actuators issue device- and network-specific concrete control commands. This system allows easy ontology-based integration of sensors and actuators. However, the execution of concrete control depends on the performance of the underlying network and the inference engine.

The benefit of decoupling policies from the underlying sensor technology via high-level context modeling is the flexibility to use different sensors dynamically. The decoupling of policies from the underlying actuators by defining a general actuation can also be beneficial when different devices are selected based on their availability. This problem was addressed by Wang and Turner (2009) who proposed a model for actuator discovery and use of an ontology for a protocol-independent action specification. The operation of actuators is modeled in an ontology, and the actuators can register themselves with a semantic service discovery module. Based on that, the actions in a policy rule can be specified using abstract operations and parameters, and only at run time will the semantic discovery module search for concrete actuator instances.

Semantically supported visualization of energy use information is another important area to be addressed. Energy usage information was fairly invisible to users in the past. Many people received usage data with their utility bills only once a year by mail. This is changing in countries that already deploy smart meters, and energy companies offer users access to their consumption diagrams.

Several companies developed products that can directly visualize usage information without interactions with energy companies. A simple device that plugs in between an outlet and an appliance to be monitored will indicate the number of watts used in real time. One representative of this type of device is the Kill A Watt of P3 International (2009). The drawback of the product is that one device is needed for each outlet, and the usage information cannot be acquired for appliances that are directly connected to a house grid. Another type of device obtains data from a power line connected to an old-style meter. The device is equipped with induction loops and does not require direct connection to a grid. An integrated transmitter delivers the data to an in-house display that visualizes current usage and can compare it with other breakpoints in its history. Some inventions show economic impacts in term of used energy cost. CurrentCost (2009), a United Kingdom company, has sold more than 600,000 such devices that may also be connected to computers to store or publish the collected data. WATTSON (2009), another device from the U.K., indicates electricity usage with different light colors and can generate statistics with the analysis software included in shipments. Devices delivering usage information to mobile phones already exist. Visual Energy (2009), a U.S. company, developed software that delivers visual feedback to mobile phones. Company hardware is needed for measuring usage at the outlets, but it is also possible to switch certain appliances on and off via phone software.

The system of Pachube (2009), a web service provider, does not fit in any of the groups described. With the challenging goal to make sharing, storing and discovering of sensor data anywhere in the world possible, this device can serve as a useful extension for the others. The web service makes several open interfaces available to interact with existing devices or with other web services.

16.4 SESAME Approach

Unlike technology focusing on the automation in the smart home domain and on users within that domain, the SESAME approach addresses new challenges from the required interactions within the user domain and among other stakeholders in the energy market. We summarize these challenges in the first part of this section, then portray and explain the architecture, highlighting all important semantic aspects of implementation of the architecture components.

16.4.1 Innovation Challenges

Major innovation pillars of the SESAME design are:

- Conceptual model-based integration of building automation; the central parts are the universal IP-based control box (UCB) and a smart meter. Smart meters are currently owned and controlled by utilities and direct integration in a home environment is not yet possible. Therefore service-based access to meter data provides bases for their integration. The research questions addressed by SESAME include which services have access rights to the smart meter, who owns the services, where they are deployed, and how they are controlled, secured, and aligned with trust and privacy models. These issues go beyond the simple question of network interfaces.
- Design of enablers for sophisticated monitoring and control of the home environment (user context). Components include the ontology-based modeling of situations that can be detected by sensors, smart meters services for

accessing energy-related data and executing actuator control, and models of user-specified policies. The cores of the system are automatic policy-based reasoning and service activation components. Policies represent complex business logic and procure automatic chaining (orchestration) of different services. An interactive graphical user interface (GUI) facilitates ontology-based policy creation.

■ Modeling of advanced energy information services for access to dynamically changing information, in particular, about the energy markets; for example, types of available energy, tariffs, and other factors, and the integration of services within the policy-based reasoning infrastructure of the user, allowing automatic triggering of relevant actions.

■ Design of sophisticated energy optimization services through which the ontology (or part of it) describing the user system and services controlling the user environment and user policies is shared with the system on the energy-provider side. Such services can be used in making higher level optimization decisions based on data from many users, and direct invocation of control services; for example, controlling the actuator regulating cooling levels in a user's refrigerator.

16.4.2 Semantics-Enabled Architecture

SESAME investigates the conceptual integration of building automation systems, smart metering, and demand management by means of semantic enablers that act as "glue" in providing flexibility in system configuration and adaptation, along with additional benefits and convenience to end customers and energy suppliers. SESAME investigates two models of integration of the user home environment and the broader demand management environment.

The first model is aligned with the current state of the art in which advanced energy meters are exclusively controlled by an external operator and a building automation system receives metering data and other energy-related information from remote sources. The second model goes further in terms of system function distribution across the boundaries of the integrated environments, and requires thorough evaluation of security trust and privacy functionalities in a new integrated system. Both settings use ontology-based modeling, multiobjective policy-based reasoning methods, and SOA designs with appropriate security and privacy preserving mechanisms.

Figure 16.1 illustrates the boundaries between the home automation and demand management environments. Currently these systems exist in parallel and are not integrated. SESAME integrates them via ontology modeling and service components to fully realize their joint potential. As depicted in the figure, a home environment has a central control (gateway and UCB) that connects to and controls the operation of devices integrated through standardized protocols and interfaces. The environmental values and control functions that can be monitored and controlled are known as user contexts. The UCB hosts

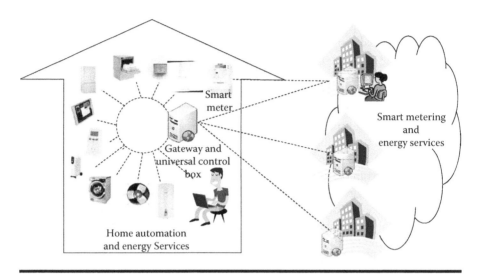

Figure 16.1   SESAME system overview.

functionalities to acquire and reason on the user contexts. The first functionality includes access to the measured environmental conditions and device status, as well as access to actuators for configuration and activation of functionalities. The second contains a variety of interactive interfaces that allow a user to specify his preferences to configure the management of resources in his environment or receive the feedback of his actions. The third is the reasoning core that maintains context information and allows the system to make automatic decisions to achieve the required actions.

The demand management environment intersects with the home environment at the smart meter. This device has a special role, as it directly measures parameters of the user context and operates under the exclusive access and control of the advanced metering infrastructure (AMI) provider. We based our design on the availability of complementary external Web information services that provide end customers with relevant energy market information (types of available energy, tariffs, criteria for selecting energy providers, etc.). We believe an innovative integration approach is required to make energy awareness a genuine parameter of cost saving and energy saving control within the home and demand management environments. The application of ontology management to create an interoperable multienvironment description will contribute to the pan-European vision of an "Internet of Things" as part of the future Internet initiative (EU Future Internet 2009).

To achieve this vision, SESAME designs architecture that brings together advanced service infrastructure, ontology and policy infrastructure, and context and policy-based reasoning. The central element is an extended ontology for the home and demand management environments that includes a model of energy-related entities, parameters, and situations; energy management and usage policies; and complementing ontologies describing home environment controls. The overall model enables automatic activation of services that encapsulate different interactions including data harvesting, actuator-based control, and interactions with users. Components of SESAME's integrated architecture are illustrated in Figure 16.2.

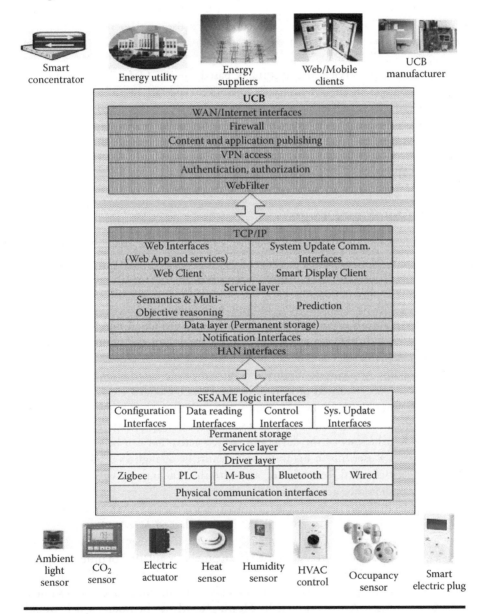

Figure 16.2 SESAME system architecture.

Services within the SESAME architecture provide different functionalities at different interfaces. For example, smart meter data is published by the AMI provider through an external SOAP-based Web service. On the same side of SESAME, the Web service client invokes this service and updates the knowledge base. Sensors, appliances, and displays are also implemented as service-based information publishers and consumers. As a home automation system is inherently an event-based system, each service interface also implements a notification passing capability for service-based interactions of users and energy providers or grid operators.

The SESAME service architecture is based on the OSGI. To account for dynamic changes in the environment and user expectations, SESAME designs flexible life-cycle management of ontologies and services. This provides means for dealing with dynamic additions of new system components (new types of devices) or adding a new user policy or workflow, a new energy provider, or a new home. The system allows "plug-in" ontologies and ontology evolution and selection driven by user needs.

16.4.3 Ontology Design

SESAME uses an ontology-based modeling approach to describe an energy-aware home and the relationships of the objects and actors within its control scenario. The SESAME ontology provides a hierarchy of concepts to model the automation and energy domains and is specified in OWL. The main components are the automation ontology, meter data ontology, and pricing ontology.

SESAME Automation Ontology (Figure 16.3) includes a number of general concepts such as Resident and Location, and concepts in the automation and in the energy domain, such as Device, and Configuration. The Device class has subclasses modeling Appliances, Sensors, or simple message-based User Interface (UI) devices. New energy-related properties in the Device model are consumption per hour, peak power, and the switch on/off status as well as the required state "to be switched on/off." For an Appliance, we also introduce the property "canBeStarted" which models the state of the devices for which activation can be scheduled. For example, after a user fills in his washing machine he configures it (via a new UI) with the "canBeStarted" set to "true," and with the time interval within which the washing task should be accomplished.

To model different types of control functionality, the SESAME ontology introduces the Configuration class, which has two subclasses: Activity (or automation activity) and EnergyPolicy. An Activity connects Appliance, Sensor, and UI Device into a joint task. A ContextBased Activity can provide regulation of different types, e.g., regulation on time, occupancy of location, or threshold value. For this purpose it includes properties including thresholds and scheduled times. An example of a ContextBased Activity would be HeatingRegulationBedroom which would connect TemperatureSensor in the Bedroom and Heater. This Activity would be

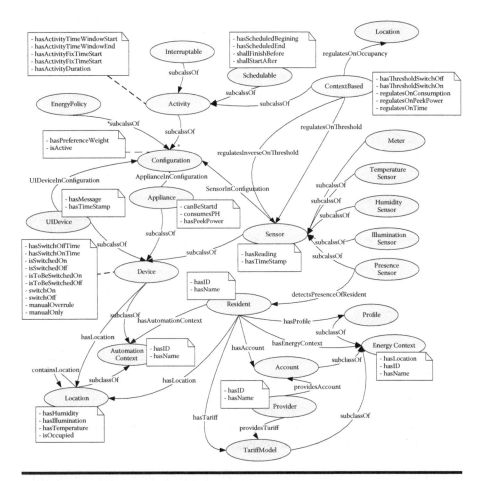

Figure 16.3   SESAME automation ontology.

configured as regulatesOnThreshold, and hasThresholdSwitchOn and hasThresholdSwitchOff would be set to 20° and 23°C, respectively.

Figure 16.3 also shows how the Automation Ontology links to the Meter Data Ontology (through the Meter class) and to the Pricing Ontology (through TariffModel and Provider classes).

SESAME meter data ontology—This ontology (Figure 16.4) is based on the DLMS standard (2009) for meter data modeling. The DLMS/COSEM specification defines a data model and communication protocols for data exchange with metering equipment.

A set of interface classes (register, activity calendar, clock) and a set of instances of these classes enable the meter to act as a server and publish its data to utilities, customers, or providers that can access the meter data as clients. A published measured object has a unique OBIS code consisting of six numbers. OBIS naming

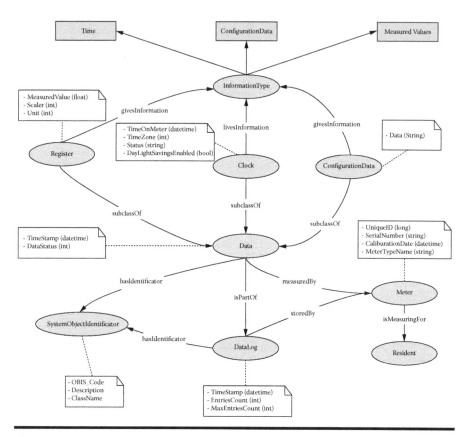

Figure 16.4   SESAME meter data ontology.

is used in logical name (LN) referencing. For a specific implementation of OBIS convention on a specific meter, a manufacturer must specify the objects supported and their OBIS codes.

As shown in Figure 16.4, stored data is of three major types, and every type provides different information. For example, the register keeps all data about active and reactive (+/–) current average power, active and reactive (+/–) energy, voltage, current, THD, cos φ, and active and reactive (+/–) maximum power for a defined period. Configuration data relates to meter status, status of all measured data, last and calibration date. The clock keeps information about time and meter time parameters. Since data can be stored on the meter in log objects (15-minute, daily, or monthly basis), they are also modeled in the ontology. Every object has a unique OBIS code that accompanies the description of what the object measures.

SESAME pricing ontology—This ontology (Figure 16.5) captures the concept of making energy-aware decisions and selecting an optimal tariff model for a specified time and energy load based on certain classes. SelectionCriteriaPonders is

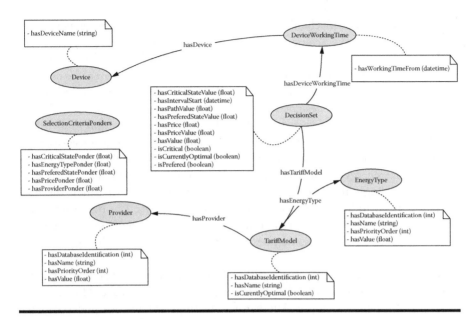

Figure 16.5   SESAME pricing ontology.

a reasoning configuration class that has only one instance; its properties represent ponders (significances of some criteria in choosing optimal tariff models). Provider and EnergyType classes represent providers and energy types that are available choices for decision making. Important properties of these classes are hasPriorityOrder and hasValue (representing pondered value for provider and energy type; depend on hasPriorityOrder value and the value of provider–energy type ponder specified in SelectionCriteriaPonder); TariffModel, which represents tariff models to which a customer is subscribed, the isCurrentlyOptimal value is a final result of ontology reasoning; DeviceWorkingTime represents device start time (e.g., a dishwasher starts at 1700 hours). DecisionSet is the main ontology class representing one combination of values specifying that a device D start at time T using an active tariff model M (hasTariffModel, hasPrice, isCritical, isPreferred), which has properties of hasPriceValue, hasCriticalStateValue, hasPreferedStateValue (pondered value for price and criticality, depend on price and critical and preferred value and value ponder specified in SelectionCriteriaPonder for those categories). The property isCurrentlyOptimal is a reasoning result and its value is set to "true" if the combination of device start time and tariff model is optimal.

16.4.4 Policies and User Interfaces for Policy Creation

Policy-based decision-making mechanisms in SESAME are parts of the policy infrastructure. Policies complement the knowledge base realized with the ontologies and capture the configuration of the system and preferences of users related to system behavior. These mechanisms are input for reasoning and specify more complex business logic and activation and orchestration of corresponding services.

The functioning of the SESAME system, specifically in terms of energy saving, depends on the quality of the installed policies or rules; however, the creation of more complex rules may overwhelm an ordinary user. Therefore, in SESAME, the creation of policies is designed as a two-stage process: (1) specific system-level policies are automatically created based on the current ontology and knowledge-base, keeping the system flexible and open for changes, (2) through a user-friendly graphical interface, the end customer specifies user-created policies (preferences) regarding the energy-aware environmental control by integrating system-level policies. By being offered selections from a set of recommended rules, the user is guarded from unintentional errors or incorrect decisions. On the other hand, within the policy, a user can customize, combine, and weight system rules to achieve personal objectives, sometimes prioritizing the quality of living to energy saving and vice versa.

We can illustrate the reasoning in SESAME with a system-level policy describing a specific activity that dictates that the heating in a living room should be reduced to 12°C if the house is empty. Another, (conflicting) system-level policy dictates that the temperature must stay between 21 and 24°C even if no one is in the house. A user-created policy describes factors affecting whether the specific system-level policy is implemented, e.g., a user may specify the ambient temperature he prefers when the house is empty and the history of the policy's adoption. The rule selection mechanisms are based on multicriteria decision making (MCDM) techniques such as analytic hierarchy process (AHP; Saaty and Vargas 2000). In addition, scenario analysis is used for complex decisions involving effects over time such as the cost of running an appliance for a specific length of time at a specific time of day.

System-level policies are classified into energy management rules and automation rules. Energy management rules are executed after automation rules to verify automation decisions based on energy constraints. For example, after the automation rule to set appliance status to isToBeSwitchedOn, the energy management rule that acts on tariff information can set the activation parameter to SwitchOn. System-level rules are created by power users who are well acquainted with the models of the devices and activities. System vendors can also create such rules for automatic implementation when devices are installed in the environment. Power user interactions for creation of preferences and policies are supported through a GUI to a rule engine, a reasoning tool that can assist in defining coherent system-level automation and energy policies.

The interface for a "normal user" is a user-friendly cockpit that grants control over the system and informs a user about his context. The user interface runs as a Web application accessible through a browser than can be installed on almost any device such as a mobile phone or home computer.

To control SESAME, a user designs policies by selecting, combining, and inserting system-level policies into the system. For example, by simple drag-and-drop, a selected policy can be added and parameterized. Sharing policies among interested users requires distributed policy and ontology infrastructure. In this framework, it is possible to differentiate different types of environments, e.g., offices and apartments require different policies from houses. The context information comes from the devices and internal and external information such as device consumption profiles, dynamic energy-related information, and real-time electricity prices. In the cockpit, energy usage is visualized based on a preselection of measurable values. Overlays of energy consumption graphs from different weeks or days show a user how input semantic policies changed overall consumption and cost. Comparing consumption patterns with friends over the Internet and sharing of semantic policies may establish visualization as a means to optimize energy use by leveraging experiences of others. Visualizing may also illustrate CO_2 footprints and financial impacts.

To investigate how different visualization approaches impact end users, an energy awareness information service was designed and a prototype implemented within the Facebook social network. Users of the prototype were shown randomly assigned visualizations of energy consumption information (as numbers and various types of graphs in Watts, trees, CO_2 footprint data, and cost in Euros) and had the opportunity to turn virtual appliances on and off in a virtual place to influence the consumption visualization. Interactions were monitored and showed that cost in Euros and real-time graphs were most effective for users trying to keep consumption low.

The participants' interactions within the virtual flat were monitored for 1 week and analyzed based on the visualization method assigned. The approach of showing consumption cost in Euros caused the highest rate of interaction (twice as much as other approaches) within the prototype, followed by the real-time graph showing immediate changes (20% more than other factors that caused almost the same interactions).

A follow-up survey of 115 participants (prototype users) gave insights about the motivations as follows: 28.95% saw their consumption clearly and most meaningfully when shown as a real-time graph; 21.05% saw their motivation best conveyed by visualization of trees needed to absorb CO_2 produced by the consumed energy. According to the participants' answers, more than 70% wanted real-time or at least timely consumption data as part of a perfect energy awareness information system. Over 60% responded that extrapolation of possible cost savings was a mandatory feature. More than 50% saw the perfect energy awareness system online through a website; only 15% wanted such information offline through a monthly bill.

16.5 Conclusions

Although the essential technology for building automation and smart metering solutions is rapidly developing and gaining maturity, there is a huge potential for innovation related to semantically enabled techniques and new approaches to make such systems truly flexible and responsive to changes in energy availability and cost, configurations of user environments, and user needs. These factors served as major motivations for cooperation and advances of technology envisaged by the SESAMEs approach. SESAME's design leverages benefits of semantic technologies and SOA so that customers can be efficiently placed in full control of their energy consumption and environment, and energy providers can efficiently channel (over the Internet) energy-relevant information to customers and improve their supply and demand management—a critical need in the energy sector. These innovations are expected to enable new business opportunities, increases of market shares, and sharpening of the competitive edge.

Acknowledgments

The work was supported by the FFG COIN funding line within the SESAME project. The Telecommunications Research Center Vienna (FTW) is supported by the Austrian government and the city of Vienna via the COMET competence center program.

References

Berners-Lee, T. and M. Fischetti. 1999. *Weaving the Web: The Past, Present and Future of the World Wide Web by its Inventor, Britain.* Orion Business.

Bonino, D., E. Castellina, and F. Corno. 2008. DOG: An ontology-powered OSGi demotic gateway. In *Proceedings of 20th IEEE International Conference on Tools with Artificial Intelligence.* pp. 157–160.

Brickley, D. and R.V. Guha. 2003. RDF Vocabulary Description Language 1.0: RDF Schema. *World Wide Web Consortium,* January.

CurrentCost. 2009. http://www.currentcost.com.

Darby, S. 2006. The effectiveness of feedback on energy consumption: A review of the literature on metering, billing and direct displays. University of Oxford, April. http://www.eci.ox.ac.uk/research/energy/downloads/smart-metering-report.pdfArt was here, but was deleted.

Dey, A. and G. Abowd. 2000. Towards a better understanding of context and context awareness. *Workshop on the What, Who, Where, When and How of Context Awareness at CHI.*

Dey, A.K., D. Salber, and G.D. Abowd. 2001. A conceptual framework and a toolkit for supporting the rapid prototyping of context-aware applications. *Human-Computer Interaction Journal, 16*: 97–166.

Diaz-Redondo, R.P., A.F. Vilas, M.R. Cabrer et al. 2008. Enhancing residential gateways: A semantic OSGi platform. *IEEE Intelligent Systems, 23*: 32–40.

DIP. 2007. EU FP6 Project Data, Information, and Process Integration with Semantic Web Services. http://dip.semanticweb.org

DLMS. 2009. Device Language Message Specification User Association. http://www.dlms.com

DPWS. 2009. Devices Profile for Web Services. www.ws4d.org

EC ICT. 2008. Impacts of Information and Communication Technologies on Energy Efficiency. Report. http://cordis.europa.eu/fp7/ict/sustainable-growth/studies_en.html

ESMIG. 2009. European Smart Metering Industry Group. http://www.esmig.eu/smart-metering

EU Future Internet. 2009. Portal http://future-internet.eu

EULER. 2009. eulersharp.sourceforge.net

Frost & Sullivan. 2009. Building Technologies, www.buildingtechnologies.frost.com

Goumopoulos C. and A. Kameas. 2008. Ambient ecologies in smart homes. *Computer Journal*, August.

Green Intelligent Buildings, 2006. Study indicates European building management and control system market booming. http://www.greenintelligentbuildings.com/Articles/Issues_and_Events/e6075eea35adc010VgnVCM100000f932a8c0____#

Gruber, T. R. 1993. A translation approach to portable ontology specifications. *Knowledge Acquisition*, 5: 199–220. http://tomgruber.org/writing/ontolingua-kaj-1993.htm

Gu, T., X.H. Wang, H.K. Pung et al. 2004. An ontology-based context model in intelligent environments. *Proceedings of Communication Networks and Distributed Systems Modeling and Simulation Conference*, pp. 270–275.

Harter, A., A. Hopper, P. Steggles et al. 2002. Anatomy of a context-aware application. *Wireless Networks*, 8: 187–197.

Henricksen K., J. Indulska, and A. Rakotonirainy. 2002. Modeling context information in pervasive computing systems. Lecture Notes in Computer Science Series 2414, pp. 167–180.

Henricksen, K., J. Indulska, and A. Rakotonirainy. 2003. Generating context management infrastructure from high-level context models. *Proceedings of Fourth International Conference on Mobile Data Management*, Melbourne.

JENA. 2009. http://jena.sourceforge.net/

Kagal, L. and T. Berners-Lee. 2005. REIN: Where policies meet rules in the Semantic Web. Technical Report, Massachusetts Institute of Technology, Cambridge, MA.

Kindberg T. and J. Barton. 2001. A web-based nomadic computing system. *Computer Networks*, 35: 443–456.

KnowledgeWeb. 2007. EU FP6 Project KnowledgeWeb, knowledgeweb.semanticweb.org

Kolovski, A., Y. Katz, J. Hendler et al. 2005. Towards a policy-aware web. *Semweb '05 and Policy Workshop*.

MESMET. 2008. Automatic Meter Reading, http://www.e-smartsys.com/en/mesmet.html

Noy, N.F., M. Sintek, S. Decker et al. 2001. Creating semantic web contents with Protégé 2000. *IEEE Intelligent Systems*, 16: 60–71.

OPC. 2009. OPC/OPC-UA Foundation, www.opcfoundation.org

OSGi. 2005. OSGi Service Platform, Core Specification, Release 4, OSGi Alliance, www.osgi.org

OSP. 2008. Open Service Platform for Automatic Meter Reading. http://www.alcatel-lucent.com/wps/portal/newsreleases/detail?LMSG_CABINET=Docs_and_Resource_Ctr&LMSG_CONTENT_FILE=News_Releases_2008/News_Article_001115.xml&lu_lang_code=en

P3 International. 2009. http://www.p3international.com/products/special/P4400/P4400-CE.html

Pachube. 2009. http://pachube.com

Papazoglou, M.G. and G. Georgakapoulos. 2003. Service-oriented computing, *CACM*, 46.

PROTÉGÉ. 2009. Protégé: http://protege.stanford.edu

PYCHINKO. 2009. www.mindswap.org/~katz/pychinko

REWERSE. 2009. EU FP7 NoE Reasoning on the Web with Rules and Semantics. http://rewerse.net/

Ricquebourg, V., D. Durand, D. Menga et al. 2007. Context inferring in the smart home: SWRL approach. *21st International Conference on Advanced Information Networking and Applications Workshops*, Vol. 2, pp. 290–295.

Saaty, L. and L.G. Vargas. 2000. *Models, Methods, Concepts and Applications of the Analytic Hierarchy Process*. Kluwer Academic, Boston, 2000.

SEKT. 2006, EU FP6 Semantically Enabled Knowledge Technologies. http://www.sekt-project.com

SESAME. 2009. Semantic Smart Metering: Enablers for Energy Efficiency. http://sesame.ftw.at

SHSG. 2009. EU FP7 Project SmartHouse/SmartGrid. http://www.smarthouse-smartgrid.eu

Smart Metering Project Map, 2009. Last accessed October 20, 2009, http://maps.google.com/maps/ms?ie=UTF8&hl=en&msa=0&msid=115519311058367534348.0000011362ac6d7d21187&ll=53.956086,14.677734&spn=23.864566,77.519531&z=4&om=1

Smith, M., C. Welty, and D. McGuinness. 2003. *Web Ontology Language (OWL) Guide.*

SOA4D. 2009. Service-Oriented Architecture for Devices. https://forge.soa4d.org

S-TEN. 2008. EU FP7 Project Intelligent Self-describing Technical and Environmental Networks. http://www.s-ten.eu/

SUPER. 2009. Semantics Utilised for Process Management within and between Enterprises. FP6 Integrated Project. www.ip-super.org

Tsai, W.T. 2005. Service-oriented system engineering: A new paradigm. *IEEE International Workshop on Service-Oriented System Engineering*, pp. 3–8.

UPnP. 2009. Universal Plug and Play Forum. www.upnp.org

VISUAL ENERGY. 2009. http://visiblenergy.com/products/display/iphone.html

Wang, F. and K.J. Turner. 2009. An ontology-based actuator discovery and invocation framework in home care systems. *Proceedings of Seventh International Conference on Smart Homes and Health Telematics*, Lecture Notes in Computer Science Series 5597, pp. 66–73.

Wang, X.H., D.Q. Zhang, T. Gu et al. 2004. Ontology-based context modeling and reasoning using OWL. *Second IEEE Annual Conference on Pervasive Computing and Communications Workshops*, p. 18.

WATTSON. 2009. http://www.diykyoto.com/uk

Xu, J., Y.H. Lee, W.T. Tsai et al. 2009. Ontology-based smart home solution and service composition. *International Conference on Embedded Software and Systems*, pp. 297–304.

Zhdanova, A.V., J. Zeiss, A. Dantcheva et al. 2009. A semantic policy management environment for end users and its empirical study. *Networked Knowledge–Networked Media: Integrating Knowledge Management*, Springer Verlag, Heidelberg.

Index

T - #0070 - 101024 - C0 - 234/156/26 [28] - CB - 9781439801567 - Gloss Lamination